Vicki
Fordham

CW00485056

Women's History: Britain, 1700–1850

Britain witnessed huge changes between 1700 and 1850, as society adapted to unprecedented urbanization, commercialization, industrialization, imperial expansion – and much more. This volume looks specifically at British women's experiences in the context of these major social, economic and cultural shifts. The chapters speak not of one overarching female historical experience, but of many experiences – of significant long-term continuities and of complex developments and changes. They speak, in particular, of tensions and opportunities, as notions of women and their place in society were examined and debated, and boundaries were extended or redrawn.

In *Women's History: Britain, 1700–1850* Hannah Barker and Elaine Chalus paint a fascinating picture of a vibrant and exciting period. In a broad-ranging and well-balanced collection of essays by established experts and dynamic new scholars, they present a comprehensive history of British women. Combining new research with discussions of current secondary literature, the contributors examine areas as diverse as the Enlightenment, politics, religion, education, sexuality, family, work, poverty and consumption.

A captivating overview of women and their lives, this book is an essential purchase for the study of women's history. With its delight in detail and the wealth of women's experiences that it reveals, it will also appeal to any reader with an interest in the topic.

Hannah Barker is Senior Lecturer in History at the University of Manchester. Her publications include *Newspapers, Politics and Public Opinion in Late Eighteenth-Century England* (1998). **Elaine Chalus** is Senior Lecturer in History at Bath Spa University College. Her publications include *Elite Women in English Political Life c.1754–1790* (2005).

Women's and Gender History
Edited by June Purvis

Emmeline Pankhurst: A Biography
June Purvis

*Child Sexual Abuse in Victorian
England*
Louise A. Jackson

*Crimes of Outrage: Sex, Violence and
Victorian Working Women*
Shani D'Cruze

*Feminism, Femininity and the Politics
of Working Women: The Women's
Co-operative Guild, 1880s to the
Second World War*
Gillian Scott

Gender and Crime in Modern Europe
Edited by Margaret L. Arnot and
Cornelie Usborne

*Gender Relations in German History:
Power, Agency and Experience from
the Sixteenth to the Twentieth Century*
Edited by Lynn Abrams and Elizabeth
Harvey

*Imaging Home: Gender, 'Race' and
National Identity, 1945–64*
Wendy Webster

*Midwives of the Revolution: Female
Bolsheviks and Women Workers in
1917*
Jane McDermid and Anna Hillyar

*No Distinction of Sex? Women in
British Universities 1870–1939*
Carol Dyhouse

*Policing Gender, Class and Family:
Britain, 1850–1945*
Linda Mahood

*Prostitution: Prevention and Reform
in England, 1860–1914*
Paula Bartley

*Sylvia Pankhurst: Sexual Politics
and Political Activism*
Barbara Winslow

Votes for Women
Edited by June Purvis and
Sandra Holton

Women's History: Britain, 1850–1945
Edited by June Purvis

*The Women's Suffrage Movement:
A Reference Guide, 1866–1928*
Elizabeth Crawford

*Women and Teacher Training Colleges
1900–1960: A Culture of Femininity*
Elizabeth Edwards

*Women, Work and Sexual Politics
in Eighteenth-Century England*
Bridget Hill

*Women Workers and Gender
Identities, 1835–1913: The Cotton
and Metal Industries in England*
Carol E. Morgan

*Women and Work in Britain Since
1840*
Gerry Holloway

*Outspoken Women: British Women
Writing about Sex, 1870–1969, An
Anthology*
Lesley A. Hall

*The Women's Suffrage Movement in
Britain and Ireland: A Regional
Survey*
Elizabeth Crawford

Women's History: Britain, 1700–1850

An Introduction

Edited by Hannah Barker and Elaine Chalus

Routledge
Taylor & Francis Group

LONDON AND NEW YORK

083066

First published 2005
by Routledge
2 Park Square, Milton Park, Abingdon, Oxon OX14 4RN

Simultaneously published in the USA and Canada
by Routledge
270 Madison Ave, New York, NY 10016

Routledge is an imprint of the Taylor & Francis Group

© 2005 selection and editorial matter, Hannah Barker
and Elaine Chalus, individual chapters © the contributors

Typeset in Garamond Book
by Keystroke, Jacaranda Lodge, Wolverhampton
Printed and bound in Great Britain
by MPG Books Ltd, Bodmin

All rights reserved. No part of this book may be reprinted or
reproduced or utilised in any form or by any electronic,
mechanical, or other means, now known or hereafter invented,
including photocopying and recording, or in any information
storage or retrieval system, without permission in writing
from the publishers.

British Library Cataloguing in Publication Data
A catalogue record for this book is available from the British Library

Library of Congress Cataloging in Publication Data
Women's history : Britain 1700–1850 : an introduction / edited by
Hannah Barker and Elaine Chalus.
p.   cm. – (Women's and gender history)
Includes bibliographical references.
1. Women–Great Britain–History–18th century. 2. Women–Great
Britain–History–19th century. I. Barker, Hannah. II. Chalus, Elaine.
III. Series.
HQ1593.W5794 2005
305.4′0941–dc22
2005004870

ISBN 0–415–29176–3 (hbk)
ISBN 0–415–29177–1 (pbk)

ॐ

Contents

Notes on contributors   vii

Introduction   1
HANNAH BARKER AND ELAINE CHALUS

1 Women and the Enlightenment in Britain *c.*1690–1800   9
JANE RENDALL

2 Women and education   33
DEBORAH SIMONTON

3 Women, marriage and the family   57
TANYA EVANS

4 Sexuality and the body   78
KAREN HARVEY

5 Women and religion   100
ANNE STOTT

6 Women and work   124
HANNAH BARKER

7 Women and poverty   152
ALANNAH TOMKINS

CONTENTS

8 Women and crime   174
   ANNE-MARIE KILDAY

9 Women, consumption and taste   194
   HELEN BERRY

10 Women and politics   217
   ELAINE CHALUS AND FIONA MONTGOMERY

11 British women and empire   260
   KATHLEEN WILSON

   Index   285

Notes on contributors

Hannah Barker is Senior Lecturer in History at the University of Manchester. Her publications include *Newspapers, Politics and Public Opinion in Late Eighteenth-Century England* (Oxford University Press, 1998); *English Newspapers and Society, 1700–1850* (Longman, 1999); and, with Karen Harvey, 'Gender and Trade in Manchester, 1780–1840', in Rosemary Sweet and Penny Lane (eds), *'On the Town': Women and Urban Life in Eighteenth-Century England, c.1660–1820* (Ashgate, 2003). She has edited, with Elaine Chalus, *Gender in Eighteenth-Century England: Roles, Representations and Responsibilities* (Longman, 1997); and, with Simon Burrows, *The Press and the Public Sphere: Newspapers, Politics and Social Change in Late Eighteenth- and Early Nineteenth-Century Europe and America* (Cambridge University Press, 2002). She has just completed her most recent book, *The Business of Women: Female Enterprise and Urban Development in Northern England, 1760–1830.*

Helen Berry is Senior Lecturer in History at the University of Newcastle. Her publications include *Gender, Society and Print Culture in Late-Stuart England* (Ashgate, 2003); 'Rethinking Politeness in Eighteenth-Century England: Moll King's Coffee House and the Significance of Flash Talk', *Transactions of the Royal Historical Society* 6th series, XI (2001); and '"Prudent Luxury": The Metropolitan Tastes of Judith Baker, Durham Gentlewoman', in Rosemary Sweet and Penny Lane (eds), *'On the Town': Women and Urban Life in Eighteenth-Century England, c.1660–1820* (Ashgate, 2003). She is co-editor, with Jeremy Gregory, of *Creating and Consuming Culture in North-East England, 1660–1800* (Ashgate, 2004). She is currently writing a book entitled *Nationalizing Taste: National Identity and Local Culture in Eighteenth-Century Britain.*

Elaine Chalus is Senior Lecturer in History at Bath Spa University College. She co-edited, with Hannah Barker, *Gender in Eighteenth-Century England: Roles, Representations and Responsibilities* (Longman, 1997). Her publications have focused on women's involvement in eighteenth-century English political culture. Her most recent publications include 'The Rag Plot: The Politics of Influence in Oxford, 1754', in R. Sweet and P. Lane (eds), *Women and Urban Life in Eighteenth-Century England* (Ashgate, forthcoming, 2003), 'How Lady Susan Wooed the Voters', *BBC History Magazine*, 2, 6 (June 2001); 'Elite Women, Social Politics and the Political World of Late Eighteenth-Century England', *Historical Journal*, 43, 3 (Sept. 2000); ' "To Serve My Friends": Women and Political Patronage in Eighteenth-Century England', in Amanda Vickery (ed.), *Women, Privilege and Power: British Politics, 1750 to the Present* (2001). She is a member of the Editorial Board of *Women's History Review* and a co-editor of the new *Women's History Magazine*. She has recently completed, *Fair and Faithful Subjects: Women's Involvement in English Political Life, 1754–1790* for Oxford University Press.

Tanya Evans is a Postdoctoral Research Fellow at the Centre for Contemporary British History at the Institute of Historical Research in London. She is working on an ESRC-funded project entitled 'Unmarried Motherhood in England and Wales, 1918–1990'. Her monograph *Unfortunate Objects: Lone Mothers in Eighteenth-Century London* will be published by Palgrave Macmillan in 2005. Other publications include: 'Blooming Virgins All Beware: Love, Courtship and Illegitimacy in Eighteenth-Century British Popular Literature', in A. Levene, T. Nutt and S. Williams (eds), *Illegitimacy in Britain; 1700–1920* (Palgrave Macmillan, 2005) and ' "Unfortunate Objects": London's Unmarried Mothers in the Eighteenth Century', *Gender and History*, 17, 1, 2005.

Karen Harvey is Lecturer in Cultural History at the University of Sheffield. Her publications include 'The Majesty of the Masculine Form: Multiplicity and Male Bodies in Eighteenth-Century Erotica', in Tim Hitchcock and Michèle Cohen (eds), *English Masculinities, 1660–1800* (Longman, 1999); 'Gender, Space and Modernity in Eighteenth-Century England: A Place called Sex', *History Workshop Journal*, 51 (2001); 'A Century of Sex? Gender, Bodies and Sexuality in the Long Eighteenth Century', *The Historical Journal*, 45, 4 (2002); and 'The Substance of Sexual Difference: Change and Persistence in Eighteenth-Century Representations of the Body', *Gender and History*, 14, 2 (2002). She is also the author of *Reading Sex in the Eighteenth Century: Bodies and Gender in English Erotic Culture* (Cambridge University Press, 2004), and editor of *The Kiss in History* (Manchester University Press, 2004).

Anne-Marie Kilday is Senior Lecturer in Early Modern History at Oxford Brookes University. She is the author of ' "A Great Effusion of Blood?" Violent Women in South-West Scotland, 1750–1815', *Journal of Legal History* (Summer, 1998); ' "Murdering Mothers": Infanticide in Eighteenth Century Glasgow', *The Journal of Family History* (forthcoming, 2006); ' "Miss Behaviour": Violent Scottish Women in the Eighteenth Century', *Women's History Review* (forthcoming, 2006); "Maternal Monsters: Murdering Mothers in Eighteenth Century Scotland", in Y. Brown and R. Ferguson (eds), *Twisted Sisters: Women, Crime and Deviance in Scotland Since 1400* (Ashgate, 2002); and *Women and Crime in Enlightenment Scotland* (Boydell and Brewer, forthcoming).

Fiona Montgomery is Head of School of Historical and Cultural Studies at Bath Spa University College. Her publications include *The European Women's History Reader* (Routledge, 2002, with C. Collette); *Into the Melting Pot* (Ashgate, 1997, with C. Collette); *Edge Hill University College: A History 1885–1987* (Phillimore, 1997); 'Mary Wollstonecraft', in P. Dematteis and P. Fosl (eds), *British Philosophers, 1500–1799* (Bruccoli Clark Layman, 2002); 'Women Who Did' in C.J. Parker, *Gender and Sexuality in Victorian England* (Scholar Press, 1995). She has also published widely on popular protest including the Unstamped Press, the Anti-Corn Law Movement and gender and suffrage, as well as on feminist pedagogy. At present she is completing a book, *Women's Rights: Feminism and Feminists in Britain c.1780s–1970s* for Manchester University Press and an article on 'Feminism in Women's Training Colleges'.

Jane Rendall is an Honorary Fellow in the Department of History and Centre for Eighteenth-Century Studies, University of York. Her publications include *The Origins of Modern Feminism: Women in Britain, France, and the United States, 1780–1860* (Macmillan, 1985); *Women in an Industrializing Society: England 1780–1880* (Basil Blackwell, 1991); (with Catherine Hall and Keith McClelland) *Defining the Nation: Class, Race, Gender and the British Reform Act of 1867* (Cambridge University Press, 2000). She has edited *Equal or Different: Women's Politics 1800–1914* (Basil Blackwell, 1987); (with Susan Mendus) *Sexuality and Subordination: Representations of Women in the Nineteenth Century* (Routledge, 1989); (with Karen Offen and Ruth Roach Pierson) *Writing Women's History: International Perspectives* (Macmillan and Indiana University Press, 1991); and (with Mark Hallett) *Eighteenth Century York: Culture, Space and Society* (Borthwick Institute of Historical Research, 2003).

Deborah Simonton is Associate Professor of British History at the University of Southern Denmark. Her publications include *A History of*

European Women's Work (Routledge, 1998), 'Age, Gender and Service in Pre-Industrial Europe,' in Christina Benninghaus, Mary Jo Maynes and Brigitte Söland (eds), *Secret Gardens, Satanic Mills: Placing Girls in Modern European History* (Indiana University Press, 2004); 'Earning and Learning: Girlhood in Pre-Industrial Europe', *Women's History Review*, 13, 3 (2004); 'Gender, Identity and Independence: Eighteenth-Century Women in the Commercial World', *Women's History Magazine*, 42 (2002); 'Schooling the Poor: Gender and Class in Eighteenth-Century England', *British Journal for Eighteenth-Century Studies*, 23 (2000); 'Gendering Labour in Eighteenth-Century Towns', in Margaret Walsh (ed.), *Working Out Gender* (Ashgate, 1999), 'Apprenticeship: Training and Gender in Eighteenth-Century England', in Maxine Berg (ed.), *Markets and Manufactures in Early Industrial Europe* (Routledge, 1991). She edited (with Mary Masson) *Women in Higher Education: Past, Present and Future* (Aberdeen University Press, 1996) and (with Terry Brotherstone and Oonagh Walsh) *Gendering Scottish History: An International Approach* (Cruithne Press, 2000).

Anne Stott is a Research Associate at the Open University and an Extra-mural Lecturer at Birkbeck College, University of London. She is the author of 'Female Patriotism: Georgiana, Duchess of Devonshire and the Westminster Election of 1784', in *Eighteenth-Century Life* (1993); 'Hannah More and the Blagdon Controversy', *Journal of Ecclesiastical History*, 51, 2 (2000); 'Patriotism and Providence: The Politics of Hannah More', in Kathryn Gleadle and Sarah Richardson (eds), *Women in British Politics, 1760–1860: The Power of the Petticoat* (Macmillan, 2000); '"A Singular Injustice towards Women": Hannah More, Evangelicalism and Female Education', in Sue Morgan (ed.), *Women, Religion and Feminism in Britain, 1750–1900* (Palgrave, 2002); *Hannah More: The First Victorian* (Oxford University Press, 2003); 'Hannah More and the Blagdon Controversy 1799–1802', in Mark Smith and Stephen Taylor (eds), *Evangelicalism in the Church of England, c. 1790–c. 1890: A Miscellany* (Boydell, 2004).

Alannah Tomkins is Lecturer in History at Keele University. She is author of 'Charity Schools and the Parish Poor in Oxford 1740–1770', *Midland History*, 22 (1997); 'Paupers and the Infirmary in Mid-Eighteenth-Century Shrewsbury', *Medical History* (1999); 'Pawnbroking and the Survival Strategies of the Urban Poor in 1770s York', in S. King and A. Tomkins (eds), *The Poor in England 1700–1850: An Economy of Makeshifts* (Manchester University Press, 2003); 'Poverty, Kinship Support, and the Case of Ellen Parker, 1818–1828', in S. King and R. Smith (eds), *The British Experience of Poverty* (Cambridge University Press, forthcoming); and *The Experience of Urban Poverty* (Manchester University Press, forthcoming).

Kathleen Wilson is Professor of History at the State University of New York at Stony Brook. She has published widely on the themes of British culture and empire, including *The Sense of the People: Politics, Culture and Imperialism in England, 1715–1785* (Cambridge University Press, 1995), which won prizes from the Royal Historical Society and the North American Conference on British Studies, and *The Island Race: Englishness, Empire and Gender in the Eighteenth Century* (Routledge, 2003). Her most recent publication is *A New Imperial History: Culture, Identity and Modernity in Britain and the Empire 1660–1840* (Cambridge University Press, 2004). She is currently working on *The Colonial Stage: Theater, Culture and Modernity in the English Provinces, 1720–1820*, which explores the politics of theatrical and social performance in the Atlantic and Pacific worlds.

ぷ

Introduction

Hannah Barker and Elaine Chalus

Britain witnessed huge changes between 1700 and 1850, not least because imperial expansion, military success, and the development of trade made the nation into the leading world power. In addition, as urbanization, industrialization, and the commercialization of agriculture served to transform the landscape of much of Britain, population growth, changes in social structure and political and religious developments greatly affected its people. The aim of this volume is to describe women's experiences in the context of the major social, economic, and cultural shifts that accompanied such transformations. It is not, however, our intention to present a picture of permanent revolution: much changed over the 150 years charted here, but many important continuities are also evident. Moreover, while this is a book specifically about women in the past, it does not pretend that we can speak of a shared female historical experience. Instead, it is assumed that factors such as social status, location, age, race, and religion could significantly affect women's lives – sometimes to the extent that gender can appear less important than other factors in determining the experiences of individual women. Finally, while this volume is about British women's history, it concentrates on the history of women in England, Scotland, and Wales. Some contributors do touch upon the experience of women in Ireland, but Irish women's history for this period is a topic in its own right and cannot be adequately addressed here.

A nation transformed?

Between 1700 and 1850, Britain was transformed from a largely rural society to an increasingly urban one. Nearly half the population of England

and Wales lived in towns by 1851. Scotland reached this level of urbanization by the later nineteenth century. In the countryside, increasing amounts of land were cultivated. Enclosure and the commercialization of farming drove some agricultural workers off the land, but they also ensured the development of a strong agricultural sector, which was vital to support the growing towns. Of the urban centres, London was unique in terms of its size from the beginning of our period. By 1801, at the time of the first census, its population was around 1 million, or 8 per cent of the population. Other provincial centres were significantly smaller: none numbered more than 100,000 inhabitants at the turn of the nineteenth century, but the growth of manufacturing, towns such as Manchester, Liverpool, Birmingham, and Leeds, was striking. Although Scotland and Wales remained less urbanized throughout our period, Edinburgh and Glasgow had sizeable populations of over 50,000 in 1801. Wales had no large towns, but, notably, its biggest urban conurbation in 1801 was Merthyr Tydfil, an entirely new town, devoted to the rapidly expanding iron industry.[1] The towns of, particularly, early nineteenth-century Britain are commonly associated with peculiarly harsh living conditions for the poorer sections of society. The second half of our period probably saw greater deprivation for urban labourers, but a decline in the standard of living was also evident among rural workers, who – like their urban counterparts – were also subject to periodic unemployment, food shortages, and price rises.[2]

The marked growth of manufacturing towns emphasizes the role played by industrial development in changing the face of Britain. Traditionally, historians have described the eighteenth and nineteenth centuries as witnessing both agricultural and industrial revolutions, although, more recently, some economic historians have argued that this period was marked as much by continuity as by revolutionary change. It is certainly true that economic change in Britain differed greatly between regions and industries, and over time,[3] and that working patterns altered in diverse ways across the country. This is not the same as saying that little changed, as contemporaries who explored Britain's industrial heartlands were keen to attest.[4] Yet it is clear that an understanding of regional and sectoral diversity is key to comprehending patterns of change between 1700 and 1850. So while towns and villages in Lancashire and Yorkshire were transformed by developments in the textile industry from the late eighteenth century, it was also the case that East London was no longer the dominant force in silk-weaving, nor was Essex of the woollen industry.[5] Moreover, while the commercialization of agriculture was marked in the South-east England and southern Scotland during the eighteenth century, it was not until the end of our period that regions such as north-eastern Scotland were affected. Farming patterns in north Wales remained virtually undisturbed throughout.[6]

2

One of the causes of Britain's economic expansion between 1700 and 1850 was the population explosion of the eighteenth century, which ensured a plentiful supply of cheap labour. In 1700, at the start of our period, around 5.8 million people lived in England and Wales, and a million in Scotland. By 1851, the population of England was around 16.7 million, Wales 1.2 million, and Scotland had 2.9 million inhabitants.[7] As the population of Britain grew, migration became more common: most notably from rural to urban areas. Some migration from the countryside to the town was temporary and seasonal, although increasingly migrants to towns relocated on a permanent basis. Britain also saw significant amounts of immigration, predominantly from Ireland and Scotland into England, although, after 1789, Britain was also home to various political refugees fleeing the French Revolution. Jewish immigration was established in Britain from the eighteenth century, as was the settlement of Africans and West Indians. Most of the latter were freed slaves or sailors who settled in port towns such as Liverpool and London.[8]

Urban expansion and the development of industry and trade in the eighteenth and nineteenth centuries are commonly associated with the emergence of a modern class system in Britain. The growth of a 'middling sort' was evident in many areas from the beginning of our period, although the use of terms such as 'middle class' and 'working class' to describe particular social groups did not emerge until the late eighteenth and early nineteenth centuries. Social status may have become increasingly tied to occupation around this time, although, even at the end of our period, Britain's social and occupation structure was extremely complex, and it is difficult to identify unified social groups with the type of 'class consciousness' that Marx described.[9] Still, contemporaries believed that major changes were taking place, especially in the second half of our period, giving rise not only to a new language of class and the growth of class-based politics in both the middle and lower classes in the first half of nineteenth century, but also to complaints that the ruling orders were abandoning their traditional patriarchal role.[10] For its part, the aristocratic élite remained virtually unchanged throughout the eighteenth and nineteenth centuries, and was notable in European terms for its wealth and power. Despite some challenges to its dominance in the shape of growing radical – and even feminist – politics from around the 1760s, aristocratic power remained largely unchanged, if not uncontested. An aristocratic and gentry élite dominated political power throughout the period, controlling Parliament and most branches of local government. It was only towards the very end of the period that this hegemony began to be undermined.[11] However, it is worth remembering that, even after the 'Great' Reform Act of 1832, the majority of British men still could not vote and that the Act conclusively removed the franchise from the few women who had previously qualified as property owners.[12]

As we shall see, this formal exclusion of women from politics does not mean that they were barred from public life altogether. Women could still be politically active and there were substantial changes, both in women's political awareness and the extent of their political involvement. The end of the period marks the birth of the women's movement and the first intimations of the feminist consciousness which would later emerge to drive the women's suffrage movement. Women were also conspicuous in the religious changes that were taking place between 1700 and 1850. The Evangelical Revival – a movement to 'rechristianize' Britain that started among the Methodists but soon spread to the Anglican Church – saw women as active participants. The same is true of other important trends in British society during our period, including the commercialization of leisure and the consumer revolution. As with other major developments, these changes did not impact on individual Britons in a uniform way. While it is undoubtedly true that more things than ever before were being made and purchased between 1700 and 1850, and that people from the lower end of the social scale could be eager consumers and followers of fashion, it is also true that urban workers, in particular, probably had less leisure time as our period progressed. Still, the growth of polite pursuits, such as theatre-going and promenading during the eighteenth century, and the expansion of popular leisure activities and the drive for 'rational recreation' in the nineteenth, undoubtedly influenced the lives of a significant number of urban dwellers, and certainly helped to shape town landscapes.[13] Coupled with such developments, the growth of print culture and other improvements in communications brought about by the spread of turnpike roads and canals, and latterly, the advent of the railway, helped Britons to assume a greater sense of a shared identity, however strong other regional and local links might have remained.[14]

Writing a history of British women, 1700–1850

The study of women's history in eighteenth- and nineteenth-century Britain is well established and the field is a diverse one. Older historical traditions tend to centre either on the way that changing economic circumstances have affected women, especially those of the lower orders, or on women's domestic and specifically female experiences, specifically those of the middling and upper ranks. Many historians have described a transformation in the relative economic and social position of men and women between 1700 and 1850. Although accounts differ as to timing, most interpretations focus on the impact of capitalism. According to this influential model, as the pre-industrial family economy gave way to an exploitative wage economy, women were increasingly marginalized, confined, and made subject to men. The model identifies the emergence of the concept of the male breadwinner with women's gradual relegation to jobs with the lowest pay and status. As their economic contributions declined and were devalued, their earlier parity with men disintegrated and, as their subordination increased, they were also confined more and more to the home.

The model of emerging capitalism has also had profound implications for historians' understanding of gender relations among the middle classes. As middle-class men embraced and came to dominate a new aggressive economic world and their womenfolk became increasingly disassociated from the workplace, they were assumed to have retreated into 'graceful indolence' in a strictly domestic setting.[15] These economic changes were presumed to have coincided with an emerging social ideology of female domesticity that was encapsulated in the notion of 'separate spheres'. Such thinking dictated that women and men were naturally suited to different spheres: for women, the private sphere; for men, the public sphere. The new, moral, world-view of the middle classes reflected their overwhelming desire for order, where femininity became decisively equated with the private sphere of the home, family, and emotion, while masculinity was linked to the public sphere of work, politics, and power.[16] Once formed, it has been argued, these ideas were not necessarily restricted to the middle classes, but could and did infiltrate and influence other sections of society.[17]

More recently, our knowledge of women's history between 1700 and 1850 has deepened and expanded. As a result, both the economic and the separate spheres' models have undergone substantial modifications, as new insights gained from a wealth of increasingly detailed, in-depth studies have begun to fill in gaps in our knowledge, revealing that women's historical experience was more complicated than had earlier been assumed and that the range of opportunities available to women could be more diverse. Informed by gender history and inflected by postmodernism, well-established subjects, such as work, religion, crime, poverty, and politics, have all been fruitfully re-interrogated, while new areas of interest – as varied as sexuality and the body, consumer society, and empire, for instance – have also been introduced.[18] The resulting historiography is rich, colourful, and wide-ranging, but the sheer variety and range of women's lives and experiences that have been uncovered mean that it can also seem less coherent and, consequently, less easily accessible to the newcomer or the student.

This volume has been designed to serve as a point of entry. The chapters reflect both traditional and significant new themes in British women's history for the period and have been designed to provide both students and academics with a useful historiographical introduction through an animated critical engagement with the sources. Contributors explore questions of continuity and change over time, stressing women's agency in the formation of modern society without ignoring the constraints and complexities of life in what was still a highly patriarchal world. Typified by an awareness of complexity and the importance of factors such as locality, age, race, class, gender, national identity, and religion in women's historical experience, the chapters make use of vivid detail and example to highlight the unevenness of historical change, identifying and explaining incremental developments and conservative reactions, while shying away from many of the more rigid models that have typified women's history between 1700 and 1850.

The volume begins with a discussion of women and ideas, as Jane Rendall traces the impact of the eighteenth-century Enlightenment, as promulgated by a wide assortment or writers and promoted through the rapid expansion of print culture, on women and gender roles. Deborah Simonton takes up some of these themes in Chapter 2, as she explores the expansion in women's education over the period. Despite significant growth, women's education continued to be shaped by contemporary understandings of class and status, and the belief that women's schooling should be tailored to their future role in society. In Chapter 3, Tanya Evans explores the variety of women's marital and familial experiences, reflecting how these were shaped by industrialization, migration, and legal change. Karen Harvey refocuses discussion on the cultural categories of sex and gender in Chapter 4. She argues that, while medical texts increasingly constructed men and women as opposites, and contemporary ideals portrayed women as passive and desexualized, working-class women in particular resisted attempts to suppress their sexuality. Anne Stott then, in Chapter 5, concentrates on the importance of religion to women in a period which was marked by evangelical fervour, maintaining that women's religious experiences provided them with both a significant spiritual outlet and the justification for creating a separate public identity.

The second half of the volume opens with Hannah Barker's exploration of women and work, concentrating on uncovering the regional and sectoral differences in female labour. In Chapter 7, Alannah Tomkins looks at those women for whom survival itself was an issue, as she discusses the ongoing problem of female poverty and the range of responses utilized by women as they sought to improve their condition. Despite the fact that most female criminals were poor, Anne-Marie Kilday argues in Chapter 8 that greed, not need, was an important motivation in female crime; more-over, as she points out, female criminals could at times be exceptionally violent in securing what they wanted. In Chapter 9, the desire for possessions forms the basis of Helen Berry's examination of women's agency in the development of a modern consumer society in Britain. Women's involvement in politics, broadly defined, serves as the subject of the last two chapters of the volume. Elaine Chalus and Fiona Montgomery jointly examine the contribution made by women of all social classes to

British political life during a period which saw politics move from the court and parliament, and the street, to issues-based campaigning. Finally, Kathleen Wilson broadens the geographical horizons of the volume to examine women's participation in Britain's imperial project.

Notes

1 John Langton, 'Urban growth and economic change: from the late seventeenth century to 1841', in *The Cambridge Urban History of Britain*, vol. II: *1540–1840*, ed. Peter Clark, Cambridge, 2000, 453–90.

2 J. Walvin, *English Urban Life, 1776–1851*, London, 1984; K. D. M. Snell, *Annals of the Labouring Poor: Social Change and Agrarian England, 1660–1900*, Cambridge, 1985.

3 See N. F. R. Crafts, *British Industrial Growth During the Industrial Revolution*, Oxford, 1985; E. A. Wrigley, *Continuity, Chance and Change: The Character of the Industrial Revolution in England*, Cambridge, 1989; Pat Hudson, *The Industrial Revolution*, London, 1992; Maxine Berg, *The Age of Manufactures, 1700–1820*, 2nd edn., London, 1994; Mark Overton, *The Agricultural Revolution 1500–1850*, Cambridge, 1996.

4 Maxine Berg and Pat Hudson, 'Rehabilitating the industrial revolution', *Economic History Review*, 45, 1 (1992).

5 Pamela Sharpe, 'Continuity and change: women's history and economic history in Britain', *Economic History Review*, 48 (1995), 353–69.

6 *The Agrarian History of England and Wales*, vol. VI: *1750–1850*, ed. G. E. Mingay, Cambridge, 1989; Malcolm Gray, 'Processes of agricultural change in the north-east, 1790–1870', in Leah Leneman and I. D. Whyte (eds), *Perspectives in Scottish Social History: Essays in Honour of Rosalind Mitchison*, Aberdeen, 1988.

7 B. R. Mitchell and P. Deane, *Abstract of British Historical Statistics*, Cambridge, 1962; E. A. Wrigley and R. S. Schofield, *The Population History of England, 1541–1871: A Reconstruction*, London, 1981.

8 Edward Royle, *Modern Britain: A Social History 1750–1985*, London, 1987, pp. 57–80.

9 P. J. Corfield, 'Class by name and number in eighteenth-century Britain', *History*, 72 (1987).

10 Gareth Stedman Jones, *Languages of Class: Studies in Working-Class History 1832–1982*, Cambridge, 1983; Patrick Joyce, *Visions of the People: Industrial England and the Question of Class, 1840–1914*, Cambridge, 1992; Dror Wahrman, *Imagining the Middle Class: The Political Representation of Class in Britain, c.1780–1840*, Cambridge, 1995.

11 J. A. Cannon, *Aristocratic Century: The Peerage in Eighteenth-Century England*, London, 1984.

12 J. A. Cannon, *Parliamentary Reform, 1660–1832*, London, 1972, Chapter 11.

13 Peter Borsay, *The English Urban Renaissance: Culture and Society in the Provincial Town, 1660–1770*, Oxford, 1989; Hugh Cunningham, *Leisure in the Industrial Revolution*, London, 1980; R. W. Malcolmson, *Popular Recreations in English Society, 1700–1850*, Cambridge, 1973.

14 Linda Colley, *Britons: Forging the Nation, 1707–1837*, London, 1992.

15 Amanda Vickery, 'Golden age to separate spheres? A review of the categories and chronology of English women's history', *Historical Journal*, 36 (1993).

16 Leonore Davidoff and Catherine Hall, *Family Fortunes: Men and Women of the English Middle Class, 1780–1850*, London, 1987, p. 30.

17 Anna Clark, *The Struggle for the Breeches: Gender and the Making of the British Working Class*, London, 1995.

18 For overviews of recent work on women and gender in this period, see Hannah Barker and Elaine Chalus (eds), *Gender in Eighteenth-Century England: Roles, Representations and Responsibilities*, Harlow, 1997; Robert B. Shoemaker, *Gender in English Society, 1650–1850*, Harlow, 1998. More detailed studies proliferate. See, for instance, Amanda Vickery, *The Gentleman's Daughter: Women's Lives in Georgian England*, London, 1998; Pamela Sharpe, *Adapting to Capitalism: Working Women in the English Economy, 1700–1850*, Basingstoke, 1996; Anna Clark, *Scandal: The Sexual Politics of the British Constitution*, Princeton, NJ, 2004.

Chapter One

ào

Women and the Enlightenment in Britain *c.*1690–1800

Jane Rendall

Our understanding of the nature of the eighteenth-century European Enlightenment has changed significantly over the past twenty years. The image of what once appeared, in Eric Hobsbawm's words, as an elitist 'conspiracy of dead white men in periwigs', of small and exclusive groups of philosophers, has been transformed by cultural-historical approaches.[1] New ideas have remained important but have been located in the context of much broader shifts in mood, in language, and in practice. Enlightened philosophies have been relocated within a rapidly expanding print culture, including newspapers, novels, and poetry, as well as theology, history, metaphysics, and science. The diffusion of ideas has been traced through circulating libraries and popular debating societies, as well as universities, salons and academies. The practitioners of Enlightenment are understood to be not only the *philosophes* of Paris or the literati of Edinburgh, but also novelists, poets, medical men, salon hostesses, utopian thinkers, and itinerant lecturers.[2] These changes have been influenced by an interest in women's and gender history, and offer opportunities for reassessing women's relationship to enlightened sociability and practice, and the significance of the Enlightenment in reshaping concepts of femininity and desired forms of gender relations.

These views of the Enlightenment have developed simultaneously with new questions about gender relations in this period. The debates among women's historians about the gendering of 'public' and 'private' worlds have actively contributed to the reinterpretation of the meaning of the 'public sphere' in the eighteenth-century culture of the Enlightenment. The interest after 1989 in Jürgen Habermas' notion of a bourgeois public sphere stimulated women's historians and historians of the Enlightenment to re-examine their assumptions, even if often to criticize Habermas' thesis, as well as to adapt and appropriate it.[3] In Britain, the concept of the 'urban renaissance' rooted in the growth of the social and cultural life of late seventeenth- and early eighteenth-century English towns recovered many forms of mixed sociability, in assembly rooms, walks, and public spaces, and was accompanied by an understanding of the forms of 'politeness' appropriate to both sexes.[4] A new interest in the history of the book and its production began a much more precise mapping of the contribution of women as printers, publishers, and especially, writers to the development of a consumer-oriented print culture.[5]

These reinterpretations remain controversial, and there are still significant differences between historians about the consequences of the Enlightenment for women and for gender relations. Some have argued that writers of the Enlightenment, such as Jean-Jacques Rousseau, who elaborated a view of women's nature as governed more by sensibility and feeling than by reason, left an oppressive, class-bound, and restraining legacy to subsequent generations of women.[6] Others have suggested that Habermas' thesis, however flawed and gender-blind, offered a way of understanding some women's sociability, and their written interventions, and allowed them a broader and sometimes political awareness, even occasionally across class boundaries.[7] Recent writing has tried to look away from such polarities towards the overlapping and fluidity of public and private worlds, and minor shifts, in degree rather than kind. Lawrence Klein identified the variety of meanings which these words could carry in different contexts, whether civic, economic, or social.[8] Harriet Guest, while recognizing the importance of the continuities in the lives of middle-class women, has suggested the possibility of 'small changes' in the positions and political awareness of such women in the course of the eighteenth century.[9]

In addition to these possibilities, historians of the Enlightenment have increasingly come to question the notion of a homogeneous Enlightenment, and to signal a different and much more pluralist world of European Enlightenments whose intellectual and social boundaries were shaped accordingly to regional and national configurations, and the social and intellectual location of different intelligentsias.[10] In trying to understand the relationships of women of different classes to the history of the Enlightenment in Britain, we have to take into account these configurations and others overlapping them – including those of the metropolis and the provinces, and of established and dissenting forms of religious belief.

The Enlightenment in England came early and its history from the late seventeenth century onwards influenced that of Europe more generally. The works of John Locke and Isaac Newton, establishing the importance of experience and empiricism in the understanding of the mental and physical worlds in the late seventeenth century, were fundamental to all later developments. The polite, urbane, and aspirational London culture of Lord Shaftesbury and of periodicals such as the *Tatler* and the *Spectator* provided another kind of model.[11] And the size, variety, and relative freedom of London intellectual life allowed such different institutions as the Royal Society, the Society of Arts, the Robin Hood Debating Society, the bluestocking salons, and the dinner table of the radical William Godwin all to function, in their own way, as centres of enlightened debate.[12] But the intellectual productions of such different circles inevitably lacked coherence. This diversity perhaps helps to explain why the English Enlightenment figures less frequently in the textbooks of the period than the Scottish Enlightenment. In the much smaller society of Lowland Scotland, where aristocracy and gentry united with important sections of the professional intelligentsia in the goals of rational social improvement, the universities of Edinburgh and Glasgow, and the Church of Scotland, provided a more homogeneous social and intellectual setting. The moral philosophy, the histories of civil society, and the scientific achievements of the Scottish Enlightenment had their roots in that milieu.

The consequences of such differences for the role of women have not yet been explored. Speculatively, the more fragmented character of intellectual debate and the strength of print culture in England from an early date may have allowed a greater degree of activity and agency to English women than the masculine institutions which so effectively underpinned the Enlightenment in Scotland. The consciousness with which the goal of improvement was pursued in Scotland, as well as the moral concerns expressed in relation to such growth, may have helped to generate the particular focus on the place of women in histories of the progress of civil society which was such a feature of Scottish historical writing by the end of the eighteenth century. At the same time, women shared in forms of patriotism which were British, English, and Scottish, especially through the imaginative literature, prose, and poetry written and read by eighteenth-century women – and men.

These differences were national, and also provincial and regional. Amanda Vickery has demonstrated how polite sociability and an engagement with print culture were characteristic not only of such towns as Bristol, Bath, and York in this period, but accessible through newspapers, circulating libraries, and reading networks from the relatively remote country homes of the women of the gentry.[13] Some enclaves had an even more clearly defined identity, whether conservative or radical, Anglican or dissenting. In Birmingham, the middle-class entrepreneurs and inventors of the Lunar Society, self-consciously committed to economic progress and rational reform, mostly sympathetic to dissent and political opposition, shared their ideas with their sisters, wives, and children, as Richard Lovell Edgeworth did with his daughter, Maria. In Warrington, the dissenting academy allowed families associated with the academy a small but effective share in its educational provision. The influential Anna Aikin, later Anna

Barbauld, grew up there and helped to contribute to the distinctive position of radical dissenters who were outside the established Church, and at the forefront of educational innovation and political opposition.[14]

Even within such different settings, the relationship of women to the Enlightenment cannot be understood through a focus on particular genres, such as political writing or imaginative literature, viewed in isolation. Changing attitudes to the situation of women and to femininity could be expressed across genres and in settings which are often unexpected, and not necessarily identical with those of the canonical literature of the Enlightenment. For women writers, the novel might be the most appropriate form for comment on the politics of the French Revolution, just as the autobiography might contribute to the prescriptive literature on women's education.

In this chapter, perspectives on the condition of women will be considered through some of the characteristic discourses of Enlighten-ment, with a particular focus on the contribution of women themselves. The emergence of a polite, sociable, and urbane culture and, along with it, the appearance of philosophies of sentiment, sympathy, and sensibility, provide an important starting point. But an earlier rationalism, which provided a basis for the claim for intellectual equality and the celebration of women's learning, remained of considerable importance and was given new inflections. Another view of gender relations was found in the histories of civil society so characteristic of the Enlightenment in Scotland from the 1760s, histories which examined the shaping of commercial civil societies, their political economy, and their gender relations from a comparative historical perspective. They also offered a way of expressing national, racial, and cultural differences in terms of European progress. They posed a direct challenge to utopian and republican visions of transformation, visions which had their roots within civic humanism, but which took on new meaning after the Revolutions in France and America. More broadly, throughout the Enlightenment in Britain, the possibilities of education for women remained a significant and recurring theme, engaging women writers of very different religious and political perspectives.

One element of enlightened thinking across Britain lay in the associations between philosophy, politeness, and sociability. Writers from John Locke onward sought to chart more closely the relationship between reason, belief, and feeling, and offered a methodology for doing this in the empirical study of human behaviour, individually and in social interaction. Locke had, in his *Essay Concerning Human Understanding* (1690), stressed the blankness of the human mind at birth and the origins of ideas in the sensations received from the external world, ideas which could be reflected upon and combined. Locke's pupil, Lord Shaftesbury, who shared his emphasis on the importance of environmental forces, developed an optimistic philosophy which assumed that the pursuit of virtue, which he compared to the aesthetic pursuit of beauty, would be undertaken as an enlightened, polite, and sociable enterprise by men of taste. In Glasgow, Francis Hutcheson explored the workings of the moral sense and emphasized the sociable and benevolent side of human nature, for which the starting point was to be found in the domestic affections of the human family, which might encourage and inspire a higher spirit of benevolence directed to the public good, the highest of aspirations. Hutcheson's interesting discussion assumed a division of labour between men and women, with citizenship remaining entirely masculine, but questioned the existence of any natural basis for male authority in marriage.[15]

Such ideas of sociable politeness were popularized in the essay period-icals founded by Joseph Addison and Richard Steele at the beginning of the eighteenth century – the *Tatler* and the *Spectator* – as well as through the club and coffee-house culture of London. This socially defined form of politeness assumed urbanity and prosperity for the well-bred and the propertied man. It attempted to define the responsibilities and lifestyle of a self-consciously modern and benevolent élite, who used the public media of a consuming society to exchange and debate its ideas. But these aspirations could be adapted. The *Female Tatler* of 1709–10, ostensibly edited by Phoebe Crackenthorpe and later a 'Society of Ladies' whose identities are unclear, was partly a scandal sheet and partly a political response to the Whiggish *Tatler*, though it also addressed issues of interest to women. More importantly, in 1744–6, Eliza Haywood, as editor of the *Female Spectator*, adopted the form of the earlier male periodical. The *Female Spectator* was less interested in stories of scandal or polit-ical intrigue than in guiding women towards right moral conduct and improving women's education. It created an imaginary audience of female readers. In its interest in defining 'the province of a Female Spectator', it differentiated itself sharply from the public interests of the earlier masculine periodical. It emphasized the significance of a female audience for such magazines, an audience which steadily expanded throughout the century, helping later to create the demand for such a long-running and successful periodical as the *Lady's Magazine* (1770–1830).[16]

By mid-century, much more attention was being given to the refining effects of mixed society. In his essays, the philosopher, David Hume, reflected on the importance of refined conversation, a conversation in which women might exercise significant influence:

> What better school for manners than the company of virtuous women, where the mutual endeavour to please must insensibly polish the mind, where the example of the female softness and modesty must communicate itself to their admirers, and where the delicacy of that sex puts everyone on his guard, lest he give offence by any breach of decency.[17]

Such a description could fit many settings. The metropolitan culture of London was viewed from Edinburgh and other English and Scottish provincial towns and cities as one worth emulating. The urban renaissance of the English provinces introduced many locations for mixed sociability and the pursuit of politeness: the assembly rooms, theatres, musical societies, walks, race-courses, and circulating libraries of such cities as Bath, Bristol, Newcastle and York.[18] Within the home, the social interchange and correspondence of women of the gentry and the middle-classes could also spread the knowledge of periodicals and printed works. The influence of the reading woman of the provinces on the social circles around her could be significant, as is demonstrated in the work of recent historians on the diaries and correspondence of Elizabeth Shackleton of Lancashire, Elizabeth Baker of Dolgellau, Elizabeth Rose of Kilravock, Nairnshire, and Katherine Plymley of Shrewsbury.[19]

The establishment of such patterns of sociability and channels of enlightenment clearly rested on new formulations of polite gender relations. Even if formally excluded from politics, except through the informal exercise of the influence of property, women could participate in and help to shape the institutions of civil society. As Hume indicated, an emphasis on their potentially refining effects rested on assumptions about masculinity and femininity, increasingly clearly spelt out in a language not only of sympathy and benevolence but also of sentiment and sensibility. The concept of 'sensibility' drew upon John Locke's philosophy of sensationalism, but, by the mid-eighteenth century, also upon many different but related fields of knowledge, including physiology, psychology, moral philosophy, history, aesthetics, and literature. Medical science suggested new ways of thinking about the body and its sensations; moral philosophers focused on the interplay of the material and the moral, of sensation, sentiment, and the power of reason; and novelists offered imaginative representations of the workings of sensibility and the passions.

Early eighteenth-century physiologists were coming to see the body not as an earlier generation had done, as a complex machine working through the mechanical relationship of material corpuscles, either solid or fluid, but rather as a vital organic entity. Leading medical teachers and writers, including Robert Whytt and William Cullen of Edinburgh, and George Cheyne of Bath wrote of the importance of the operations of the nervous system, which through its properties could determine individual degrees of sensibility and receptivity to external impressions. The workings of sensibility could vary according to class and gender. Cheyne viewed women, especially those of the upper and middle classes, as having a more delicate nervous system and a greater degree of sensibility than men, signalling both a greater refinement and politeness, and greater susceptibility to weakness and disorder. By the mid-eighteenth century, gendered aspects of sensibility were much more sharply delineated by medical theorists and associated with increasing emphasis on the fundamental biological differences between women and men, especially differences in their reproductive systems which would determine their separate destinies.[20]

David Hume's sceptical philosophy suggested not only that knowledge must rest on experience and custom, rather than reason, but also that human actions were shaped by sentiments and not reason, though they could also arise from reflection and calculation on the overall desirability or utility to society of particular actions. In his *Treatise of Human Nature* (1739), Hume indicated the possibility of different implications for women and for men, as in what he had to say of the 'artificial' and the 'natural' virtues. For him, chastity, like justice, was an artificial, socially acquired virtue, based originally on self-interest but strengthened through sympathy with the sentiments of (masculine) others, or internalized through the working of the (female) conscience. But, at the same time, Hume also identified the existence of the 'natural virtues', including the love of relations and those close to us, pity, benevolence, meekness, and generosity.[21] And both the natural and the artificial virtues were rooted in the sympathy of individuals with the feelings of others. Passions and feelings in both sexes could be destructive to society, yet, when ordered and regulated, provided the basis of the social virtues. Adam Smith elaborated on Hume's concept of sympathy in *Theory of the Moral Sentiments* (1759), in language which occasionally explicitly suggests the gendered nature of such sentiments:

> Generosity is different from humanity. Those two qualities, which at first sight seem so nearly allied, do not always belong to the same person. Humanity is the virtue of a woman, generosity of a man. The fair sex, who have commonly much more tenderness than ours, have seldom so much generosity.[22]

In a different context, Edmund Burke's *A Philosophical Enquiry into the Origin of our Ideas of the Sublime and the Beautiful* (1757/9) identified the gendered nature of aesthetic perceptions and sensations, distinguishing the masculine experience of the sublime from perceptions of the beautiful associated with a particular kind of femininity. Beauty, for Burke, carried with it the implication of weakness and imperfection, with which women themselves colluded: 'they learn to lisp, to totter in their walk, to counterfeit weakness, and even sickness'.[23] The very presence of beauty could induce a dangerous relaxation, 'an inward sense of melting and languor'.[24]

Such themes were also widely found in imaginative literature. In Samuel Richardson's *Clarissa* (1748), *Pamela* (1740–1) and *Sir Charles Grandison* (1753–4) the feeling, sentimental, and moral hero or heroine would confront the world, and, sometimes, older more libertine manners, through many traumas and sufferings related through letters, engaging and identifying the reader with the emotions of the central character. Each has an instructive purpose, dominated by a view of feminine virtue identified with feeling and with sentiment. Richardson's influence on the most significant novel of sentiment written during the Enlightenment, Jean-Jacques Rousseau's *La Nouvelle Héloïse* (1761), was considerable. Its full title was very rapidly translated into English as *Julie, or the New Eloise: Letters of Two Lovers, Inhabitants of a Small Town at the Foot of the Alps* (1761), and ten editions appeared in English before 1800. In this love story, related through letters, the heroine Julie, a woman of great moral seriousness, returned the passion of her tutor, Saint-Preux. Renouncing her lover, she resolved to do her duty and to marry her father's old friend, Baron Wolmar, she became a model wife and mother on a secluded estate, Clarens, in Switzerland, devoted to the care of her sons and far from the corruptions of the world. Hoping to end the affair, her husband brought Saint-Preux to Clarens. No unambiguous lesson could be drawn from the novel. When caught with her lover in a storm on Lake Geneva, Julie saved one of her children from drowning, but when dying confessed that she had never ceased to love Saint-Preux.[25]

The attractions of *La Nouvelle Héloïse*, and of the imagining of emotional experience through epistolary exchanges, were considerable. Many authors followed Rousseau's lead, including the Scottish writer, Henry Mackenzie, who in his *Man of Feeling* (1771) and *Julia de Roubigné* (1777) also used the exchange of letters to represent subjective feeling. Mackenzie's Julia, though preserving her chastity, died at the hands of her upright though wrongly jealous husband, a death which again signalled the incompatibility of fulfilled passion and social order. In Britain in the 1770s and 1780s just over 40 per cent of all novels were published in the form of letters.[26]

Women's responses as readers and as writers to the literature of sensibility and the prescriptive writing which drew upon it were very diverse. Before 1789 in particular, many, though not all, respectable women read such texts with sometimes guilty pleasure, though they might criticize aspects of them. Women readers not only identified with the representation of emotion, but found in such novels the empowering of emotional expression. They might, however, criticize the weight placed upon a feminized sensibility or find new uses for it.[27]

The English dissenter and liberal reformer, Anna Aikin, later Barbauld, brought up in one of the great seminaries of the English Enlightenment, Warrington Academy, was well acquainted with the literature of sensibility. She accepted and traced the different attributes of women and men, and wrote of women's greater capacity for sentiment and feeling. But she also asserted the relationship of emotion and sensibility to the critical use of reason and moral sense, and chose to write in areas of moral philosophy, religion, and politics as well as on education. So, in her essay 'An Enquiry into those Kinds of Distress which excite Agreeable Sensations' (1773), she followed Burke in exploring the appropriate ways in which the emotions of love and pity should be represented, but differed from him in her claim for their moral stature. Critical of lachrymose sentimentality for its own sake, she wrote that 'no scenes of misery ought to be exhibited which are not connected with the display of some moral excellence or agreeable quality'.[28] Her 'Thoughts on Devotional Taste' (1775) continued the same kind of enlightened and 'scientific' exploration in a study of religious emotion and of the relationship between establishments and sects. Her focus here was on 'religion as a taste, an affair of sentiment and feeling', with 'its seat in the imagination and the passions'.[29]

After 1789, however, the philosophy of sentimentalism and the reading of *La Nouvelle Héloïse* carried what could be dangerous associations with French revolutionary politics.[30] One of the outstanding women writers on the French Revolution, also a poet and dissenter, Helen Maria Williams, used the language of sensibility throughout her political commentary in epistolary form, the eight-volume *Letters from France* (1790–6).[31] Her earlier novel, *Julia* (1790), had focused on an intense triangle of relationships, between Frederick Seymour, Charlotte, his future wife and Julia's friend and cousin, and Julia herself. To Williams, like Barbauld, 'in a mind where the principles of religion and integrity are firmly established, sensibility is not merely the ally of weakness, or the slave of guilt, but serves to give a stronger impulse'.[32] Frederick Seymour's passion for Julia, spoken but never consummated, ended only in his death. Julia, refusing to marry, devoted herself to Charlotte and the education of her child, to religious and benevolent projects, and to 'the society of persons of understanding and merit'.[33] Williams' *Letters* consistently represented the revolution in terms of the transformation of feeling. In 1789–90, she wrote of the possibility of a world of affection and greater equality, and of the restructuring of the hierarchy of state and family in parallel, though in 1793–4 she showed the terrible effects of the Jacobin betrayal on men, women, and families, revolutionary sympathizers and royalists. Williams' politics had a place for a radical sensibility, though subsequent British women writers of the 1790s, such as Mary Wollstonecraft, were to struggle with the relationship between passion and politics, sentiment and reason.[34]

Yet, at the same time, it has to be stressed that older ways of thinking about the relative situation of the sexes retained considerable force during the European and British Enlightenments. The *querelle des femmes* – the debate about the relative capacities of men and women, which looked back to the celebratory biographies of Plutarch's *Bravery of Women* and Boccacio's *Concerning Famous Women* (c.1360), and gathered strength with the Renaissance – had left a legacy.[35] Seventeenth-century rationalism, which emphasized the separation of mind and body, seemed to make the physical differences between the sexes less significant and provide new ground for the assertion of intellectual equality. The French writer, Poullain de la Barre, did just that in his influential *The Woman as Good as the Man* (1673). Translations and adaptations of Poullain's work were still being published in Britain as late as 1751.[36] Women writers restated the case for intellectual equality in these terms from the beginning of the eighteenth century onwards, and they shared also in the celebration of women of learning. Damaris Lady Masham, Catharine Trotter, and Mary Astell wrote as participants in philosophical debate, with their own political and religious priorities. Mary Astell, the best-known defender of women's intellectual abilities in these years, was a conservative Anglican whose major works on this subject were her *Serious Proposal to the Ladies* (1694; 1697) and *Some Reflections upon Marriage* (1700).[37] In the first volume of the *Serious Proposal*, Astell, thinking 'women as capable of learning as men', called for them to counter the masculine monopoly of learning – 'to Tast [*sic*] of that Tree of Knowledge [men] have so long unjustly monopolised' – in the setting of a female academy devoted to the pursuit of religion, virtue, and reason.[38] In the second volume, stimulated by the support of Damaris Lady Masham for John Locke, she transformed her work into a philosophical and epistemological critique of Locke and his interpreters. In rejecting empiricism as condemning women to the environment in which they lived, she challenged Lockean orthodoxy in the name of a religious and Platonic philosophy which allowed her to assert the autonomy of the rational will, for women and for men, to understand and to pursue virtuous conduct.[39] Her challenge to Locke's political philosophy in *Some Reflections upon Marriage* is well known:

> If all men are born free, how is it that all women are born slaves? as they must be if the being subjected to the inconstant, uncertain, unknown arbitrary will of men, be the perfect condition of slavery?[40]

But such a comment was an ironic one, intended to demonstrate that though reason might be the preserve of all, both marriage and the social order were divinely ordained as hierarchical; for her, marriage was not a contract between individuals but an institution whose rights and duties were ordained by God.

Judith Drake's *Essay in Defence of the Female Sex* (1696) attacked masculine self-interest and intellectual authority, 'the Usurpation of Men, and the Tyranny of Custom', and traditional male classical learning, suggesting the potential of a modern, rational education.[41] Unlike Astell, Drake combined a Tory perspective with a Lockean outlook and concepts of 'politeness' to trace an early Enlightenment vision of a sociable and conversational learned world. In *Anthropologia Nova; or, A New System of Anatomy* (1707), which she, an unlicensed practitioner herself, wrote with her husband, James Drake, the English physician, Drake emphasized the contribution of both sexes to conception and to heredity, challenging any view of female passivity in the reproductive process.[42]

Many individual women were able to demonstrate, and were celebrated for, their considerable intellectual achievements. In the process, they became a part of a polite and conversational culture of the kind that both Judith Drake and David Hume anticipated. Lady Mary Wortley Montagu, poet, traveller, supporter of inoculation against smallpox, and woman of letters, was an outstanding figure in the literary world of early eighteenth-century London. Even she, however, experienced 'a life of struggle in almost all its phases' to fulfil her intellectual ambitions, and, as she did so, moved towards questioning the inequities of women's situation in her society.[43] The women known as the bluestockings – especially Elizabeth Carter and Catherine Talbot, and the sisters Sarah Scott and Elizabeth Montagu – defended women's learning as part of an Anglican and domesticated mixed sociability, a salon culture which set itself in opposition to courtly and aristocratic networks.[44] In this, letters, conversation, and friendship with male supporters such as Dr Johnson and Lord Kames were perhaps more to the fore than publication. But a few publications across a variety of genres demonstrated the range of the learning of the women known as the 'bluestockings'. Elizabeth Carter translated the works of the Stoic, Epictetus. Elizabeth Montagu's *Essay on the Writings and Genius of Shakespear [sic]* (1769) defended the playwright against Voltaire's criticisms. Carter's *Remarks on the Athanasian Creed* (1752) and Catherine Talbot's *Reflections on the Seven Days of the Week* (1770) both demonstrated a desire for a feminized Anglican theology. And Sarah Scott, in *A Description of Millenium Hall* (1762), transformed the bluestocking programme into a utopian vision of a retreat for privileged women, sharing learning, piety, and philanthropy, away from the oppression of husbands and fathers By the middle of the eighteenth century, many writers and intellectuals, both women and men, were attempting to elaborate a balance between the acceptance of a degree of sexual difference and a continuing claim for intellectual and moral equality.

The existence of such a group of women writers allowed the continuing celebration of a genealogy of learned women. The best known of a number of such works was probably George Ballard's *Memoirs of Several Ladies of Great Britain* (1752), a collection which celebrated learning in women as an appropriately feminine accomplishment and appropriate to the national identity of a commercial and civilized society. John Duncombe's *Feminiad: A Poem* (1754) wrote of twenty-one learned British women, extending well into the eighteenth century and including the philosopher, Catherine Cockburn, and the working woman poet, Mary Leapor. In 1774,

Duncombe was mildly criticized for the small number identified by Mary Scott, who in her *The Female Advocate* described herself as 'being too well acquainted with the illiberal sentiments of men in general in regard to our sex, and prompted by the most fervent zeal for their privileges'.[45] Scott's fifty women included many still in the early stages of their writing careers: Anna Barbauld, Charlotte Lennox, Catherine Macaulay, Elizabeth Montagu, Hannah More, and also Phillis Wheatley, the black Boston slave. She not only praised past writings in literature, religion, and education but also looked to women's future achievements, including their potential to rival a Shakespeare or a Newton, and the extension of their interests to astronomy, natural history, botany, and moral philosophy.[46] That vision of future possibilities was, in the next decades, to be echoed by many and to interact with the languages of republican or utopian expectations, or of progressive history.

One important strand in eighteenth-century British social and political thought was that of republicanism, a word used with many different nuances in the course of the century. Republican political theory had its origins in the Renaissance recovery of the ideal republic, but had been translated during the early modern period to a philosophy more appropriate to the needs of a reforming gentry, concerned to preserve civic virtue and counter corruption in the court and the executive. James Harrington's *Oceana* (1656), and David Hume's 'The Idea of a Perfect Commonwealth' (1754) both had at their heart the classical ideal of the citizen as an independent and armed proprietor, who was also the head of a household and an active participant in representative government. This masculine republican ideal was hostile to the expansion of wealth and luxury, and the potential moral corruptions of commerce. It was no accident that the image of Credit was a feminine one or that the dangers of the court were so often expressed in feminized terms.[47] Among English dissenters, the most active spokesmen for this tradition were the 'commonwealthsmen' (a term implying awareness of the legacy of the seventeenth-century British revolutions) such as Richard Price and James Burgh.[48] One of the most outstanding writers in this group was the 'commonwealthswoman', Catherine Macaulay. Between 1763 and 1783, Catherine Macaulay completed a major contribution to republican thinking in her *History of England* (1763–83). Unlike earlier writers she drew upon wide-ranging resources, including women's petitions, to represent the republicanism of many different political groupings and sects in the revolutions of the seventeenth century. At the same time, she remained constantly aware of the ideal represented by the early Greek and Roman republics, here viewed as exemplars of Liberty:

> From my earliest youth I have read with delight those histories that exhibit Liberty in its most exalted state, the annals of the Roman

and the Greek republics. Studies like these excite that natural love of freedom which lies latent in the breath of every rational being, till it is nipped by the frost of prejudice or blasted by the influence of vice.[49]

For Francis Hutcheson in Glasgow, the public good had required a state committed to the pursuit of virtue, united by industry and not excess, encouraged by the moral potential of domestic and family affections. And the paradigm which looked to the republican home – whether that of the classical Roman matrons such as Cornelia, mother of the Gracchi, or Veturia, the mother of Coriolanus, or seventeenth-century Whig heroines such as Lucy Hutchinson or Rachel Russell – was one which tended to celebrate a domesticated and patriotic republican motherhood, committed to the education of children in the interests of new or reforming nations. Both Anna Barbauld and Catherine Macaulay were portrayed as Roman matrons, their images also associated with the allegorical figure of Liberty.[50] Such themes, however gender-specific, oriented women through the domestic affections towards the public good and the responsibilities of a civic culture.

Republican political ideas, however, took many different forms. Jean-Jacques Rousseau's *Social Contract* (1762) imagined the will of the individual citizen absorbed within the collective goals of the ideal republic. In 1776, Thomas Paine's *Common Sense* united a devotion to the public good with a philosophy of individual natural rights, and a commitment to a progressive and peaceful society, which did not reject the benefits of commerce and prosperity. Both assumed the masculinity of citizenship, but that assumption was challenged from within reforming and republican circles. The political radical, Ann Jebb, married to a Unitarian minister, John Jebb, came from the milieu of rational dissent and wrote in support of religious toleration and the movement for political reform in Britain.[51] Catherine Macaulay's *Letters on Education* (1790) was shaped by a republican perspective, which, though asserting 'the great difference . . . observable in the characters of the sexes . . . as they display themselves in the scenes of social life', denied such a difference in the intellectual and moral powers of women and men, and attacked the 'absurd notion of a sexual excellence', blaming the corrupt conditions and gallantry of modern Europe for the weaknesses of modern women. For 'when the sex have been taught wisdom by education, they will be glad to give up indirect influence for rational privileges'.[52]

In December 1790, Mary Wollstonecraft wrote to Catherine Macaulay: 'You are the only female writer who I coincide in opinion with respecting the rank our sex ought to endeavour to attain in the world.'[53] In her *Vindication of the Rights of Men* (1790), Wollstonecraft deliberately opposed Burke's 'equivocal idiom of politeness' to a 'manly definition' of the 'rights of men' and looked towards a world which would inspire not the misery and poverty and false sensibility of 'civilized' contemporary Britain, but 'a manly spirit of independence' and 'a virtuous ambition'.[54]

The very term 'civilization', used in this sense, was a product of the Enlightenment in Britain and, more specifically, Scotland. By 1771, as used in John Millar's *Observations Concerning the Distinction of Ranks*, it was no longer a technical legal term drawn from Scottish law, but a self-conscious description of the state of modern commercial society, which implied refinement and prosperity.[55] Adam Smith, as part of his lectures on jurisprudence, had considered the history of women and of marriage against a framework of staged economic development. The condition of women was central to the work of Smith's pupil and successor, John Millar. It was also important to the work of other Scottish 'philosophical' historians of the period who wrote not of politics and constitutional change but of the progressive emergence of civil societies through different social and economic stages from 'ignorance to knowledge and from rude to civilized manners'.[56] In such works, the history of the condition of women, the state of marriage, the relationship between parents and children, and manners and morals in general were not separated from the history of economic development and political forms, but were integrally related to them. The condition of women became an index of the state of civilization: 'the rank and condition, in which we find women in any country, mark out to us with the greatest precision, the exact point in scale of civil society, to which the people of such country have arrived'.[57]

Such histories traced a history of European progress, with particular attention to the impact of material wealth and the coming of chivalry. Progress was constantly contrasted with the barbarism of earlier periods, of the Germanic tribes as of the American Indians, and with the 'despotism' of Asian governments and harems. The impact of chivalry, here read rather as an aspect of late medieval society which looked towards modernity, brought 'a great respect and veneration for the female sex'. This was not, however, an unproblematic tale of improvement, for the moral dangers of excessive wealth and luxury, in the corruption of manners, morals, and institutions still had to be avoided. Material progress should be measured, steady and temperate towards an industrious society, in which learning, sociability, and good conversation could still flourish in social and domestic settings where 'women become neither the slaves nor the idols of the other sex, but the friends and companions'.[58]

Women's position was here regarded as central to the emergence of modern civil society. Mary Catherine Moran has argued that the focus in such histories lay in the improvement of masculine manners, while the qualities attributed to women, by Millar, Kames, Alexander, and others remained relatively unchanged. If women were agents of civilization, it was as passive conduits of sentiment and refinement. Nevertheless, these formulations allowed discussion and approval of women's roles in settings which were both domestic and social, neither public nor private.[59]

It is not easy to trace the immediate reception of such histories. History was widely recommended as appropriate reading matter for girls and young women by reformers and conservatives alike. If Jane Austen represented Catherine Morland in *Northanger Abbey* (1818, but drafted by 1803) as finding in history only vexations, 'the quarrels of popes and kings, with wars or pestilences, in every page', she countered that with the pleasure taken by the sensible Eleanor Tilney in the works of David Hume and William Robertson.[60] Hume and Robertson appeared also in Wollstonecraft's anthology, *The Female Reader* (1789). Wollstonecraft's *Vindication of the Rights of Woman* (1792) asserted a progressive historical framework and a view of the unintended nature of historical change against the primitivism of Jean-Jacques Rousseau, though Wollstonecraft remained ambivalent as to the future direction of such progress. In her *Historical and Moral View of the Origin and Progress of the French Revolution* (1794), she stated her ambition to write a historical narrative of the French Revolution informed by a 'philosophical eye'; and in this and her *Letters . . . in Sweden . . .* (1796), she was committed to an understanding of 'the grand causes which combine to carry mankind forward'.[61] Yet, her history of the French Revolution concluded with a discussion of the 'destructive influence' of an unregulated and grasping commerce, and of Adam Smith's understanding of the damaging effects of the division of labour on human character.[62]

While few women writers followed Macaulay and Wollstonecraft in the writing of history, many were to take up and identify with the possibilities of progressive improvement in the condition of women so clearly signalled. Mark Phillips has suggested that such historical approaches should be read in the context of more general shifts in the nature of historical writing – no longer simply a matter of the formal public and political record, but also a question of sentiment and identification. Though Lucy Aikin, in her poetic *Epistles on Woman* (1810), denied 'the absurd idea that the two sexes ever can be or ever ought to be, placed in all respects on a footing of equality', she appealed to 'the impartial voice of History' to 'testify for us', so that the 'Juvenals and Popes of future ages' will no longer express their misogyny and scorn. Her aim was to trace the 'progress of human society', and the 'accompanying and proportional elevation or depression of woman in the scale of existence'.[63] She asked 'enlightened Man' to lift the 'barbarous shackles', to 'loose the female mind', and to erase the 'slavish stigma seared on half the race'.[64]

Such historical perspectives can be associated with the literature of conduct and education focused on and directed towards women. For it was this literature – though no guide to experience – which represented the most significant site of contest, contest about the nature of women and

the nature of historical progress. The conduct-book was not an Enlightenment invention, though eighteenth-century versions incorporated
prescriptions of conduct which owed much to the contemporary language
of gender difference, whether in terms of polite society, Enlightenment
psychology, or progressive history. The conduct-book could express social
aspirations reflecting shifting class boundaries, and educational advice
could provide an opportunity for public and political intervention, for
radicals, liberals, and conservatives. Education and intellectual development, seriously conceived, were central to the concerns of enlightened
women and capable of expansion towards a broader moral and social role.
Educational employment and the writing of practical educational texts
became and remained one of the most important sources of income for
middle-class women.[65]

Such works had many contradictions, as did the popular and frequently
reprinted John Gregory's *A Father's Legacy to His Daughters* (1774), in
which he wrote of women as 'designed to soften our hearts and polish our
manners'. But Gregory was also a Scottish historian, whose writings
constantly reflected a tension between assumptions of natural sexual
difference and of women as agents of refinement and civilization.[66] Hester
Chapone's *Letters on the Improvement of the Mind* (1773) was also
reprinted many times. In it she described a serious and systematic
programme of study intended to 'form and strengthen your judgement'
and, at the same time, indicated that 'the private and domestic happiness'
of women would depend on their capacity to control and regulate their
own affections and temper. As Kathryn Sutherland has pointed out,
however, this conjunction of an intellectual curriculum with a limited and
private future was by no means new, even though it could be identified
with the bluestocking circle. A major source for Chapone's work was the
Revd Wetenhall Wilkes, *A Letter of Genteel and Moral Advice to a Young
Lady* (1741).[67]

In the 1790s, such works continued to be reprinted. *The Young Lady's
Pocket Library, or Parental Monitor* (1790) included not only *A Father's
Legacy*, but three earlier works, Edward Moore's poetic *Fables for the
Female Sex* (1744), Sarah Pennington's *An Unfortunate Mother's Advice to
Her Daughter* (1761), and the Marquise de Lambert's *Advice of a Mother
to Her Daughter* (1727). However, writing about the education of women
took on new significance as the full impact of the French Revolution and its
implications for gender roles was appreciated. Catherine Macaulay's *Letters
on Education* (1790) offered one model of a politicized approach, rapidly
appropriated in a spirit of intellectual sympathy by Mary Wollstonecraft,
who had already served her apprenticeship in the field of educational
writing in her *Thoughts on the Education of Daughters* (1787), *Original
Stories* (1788), and *The Female Reader* (1789). Wollstonecraft, like
Macaulay, wrote in her *Vindication of the Rights of Woman* against: 'those

pretty feminine phrases, which the men condescendingly use to soften our slavish dependence, and despising that weak elegancy of mind, exquisite sensibility, and sweet docility of manners, supposed to be the sexual characteristics of the weaker vessel'.[68] In her committed and philosophically informed chapters, Wollstonecraft condemned not only the portrait of Sophie in Rousseau's *Emile* (1761), but also all those writers of conduct-books who had associated themselves with his outlook, including John Gregory, whose 'opinions . . . have had the most baneful effect on the morals and manners of the female world'.[69]

The *Vindication* was not only, however, a criticism of conduct literature nor was it in spite of its title, straightforwardly a political pamphlet. It marked Wollstonecraft's complete engagement with the political and historical themes of the Enlightenment that have been traced here. Tracing the internalization of the qualities attributed to women through the early association of ideas in children, she looked to the creation of a new kind of educational system which would allow women intellectual and human autonomy, though it would not displace the division of labour or the responsibilities of motherhood. Such an outcome would depend upon a transformative republican politics, which would ultimately enable 'a revolution in female manners', a revolution which would spread 'that sublime contentment which only morality could diffuse'.[70] At the heart of Wollstonecraft's *Vindication* lay the goal of a virtuous society. That virtue could be defined in republican terms which owed something both to Rousseau and to the commonwealth tradition. It required the continuing improvement of the powers of reason and the human mind, the worth-while fruits of civilization. And it was also suffused with the rhetoric of religion and the contemplation of God. Barbara Taylor has recently argued that this classic feminist text can only be fully understood if we recognize the strength of Wollstonecraft's representation, sometimes in erotic terms, of the transcendent perfection of the Deity.[71]

Other texts fully recognized the political charge as well as the educational importance of the subject. Maria Edgeworth's *Letters for Literary Ladies* (1795) used epistolary forms and both male and female voices to argue for a serious and modern plan of instruction. Such a plan would abandon the old assumptions of chivalry and the attractions of a sexualized sensibility for a future which would be that of rational agency, even if it were also focused on domestic and social duties. Hannah More's *Strictures on Female Education* (1799), however conservative, may also be read as a text of the Enlightenment. As a former member of the bluestocking circle, a poet, dramatist, political writer, and novelist, she was a woman of learning and wit, qualities which are very evident in her educational writing. She, like Edgeworth, Macaulay, and Wollstonecraft, also dissented from Edmund Burke's representations of female attributes and argued for a serious and rational curriculum for women, though she did not envisage education as allowing women intellectual confidence or autonomy. For her, the hierarchy of marriage continued to mirror that of divinely ordained social order.

Wollstonecraft's *Vindication of the Rights of Woman* had been favourably received on its publication in 1792. By 1800, however, the climate of opinion had shifted significantly against her reforming, or radical, politics. In part, this was because of the consequences of the French Revolution and in part because of the notoriety of Wollstonecraft herself after her sexual relationships with Gilbert Imlay and William Godwin had been posthumously publicized in Godwin's *Memoirs* (1798).[72]

It is not easy to trace the legacy of the eighteenth-century Enlightenment for women and for gender roles. In the aftermath of the political conflicts of the 1790s, the 'enlightened' qualities of women's writing may appear more subdued, as the force of conservative reaction was felt among dissenters, radicals, and Whigs during and after the Napoleonic Wars.[73] The extent of writing on women's education was not matched by any broad initiative, though private, religious, and entrepreneurial expansion continued. The boundaries between the legacies of the Enlightenment and the attractions of Romanticism were fluid ones. The period between 1800 and 1830 remains understudied, although there are signs of some of those 'small changes' of which Harriet Guest has written.

The Enlightenment certainly left a legacy to radical politics in the democratic, utopian, and secularizing ideologies of the early nineteenth century. So, for instance, the politics of the utopian communitarian, Frances Wright, and of the freethinker, Eliza Sharples, drew extensively upon its transforming possibilities.[74] Less dramatically, the republican commitment to the public good could be translated into local benevolence. Early nineteenth-century women's philanthropy has generally been interpreted in terms of expanding evangelical commitment, but other interpretations are possible. The Quaker, Priscilla Wakefield, suggested in her *Reflections on the Present Condition of the Female Sex* of 1798, that for women of the upper and middle classes a commitment to 'the reformation of vice, the instruction of ignorance, and the promotion of virtue' was not merely a leisure activity but a civic duty, conducive 'to the improvement of public morals, and the increase of public happiness'.[75] The different strands which made up the philanthropy of urban civic élites in the early nineteenth century still await further study. There is a much broader history also to be written of women as writers and participants in print culture in these years. We know that women novelists increased proportionately to men steadily until the 1790s, though not how this was reflected across other genres. That increase was to continue until the 1820s.[76]

By the early nineteenth century, there appears to be a sharpening of definitions of masculinity and femininity, definitions which could be expanded into the familiar trope of separate spheres. Constructions of femininity continued to draw upon the vocabularies of sensibility, privacy, and domesticity. Yet it is also possible to read across these definitions a continuing process of negotiation about gender boundaries, often reactive, and frequently tested and manipulated. If the Enlightenment had clearly given the authority of nature to particular gender attributes, it had at the same time encouraged and drawn upon the rapid expansion of print culture and associational life, suggested a language of progressive improvement, fostered intellectual ambition, and reshaped the ideal of the public good. The dominant response may have been the desirability of limiting the boundaries of women's action and their social and political roles, but the divisions of opinion and practice among the women and men of the cultural and professional élite, especially among liberals and radicals, perhaps also indicate the diversity of the opinions that were to crystallize around women's political and social claims by the mid-nineteenth century.

Notes

1 E. Hobsbawm, *On History*, London, 1997, p. 254, as quoted in R. Porter, *Enlightenment: Britain and the Creation of the Modern World*, London, 2000, p. xxi.

2 For the most useful discussions of these reinterpretations generally, see D. Outram, *The Enlightenment*, Cambridge, 1995; T. L. Munck, *The Enlightenment: A Comparative Social History, 1721–1794*, London, 2000; R. Porter and M. Teich (eds), *The Enlightenment in National Context*, Cambridge, 1981. For Britain, see Porter, *Enlightenment, passim*; J. Brewer, *The Pleasures of the Imagination: English Culture in the Eighteenth Century*, London, 1997.

3 J. Habermas, *The Structural Transformation of the Public Sphere*, trans. T. Burger, Cambridge, 1989; J. Meehan (ed.), *Feminists Read Habermas*, London, 1995; J. Brewer, 'This, that and the other: public, social and private in the seventeenth and eighteenth centuries', in D. Castiglione and L. Sharpe (eds), *Shifting the Boundaries: Transformation of the Languages of Public and Private in the Eighteenth Century*, Exeter, 1995; H. Barker and E. Chalus (eds), *Gender in Eighteenth-Century England: Roles, Representations, Responsibilities*, Harlow, 1997; E. Eger, C. Grant, C. Ó Gallchoir, and P. Warburton, 'Introduction: women, writing and representation', in Eger *et al.* (eds), *Women, Writing and the Public Sphere, 1700–1830*, Cambridge, 2001.

4 P. Borsay, *The English Urban Renaissance: Culture and Society in the Provincial Town, 1660–1770*, Oxford, 1989; A. Vickery, *The Gentleman's Daughter: Women's Lives in Georgian England*, London, 1998.

5 See J. Raven, H. Small and N. Tadmor (eds), *The Practice and Representation of Reading in the Eighteenth Century*, Cambridge, 1995; James Raven, *Judging New Wealth: Popular Publishing and Responses to Commerce in England, 1750–1800*, Oxford, 1992; P. Garside, J. Raven and R. Schöwerling (eds), *The English Novel, 1770–1829: A Bibliographic Survey of Prose Fiction Published in the British Isles*, 2 vols, Oxford, 2000; P. McDowell, *The Women of Grub Street: Press, Politics and Gender in the London Literary Marketplace, 1678–1730*, Oxford, 1998.

6 J. Landes, *Women and the Public Sphere in the Age of the French Revolution*, Ithaca,

NY, 1988; J. Schwartz, *The Sexual Politics of Jean-Jacques Rousseau*, Chicago, 1984; M. S. Trouille, *Sexual Politics in the Enlightenment: Women Writers Read Rousseau*, Albany, NY, 1997. More generally, see L. Steinbrugge, *The Moral Sex: Woman's Nature in the French Enlightenment*, New York, 1995.

7 For instance, see M. Jacob, 'The mental landscape of the public sphere', *Eighteenth Century Studies*, 1994, vol. 28, pp. 95–113; also, *Living the Enlightenment: Freemasonry and Politics in Eighteenth-Century Europe*, New York, 1991, Chapter 5; Dena Goodman, *The Republic of Letters: A Cultural History of the French Enlightenment*, Ithaca, NY, 1994; M. Bolufer Peruga and I. Morant Deusa, 'On women's reason, education and love', *Gender & History*, 1998, vol. 10, pp. 183–216; C. Hesse, *The Other Enlightenment: How French Women Became Modern*, Princeton, NJ, 2001.

8 L. Klein, 'Gender and the public/private distinction in the eighteenth century: some questions about evidence and analytic procedure', *Eighteenth-Century Studies*, 1995, vol. 29, pp. 97–109.

9 H. Guest, *Small Change: Women, Learning, Patriotism, 1750–1810*, Chicago, 2000.

10 See especially Porter and Teich (eds), *Enlightenment in National Context*.

11 Porter, *Enlightenment*, Chapters 2–3; L. Klein, *Shaftesbury and the Culture of Politeness: Moral Discourse and Cultural Politics in Early Eighteenth-Century England*, Cambridge, 1994.

12 For these different worlds, see Porter, *Enlightenment*, pp. 34–40; P. Clark, *British Clubs and Societies, 1580–1800: The Origins of an Associational World*, Oxford, 2000; G. Kelly, 'Bluestocking feminism', in Eger *et al.* (eds), *Women, Writing and the Public Sphere*; M. Philp, *Godwin's Political Justice*, London, 1986, Appendices A–D.

13 Vickery, *Gentleman's Daughter*, Chapter 7.

14 J. Uglow, *The Lunar Men: The Friends who Made the Future, c.1730–1810*, London, 2002, Chapters 27, 40, epilogue; B. Rodgers, *Georgian Chronicle: Mrs Barbauld and Her Family*, London, 1958.

15 Porter, *Enlightenment*, Chapter 7; Klein, *Shaftesbury and the Culture of Politeness*, *passim*; G. J. Barker-Benfield, *The Culture of Sensibility: Sex and Society in Eighteenth-Century Britain*, Chicago, 1992, pp. 105–19; J. Rendall, *The Origins of the Scottish Enlightenment, 1707–1776*, London, 1978, Chapter 2.

16 Ros Ballaster *et al.* (eds), *Women's Worlds: Ideology, Femininity and the Woman's Magazine*, London, 1991, Chapter 2. See also K. Shevelow, *Women and Print Culture: The Construction of Femininity in the Early Periodical*, London, 1989.

17 Hume, 'Of the Rise and Progress of the Arts and Sciences', as quoted in G. Kelly, 'Bluestocking feminism', p. 166.

18 Borsay, *English Urban Renaissance*; Vickery, *Gentleman's Daughter*, Chapter 7.

19 L. Klein, 'Gender, conversation and the public sphere in early eighteenth century England', in J. Still and M. Worton (eds), *Textuality and Sexuality: Reading Theories and Practices*, Manchester, 1993; ibid., *passim*, especially pp. 202ff., 258–60; S. Clarke, 'The construction of genteel sensibilities: the socialization of daughters of the gentry in seventeenth- and eighteenth-century Wales', in S. Betts (ed.), *Our Daughters' Land: Past and Present*, Cardiff, 1996; also, 'Visions of community: Elizabeth Baker and late eighteenth-century Merioneth', in M. Roberts and S. Clarke (eds), *Women and Gender in Early Modern Wales*, Cardiff, 2000; M. C. Moran, 'From rudeness to refinement: gender, genre and Scottish Enlightenment discourse', DPhil thesis, Johns Hopkins University, 1999, pp. 76–90; K. Gleadle, ' "Opinions deliver'd in conversation": gender, politics and conversation

in the late eighteenth century', in J. Harris (ed.), *Civil Society in History*, Oxford, 2003.

20 C. Lawrence 'The nervous system and society in the Scottish Enlightenment', in B. Barnes and S. Shapin (eds), *Natural Order: Historical Studies of Scientific Culture*, Beverley Hills, 1979; Barker-Benfield, *Culture of Sensibility*, Chapter 1; A. Van Sant, *Eighteenth-Century Sensibility and the Novel: The Senses in Social Context*, Cambridge, 1993; M. Ellis (ed.), *The Politics of Sensibility: Race, Gender and Commerce in the Sentimental Novel*, Cambridge, 1996, Chapter 1.

21 D. Hume, *A Treatise of Human Nature*, ed. E. C. Mossner, Harmondsworth, 1969, pp. 629–31; see also A. C. Baier, 'Hume on women's complexion', in P. Jones (ed.), *The 'Science of Man' in the Scottish Enlightenment: Hume, Reid and their Contemporaries*, Edinburgh, 1989; J. Mullan, *Sentiment and Sociability: The Language of Feeling in the Eighteenth Century*, Oxford, 2002, Chapter 1.

22 A. Smith, *The Theory of Moral Sentiments*, ed. D. D. Raphael and A. L. Macfie, Oxford, 1976, p. 190; J. Rendall, 'Virtue and commerce: women in the making of Adam Smith's political economy', in E. Kennedy and S. Mendus (eds), *Women in Western Political Philosophy*, Brighton, 1987; Mullan, *Sentiment and Sociability*, pp. 43–56. H. C. Clark, in 'Women and humanity in Scottish Enlightenment social thought: the case of Adam Smith', *Historical Reflections/Réflexions historiques*, 1993, vol. 19, 334–61, takes a different view of Smith.

23 E. Burke, *A Philosophical Enquiry into the Origin of our Ideas of the Sublime and the Beautiful*, ed. J. T. Boulton, Oxford, 1958, p. 110.

24 Ibid., p. 149.

25 See, for discussion, among much recent work, N. Fermon, *Domesticating Passions: Rousseau, Woman and Nation*, Hanover, NH, 1997; J. Schwartz, *The Sexual Politics of Jean-Jacques Rousseau*, Chicago, 1985; Trouille, *Sexual Politics in the Enlightenment*; V. G. Wexler, ' "Made for Man's Delight": Rousseau as anti-feminist', *American Historical Review*, 1976, vol. 81, pp. 266–91.

26 J. Raven, 'Historical introduction: the novel comes of age', in J. Raven *et al.* (eds), *The English Novel, 1770–1829*, vol. I: *1770–1779*, p. 31.

27 Trouille, *Sexual Politics in the Enlightenment*, pp. 54–60; J. Pearson, *Women's Reading in Britain, 1750–1835: A Dangerous Recreation*, Cambridge, 1999, especially Chapter 2.

28 W. McCarthy and E. Kraft (eds), *Anna Letitia Barbauld: Selected Poetry and Prose*, Peterborough, ON, 2002, p. 198.

29 Ibid., p. 211.

30 See, on this theme, M. Butler, *Jane Austen and the War of Ideas*, Oxford, 1987, pt 1; 'Introduction', in A. Craciun and K. E. Lokke (eds), *Rebellious Hearts: British Women Writers and the French Revolution*, Albany, NY, 2001; W. Stafford, *English Feminists and their Opponents in the 1790s*, Manchester, 2002, Chapters 1–2.

31 These volumes were published serially under various titles; the only modern edition is H. M. Williams, *Letters from France*, 2 vols, Delmar, NY, 1975; see, for bibliographical details, H. M. Williams, *Letters Written in France*, ed. N. Fraistat and S. Lanser, Peterborough, ON, 2001; J. Fruchtman (ed.), *An Eye-Witness Account of the French Revolution by Helen Maria Williams*, New York, 1997; D. Kennedy, *Helen Maria Williams and the Age of Revolution*, Lewisburg, PA, 2002.

32 H. M. Williams, *Julia: A Novel*, intro. P. Garside, 2 vols, London, 1995, Vol. 1, p. 178.

33 Ibid., Vol. 2, p. 244.

34 See C. B. Jones, *Radical Sensibility: Literature and Ideas in the 1790s*, London,

1993; G. Kelly, *Women, Writing and Revolution, 1790–1827*, Oxford, 1993, Chapter 2; V. Jones, 'Women writing revolution: narratives of history and sexuality in Wollstonecraft and Williams', in S. Copley and J. Whale (eds), *Beyond Romanticism: New Approaches to Texts and Contexts, 1780–1832*, London, 1992.

35 For a bibliography and discussion of this tradition, see S. Oldfield, *Collective Biography of Women in Britain, 1550–1900: A Select Annotated Bibliography*, London, 1999; Gianna Pomata, 'History, particular and universal: on reading some recent women's history textbooks', *Feminist Studies*, 1993, vol. 19, pp. 7–49.

36 E. Cohen, ' "What the women at all times would laugh at": redefining equality and difference, circa 1660–1760', *Osiris*, 1997, vol. 12, pp. 121–42.

37 Generally, on these three women, see R. Perry, *The Celebrated Mary Astell: An Early English Feminist*, Chicago, 1986; S. Hutton, 'Damaris Cudworth, Lady Masham: between Platonism and Enlightenment', *British Journal for the History of Philosophy*, 1993, vol. 1, 29–54; A. Kelley, ' "In search of truths sublime": reason and the body in the writings of Catherine Trotter', *Women's Writing*, 2001, vol. 8, pp. 235–50.

38 M. Astell, *A Serious Proposal to the Ladies*, pts 1–2, ed. P. Springborg, Peterborough, ON, 2002, p. 83.

39 See P. Springborg, 'Introduction' to Astell, *A Serious Proposal*; 'Astell, Masham and Locke: religion and politics', in H. Smith (ed.), *Women Writers and the Early Modern British Political Tradition*, Cambridge, 1998.

40 Astell, *Some Reflections upon Marriage*, in Astell, *Political Writings*, pp. 18–19.

41 Drake, *Essay in Defence of the Female Sex*, reprinted in Astell, *A Serious Proposal*, p. 238; H. Smith, 'English "feminist" writings and Judith Drake's *An Essay in Defence of the Female Sex* (1696)', *Historical Journal*, 2001, no. 44, pp. 727–47.

42 Cohen, ' "What the women at all times would laugh at" '.

43 See I. Grundy, *Lady Mary Wortley Montagu*, Oxford, 1999, p. xxi.

44 For a very thorough bibliography and survey of recent scholarship on the bluestocking group, see *Huntington Library Quarterly*, 65, 2002, nos 1 and 2, special issue, 'Reconsidering the bluestockings', ed. N. Pohl and B. A. Schellenberg, *passim*; E. Eger, ' "The noblest commerce of mankind": conversation and community in the bluestocking circle', in S. Knott and B. Taylor (eds) *Feminism and the Enlightenment*, London, 2005.

45 M. Scott, *The Female Advocate: A Poem Occasioned by Reading Mr Duncombe's Feminead*, London, 1774, p. v.

46 Ibid., pp. 36–7.

47 See, generally on the language of republicanism, J. G. A. Pocock, *The Machiavellian Moment: Florentine Political Thought and the Atlantic Republican Tradition*, Princeton, NJ, 1975; also his, *Virtue, Commerce, and History: Essays on Political Thought and History, Chiefly in the Eighteenth Century*, Cambridge, 1985. Most recently, see the articles by C. Fauré, C. Larrère and J. Vega, in M. Van Gelderen and Q. Skinner (eds), *Republicanism: A Shared European Heritage*, 2 vols, Cambridge, 2002, vol. 2, pt 2: 'The place of women in the republic'.

48 See C. Robbins, *The Eighteenth-Century Commonwealthman*, Cambridge, MA, 1959.

49 Catherine Macaulay, 'Introduction', *History of England*, vol. 1, as quoted in S. Wiseman, 'Catharine Macaulay: history and republicanism', in Eger *et al.* (eds), *Women, Writing and the Public Sphere*. See also on Macaulay, B. Hill, *The Republican Virago: The Life and Times of Catharine Macaulay, Historian*, Oxford, 1992; N. Z. Davis, 'History's two bodies', *American Historical Review*, 1988, vol. 93,

pp. 1–30; J. G. A. Pocock, 'Catharine Macaulay: patriot historian', in Smith (ed.), *Women Writers and the Early Modern British Political Tradition*; D. Looser, *British Women Writers and the Writing of History, 1670–1820*, Baltimore, 2000, Chapter 5.

50 Guest, *Small Change*, pp. 195–208, 236–51.

51 G. M. Meadley, *Memoir of Mrs Jebb*, London, 1812; A. Page, *John Jebb and the Enlightenment Origins of British Radicalism*, Westport, CT, 2003.

52 C. Macaulay, *Letters on Education*, London, 1790, pp. 203, 208, 215.

53 B. Hill, 'The links between Mary Wollstonecraft and Catherine Macaulay: new evidence', *Women's History Review*, 1995, vol. 4, p. 177.

54 M. Wollstonecraft, *Vindication of the Rights of Men*, in M. Butler and J.Todd (eds), *Collected Works of Mary Wollstonecraft*, 7 vols, London, 1989, vol. 5, pp. 7, 16, 24; G. J. Barker-Benfield, 'Mary Wollstonecraft: eighteenth-century commonwealths-woman', *Journal of the History of Ideas*, 1989, vol. 50, pp. 95–116.

55 The work was retitled *Origins of the Distinction of Ranks*, 3rd edn, London, 1779; G. Caffentzis, 'On the Scottish origin of "civilization"', in S. Federico (ed.), *Enduring Western Civilization: The Construction of the Concept of Western Civilization and its 'Others'*, Westport CT, 1995, pp. 14–15, as cited in Moran, 'From rudeness to refinement', pp. 45–6.

56 Millar, *Origins*, repr. in W. C. Lehmann, *John Millar of Glasgow, 1735–1801: His Life and Thought and his Contributions to Sociological Analysis*, Cambridge, 1960, p. 176. See Rendall, 'Virtue and commerce'; Moran, 'From rudeness to refinement', Chapter 2; also, '"The Commerce of the Sexes": gender and the social sphere in Scottish Enlightenment accounts of civil society', in F. Trentmann (ed.), *Paradoxes of Civil Society: New Perspectives on Modern German and British History*, New York, 2000.

57 Jane Rendall, 'Introduction', in W. Alexander, *The History of Women, from the Earliest Antiquity to the Present Time*, 2 vols, 1782 edn, reprinted with introduction by J. Rendall, Bath, 1995, vol. 1, p. 151.

58 Millar, *Origins*, in Lehmann, *John Millar of Glasgow*, pp. 214, 219.

59 Moran, '"Commerce of the sexes"', pp. 71–4.

60 Pearson, *Women's Reading in Britain*, pp. 49–55; Jane Austen, *Northanger Abbey*, London, 1965, p. 92; Looser, *British Women Writers*, pp. 16–21; M. S. Phillips, *Society and Sentiment: Genres of Historical Writing in Britain, 1740–1820* Princeton, NJ, 2000, Chapter 4.

61 Mary Wollstonecraft, *An Historical and Moral View of the Origin and Progress of the French Revolution*, in *Works* ed. Butler and Todd, vol. 6, p. 235; *Letters Written in Sweden, Norway and Denmark*, ibid., p. 346; J. Rendall, '"The grand causes which combine to carry mankind forward": Wollstonecraft, history and revolution', *Women's Writing*, 1997, vol. 4, pp. 155–72.

62 Wollstonecraft, *Historical and Moral View*, pp. 233–4.

63 L. Aikin, 'Introduction', in *Epistles on Women, Exemplifying Their Character and Condition in Various Ages and Nations*, London, 1810; see also Guest, *Small Change*, pp. 335–8.

64 Ibid., pp. 72–7, 80.

65 J. Hemlow, 'Fanny Burney and the Courtesy Books', *Publications of the Modern Languages Association of America*, 1950, vol. 65, pp. 732–61; M. Poovey, *The Proper Lady and the Woman Writer: Ideology as Style in the Works of Mary Wollstonecraft, Mary Shelley and Jane Austen*, Chicago, 1984; M. Myers, 'Servants as they are now educated: women writers and Georgian pedagogy', *Essays in Literature*, 1989, vol. 16, pp. 51–69; N. Armstrong, *Desire and Domestic Fiction: A*

Political History of the Novel, New York, 1987; V. Jones, 'Introduction', to *The Young Lady's Pocket Library, or Parental Monitor*, 1790, repr. Bath, 1995; also 'The seductions of conduct: pleasure and conduct literature', in R. Porter and M. M. Roberts (eds), *Pleasure in the Eighteenth Century*, Basingstoke, 1996; K. Sutherland, 'Writings on education and conduct: arguments for female improvement', in V. Jones (ed.), *Women and Literature in Britain 1700–1800*, Cambridge, 2000.

66 Dr John Gregory, *A Father's Legacy to His Daughters*, in V. Jones (ed.), *Young Lady's Pocket Library*, p. 3; M. C. Moran, 'Between the savage and the civil: Dr John Gregory's Natural History of Femininity', in Knott and Taylor (eds), *Feminism and the Enlightenment*.

67 Sutherland 'Writings on education and conduct', pp. 28–9.

68 Wollstonecraft, *Vindication*, in *Works*, vol. 5, p. 75.

69 Wollstonecraft, *Vindication*, in *Works*, vol. 5, p. 166.

70 Ibid., p. 265.

71 See, from an extensive literature, G. Kelly, *Revolutionary Feminism: The Mind and Career of Mary Wollstonecraft*, Basingstoke, 1992; V. Sapiro, *A Vindication of Political Virtue: The Political Theory of Mary Wollstonecraft*, Chicago, 1992; C. Johnson, *The Cambridge Companion to Mary Wollstonecraft*, Cambridge, 2002; B. Taylor, *Mary Wollstonecraft and the Feminist Imagination*, Cambridge, 2003.

72 R. M. Janes, 'The reception of Mary Wollstonecraft's *Vindication of the Rights of Woman*', *Journal of the History of Ideas*, 1978, vol. 39, pp. 293–302; W. Godwin, *Memoirs of the Author of a Vindication of the Rights of Woman*, ed. R. Holmes, London, 1987.

73 Butler, *Jane Austen and the War of Ideas*, Chapter 4; M. O. Grenby, *The Anti-Jacobin Novel: British Conservatism and the French Revolution*, Cambridge, 2001.

74 C. Eckhardt, *Fanny Wright: Rebel in America*, Cambridge, MA, 1984; H. Rogers, *Women and the People: Authority, Authorship and the Radical Tradition in Nineteenth-Century England*, Aldershot, 2000, Chapter 2.

75 P. Wakefield, *Reflections on the Present Condition of the Female Sex; With Suggestions for its Improvement*, London, 1798, pp. 88, 97.

76 See Garside *et al.* (eds), *The English Novel, 1770–1829*, vol. 2, pp. 72–6.

Chapter Two

৯৯

Women and education

Deborah Simonton

> It is astonishing how little qualification was thought on in [those] days. Not
> one of the Governesses it was my fate to be placed under knew as much of
> education as could now be found in any Mistress of any village Charity
> School.[1]

This is how Elizabeth Ham, looking back at her childhood in 1820
described her experience of education in the last years of the eighteenth
century. For her, education had improved considerably in that short time.
She reflects a popular conception, still held today, that many girls
remained largely uneducated from 1700 to 1850. Indeed, historians of
education appear only to have discovered girls around the middle of the
nineteenth century. The historiography of female education owes much of
its construction to the women's movement of the nineteenth century and
to a preoccupation with suffrage and the desire to understand the origins
and underpinning social structures of the suffrage movement. Thus, much
of the research has concentrated on the period from about 1840, focusing
in particular on the achievement of women's higher education, the impact
of state intervention, and the implication of Victorian values on girls'
education. We are left with a virtual desert in the period before that:
educational history for 1700 to 1850 is remarkably gender blind.

There are some notable exceptions in a few good surveys of girls'
education, such as Dorothy Gardiner's magisterial survey *English Girlhood
at School* (1929) and Josephine Kamm's survey of girls' education, *Hope
Deferred* (1965).[2] Recent attention to female influence on educational
ideas and their contribution to reform in this period has been an important
development.[3] The formative period before the mid-nineteenth century

has also received welcome attention with Ruth Watts' work on the Unitarian influence in education and Susan Skedd's study of teachers, 1760–1820. My work on English girls' education in the eighteenth century has added to what is clearly a growing literature.[4] Girls in Scotland, Wales, and Ireland have received even less attention, although Lindy Moore is filling this gap with studies of Scottish girls' education, disaggregating it from both its male counterpart and from an elision with English girls' education.[5]

This chapter will focus primarily on schooling. However, education in its broadest liberal sense certainly included far more than schools. Apprenticeship and service also provided learning for children, sometimes in succession to schools; other children learned far more in informal settings, while home education was important to girls of all social classes.[6] There were gaps in schooling; not only was a great deal of knowledge excluded, but also many children never came into contact with schools and teachers. The oral tradition remained the fundamental mechanism of transmission of values, work practices, customs, and entertainment, despite the gradual emergence of a literate society. In this context, widespread reliance upon written material for instruction was relatively new.

Between 1700 and 1850, schooling was framed in this less formal culture, and local rules, regulations, and practices dominated. Attendance was certainly voluntary and the provision of schools was widely disparate. Despite the increasing importance of schooling to many in British society, a resistance to governmental intervention, and an appreciation of the contradictory ways in which schooling could be used meant that a voluntary approach to educational provision was widely accepted and continued far into the nineteenth century. Even in Scotland, where an Act of 1696, motivated by Presbyterian concern with being able to read, confirmed the principle that there should be a school in every parish, education was largely a local issue. It remained a matter of individual choice, with provision resting in the community. By the end of the period, however, the perception of schooling as a public good requiring state intervention meant that the first steps to state education had been taken.

Ideological constraints and opportunities

Educational practice had firm roots in contemporary political and philosophical debates. First, education was central to the Enlightenment world-view. With it came the belief that children were innocent and that the impressions and environmental influences of their early years shaped them for adulthood. As John Locke explained: 'We have reason to conclude, that great Care is to be had of the forming Children's *Minds*, and giving them that seasoning early, which shall influence their Lives always after.'[7] In 1762, Jean-Jacques Rousseau's *Emile* was published in Britain. Arguing that the child was born good and was corrupted by society, Rousseau even more forcefully focused attention on those influences that shaped children's character. Education was recast, with implications for how schooling would be perceived across society.

The second influence of the Enlightenment was the reformulation of gender. The increased emphasis on early formation of character meant that the child's upbringing gained in importance. Mothering took on new prominence. As Jane Rendall has shown in Chapter 1 of this book, there were important contradictions in Enlightenment construction of femininity, which 'had clearly given the authority of nature to particular gender attributes', but it had also, 'suggested a language of improvement, fostered intellectual ambition, and reshaped the ideal of public good'.[8] These new ideas specifically focused responsibility on mothers for the early education of children. They also ultimately charged them with the morality of society through the education of their children. In the process of identifying women with sensibility and with a responsibility for setting standards of morality and behaviour, new semi-permeable boundaries were set around female activities. As Hannah More explained:

> the man whose happiness she is one day to make, whose family she is
> to govern, and whose children she is to educate . . . he will seek for
> her in the bosom of retirement, in the practice of every domestic virtue
> . . . to embellish the narrow but charming circle of family delights.[9]

However, as Hugh Cunningham has noted, the 'move towards a more child-oriented society was challenged at every stage, and never completed. Both in attitudes . . . and behaviour . . . we are confronted at every turn by ambivalence and contradictions.'[10] Moreover, the cultural and economic nexus of labouring life meant that the image of the child-oriented mother remained alien among the lower classes. The experiences and expectations of middle- and upper-class girls were significantly different from those of poor, artisan, or labouring girls.

The fundamental view was that nature had created men and women differently, each with his or her unique role. Since the female mind could be shown to be unlike the male mind in quality and character, it followed naturally that women's education should be different in content as well as essence. In 1805, Catherine Cappe of York explained: 'cultivation of social and pious affections, gentleness of temper and resignation to the will of God [were] as important to the female character in the lowest as well as the highest forms of life'.[11] These ideas had particular resonance for the middle classes, who not only increasingly adopted the domestic vision, but also influenced schooling for poorer girls through their writing and their contact with – and management of – local schools. Girls' education and function in society was consequently depicted in language that owed its tenor to the faith in human perfectibility. Education was a double-edged sword: on the one hand, limiting spheres of action, while, on the other, beginning to provide the schooling to expand those limits. The interest in female education probably also meant that between 1700 and 1850 more girls had more education than former generations.

Education was embedded in ideas of social difference. Along with the sense of industrial and scientific improvement and a feeling of growing prosperity, social aspirations governed the actions of wide sections of society. Not surprisingly, education was an important vehicle of social elevation and emulation. However, a resurgence in educational interest was also a response to new social problems arising from economic and demographic changes, and, from the last quarter of the eighteenth century, these insecurities were compounded by fears arising from the French Revolution. Concern about the security of the social system led people to turn to education as a preventative measure.

Girls' education was at the forefront of the debate about social mobility and contemporary concerns were as much about middle-class girls being educated above their station as they were about working-class girls learning their place in society. To many among the élite, the framework of society was threatened not only by radical ideas, but also by the increasing wealth and social ambition of the middle classes. Similarly, they believed that the dissatisfaction of the middle classes was transmitted to the 'inferior orders' so that the whole of society based on rank and subordination was under threat. Representative of this anxiety, Clara Reeve of Ipswich complained: 'Every rank and degree of people bring up their children in a way above their station and circumstances; they step over their proper place and seat themselves upon a higher form.'[12] Such an education was assumed to make girls idle and fit for nothing.

Appropriate schooling and training for girls maintained social distance, prepared labouring girls for a life of work, and aimed to bring about an improvement in manners and morals for the benefit of all of society. Particular criticism was levelled at working-class mothers' childrearing. Cappe argued that mothers of poor girls were unable to instruct their daughters properly because of their own want of education. She preferred to educate 'female children of the honest, virtuous and industrious poor' at home, but 'where a child is ill-treated, or has a bad example set before her, the sooner she can be removed from under the pernicious influences the better'.[13] Sarah Trimmer of Ipswich, put it somewhat more picturesquely:

> it is observable that poor children have a greater regard to their behaviour when they are lifted from the dunghill, decently clothed, and noticed by their betters, than when they are driven away to associate with their own abject class, and to eat husks with swine.[14]

The solution was to educate girls in good morals and behaviour, in order to ameliorate the manners of their future children: the right sort of education for poor girls would then, ultimately, create reformation in every department of society.[15]

The crucial class difference in education was the recognition that plebeian girls had to support themselves. The other prong of the argument about poor girls' schooling was that education should train them to provide their own living:

> Their employment and duty in life will probably be to discharge the several offices at first of menial servants, and afterwards of wives and mothers, with the fear of God before their eyes; as well as to assist in the maintenance of a family by some species of profitable industry. Let their education, therefore be calculated to impress them with a sense of religious obligation as also to prepare them for the various employments of the stations they are expected to occupy, as far as is practicable in a school.[16]

The Quaker, Priscilla Wakefield of Tottenham, also advised 'useful occupations . . . without destroying the peculiar characteristic of the sex'.[17] Schools were advised to teach religion and domestic arts to provide the skills for domestic service and for the natural female positions of wife, mother, and homemaker, emphasizing industry, frugality, diligence, and good management.

Schooling for plebeian girls

As we have seen, for poor girls 'character moulding' and 'early influences' took on a rather different connotation than they did in middle-class education. In *The Christian Schoolmaster*, a manual for charity schools, Dr James Talbot acknowledged the child's susceptibility:

> As to the Business of *Instruction*, it must be consider'd, that the Minds of Children, like blank Paper, or smooth wax, are equally capable of any Impression: the Use and Exercise of our Understanding advances by slower Degrees than that of our Limbs, and requires more Assistance from without, to Guide and Direct it.[18]

A major influence at both parish and national level was the response of the conservative sectors of society, who reacted strongly to Rousseau's 'natural' education and feared too much freedom for children of the lower orders. Similarly, evangelical religion and revolutionary reaction influenced the education of the poor. Hannah More consistently stressed that the purpose of education was not to allow free rein to childish curiosity but to counteract the innate depravity of children:

> Is it not a fundamental error to consider children as innocent beings, whose little weaknesses may perhaps want some correction, rather than as beings who bring into the world a corrupt nature and evil dispositions, which it should be the great end of education to rectify.[19]

Despite the optimism and energy generated by the hopes of human perfectibility, many during this period held more traditional, orthodox views.

A girl's opportunities were roughly determined by her family's financial situation and its interest in educating her. If able and willing to pay a modest sum for education, girls had access to many parish, village, and dame schools on much the same terms as boys – and sometimes to a grammar school or boys' schoolmaster for certain lessons. In Scotland, parochial schools were the main providers of education for girls; in towns, burgh schools also catered for girls, at least in theory. After the creation of the National and British Schools in the early nineteenth century, girls in principle had equal and free access to them.[20] Some charity and Sunday-School foundations restricted access to the poorest children, others specifically excluded paupers (that is, those on parish relief), while yet others admitted children of the trades and artisan classes. Romford Charity School dismissed children if they went into the workhouse; however, the master of the Chelmsford workhouse paid the Charity School to teach children in his care. At Ashdon in Essex, the overseers of the poor paid for three pupils each quarter. Tradespeople's children attended Chelmsford Charity School, while children of tradespeople, artisans, and labourers attended the Mitcham National School in the 1830s.[21] In Scotland, the Kirk was expected to assist poor children to attend; nevertheless, the number of places available probably neither satisfied actual demand nor the desire to educate the poor. Research on schools in Essex and Staffordshire has shown that places were less frequently provided for girls than they were for boys.[22] On average, there were about nine schools for boys to every eight for girls, while schools consistently provided fewer places for girls in a ratio of between 1.5–2 boys admitted to 1 girl. The overwhelming trend was to give preferential treatment to boys, both in admissions policies and practices.

Reading was taught to both sexes primarily to promote moral education. Sunday Schools, which probably reached the greatest number of girls, tended to restrict the curriculum at this point, since writing and arithmetic were seen as secular and therefore unsuitable for the Sabbath. For example, Coggeshall Sunday School in Essex stipulated:

The religious observation of the Christian Sabbath being an essential object with the Society . . . the exercise of the scholars on that day shall be restricted to reading in the Old and New Testament and to spelling as a preparation for it.[23]

Scientific, technical, and economic changes gradually enhanced the need for reading, writing, and arithmetic. Indeed, accounts, arithmetic or 'ciphering' were fairly common parts of the syllabus for both sexes by the nineteenth century. With writing, they were seen as preparation for service and apprenticeship. However, boys were more often taught writing and arithmetic than girls. The curricula of single-sex charity schools brought this into stark relief. While the pattern for boys was reading, writing, and arithmetic, it was reading, religion, and needlework for girls. Despite this, it is worth noting that a sizeable proportion of girls in charity schools obtained more academic schooling than the average: 25 per cent received instruction in arithmetic and 40 per cent in writing.[24]

The inclusion of work skills was a positive way to inculcate proper attitudes in the young; they helped to support schools dependent upon voluntary contributions and they improved attendance if children were allowed a small income from their work. In some schools, girls made their own and boys' stockings and uniforms; in others, their output was sold to supplement income.[25] 'Working' was a dominant theme in poorer girls' education. Trimmer proposed that they should spin wool and flax, clean the school, and sew. She declared: 'No Charity Girl can be deemed properly educated who has not attained to a tolerable proficiency at her needle.'[26]

Needlework was deemed particularly relevant. First, it was part of the appropriate domestic province of women. Second, it was an essential skill for a frugal housewife or a domestic servant. Providing these girls with the knowledge and opportunity to attain a place in service was tacitly accepted by schools. At Wolverhampton Charity School, some girls were not allowed to leave until they had gained a place. In one instance, a younger sister was prevented from entering the school until the elder one had gone into service. Romford and Chelmsford intended to teach girls reading, knitting, sewing, and all other requisites to make them good servants.[27]

At Chelmsford, 'from time to time', boys were set such work as the trustees saw fit, such as picking stones or cleaning the town;[28] otherwise, little mention was made of what work, if any, they were to do. Educational tracts were much vaguer about the opportunities or expectations for boys than for girls. The importance of domestic service to a girl permeates the literature, minute books, and schools' rules. Except for general and occasional references to apprenticeship, boys' occupations or expectations receive little or no mention. Trimmer made this distinction in *The Charity Spelling Book*, admonishing girls to follow the appropriate strictures to 'get a good place', while boys were simply to use school to improve themselves.[29] She allowed that they could learn to mend shoes, so that they did not get 'too much learning'.[30]

The gender difference in attitudes to social mobility suggests a tension around class. Poor boys were, of course, expected to work, and encouraged to improve their occupational prospects, but within the broad band of their class. They were not to encroach upon middle-class prerogatives. For girls, ideology was formulated around a domestic image of woman, so that the middle class viewed only certain kinds of work as appropriate for labouring women. Yet, as it was recognized they would have to contribute to family income, their education had to be suitable to their station: 'inappropriate' education would disqualify a girl for work. The boundary between 'working' women and 'leisured' genteel females was one the middle classes were keen to maintain, despite imposing their own behavioural values on plebeian women. However, in improving girls, providing them with the manners and norms which set them apart from the rest of the lower orders, they gave them a 'leg up' the social ladder.

School attendance regulations varied by sex, reflecting the effect of gender on education. As has been noted, attendance was not obligatory and numerous factors affected the regularity and length of attendance. Trustees tended to admit children around 7 years of age and discharge them at age 14. This is comparable to the practices in apprenticeship and domestic service where 14 was considered the appropriate age for placing children, although parish apprentices were indentured younger.[31] Few children stayed in schools for seven years, but school records show an average duration of nearly 3.5 years, although daily attendance was irregular.[32] Girls tended to attend school longer than boys. In Staffordshire, girls remained at school on average three months longer, and in Essex about two months longer. Comparing individual schools instead of county averages, some girls stayed as much as six to nine months longer than boys in the same school. Over 10 per cent of girls, but less than 2 per cent of boys, stayed for six years or more. Similar attendance patterns operated in the Mitcham National School early in the nineteenth century, where girls stayed an average of nearly eight months longer.[33] Nevertheless, three years was a substantial period of time to attend school in an age in which we regard child labour to have been all-pervasive and when the length of the school day left only small amounts of time for part-time work. Historians estimate that it took a year to teach reading and writing, and arithmetic another three or four years.[34] Therefore, many children at these schools could have achieved a reasonable reading standard, as well as some writing and arithmetic. Although fewer girls learnt to write and do arithmetic, those girls who did stayed in school long enough to achieve good comprehension in reading, some competence in writing and arithmetic, and were in fact more likely than boys to stay long enough to achieve a lasting education.

Despite the possibilities for schooling outlined above, one of the key concerns at the beginning of the nineteenth century was the small proportion of working-class children who had access to schools. The Brougham Report in 1819 estimated that about 30 per cent of children had a little schooling. The Children's Employment Commission of 1833 concluded that only 10 per cent of children had satisfactory schooling, whereas 40 per cent had none at all. Calculations based on the Brougham Report suggest about 23 per cent of children in Essex and 21 per cent in Staffordshire were in day schools, and perhaps 18 and 22 per cent, respectively, were enrolled at Sunday Schools.[35] Commercial schools also existed in some parishes, so figures probably underestimate the extent of schooling, but not necessarily schooling for the labouring classes. If only poor children attended these schools, and about half the population was poor, then about 40 per cent of poor children in the parishes studied could have had access to a free day school. Educational opportunity depended very much upon local variation and the period from which the figures are taken. Average access to school ranges from 40 per cent of children in Romford at mid-century to 7.6 per cent in Wolverhampton by 1801. Because fewer places usually were allocated for girls in the schools, and girls, on average, stayed longer than boys, vacancies for girls were created at a slower rate than for boys. Logically then, a smaller proportion of girls than boys could have attended these schools. Moreover, because population increased during the century, unless schools expanded, by 1801 they catered for a smaller proportion of children than they had at their foundation. Scottish schools also felt the pressure of population and it is probable that as fewer children gained entry, girls were disadvantaged over boys.[36]

Schooling for the 'better off'

Élite and middling women's life stories confirm a high incidence of home education, showing that it was often preferred even when schools were available. With time, competence, and interest, mothers taught daughters themselves, but the period also saw the rise of the governess as an important part of the educational structure. One study of English women showed that 60 per cent of middle-class girls were educated at home, and the trend is similarly pronounced among girls of the élite.[37] Another small study of English autobiographers showed that their mothers or other women in the household taught nearly all of them at some point. Half of the group of twenty-two were taught exclusively at home, whereas another seven were taught at home for some of their education. There are a number of reasons for the significance of home education. Girls were expected to focus their life on the world of house and home, while their brothers anticipated a life of work, politics, and public affairs. This contrast between male and female expectations was probably more pronounced in the middle and upper classes than among the labouring sectors of society. Maternal affection and the perceived need to shelter and protect young women may have contributed to the tendency to keep girls at home – ideology and expectation operating together may have encouraged home education where a daughter was under her mother's care.

Academic education could be identified from these accounts since the women tended to chronicle learning to read and write, followed in many cases by other subjects commonly taught at schools. These women described a wide range of education, including physical exercise, learning 'the first lessons of parental obedience', being 'educated . . . in industry', or being 'brought up strictly in . . . religion'.[38] Other references were more vague, crediting parents or mothers with 'tenderness and solicitude for . . . [my] best welfare'.[39] Ruth Fellows wrote only that, 'my dear parents taught me, both by example and precept, to live a sober and godly life'.[40] These women identified important educational influences other than purely academic learning.

Mothers were explicitly mentioned in the education of thirteen of the twenty-two women, but because several referred only vaguely to the parental home, or only wrote about schooling, the total is probably higher. Other women, excluding schoolmistresses, taught eight of them, suggesting interesting female networks, including Methodist servants, friends, a neighbour, an uncle's housekeeper, an aunt, and a female household of relatives.[41] Such women tended to supplement home instruction, but in two cases they virtually replaced it. Elizabeth Ham was sent to an aunt's house, which alternated with spells at home or school. Her family's financial situation meant that two sons were also sent to uncles; one was eventually adopted. Margaret Lucas, orphaned at age 7, was partly reared by her uncle's housekeeper. Women remained the strongest educational influence on girls, even for those women whose mothers died while they were young. Elizabeth Fry was taught by her mother until the age of 12, and then by a governess. Margaret Lucas was taken in hand by her uncle's housekeeper until she was sent to school at about age 12 or 13. Sarah Grubb, whose mother died before she was 5, praised her stepmother, whom her father married when she was about 10, for her 'care and regard', and wrote that she was instrumental in the 'watchful and religious education' she received.[42]

Fathers also played a significant role in the home education of three of the female autobiographers: Ann Gilbert, Mary Alexander and Mary Fletcher. Mary Alexander, whose mother died when she was young, credited her early education to her father's concerns for her education, but claimed that most of her learning was self-taught. Ann Gilbert provides a valuable case study, however. Both of her parents were well educated, but for health reasons her father reverted to his trade as an engraver, working from home. He taught his daughters, his apprentices, and his pupils both his trade and an academic education. As the girls became older, they took turns learning drawing and engraving from him and domestic skills from their mother.[43] The educational climate of the home was exceptional in many respects, and several family members became published authors.

Boarding schools and day schools were the other routes for families who wished to educate their daughters, and many girls experienced a mixed approach. Parents frequently provided lessons at home, but used schools for 'finishing'. Some middle-class families paid to send their daughter to an 'English' school, which taught the basics of reading and writing, and some certainly attended charity and village schools. The small commercial schools that emerged during the seventeenth and eighteenth centuries were an innovation in girls' education, providing an alternative to home education. They were extraordinarily popular in a climate of widespread interest in female education. Most middle-class institutions were small and privately run, depending heavily upon individual efforts, ingenuity, and ability, both for survival and provision of a broad education. While many did not survive their founder, some were passed from mother to daughter, or sometimes to former pupils. Some premises did become associated with schools and passed through many hands, but most of these schools were commercially fragile and transient.[44]

Boarding schools were problematic. The range and quality were staggeringly broad. Not only could they cost very large sums of money, but they also meant taking girls away from home. Many had an unsavoury reputation, which restrained some parents from sending their daughters unless they could financially ensure their health and well-being. Martha Young died within months of going to school for the first time and her father condemned himself for sending her:

> Oh! What infatuation ever to send her to one. In the country she had health, spirits, and strength, as if there were not enough with what she might have learned at home, instead of going to that region of constraint and death, Camden House.[45]

Yet parents also willingly paid handsomely to prepare their daughters to compete effectively in the marriage market. The cost of educating girls at 'fashionable' boarding schools could be as high as £200 p.a. A hopeful parent could find a cheap copy for as little as £12–14 p.a., or even less.[46] Day scholars certainly paid less.

For some women, school was either a short-lived or a haphazard experience. Elizabeth Ham attended seven different schools, with frequent breaks between and during attendance at any one of them. Writing in 1849, when she was 66, she commented on the poor qualifications of her teachers and the paucity of her education. All of her schools had charged fees and the curriculum had varied from an evening writing school to a boarding school with an extra dancing master. On the whole, though, her experience was of unpretentious day schools with a curriculum typical of charity schools. Eliza Fletcher would have agreed. Referring to Manor House School in York between 1760 and 1785, she said: 'Mrs. Forster was a very well disposed conscientious old gentlewoman, but incapable of proper superintendence . . . Four volumes of the *Spectator* constituted the whole school library . . . Nothing useful could be learned in that school.'[47] Eliza Fox, who experienced day schools between the ages of 7 and 16, at the start of the nineteenth century, noted a broader curriculum including history, geography, French, and dancing, this last which her father insisted she study in order to have a 'good carriage'. Her parents felt she had to learn 'to behave like a "young lady" . . . It *was* proper I should leave off being a "*Tom-boy*" at age seven!'[48]

Fashionable schools in England were centred on London and provincial towns, such as Bath, and Oxford. Private girls schools also proliferated in Edinburgh, Glasgow, and Aberdeen, so that, in 1825, Edinburgh had thirty-three, Glasgow eighteen and Aberdeen fifteen.[49] The frequent perception that schoolmistresses were distressed gentlewomen contains a half-truth. Certainly many middle-class women without alternatives turned to teaching and often relinquished it if the opportunity arose, but there were also many single and married women who undertook it out of choice or vocation. Hannah More, who worked near Bristol, and Mary Wollstonecraft, who had a school in Newington Green, both did so, as did Wollstonecraft's childhood friend, Jane Arden. Arden represents some of the best in eighteenth-century schoolteachers. Staying in school until 16 or 17, and then testing her craft during six years as a governess, she went on to run a school, first with her sister in Bath, and then, by herself, for sixteen years in her native Beverley. A conscientious teacher, she dedicated her life to her pupils, building a large library in multiple languages for their use and writing her own successful teaching books.[50]

For many women, teaching involved a balancing act between retaining their gentility and commercial gain, and, for most, gentility was essential to acquiring and maintaining an appropriate clientele. Good networks and location in a reasonably large town were the key to a steady flow of pupils, especially those who could pay. By aiming to secure pupils of a sufficiently high status as boarders and sloughing off the less lucrative day pupils, successful women combined gentility and personal gain to create the exclusive, small, private boarding school.[51]

For élite and middle-class girls the curriculum varied considerably. Certainly some girls received a scholarly education but these are exceptions. Most institutions and home tuition offered a typical curriculum which included various needlecraft skills, the art of polite conversation, dancing, music, drawing, painting, French, perhaps Italian, and subjects such as history, geography, and astronomy, with which to make polite conversation. Most schools provided a core of subjects for a set fee; others, such as music and dancing, cost extra. Masters were frequently brought in on a peripatetic basis for these specialist subjects. Where a school offered a wide curriculum taught by one or two women, most lessons were mere glosses of the subject, particularly as the majority of teachers were not particularly well educated themselves.

The popular fashionable education served little practical purpose; indeed, its main function was to present a girl in the best light in the marriage market and to make her a suitable ornament in marriage. Adam Smith illustrated this view arguing that there was nothing wrong with girls' education. They were taught what their parents or guardians judged necessary or useful and their education rendered 'them both likely to become the mistresses of a family and to behave properly when they have become such'.[52] 'Accomplishments' became entrenched in the curriculum as a response to this goal, overshadowing 'useful' housewifery skills. As Hannah More put it, girls were educated, 'either to make their fortune by marriage, or if that fail, to qualify them to become teachers of others: hence the abundant multiplication of superficial wives, and of incompetent and illiterate governesses'.[53]

By the last quarter of the eighteenth century, powerful criticisms were raised against girls' education, criticisms that were embedded in a wider European debate about women's rights in which education was seen as a key plank. Importantly, not all critics were liberals, and the strong evangelical belief in virtue played an important role. Enlightenment emphasis on the development of the individual and the female contribution to family and civic society combined with a concern for mothers to educate both themselves and their children appropriately. The emphasis on education for virtue led authors like the Scots educationalist, Elizabeth Hamilton, to argue that, 'to be virtuous, women needed to be educated in morals rather than manners', while Irishwoman, Maria Edgeworth defended the right of women to useful knowledge, including the sciences, rather than be kept in 'Turkish Ignorance', with 'every means of acquiring knowledge was discountenanced by fashion, and impracticable even to those who despised fashion'.[54] Hannah More and the radical Mary Wollstonecraft condemned what More termed, 'this phrenzy of accomplishments'. More also criticized female education because it was geared exclusively for the transient period of youth and beauty: 'We educate them for a crowd, forgetting they live at home, for the world and not for themselves, for show and not for use, for time and not for eternity.' The real object of education for More was to make girls into 'good daughters, good wives, good mistresses, good members of society, good Christians'.[55] Wollstonecraft agreed insofar as improved education would make women better companions to men and better citizens. She believed that the false system of education prepared women to be the mistresses of men rather than affectionate sisters, more faithful wives, more reasonable mothers – in a word, better citizens.[56] She also agreed with Englishwoman, Catherine Macaulay, who denounced Rousseau's construction of the female in her *Letters on Education* (1790), arguing that there was no inherent disparity between men and women in their potential for learning, a view that contributed to the newer curricula developing in the better and more innovative schools.[57]

This impetus led to an increasing recognition that a more intellectual education held advantages for girls and for the future of society.[58] Some teachers began to devise curricula that increasingly prepared pupils for lives that were not solely bound up in the home. Mrs Margaret Bryan ran boarding schools in greater London, c. 1795–1815, in which she delivered lectures on Astronomy and Mathematics She also published a series of lectures in 1806, subscribed to by 157 women, many of whom were former pupils.[59] A detailed advertisement for Mrs Florian's boarding school in Leytonshire explained:

> Among the multifarious attempts for making the education of young women keep pace with the general diffusion and rapid progress of useful knowledge which distinguishes this age, . . . The elements of Geometry and Trigonometry are also taught as far as is requisite for a perfect intelligence of the principles of Astronomy, of the geographical knowledge of our globe and of Natural Philosophy, which are illustrated by experiments and machines.[60]

Notably she refers to 'young women' [not ladies] and emphasized 'useful knowledge'. This marks an important shift in thinking, one which also took place in Scottish education.

For the most part, the sort of education available to Scots girls was not very different from that available in England, though the fashion for 'taking classes', whereby a girl attended a number of 'private classes' spread across the town appears to have been more common in Scotland than England.[61] But as Lindy Moore has shown, by the 1820s a number of educational experiments were taking place across Edinburgh. Edinburgh Academy, a boys' private school, and the Circus Place School, a mixed-sex elementary school for the middle classes, were organized with specialist masters and shareholders who elected the board of directors. This innovation led to private masters combining into academies. The Southern Academy opened in 1829, followed by a 'sister' school based on subscriptions, the Young Ladies' Seminary for the Southern Districts, in 1833, and the Scottish Institution for the Education of Young Ladies in 1834. The latter is particularly significant because it was formed by teachers influenced by the contemporary reform movement who came together as specialist masters to offer a sound curriculum including science in one setting, where students could read and relax between lessons, and where masters could assess pupils more holistically. The Edinburgh Institution for the Education of Young Ladies opened in 1835. These three institutions rapidly became the leading girls' schools in Edinburgh. They attracted girls from the upper middle class, though girls from the lower ranks occasionally attended for a short while or took some classes. Some of the institutions also ran special classes for prospective governesses. Three key features stand out in addition to their 'modern' curriculum and clientele: the schools were large in comparison to most contemporary schools; their very 'public' stance (courting publicity and advertising); and, significantly for Scottish education, the fact that the managers and masters were virtually all male. Schools appointed women as a 'supporting cast' of governesses, a few teachers, and the Lady Superintendent. Thus, the ultimate message was that academic teaching was male, a factor that inevitably influenced admissions to teacher training in Scotland.[62] Newer approaches in girls' education resulted from developments such as these, and while the second half of the nineteenth century is credited with innovation in girls' schooling, the antecedents were clearly present before 1850.

Further and higher education

Further and higher education are contemporary terms, but they best describe the additional education that was available to young women during the period. Such education was central to raising the standards in schools by providing further education for potential teachers and governesses, but it was also fundamental to bringing female opportunities within the ranges of males' education. Sarah Smith has fruitfully argued that this early period has been largely ignored in the literature because historians looked for the kinds of institutional forms that existed in the twentieth century. That is, usually framed by a feminist agenda, historians have looked for institutions that gave qualifications and access to professional standing. Smith argues that 'the basis of this historiography lies . . . in the preoccupations of certain theoretical trends in women's history', which describe 'a period of total exclusion . . . followed by a push by women for full educational rights after 1860'.[63]

In fact, a range of training and educational genres existed, including midwifery training, 'teacher training', and liberal arts or scientific studies, to which numerous women turned in their efforts at 'improvement'. Such opportunities could be structurally very casual, relying upon improving 'leisure' activities. Indeed, the line between entertainment and instruction was as ill-defined as in today's extramural classes. In 1701, Mr Margetts of Bedfordshire reported:

twice in the Week [John Pierson] meets' another Company of Adult Persons (about 8 in number) in the Town, and hears them read, and train's them up in Bishop William's Exposition of the Church Catechism. [John Reynolds] instructs' gratis another Company every night at his house, in the Catechism, in Reading and Serious Principles, and indeavours to bring them to an awful sence of God and man.[64]

In 1739, Griffith Jones, reporting on Welsh circulating schools, claimed:

In most of the schools, the adult persons do make about two thirds of the number taught in them . . . I am informed of two or three women aged about sixty, who knew not a letter before, did attend constantly everyday, except sometimes when they were obliged to seek abroad for a little bread; . . . and lamenting that they had not an opportunity of learning forty or fifty years earlier.[65]

In the north of England and Wales, adults attended Sunday Schools alongside children, while in other areas adult schools connected to Sunday Schools were established. For example, Manchester Sunday Schools taught reading to adults on Sunday evenings.[66] By 1813 in Bristol, there were twenty-one such schools teaching 540 men and twenty-three teaching 708 women.[67] Jonas Hanway commented: 'In some young women learn to read. As to men, they do not appear to have any such ambition. If they have not been taught in their childhood they prefer ignorance.'[68]

The first fully documented English adult school was founded in 1798 in Nottingham for young women in the lace and hosiery factories. 'It was a thing understood in the old-fashioned Quakerish economy, that all the shop assistants, male and female – they were principally female – should help at the Adult School on First Day morning.' A Sunday school for Bible reading, it also taught women 'the secular arts of writing and arithmetic'.[69] The adult Sunday School idea blended with self-help attempts by the working classes to improve their education. The bulk of the evidence describes male 'mechanics' groups, but here and there are glimpses of women. A concerted effort was the Birmingham Sunday Society created in 1789 by Sunday School teachers to instruct young men in writing and arithmetic. Both the Old and New Meeting Sunday Schools provided places for girls, with paid female teachers. Women as well as men attended the Birmingham Sunday Society lectures, as a member described:

The admission to all these lectures was gratuitous, and as the style of the lecturer was remarkably simple, his manner earnest and unassuming, and his illustrations particularly felicitous, the interest which they excited occasioned them to be very numerously attended by persons of both sexes.[70]

While a 'movement' hardly existed, there was a multiplicity of local, casual attempts to provide further education in basic and more sophisticated branches of knowledge. These are clear indications that women were offered and sought further forms of education.

Lecture series were also offered in many British towns throughout the century. Most were open to women; some even offered women concessions. Large numbers of women attended in Manchester, London, Bristol, and Newcastle. In 1803, it was noted: 'Even some ladies talk with facility about oxygen . . . hydrogen and the carbonic acid.'[71] By the 1840s, most Mechanics' Institutes also had women members. Some of these series were clearly associated with the universities. Lectures on Experimental Philosophy at Oxford included women from 1710, while other lectures were attended by 'persons', or in the case of Glasgow, by the 'town's people of almost every rank, age and employment'.[72] Lectures at University College, London, were open to women from its foundation in 1825. Announcing its [failed] intention in 1742, an advert stated, 'all liberal Arts and Sciences will be most usefully, critically and demonstratively taught in the mother tongue in a proper course of lectures . . . so as to be entertaining to all and particularly to the ladies'.[73] The Royal Institution in London admitted women from its inception.

Ladies were encouraged at the Robin Hood Free Debating Society and the Amicable Debating Society in Birmingham. On 2 May 1774, the Robin Hood Society resolved:

> That as this Society is intended to be of general Advantage that such Ladies who choose to hear the Debates shall be admitted. – The President therefore gives Notice that the Upper Part of the Room will be railed in for the Reception of Ladies, that they may sit without interruption, but no Gentleman is to be permitted to sit within side of the Rail. – The Ladies will be admitted without Expense. – Admittance 6d. each Gentleman.[74]

Later that summer, it announced that ladies were to be allowed to speak to the proposed questions.[75] The 'Gentlemen' referred to included artisans or other workingmen. As one critic wrote:

> Besides the outward Garb of many of those who spoke was rather indecent; a clean Shirt and Stock should surely be procured for this night, even though Sunday went unprovided; the Ladies are permitted Gratis, and Cleanliness is a Compliment due to the Sex everywhere.[76]

Whether ladies were always 'ladies' is not possible to tell.

Such activities were more likely to take place in urban rather than rural areas. Intellectual activity also seemed to emanate from, and to be directed toward, the upper echelons of the working classes. Women may have been further restrained by familial responsibilities, so that the influence was probably nominal on the typical working-class woman. Many who could took advantage of such opportunities. Such lectures could be seen as merely leisure-time activities, but society also had come to believe that education could and should be amusing and entertaining, as well as intellectual.

An important feature of 'higher' education during this period was that graduation was not the focus of study – learning was. At Edinburgh, 'graduation was simply unimportant' before the nineteenth century and fewer than 12 per cent of medical students 'bothered to graduate' each year. Indeed, 'graduation before 1858, except perhaps in Aberdeen, seems to have been something of an eccentricity'.[77] It was similar in the ancient English universities, so while 70 per cent graduated, the absolute number was small, and the value of a degree was in itself minimal.[78] Therefore, the degree was of less relevance than access to courses of study, lectures and exposure to a range of educational experiences. Similarly, the growth of 'dissenting academies' represented the need for a different sort of education – that is, the social education of Locke and an interest in science and commerce among the middle classes.

In Scotland, the broader curriculum already existed, and universities were non-residential, making access easier for women.[79] John Anderson, professor at Glasgow for over forty years, and strongly committed to the application of democratic principles through higher education, was instrumental in founding a unique institution that from its inception included women. His bequest in 1796 proposed a 'Ladies course' and that women might attend several of the lecture courses in order to gain an education which would 'make them the most accomplished Ladies in Europe'.[80] As Smith suggests, there seems to have been no question of women's education, and the first Professor of Natural Philosophy, Thomas Garnett, utilized a system in which each ticket admitted either 'a Gentleman and a Lady,' or 'Two Ladies', thus actively encouraging female attendance.[81] This was so successful that Garnett reckoned that half of the attendees at his first course of lectures were female, commenting that the Andersonian was 'the first regular institution in which the fair sex have been admitted to the temple of knowledge on the same footing with men; and it must be said in their praise, that they have not neglected to avail themselves of it'.[82] It continued to admit women, and as it developed into a full university, women had access to a more varied curriculum.

Professors of medicine also began to give courses of lectures specifically to women who wished to qualify as midwives. In the 1760s, John Memus of Marischal College, Aberdeen, advertised regularly in the *Aberdeen Journal*,[83] and Thomas Young, Professor of Midwifery at Edinburgh University, signed certificates confirming the strenuous nature of the courses. Women passed admission interviews and attended three full courses of lectures, followed by practical tuition at Edinburgh Royal Infirmary. They then passed examinations – having paid six guineas for the privilege. James Hamilton, Young's successor, estimated that he had taught 1,000 women between 1760 and 1817.[84]

Within women's educational history, the foundation of Queen's College, London, in 1848, is seen as a landmark. It provided a foundation to give governesses and teachers a better educational grounding, thus marking the beginning of higher education for women in Britain. However, Sarah Smith has documented the emergence of Queen's College, Glasgow, in 1842, as a women's higher education institution, some six years earlier.[85] It operated four departments – Religion, Literature, Science, and Fine Art – with a wide curriculum and high-calibre lecturing staff. Its aim was to provide a solid educational experience, and 'induce habits of sustained and steady application, instead of . . . the desultory and irregular mode hitherto so characteristic of female education'.[86] The aim was to provide full-time education and innovative 'clash-free' timetabling allowed the students to attend classes across the academic spectrum rather than limiting them to their chosen fields of study. It was also clearly higher education: 'intended principally for Ladies who have completed the ordinary courses of education given in schools [who] are desirous of pursuing branches of Literature and Science hitherto partially or entirely inaccessible'.[87] The institution had high-level support from the outset, as specifically higher education for women, and by implication, women from the middle classes who could afford the money and time and who were most likely to meet the educational prerequisites. However, it lasted only four years.

One of the motivations for providing women's higher education was the need for teachers. While the relative lack of good widespread education for girls was a limiting factor in providing the students and the impetus to provide higher education, the need to address the growing pressure for more teachers and better education for all children also contributed to opening the door to higher education and providing the venues to pursue it.

Conclusion

The patterns of girls' education and training in eighteenth- and early nineteenth-century Britain were varied and diverse. Changing social relationships could be felt in the workplace and across the commercial world, and aspirations for social mobility underpinned much of the vibrancy of social and cultural attitudes. Enlightenment thought, the democratizing influences of the 'rights of man' and a wider respect for education shaped approaches to women and their education. The effect on women was ambivalent, certainly in the short term. Since the rights of man did not actually mean women, their role was recast in an ideology that valued their mothering and homemaking skills. The level of debate at the end of the eighteenth century and the beginning of the nineteenth about popular education in general, and female education in particular, reveals the underlying tensions in society. It illustrated the forces of liberal radicalism and the threat posed to the conservative view of society and to a perception of woman's place within it. But these influences, and particularly the debate on the purposes, quality, and quantity of women's education, led to more education generally, and specifically to a 'useful' education that had democratizing tendencies. Thus, across Britain, and particularly after c. 1750, more schools were founded and gradually a wider curriculum was produced.

Nevertheless, education was shaped by perceptions of class and status, and the need for girls to be educated in certain ways for the good of society as a whole. The impact on girls of the 'lower orders' was to promote their education in the context of providing the skills these girls would require in order to work and to care for their own 'little families'. Specifically, domestic service was highlighted as appropriate work. For girls from better-off families, education shifted from accomplishments to a more academic content, not to make scholars of them so much as to provide a more well-rounded knowledge and make them better companions to the men they would marry. Importantly, girls and their families may well have had different motives from those providing schools. Across the spectrum, girls and their families were active in taking advantage of, and shaping, their education. They sought out schooling, informal avenues of learning, and forms of higher education. They stayed at school frequently longer than historians have suggested. Overall, the extent and quality of their education, though sharply restricted in some respects by social strictures and preconceptions, were far greater than earlier impressions indicated.

Notes

1 Elizabeth Ham, *Elizabeth Ham, by Herself: 1783–1820*, ed. Eric Gillet, London, 1945, p. 42.
2 Dorothy Gardiner, *English Girlhood at School: A Study of Women's Education through Twelve Centuries*, London, 1929; Josephine Kamm, *Hope Deferred: Girls Education in English History*, London, 1965; Mary Cathcart Borer, *Willingly to School: A History of Women's Education*, London, 1975.
3 Mary Hilton and Pam Hirsch (eds), *Practical Visionaries: Women, Education and Social Progress, 1790–1930*, London, 2000; Jane Nardin, 'Hannah More and the rhetoric of educational reform', *Women's History Review*, 2001, vol. 10, pp. 211–27; Joyce Goodman, 'Undermining or building up the nation? Elizabeth Hamilton (1758–1816), national identities and an authoritative role for woman education-alists', *History of Education*, 1999, vol. 28, pp. 279–96; Anne Stott, *Hannah More: The First Victorian*, Oxford, 2003.

4 Ruth Watts, *Gender, Power and the Unitarians in England, 1760–1860*, London, 1998; also Ruth Watts, 'Knowledge is power: Unitarians, gender and education in the eighteenth and early nineteenth centuries', *Gender and Education*, 1989, vol. 1, pp. 35–50; Susan Skedd, 'Women teachers and the expansion of girls' schooling in England, *c.*1760–1820', in Hannah Barker and Elaine Chalus (eds), *Gender in Eighteenth-Century England: Roles, Representations and Responsibilities*, Harlow, 1997, pp. 101–25; see also Deborah Simonton, 'Earning and learning: girlhood in pre-industrial Europe', *Women's History Review*, 2004, vol. 13, pp. 363–85; Simonton, 'Schooling the poor: gender and class in eighteenth-century England', *British Journal for Eighteenth-century Studies*, 2000, vol. 23, pp. 183–202; Simonton, 'Bringing up girls: work in pre-industrial Europe', in Christina Benninghaus, Mary Jo Maynes, and Brigitte Söland (eds), *Secret Gardens, Satanic Mills: Youth and Gender in European History*, Bloomington, IN, 2004; and Simonton, 'The education and training of eighteenth-century English girls, with special reference to the working classes', PhD thesis, University of Essex, June 1988.

5 Lindy Moore, 'Educating for the "woman's sphere": domestic training versus intellectual discipline', in Esther Breitenbach and Eleanor Gordon (eds), *Out of Bounds: Women in Scottish Society, 1800–1945*, Edinburgh, 1992, pp. 10–41; Lindy Moore, 'Young Ladies' institutions: the development of secondary schools for girls in Scotland, 1833–*c.*1870', *History of Education*, 2003, vol. 32, pp. 249–72; also Moore, 'Gender, education and learning', in Lynn Abrams, Eleanor Gordon, Deborah Simonton, and Eileen Yeo (eds), *Gender in Scottish History, 1700 to the Present*, Edinburgh, forthcoming. For Wales, see Eryn M. White, 'Women, religion and education in eighteenth-century Wales', in Michael Roberts and Simone Clarke (eds), *Women and Gender in Early Modern Wales*, Cardiff, 2000, pp. 210–32.

6 This argument is developed more fully in Simonton, 'Earning and learning', and 'Bringing up girls'.

7 John Locke, *The Educational Writings of John Locke* (1693), ed. James L. Axtell, London, 1968, p. 138.

8 See Jane Rendall's chapter, 'Women and the Enlightenment in Britain, *c.*1690–1800', pp. 9–32.

9 Hannah More, *Essays on Various Subjects, Principally Designed for Young Ladies*, London, 1777, p. 135.

10 Hugh Cunningham, *Children and Childhood in Western Society since 1500*, London, 1995, p. 62. These ideas were extended to the lower classes through schools, schoolbooks, and sermons, such as John Burton, *Religious Education for Poor Children Recommended*, London, 1759, and John Chapman, *The Ends and Uses of Charity Schools for Poor Children*, 30 April 1752.

11 Catharine Cappe, *Observations on Charity Schools, Female Friendly Societies and Other Subjects Connected with the Views of the Ladies' Committee*, London, 1805, p. 31.

12 Clara Reeve, *Plans of Education*, London, 1792, p. 60.

13 Cappe, *Observations on Charity Schools*, pp. 32, 23.

14 Sarah Trimmer, *The Oeconomy of Charity: Or, An Address to Ladies Concerning Sunday Schools*, London, 1787, p. 46.

15 John Moir, *Female Tuition: Or, An Address to Mothers on the Education of Daughters*, London, 1784, Preface.

16 Robert Acklom Ingram, *An Essay on the Importance of Schools of Industry and Religious Instruction*, London, 1800, p. 37.

17 Priscilla Wakefield, *Reflections on the Present Condition of the Female Sex with Suggestions for its Improvement*, London, 1798. pp. 8–9.

18 James Talbot, *The Christian Schoolmaster*, London, 1707, p. 24.

19 Hannah More, *Strictures on the Modern System of Female Education, with a View of the Principles and Conduct Prevalent among Females of Rank and Fortune*, London, 1799, vol. i, p. 64.

20 By 1832, the National Society, supported by the Church of England, had established some 12,000 schools. Far fewer were founded by the Lancastrian group, supported by dissenters, although by 1810 it was estimated that they had taught 14,000 'scholars'.

21 Essex Record Office (hereafter ERO), T/A 461, Romford Charity School Minutes and Accounts, 1762–1803; ERO, D/Q 24/2, Ashdon, Draft Returns to the Bishop of London, 1810, 1814; ERO, D/P 18/2/2; Beryl Madoc-Jones, 'Patterns of attendance and their social significance: Mitcham National School. 1830–39', in Phillip McCann (ed.), *Popular Education and Socialization in the Nineteenth Century*, London, 1977, pp. 53–4.

22 See Simonton, 'Education and training', App. 3.2, for a digest of the case studies on which much of this section relies.

23 ERO, D/NC 1/9, Coggeshall, Minutes of the Congregational Sunday School, and Accounts, 1788–1800.

24 Charities Commission, *Reports* for Staffordshire and Essex, and Essex and Staffordshire Record Office school records, as described in Simonton, 'Education and training', App. 3.2.

25 Staffordshire Record Office (hereafter SRO), D1157/1/5/1; ERO, T/A 461; Philip Morant, *The History and Antiquities of the County of Essex*, London, 1768, vol. 2, p. 6.

26 Trimmer, *Reflections on Education*, pp. 21–2.

27 SRO, D1157/1/5/1, 5 February 1729, 1 October 1730; ERO, D/Q 24/2, 10 April 1794; Morant, *History and Antiquities of the County of Essex*, vol. 2, p. 6.

28 ERO, D/Q 8/3.

29 Sarah Trimmer, *The Charity Spelling Book*, 5th edn, London, 1799, pt 1, p. 115.

30 Trimmer, *Reflections on Education*, p. 21.

31 See Simonton, 'Education and training', Chapter 5B.

32 Note that all statistics are based on traceable children, not the total intake of schools.

33 ERO, D/P 18/12/3, D/P 18/12/4, D/P 18/11/3, D/Q 8/3, D/Q 8/1, T/A 461, D/Q 24/2, D/P 30/1/2A; SRO, D260/M/F/120, D1157/1/5/1; Madoc-Jones, 'Patterns of attendance', p. 45.

34 Roger Schofield, 'The measurement of literacy in preindustrial England', pp. 311–25, in Jack Goody (ed.), *Literacy in Traditional Societies*, Cambridge, 1968, p. 317.

35 Parliamentary Papers, *Report from the Select Committee on the Education of the Lower Orders in the Metropolis* (Brougham) 1819, vol. 9; Parliamentary Papers, Factories Inquiry Commission, *First Report, Employment of Children in Factories, with Minutes of Evidence and Reports by the District Commissioners*. 1833.

36 David Allan, *Scotland in the Eighteenth Century*, London, 2002, p. 120.

37 N. Hans, *New Trends in Education in the Eighteenth Century*, London, 1951, pp. 194–6.

38 Mary Capper, 'A memoir of Mary Capper', ed. Katherine Backhouse, *The Friends' Library*, 1848, vol. 12, p. 2; Eliza Fox, *Memoir of Mrs. Eliza Fox*, ed. Franklin Fox, London, 1869, p. 6; Margaret Lucas, 'An account of the convincement and call to the ministry of Margaret Lucas', *The Friends' Library*, 1849, vol. 13, p. 170.

39 Sarah Grubb, 'Some account of the life and religious labours of Sarah Grubb', *The Friends' Library*, 1848, vol. 12, p. 256.

40 Ruth Follows, 'Memoirs of Ruth Follows', *The Friends' Library*, 1840, vol. 4, p. 25.

41 Henry Moore (ed.), *The Life of Mrs. Mary Fletcher*, 3rd edn, London, 1818, pp. 3, 7, 9; Ann Taylor Gilbert, *Autobiography and other Memorials of Mrs. Gilbert*, ed. Josiah Gilbert, 2 vols, London, 1874, p. 108; Lucas, 'Account of the convincement', p. 179; Capper, 'Memoir of Mary Capper', p. 2; Ham, *Elizabeth Ham*, p. 16.

42 K. and C. Fry, *Memoir of the Life of Elizabeth Fry with Extracts from Her Journal and Letters*, 2nd edn, 2 vols, London, 1848, p. 11; Lucas, 'Account of the convincement', p. 179; Grubb, 'Some account of the life', p. 256.

43 Gilbert, *Autobiography*, p. 114.

44 Susan Skedd, 'Women Teachers'.

45 M. Bentham-Edwards (ed.), *The Autobiography of Arthur Young with Selections from his Correspondence*, London, 1898, p. 263.

46 J. L. Chirol, *An Inquiry into the Best System of Female Education*, London, 1809, p. 9; *The Governess: Or, the Boarding School Dissected: A Dramatic Original*, London, 1785, pp. 58–9.

47 Quoted in Hans, *New Trends in Education*, p. 196.

48 Fox, *Memoir of Mrs. Eliza Fox*, p. 6.

49 Moore, 'Young Ladies' institutions', p. 249.

50 Teachers have been given little attention in this chapter, due to the constraints of space, but for a detailed look at the profession in England in these years, see Skedd, 'Women teachers'.

51 Joyce Senders Pedersen, 'Schoolmistresses and headmistresses: elites and education in nineteenth-century England', *Journal of British Studies*, vol. 15, no. 1 (Autumn 1975), especially pp. 140–2.

52 Adam Smith, *An Inquiry into the Nature and Causes of the Wealth of Nations*, ed. R. H. Campbell and A. S. Skinner, 2 vols (1776; Oxford, 1976), p. 781. Smith made this comment while criticizing the uselessness of most boys' public-school education. In part, his point was that girls' education was more appropriate than boys', because it was more geared to their ultimate future.

53 More, *Strictures on Female Education*, p. 39.

54 Goodman, 'Undermining or building up the nation?', p. 290; Maria Edgeworth, *Letters for Literary Ladies: To Which Is Added, An Essay on the Noble Science of Self-Justification*, 2nd edn, 1798, http://digital.library.upenn.edu/women/edgeworth/ladies/ladies.html: accessed 11 January 2005.

55 More, *Strictures on Female Education*, pp. 72, 74.

56 Mary Wollstonecraft, *A Vindication of the Rights of Women*, London, 1792, Chapter IX.

57 Catherine Macaulay, *Letters on Education*, London, 1790, pt 1.

58 See Goodman's argument about how many of these female educationalists contributed to the re-constructions of national identity in 'Undermining or building up the nation?'.

59 Hans, *New Trends in Education*, p. 203.

60 As quoted in ibid., pp. 204–5.

61 This paragraph draws upon Lindy Moore, 'Young Ladies' institutions', pp. 249–50.

62 See work by Helen Corr, including, 'The sexual division of labour in the Scottish teaching profession, 1872–1914', in Walter Humes and Hamish M. Paterson (eds), *Scottish Culture and Scottish Education, 1800–1980*, Edinburgh, 1983, pp. 137–50; or, 'Teachers and gender; debating the myths of equal opportunities in Scottish Education, 1800–1914', *Cambridge Journal of Education*, 1997, vol. 27, pp. 355–63.

63 Sarah Smith, 'Retaking the register: women's higher education in Glasgow and beyond, *c*.1796–1845', *Gender and History*, 2000, vol. 12, p. 311. Much of the information on Scotland comes from this article and I am grateful to Sarah for sharing a pre-publication version.

64 Society for the Propagation of Christian Knowledge (hereafter SPCK), *Early Eighteenth-Century Archives, Part C: Letters and Memorials, Abstract Letter Books* (Correspondence received and sent), 1699–1701, vol. 1, 8 March 1700/01.

65 Griffith Jones, *Selections from the Welch Piety*, ed. W. Moses Williams, Cardiff, 1938, p. 35.

66 A. P. Wadsworth, 'The first Manchester Sunday Schools', as cited in M. W. Flinn and T. C. Smout (eds), *Essays in Social History*, Oxford, 1974, p. 315.

67 Robert Peers, *Adult Education: A Comparative Study*, ed. W. J. H. Sprott, London, n.d., p. 11.

68 Jonas Hanway, *A Comprehensive View of Sunday Schools for the Use of the More Indigent Inhabitants of Cities, Towns and Villages, through England and Wales*, London, 1786, p. 32.

69 As quoted in Thomas Kelly, *A History of Adult Education in Great Britain*, Liverpool, 1970, p. 80.

70 The prime sources for its history are by one of the founders, James Luckock, in *Moral Culture, to which is Appended an Account of the Origin, Progress and Success of the Birmingham Sunday Society, 1816*, and his 'Narration of Proceedings relative to the erection of the Old Meeting Sunday Schools, Birmingham,' MS *c*.1832; and by a member of the Society, William Matthews, *A Sketch of the Principal Means which Have Been Employed to Ameliorate the Intellectual and Moral Condition of the Working Classes at Birmingham*, London, 1830, p. 15.

71 As quoted in William Page (ed.), *The Victoria History of the County of Warwickshire*, Oxford, 1904, vol. 7, p. 212.

72 See Smith, 'Retaking the register', p. 311, n. 20.

73 Hans, *New Trends in Education*, pp. 136–7.

74 *Aris' Birmingham Gazette*, 2 May 1774, p. 3.

75 Ibid., 6 June 1774, p. 3.

76 Ibid., 20 June 1774, p. 3.

77 J. B. Morrell, 'The University of Edinburgh in the late eighteenth century', *Isis*, 1971, pp. 168–9; J. Scotland, *The History of Scottish Education: I*, London, 1969, p. 153.

78 Hans, *New Trends in Education*, pp. 43–5.

79 Christina Struthers, *The Admission of Women to the Scottish Universities*, Aberdeen, 1883, p. 13.

80 Strathclyde University Archive, B1/1, John Anderson's Will, Andersonian Minute Book, as cited in Smith, 'Retaking the register,' p. 317.

81 S. G. E. Lythe, *Thomas Garnett, 1766–1802*, Glasgow, 1984, p. 17.

82 Thomas Garnett, *Observations on a Tour through the Highlands*, as quoted in Smith, 'Retaking the register', p. 318.

83 See *Aberdeen Journal*, 2 September 1765, advertising his book, *The Midwife's Pocket Companion*, praised by Thomas Young.

84 Elizabeth C. Sanderson, *Women and Work in Eighteenth-Century Edinburgh*, Basingstoke, 1996, pp. 53–4, 59.

85 Smith, 'Retaking the register', pp. 322–5.

86 *Glasgow Constitutional*, 3 November 1842.

87 Ibid., 15 October, 1 November 1842.

Chapter Three

ぇ♣

Women, marriage and the family

Tanya Evans

The family and marriage were central to contemporary British social, political, and cultural concerns between 1700 and 1850. Numerous commentators identified both units as vital for the maintenance of social order and the promotion of national prosperity and expansion, especially during a period characterized by extensive warfare and imperial growth. Although the law on marriage was codified by the end of our period, understandings of family and marriage continued to differ. Recent historians of women and gender have focused on how the meanings of marriage and the family were transformed. In order to move beyond the primary conceptualization of women as wives and mothers, they have concentrated on detailing the ways that ideas about, and the experience of, courtship, sex, marriage, and motherhood changed over time.[1] By outlining the major changes that occurred to family and marital life over the period, and the effects of these historical processes on women's lives, this chapter will emphasize the diversity of the experience of marital and familial relationships for women of different social status, geographical location, age, and gender between 1700 and 1850.[2] In particular, it will shine a spotlight on the familial experiences of poor women who have remained beyond the gaze of most observers.

Our knowledge of women in the past has long been focused on their familial roles and relationships. In part, this reflected the fact that women tended to be defined only in relation to the family since it was assumed that all women became wives and mothers, and, if they did not, then prescriptive literature, the law, and much of society, labelled them deviants.[3] Women's familial and marital identity was framed by a combination of legal, religious, medical, and popular ideas, all of which proclaimed that familial relations should be patriarchal, but companionate. The family has long been identified as a crucial arena for the construction of gender relations and the formulation of patriarchy. Early women's historians explained how the subordination of women as a group could only be understood with reference to the family and marriage.[4] Men's legal, social, and political power over women was located, as well as learned, it was argued, within the home.[5] Prescriptive literature expounded a husband's authority over his wife and delineated the strict hierarchies to be maintained within households between husbands and wives, parents and children, and masters and their servants. At their wedding ceremonies, women in England and Wales effectively kissed goodbye to their status as individuals, as husbands subsumed their legal rights according to the law of *coverture*. Theoretically, women and everything they owned, became the property of their husbands. In his 1765 *Commentaries on the Laws of England*, Sir William Blackstone declared:

> By marriage, the husband and wife are one person in law: that is, the very being, or legal existence of the woman is suspended during the marriage, or at least is incorporated and consolidated into that of the husband . . . [her property] becomes absolutely her husband's which at his death he may leave entirely from her.[6]

Yet even if women's legal rights within marriage were clear on paper, the way that marriage was defined and experienced during this period certainly was not.[7] Recourse to equity and ecclesiastical law, and the use of marriage settlements, allowed women of all social classes to retain control over their property. It meant that they managed finances on their own behalf, as well as with their husbands. Marriage settlements became increasingly popular among wives, at all levels of society, eager to control their own property.[8] Moreover, the use of *coverture* was particular to English law. Scottish women experienced very different systems of marriage and divorce throughout this period, and may well have been less constrained upon marriage, both in theory and practice.[9] The patriarchal model of marriage set down in the statute books, therefore, needs to be tested carefully in the context of the emergence of modern family life. If too much attention is paid to prescriptive literature and the law, then we remain blind to the changing meanings of marriage and the family, as well as to the much more complicated power relations experienced by women within these institutions.[10] Women were expected to 'love, honour, and obey' their husbands – and most did so – but within reason. We therefore need to understand how social practice diverged from representations of the 'ideal family'.

Changing meanings of marriage and the family

During the eighteenth century, people were marrying earlier. They were also having more children than at any time before, both inside and outside of marriage. In the first half of the century, the mean age at first marriage was 27.5 years for men and 26.2 years for women; by mid-century, it had dropped to 26.4 for men and 23.4 for women.[11] The significant rise in population during the eighteenth century was due to an increase in fertility precipitated by this decline in the age of marriage.[12] Until the twentieth century, however, there was no consensus between the state, church, and popular opinion as to how marriage should be defined; thus, meanings of marriage and the family remained unstable until the end of our period.

Some historians have claimed that a surge in sentiment from the eighteenth century facilitated the disintegration of the traditional family.[13] Economic change dominated Shorter's interpretation, while, for Lawrence Stone, it was cultural transformation and the rise in sentiment that were crucial. Stone argued that the family changed in structure from one based upon deference and patriarchy in the sixteenth century to one grounded in affective individualism by the nineteenth.[14] Although families still tended to share their resources, economic change, urbanization, and enclosure meant that many young men and women were forced to travel far from the family home in order to find sufficient work to survive. Migration and increased mobility disrupted long-standing marital practices.[15] Migrants who moved away from home in search of work left behind parental and familial support, as well as constraint. Throughout the period, urban centres remained magnets for a continual stream of young men and women looking for work in the growing service sector and in the huge variety of relatively well-paid trades on offer.[16] Mobility remained common for people at a particular point in their life-cycle – usually their late teens to mid-to-late-twenties, before marriage.[17] As one contemporary ballad put it:

Since life in London's all the rage
A country life deserted
And all the lads and lasses come.
To Town to be diverted.[18]

Before the passage of Lord Hardwicke's Marriage Act of 1753 (which affected only England and Wales), there was little consensus as to what constituted a legal marriage. For centuries a gulf had existed between the ways in which the élite and poor had married. Wealthy members of society would celebrate their unions in public, often in church, after declaring the banns and buying a licence. The poor would marry in much more informal circumstances, often using verbal contracts and folklore customs familiar to the local community. When relationships were subject to greater surveillance by society, a 'promise of marriage' was sometimes enough to formalize a union between a couple. In the south-west of England, Wales, and in the borders between Scotland and England, couples often agreed to marry verbally, without exchanging legal contracts. Others jumped over broomsticks placed across their thresholds to officialize their union and create new households.[19]

During the early modern period, London developed the widest range of opportunities for clandestine marriages. These irregular marriages threatened to replace marriages formalized through private contract or betrothal, particularly among the poor.[20] They were particularly popular among artisans and sailors on leave, but wealthy individuals hoping to avoid parental intervention also resorted to them. The elopements of the latter became the butt of much society gossip.[21] In Scotland, Edinburgh was the capital of irregular marriage. Indeed, Scotland remained unaffected by Hardwicke's Act. Contract and clandestine marriages remained legal, and popular, throughout our period.[22] In 1751, Margaret Lindsay disobeyed her father by eloping with the portrait painter, Allan Ramsay. They married in Edinburgh before moving south. Although their marriage was happy and successful, she remained estranged from her family until her father's death. Other couples were luckier. In 1744, Lady Caroline Lennox eloped with the rising politician (but not her social equal), Henry Fox. Caroline's parents originally banned her from her childhood home and from making contact with her siblings, but by 1748 they had forgiven the couple and the family was reconciled.[23]

The popularity of informal marriage arrangements rested upon the belief that they, 'saved time, hindrance of business and knowledge of friends'.[24] But people resorted to private marriages for a multiplicity of reasons. Marriage ceremonies, then as well as now, were expensive. Celebrations shared among friends and family involved spending money on food and drink. They required purchasing presents for those participating in the ceremony and buying the wedding licence or paying parish fees.[25] Parish records attest to the popularity of informal, as well as illegal, unions among poor Britons throughout our period. Many other individuals found that keeping unions secret from family and parish authorities gave them some flexibility in future relationships.[26] There were also always some people, such as Catholics and Dissenters, who married, but whose marriages were not recognized because they practised their own religious ceremonies.

Concern over the transfer of property, coupled with the fear that children would run off and marry unapproved lovers in secret, encouraged élite men to lobby Parliament for change in the middle of the eighteenth century.[27] The furore that came to focus on informal marital practices was the catalyst for legal reform in 1753.[28] Hardwicke's Marriage Act prohibited Fleet chapels and marriage shops, and ensured that the registration of marriages became a much more public affair.[29] Parental consent became necessary for any individual hoping to marry aged under 21 and all marriages had to take place in an Anglican church, either after banns had been called or a licence had been purchased. The law exempted Quakers, Jews, and royalty, but not Catholics.[30] Consequently, Britain's Irish communities continued to practise their own marriage customs, although their unions were officially categorized as illegal and the children born within them were deemed illegitimate. In 1789, for instance, Martha Cropper was advised by parish authorities that her nine-year marriage to Patrick Burn, which had been presided over by a Catholic priest in a chapel in Virginia Street in the East End of London, was a 'pretended Solemnisation of a Marriage' and that she and her husband were actually cohabiting together, not married.[31] Catholic marriages were finally recognized as legal by English authorities with Catholic Emancipation in 1829. The introduction of the Civil Marriages Act in 1836 then allowed Dissenters to marry in their chosen places of worship with documents provided by civil registrars.[32] Despite the fact that anyone caught flouting the law might be liable to transportation for fourteen years, and even though legal marriage in church became increasingly widespread among the population as a whole, the tradition of informal marriage continued among the poor well into the nineteenth century.

Private contracts or betrothals had worked well for years in smaller communities where parental supervision ensured that contracts could not be broken and the responsibilities of putative fathers guaranteed. But in late eighteenth-century Britain, individuals were rarely subjected to the same level of familial and community control. Informal contracts continued, but were more likely to be broken, and it was women who bore the brunt of these unstable relationships. The absence of traditional community constraints led not to the desire to be free, as Shorter has suggested, but to frustrated marital expectations.[33] Marriage was most women's ticket to some semblance of economic security. Nevertheless, as Alannah Tomkins discusses in more detail elsewhere in this volume, unemployment, migration, the anonymity of urban life, high mortality rates, war, and desertion, meant that a stable, long-term marriage was often unattainable for poor women in eighteenth-century Britain, especially in its urban centres.[34]

Before the passage of the Marriage Act, the legal age of consent was 12 for girls and 14 for boys, but many of society's poorest delayed marriage until much later in their lives when sufficient resources had been accumulated to set up independent households. Young women who migrated tended to marry later than women who stayed within the same geographical area for most of their lives. Many of the Irish, Welsh, and Scots women who moved to London or other provincial cities, or to the new industrial centres in search of work spent longer saving up the money that would allow them to set up an independent household with their husbands. This left them at risk of seduction and the consequences of consensual premarital sexual relations.[35] Many pregnancies were the result of sexual relationships which had begun with marriage in mind but had been disrupted by war, abandonment, death, and illness. Mary Bennett, a migrant domestic servant with few friends in London, petitioned for the admission of her illegitimate child into the Foundling Hospital in 1774, explaining that, 'being young . . .[she] admitted a Young man to Pay his addresses, and they were even asked at Church for Matrimony . . . but she had been too weak as to consent to his Desires too soon'.[36]

It seems likely that marriage became harder to achieve for poor men and women, many of whom worked as servants and apprentices in eighteenth-century towns because the nature of their work delayed their quest for economic independence.[37] The insecurity associated with migration and declining economic independence affected women who were married, as well as those who were not. Thousands of wives were deserted by their husbands or found themselves the victims of bigamy or widowhood during this period.[38] In 1752, for example, Elizabeth Benstead travelled from London to Leith in Edinburgh to complain about the desertion of her husband, James Adams.[39]

Patriarchal but companionate?

Social status remained a crucial determinant in the experience of marriage during this period. Although they suffered most in many other respects, poor women had rather more choice over who they married than richer women whose parents were concerned about the transferral of property.[40] Poor parents could offer relatively little in the way of a dowry which could be used to wield power over their children's choices.[41] Nevertheless, a number of historians have suggested that élite marriage also became more egalitarian during the eighteenth century, as women came to exercise a greater degree of choice over their partners and expect more equality with their husbands.[42] However, many élite women still found that their marriage contracts and their married lives remained out of their control.[43] Lady Sarah Pennington, for instance, claimed never to have met her husband before they were married in the mid-eighteenth century.[44] Most women, however, were allowed a degree of latitude when it came to whom they courted. Many élite women were actively involved in their choice of husbands, prevailing upon their parents to accept their lovers.[45] Couples throughout this period married for reasons that could be described as both strategic and emotional, and many continued to rely on the advice of family and friends before making their decisions.

Many historians have disputed whether affective relations between husbands and their wives were new to this period and have suggested that romantic love and marital companionship have a much longer chronology.[46] Of course, there is a limit to what historians can ever learn about the intimate personal lives of those in the past, but women's diaries, letters, and journals have been culled to good effect.[47] Recent historical work has cast aside the preoccupation with continuity and change, and suggested instead that marriage was not transformed from a patriarchal to a companionate model during this period, but remained a combination of both.[48] In her study of marriages among the middling sorts and labouring classes in seventeenth- and eighteenth-century England, Joanne Bailey has argued that a model of 'co-dependency' best describes most marriages. Women were not, she asserts, entirely subordinate to their husbands, but played an important role in the household economy, household management and childcare which made them indispensable to their husbands.[49]

All women hoped to marry wisely and be happy ever after, but conflict of varying degrees was a characteristic of most unions. Successful marriages depended upon mutually agreed duties shared between husbands and wives. Women, as mistresses of households, were responsible for the household's orderly and successful management, while their husbands had a duty to provide and care for their family.[50] Both roles involved public, as well as private, functions and both were deemed to be crucial. Women certainly owed their husbands obedience, but men were also expected to respect and support their wives. Women's writings frequently emphasize passion for their husbands and it is clear that love was possible despite the strict demarcation of gender roles within the household. Frequently, both husbands and wives learned how to manipulate each other after years spent living together. In the mid-eighteenth century, for instance, Emily, Duchess of Leinster, was renowned for exchanging her sexual charms in return for her husband's affection and money. It is little wonder that their relationship led to the birth of nineteen children and the accumulation of huge debts. Although the duke was easily bored by the domestic minutiae of his wife's world, he often asked her opinion and took her advice on how to steer his way through the vagaries of Irish political life at the time. Despite both of their infidelities, they considered their marriage to be successful.[51]

Some wives were absolutely crucial to their husband's economic success. Élite women often brought considerable personal wealth and status to a marriage, and many husbands continued to respect this. Others used their skills to augment the family's income. Lady Charlotte Guest, wife of Sir Josiah John Guest, owner of the largest ironworks in the world during the 1830s, was deeply involved in her husband's business. Not only was she devoted to her spouse but she was also ambitious for herself and their family. For his part, Guest was supremely confident of his wife's abilities and often used her as his business representative.[52] For families of all social classes, the paid and unpaid labour of wives was often crucial to the successful running of households. In middling marriages, the role of wives in running family businesses was likely to be particularly important and far more common than among the élite.[53] Working-class women's economic partnership in marriage also gave them status: wives in rural areas of Wales were instrumental to the success of small family farming enterprises, for instance.[54]

Husbands, it was argued, were best managed if they were unaware of the process. As an article in the *Scots Magazine* of 1765 advised, wives should aim to enjoy, 'the amiable female privileges of ruling by obeying, of commanding by submitting, and of being perfectly happy from consulting another's happiness'. From the voluminous correspondence of the Carlyles we discover that they had greater difficulty learning how to deal with each other than other famous couples. All Thomas Carlyle's friends and family knew how hard he could be to live with and his wife Jane spent the forty years of their marriage from the 1820s learning how to negotiate the moods and idiosyncrasies that accompanied his intellectual exertions. As she aged, she became increasingly obsessed with the lack of power women had within marriage, but she did little to stake her own claim for equality, despite knowing many women, including George Eliot and Harriet Taylor, who openly challenged the power of their husbands.[55] The happiest wives during this period accepted the inequalities of power that were integral to their marriages, but not without exercising considerable autonomy over their relationships, the running of their households, and many other aspects of their lives.[56]

Marital harmony remained an elusive dream for many couples during this period, however. In Yorkshire, Elizabeth Parker eloped to Gretna Green with John Shackleton in 1765, seven years after the premature death of her first husband. Her family was outraged by her behaviour and, despite a few happy early years of marriage, John's drinking led to increasing verbal and physical abuse. As she stated in her diary, he said: 'I was . . . nought to him, he co'd not live with me, Nor wo'd not. He quite hates me, dos not like me. He behaves most cruelly to me.' Despite his violence, she could not leave him for fear of the scandal that would ensue, and her own family refused to help her because she had married below her station and without their consent. She died lonely and embittered in 1781.[57]

Theoretically, women continued to be defined as the property of their husbands and at no time during this period was the sexual double standard threatened. The adultery of a woman was always treated with more severity than that of a man. In England, élite men could sue their wives' lovers, effectively for trespassing on their property, through criminal conversation proceedings. Occasionally, poor men sold their wives in the market when they tired of them.[58] Husbands were expected to enforce the obedience of their wives and the records show that many women, mostly among the poor, were subjected to domestic violence.[59] It has been suggested that working-class unions were characterized by conflict and the 'struggle for the breeches' as wives wrestled with their husbands over control of the marriage. In the early nineteenth century, working-class men increasingly aspired to the middle-class model of separate spheres. While they aimed for a patriarchal marriage, their wives desired love and companionship. Anna Clark has argued that working-class men utilized the language of domesticity to bind women to the home and to prevent them from competing for wages and being treated as social and political equals. These struggles often resulted in wives being assaulted by their husbands.[60] This did not mean, however, that plebeian men and women could not expect to find love and companionship within the family.[61] As Francis Place said of his early years:

> It may be supposed that I led a miserable life but I did not I was very far indeed from being miserable at this time when my wife came home at night, we had always something to talk about, we were pleased to see each other, our reliance on each other was great indeed, we were poor, but we were young, active, cheerful.[62]

It is, however, important to acknowledge that conflict rather than companionship is more likely to leave its mark on the historical record and that that patriarchal power had limits. Most women would not tolerate violence against their persons and took measures to prevent it. Mary Taylor told the courts in 1785 that her spouse had 'treated her with "inhumanity" by spending all his money on "naughty women" and depriving her of the "necessaries of life" '.[63] Margaret Hunt has explained that married women of the middling sorts believed they had the right to expect maintenance, protection, and freedom from assault from their husbands, as well as a say in the family finances.[64] Abused wives could often also expect to find support and a safe haven among kin and neighbours.[65] In 1843, forty Pontarddulais women participated in a rough music ritual in order to humiliate a neighbour renowned for beating his wife and encourage him to change his habits.[66] Although economic dependency on a husband prevented most women from escaping abusive relationships, few wives remained passive partners in marriages controlled by violent and domineering husbands.

By the early nineteenth century, as more women resisted the power of their spouses, public opinion and the law increasingly demanded that husbands treat their wives with humanity. Men's violence towards women came to be interpreted as the neglect of male duties. Nineteenth-century notions of respectability defined such behaviour as unmanly. Widespread protests against violence within marriage, most famously perhaps in the case of Caroline Norton, became part of a wider debate about husbands' power over wives that reached a peak in the marriage debates of the later nineteenth century. The struggle for a mother's rights over her children was partly resolved in the passage of the Infant Custody Act of 1839, which stipulated that a mother of legitimate children had legal rights over her offspring until they reached seven years of age, in the event of marital separation. In the nineteenth century, middle-class women increasingly used their writings and actions openly to criticize the subordination of women within marriage. Owenite women in particular insisted on the equality of wives before wider social justice could be implemented.[67] The many women of all social classes who rallied to the defence of Princess Caroline in the 1820s actively involved themselves in the public discussion of the rights and responsibilities of husbands and wives.[68] Nevertheless, feminist demands for a wife's control over her own property were not met until the passage of the Married Women's Property Acts in 1870 and 1886 (Scotland Conjugal Rights Act 1861; Married Women's Property Act 1877).[69]

Women-headed households

Women rarely chose to separate themselves from men because so few, rich or poor, could survive without the financial support of their fathers or husbands. Divorce remained rare throughout this period. Between 1670 and 1857 there were only 325 divorces recorded in England, and all except four were initiated by men.[70] The sole grounds for full divorce in England was the adultery of a woman, but in Scotland divorce for adultery or desertion by a husband or wife had been allowed since the mid-sixteenth century. Nonetheless, rates remained low, and between 1836 and 1841 only nineteen per annum were granted, although 40 per cent of plaintiffs were wives.[71] In England, under canon law a legal separation could be obtained if one-half of the partnership was successfully accused of adultery, cruelty, heresy, or apostasy; however, few followed this route. Others obtained a divorce using the costly and lengthy process of the private Act of Parliament (expenses could rise to £700).[72] Only rich men seeking to protect their property avenged the adultery of their wives in this way.

To avoid these costs, couples often agreed to separate informally, but many men also simply abandoned their wives. Few women, especially if they had children to support, could afford to do the same. Mothers, particularly if they were single, struggled to combine work with motherhood. They could rarely do both adequately if they were left on their own. If a marriage ended as a result of death or desertion, then remarriage was often a necessary requirement for economic survival. While remarriage intervals were often short for eighteenth-century Britons, Peter Laslett has calculated that as many as one-fifth of the households in any early modern

English community were headed by widows.[73] As has been noted, unemployment, death, and desertion by husbands and lovers were frequent occurrences.[74] Peggy Smith, who lived in St Botolph's Aldgate in the East End of London, came with her illegitimate children before the parish for relief in 1794. She told the parish officers that in 1780 she had married John Smith in the church at Rotherhithe before discovering he had a wife in every port across the world, one in Cork, Barbados, Plymouth, and Dartmouth, and had obviously abandoned her and her children for another lover.[75] John Smith was not alone: significant numbers of men simply disappeared during this period. Defoe's Roxana faced destitution when her husband vanished out of her life leaving her with five children to support. She exclaimed that it was as if, 'the Ground had open'd and swallow'd [him] all up, and no-body had known it'.[76]

Until recently, historians have largely ignored those women who did not follow the path to marriage and motherhood.[77] Yet what has been described as a 'significant minority' of women, calculated between 1250 and 1800 as 10–20 per cent of all adult women, remained unmarried.[78] Women of independent means could live their lives largely as they wished. Many chose not to marry or to tie themselves to men. Anne Lister was an upper-class woman who never married but lived an outwardly respectable life in Yorkshire in the late-eighteenth and early-nineteenth centuries. Following the death of her brother and then her uncle, she was left to manage the family estate. Economic freedom allowed her an advanced education, travel, and passionate relationships with lesbian lovers that she detailed in her carefully coded diaries.[79] For wealthy women, widowhood could provide the key to similar economic independence and relative social freedom. Indeed, widows and single women need to be differentiated because widows enjoyed far greater economic security as heads of households and social status.[80] Many poorer single women led a life of unremitting poverty and their singleness was rarely a self-conscious choice. Most women-headed households were among the poor and in urban rather than rural areas. As few women could earn enough to support themselves without board and lodgings provided by an employer, father, or husband, many single women had to rely upon ties of support outside the familial realm to survive.[81] Some women had no choice but to set up households with other women in order to guarantee their survival – what Olwen Hufton has labelled 'spinster-clustering'.[82] Some supported themselves through the teaching and philanthropic work that expanded across the country in the nineteenth century. Other women had to resort to varied 'economies of makeshift' to make ends meet.

Motherhood

The duties of mothers and fathers were fundamentally gendered and differed ideologically as well as in practice. Theological, medical, social, and legal understandings of women were intimately bound up with their capacity to bear children.[83] A woman's reproductive status defined her and motherhood was deemed her natural role. In a period when access to trustworthy contraception was limited, sex within and outside of marriage was usually tantamount to motherhood.[84] The physical relationship between women and their children explained why maternal affection was deemed to be stronger than the love of fathers for their offspring.[85]

Both Stone and Shorter, drawing on the pioneering work of Philippe Ariès, suggested that the emergence of modernity produced a trans-formation not only in affective relations between lovers and marriage partners, but also between parents and their children.[86] Elizabeth Badinter, arguing that motherhood was an invention of capitalism, suggested that the élite's practice of wet-nursing children and the poor's propensity to abandon theirs, proved that early modern mothers and fathers felt little love for their offspring.[87] Only in the eighteenth century did childhood come to be acknowledged as a separate stage in the life-cycle and children valued. The staggeringly high rate of infant mortality up until the mid-1700s had supposedly encouraged parents to make less investment in the lives of their newborns[88] and even until the nineteenth century, it has been argued, indifference towards infant life and death was common.[89] The decline in infant mortality, deemed to be a direct result of the increase in breastfeeding among the aristocracy and bourgeoisie, as well as a philosophical reassessment of the role of mothers within the family, precipitated this change.[90] For Ruth Perry the ideological shift was a response to the new political and economic forces creating the British empire and was signified by an increasing cultural emphasis, promulgated by political commentators as well as the medical establishment, on breastfeeding.[91] Rousseau, in particular, has been credited with the revaluation of maternity. Many became convinced that women had a vital role to play in the education of their children and the future citizens of nation-states. Good mothering and responsible childrearing became women's social duty.[92]

It is clear that the cult of breastfeeding made little impact on the lives of the poor because they had no choice but to nurse their own children. Nevertheless, the eighteenth-century revaluation of motherhood was to have enormous implications for the lives of pauper women, especially in Britain's cities, following the establishment of charitable institutions, lying-in hospitals, and Foundling Hospitals, all intended for the pregnant poor.[93] Charity sermons and fundraising appeals for hospitals set up from the 1750s exhorted the benefits of these institutions for Britain at a time when child mortality and the increasingly visible problem of abandoned children occupied the minds of the 'polite and commercial people' of eighteenth-century Britain.[94] Toni Bowers has used the literary creations of Defoe to explore the impossibility of becoming the perfect mother for most women in eighteenth-century England. Both Moll Flanders and Roxana represented the conflict between motherhood and survival. Bowers suggests that eighteenth-century literature, pamphlets, and broadsides dwell on representations of 'unnatural mothers'. These were women who were too poor to conform to the middle-class definition of maternity promulgated in *Pamela*, which was increasingly forced on women by the end of the century.[95]

Although motherhood became much more ideologically significant over the course of our period and contributed to the transformation of the experience for some élite and middling women, many women continued to mother in much the same way that women had for centuries.[96] Historians who have researched childcare manuals and élite diaries have been quick to counter the claims that parents did not love their children before the eighteenth century. Evidence of early modern maternal affection and the value placed on infant life is not hard to find.[97] It is clear that many parents felt deep affection for their children and, despite the frequency with which they faced their deaths, grief was both widely experienced and expressed in early modern England.[98] Instead of emphasizing change, historians now insist on the value of studying continuity as well as change while highlighting the enduring characteristics of parental care and emotion.[99] Fewer historians have attempted to reveal the maternal care and emotions of the poor because such evidence is harder to find and much more difficult to interpret. But it has been argued that the eighteenth-century emotional revolution was limited to those who could afford to care, and that the obsession with economic survival within plebeian families meant that the maternal revolution passed the poor by. Once again, recent research has suggested otherwise.[100]

Social historians have revealed the significant experiential differences between mothers of different social groups, marital status, and age, and have emphasized that women did not experience motherhood as an homogeneous group.[101] Unmarried mothers were far less likely to look forward to the births of their children due to the disruption caused to their working lives, fear over the loss of reputation, familial displeasure, and communal rejection. Even married women might not welcome the birth of another mouth to feed or child to care for, however, and many feared the processes of childbirth and motherhood that remained out of their control.[102] Maternal mortality was a substantial danger for women throughout this period and first births were known to be the most precarious.[103] In her letters, Jane Scrimshire of Yorkshire described her fear of her approaching labour: 'I do assure you I dread the approaching time very much as I suffer'd so greatly before.'[104] For poor families the birth of children, legitimate or not, resulted in increased poverty.

Women rather than men were primarily responsible for childcare on a day-to-day basis. Most wives spent almost their entire married lives pregnant or caring for children. Women on average bore 6–7 live children, although some mothers never bore any at all. This role left them little time to themselves – for friends, correspondences, shopping, and amusement if they were élite women – for work, if they were poor. At the highest echelons of society, some women kept aside very little time for childcare and their progeny spent much of their time, especially in their early years, with servants.[105] Some loathed the tedium of childcare and the difficulty of caring for a family, while others revelled in the joys of motherhood like the Duchess of Leinster – even following the birth of her nineteen children. In Glamorgan, Julianna Mackworth was so enraptured by her children in the 1730s that she was 'content to play with them all day long, for though it be ninny, 'tis very natural and quite in her character'.[106] Each woman's personal experience of parenthood was different despite the significance of her material circumstances.[107]

The turn of the nineteenth century saw the rise of a domestic ideology that encouraged the separation of the public world of work from the private sphere of home and family life.[108] The rising popularity of Evangelicalism among the middle classes led to an increased stress on the moral significance of women's domestic role and the emergence of the virtuous, moral, and religious mother as a major trope of early Victorian ideology.[109] Motherhood gave middle-class women a voice in this culture that they used to promulgate the 'ideal family'. Popular writers on morality and proponents of separate spheres, such as Hannah More and Sarah Stickney Ellis, believed that it was women who, 'had both the time, the moral capacity and the influence to exercise real power in the domestic world. It was their responsibility to re-create society from below'.[110] Plebeian and working-class family life all too often fell outside the boundaries of their model and were subject to criticism. Informal marriages, cohabitation, and premarital sex, which had remained widespread during the eighteenth century, were increasingly rejected in the nineteenth. Britain's poor were continuously derided for their inability to 'do their duty', to maintain, protect, and educate their offspring. The influence of Evangelicalism, the increasing popularity of Malthusianism, the rise in population, continued urbanization, the impact of the French Revolution, and the belief in the increasing dependence of the poor served to transform attitudes towards poor families during the nineteenth century. Respectability and moral responsibility within the family became the cornerstone of the Poor Laws, employment legislation, and philanthropic and charitable endeavours.

Conclusion

The family and marriage underwent enormous transformations during our period. Industrialization, migration, and legal change resulted in the decline of stable family life and long-standing courtship and marital practices. Many young men and women were forced to travel far from home to find work, leaving the support and control of their families and communities behind. Such developments destabilized personal relationships and many women were left to rear children on their own. Other couples in small rural communities, untouched by economic change, experienced marriage and the family in much the same way as their ancestors. But war or the promise of work attracted lovers, fathers, and husbands away from their partners and wives across Britain. Most women remained economically dependent upon fathers and husbands during this period and few could afford to support a family on their own. Others actively avoided marriage, as well as childbearing, and the consequent constraints on their freedom. Women of independent means found that economic self-sufficiency, sometimes as a result of the death of a husband, bought substantial social liberty.

During the nineteenth century, the institution of marriage came under increasing criticism, particularly from middle-class women following the growth of political radicalism and the anti-slavery movement. Women's involvement in movements for political reform encouraged them to analyse their lack of power within the family. The early nineteenth century was thus a crucial period when the foundations were laid for the important reforms of marriage that were to reconfigure the relationship between men and women later in the century. Criticisms of marriage, however, did not affect the search for husbands. Marriage and the family were patriarchal structures for all, but, as many historians have been at pains to point out, patriarchy was usually coupled with companionship. Women's power within marriage and the family remained circumscribed throughout this period, but many negotiated rather more power than was legally entitled to them. Although the sexual division of labour within the household remained unchanged, few women allowed their husbands to dominate them unquestioningly. Wives of all social classes resisted the power of their husbands within the home and in public, yet all Chartist women and anti-slavery campaigners justified their political activism as wives and mothers. As the period progressed, women increasingly drew on the language of domesticity to justify their intervention in the public, political world.

Notes

1 Hannah Barker and Elaine Chalus (eds), *Gender in Eighteenth-Century England: Roles, Representations and Responsibilities*, Harlow, 1997, p. 16.

2 M. Anderson, *Approaches to the History of the Western Family, 1500–1914*, London, 1980, p. 14.

3 S. Mendelson and P. Crawford, *Women in Early Modern England, 1550–1720*, Oxford, 1998, p. 165.

4 A. Clark, *Working Life of Women in the Seventeenth Century*, London, 1919.

5 J. Bennett, 'Feminism and history', *Gender and History*, 1989, vol. 1, 3, pp. 251–72.

6 W. Blackstone, *Commentaries on the Laws of England in Four Books*, 4 vols, London, 1793, vol. 1, pp. 441–5, n. 23.

7 B. Hill, *Women, Work and Sexual Politics in Eighteenth-Century England*, London, 1994, p. 202.

8 A. L. Erickson, *Women and Property in Early Modern England*, London, 1993, pp. 19, 225–33; A. L. Erickson, 'Common law versus common practice: the use of marriage settlements in early modern England', *Economic History Review*, 2nd series, 1990, vol. 18, pp. 21–40; S. Staves, *Married Women's Separate Property, 1660–1833*, London, 1990, p. 10; M. Finn, 'Women, consumption and coverture in England, c. 1760–1860' *Historical Journal*, 1996, vol. 39, pp. 703–22.

9 For further discussion, see pp. 60, 64, 66.

10 Hannah Barker and Elaine Chalus, 'Introduction', in Barker and Chalus (eds), *Gender in Eighteenth-Century England*, pp. 16–24.

11 P. Laslett, *Family Life and Illicit Love in Earlier Generations*, Cambridge, 1978, pp. 26–7.

12 E. A. Wrigley, 'Marriage, fertility and population growth in eighteenth-century England', in R. B. Outhwaite (ed.), *Marriage and Society: Studies in the Social History of Marriage*, London, 1981, pp. 140–65.

13 E. Shorter, *The Making of the Modern Family*, London, 1976, p. 5.

14 L. Stone, *The Family, Sex and Marriage in England, 1500–1800*, London, 1990, p. 22. Stone and Shorter's work has fruitfully prompted continued research on the history of the family and sexuality and their work always forms the basis of contemporary debates, but it is now widely accepted that both of their models of the modern family are flawed.

15 Hill, *Women, Work and Sexual Politics*, pp. 174–95, 202–11.

16 N. Rogers, 'Carnal knowledge: illegitimacy in eighteenth-century Westminster', *Journal of Social History*, 1989, vol. 23, p. 355.

17 R. Finlay and B. Shearer, 'Population growth and suburban expansion', in A. L. Beier and R. Finlay (eds), *London, 1500–1700: The Making of the Metropolis*, Harlow, 1981, p. 46.

18 New York Public Library (hereafter NYPL), KVB (Ballads), p.v.1, *Peep at Life in London* (n.d.).

19 J. Gillis, 'Married but not churched: plebeian sexual relations and marital nonconformity in eighteenth-century Britain', *Eighteenth-Century Life*, 1985, vol. 9, pp. 32–4; Leah Leneman, *Promises, Promises: Marriage Litigation in Scotland, 1698–1830*, Edinburgh, 2003, pp. x–xi.

20 R. B. Outhwaite, *Clandestine Marriage in England, 1500–1850*, London, 1995, p. xxi.

21 Hill, *Women, Work and Sexual Politics*, p. 204.

22 L. Stone, *Road to Divorce; A History of the Making and Breaking of Marriage in England*, Oxford, 1995, p. 80.

23 R. Marshall, *Virgins and Viragos: A History of Women in Scotland from 1080 to 1980*, London, 1983, pp. 184–5. See also L. Leneman and R. Mitchison, *Sin in the City: Sexuality and Social Control in Urban Scotland, 1660–1780*, Edinburgh, 1998, pp. 132–3. S. Tillyard, *Aristocrats: Caroline, Emily, Louisa and Sarah Lennox, 1740–1832*, London, 1995, pp. 28–30, 48, 76.

24 Hill, *Women, Work and Sexual Politics*, p. 124.

25 Boulton, 'Itching', pp. 16–17; J. Gillis, 'Conjugal settlements: resort to clandestine and common law marriage in England and Wales, 1650–1850', in J. Bossy (ed.), *Disputes and Settlements: Law and Human Relations in the West*, Cambridge, 1983, p. 266.

26 Gillis, 'Conjugal settlements', p. 264.

27 D. Lemmings, 'Marriage and the law in the eighteenth century: Hardwicke's Marriage Act of 1753', *Historical Journal*, 1996, vol. 39, pp. 339–60.

28 Boulton, 'Itching', p. 15.

29 Outhwaite, *Clandestine Marriages*, pp. 125–31.

30 Ibid. p. 85.

31 Guildhall Library, London, MS2676/18, Bastardy Examination for St Botolph's Aldgate, 18 May 1789.

32 Gillis, 'Conjugal settlements', p. 273; also J. Gillis, *For Better, for Worse: British Marriages, 1600 to the Present*, Oxford, 1988, p. 140; Outhwaite, *Clandestine Marriages*, pp. xxiii, 139–40.

33 L. Tilly and J. W. Scott, *Women, Work and Family*, London, 1987, p. 98; C. Fairchilds, 'Female sexual attitudes and the rise of illegitimacy: a case study', *Journal of Interdisciplinary History*, 1978, vol. 7, pp. 627–67.

34 Leneman and Mitchison, *Sin in the City*, p. 7; S. J. Connolly, 'Marriage in pre-famine Ireland', in A. Cosgrove (ed.), *Marriage in Ireland*, Dublin, 1985, p. 91; G. DeBrisay, 'Wet nurses and unwed mothers in seventeenth-century Aberdeen', in E. Ewan and M. Meikle (eds), *Women in Scotland, c.1100–c.1750*, East Linton, 1999, p. 213.

35 J. Bennett and A. Froide (eds), *Singlewomen in the European Past, 1250–1800*, Philadelphia, PA, 1999, p. 11; T. Evans, '"Unfortunate Objects": London's Unmarried Mothers in the Eighteenth Century', *Gender & History*, 2005, vol. 17.

36 LMA/A/FH/A8/1/1/5, Petition for Admission to the Foundling Hospital, 13 April 1774.

37 On the increasing difficulties the poor had in achieving marriage in the late seventeenth century, see Keith Wrightson, *English Society, 1580–1680*, London, 1982, p. 70; Steve Hindle, 'The problem of pauper marriage in seventeenth-century England', in *Transactions of the Royal Historical Society*, Cambridge, 1998, p. 73.

38 A. Erickson, 'Family, household and community', in J. Morrill (ed.), *The Oxford Illustrated History of Tudor and Stuart Britain*, Oxford, 1996, p. 109.

39 Leneman and Mitchison, *Sin in the City*, p. 134.

40 A. Vickery, *The Gentleman's Daughter: Women's Lives in Georgian England*, New Haven, CT, 1998, pp. 40–5.

41 Hill, *Women, Work and Sexual Politics*, p. 185.

42 Stone, *Family, Sex and Marriage*, pp. 325–404; R. Trumbach, *The Rise of the Egalitarian Family: Aristocratic Kinship and Domestic Relations in Eighteenth-Century England*, New York, 1978, pp. 97–117.

43 See M. Hunt, 'Wife beating, domesticity and women's independence in eighteenth-century London', *Gender and History*, 1992, vol. 4, p. 27.

44 Lady S. Pennington, *An Unfortunate Mother's Advice to her Absent Daughters*, London, 1770, pp. 9–10.

45 Vickery, *Gentleman's Daughter*, p. 8; P. Jenkins, *The Making of a Ruling Class: The Glamorgan Gentry, 1640–1790*, Cambridge, 1983, p. 257; D. U. Stiubhart, 'Women and gender in the early modern Western Gaidhealtachd', in Ewan and Meikle (eds), *Women in Scotland*, p. 243.

46 A. Fletcher, *Gender, Sex and Subordination in England, 1500–1800*, New Haven, CT, 1995, p. 395; Mendelson and Crawford, *Women in Early Modern England*, pp. 131–2.

47 Nonetheless, most research has been focused so far on the writings of élite women, predominantly in England. Work on the experience of marriage and the family is recent in Scottish, Welsh, and, particularly, Irish history. See Ewan and Meikle (eds), *Women in Scotland*, p. xxviii, and 'Introduction', in M. Roberts and S. Clarke (eds), *Women and Gender in Early Modern Wales*, Cardiff, 2000. Much less is known about poor marriages and family life, although some fascinating work has been done on eighteenth-century illegitimacy in Scotland, see Mitchison and Leneman, *Sin in the City*; Leneman, *Sexuality and Social Control Scotland, 1660–1780*, Oxford, 1989, and A.-M. Kilday, 'Maternal monsters: murdering mothers in south-west Scotland, 1750–1815', in Y. Brown and R. Ferguson (eds), *Twisted Sisters: Women, Crime and Deviance in Scotland since 1400*, East Linton, 2002. We know even less about married and family life in British rural areas prior to the mid-nineteenth century.

48 Vickery, *Gentleman's Daughter*, 86.

49 J. Bailey, *Unquiet Lives: Marriage and Marriage Breakdown in England, 1660–1800*, Cambridge, 2003.

50 Ibid., p. 8.

51 Tillyard, *Aristocrats*, pp. 58, 64, 267.

52 A. V. John, 'Beyond paternalism: the ironmaster's wife in the industrial community', in A. V. John (ed.), *Our Mother's Land: Chapters in Welsh Women's History 1830–1939*, Cardiff, 1991; *Lady Charlotte Guest; Extracts from her Journal 1833–1852*, ed. Bessborough, London, 1950.

53 Margaret Hunt, *The Middling Sort: Commerce, Gender and the Family in England 1680–1780*, Berkeley, CA, 1996; L. Davidoff and C. Hall, *Family Fortunes: Men and Women of the English Middle Class, 1780–1850*, Chicago, IL, 1987, Chapter 6.

54 John, *Our Mother's Land*, p. 8.

55 R. Ashton, *Thomas and Jane Carlyle; Portrait of a Marriage*, London, 2002.

56 Vickery, *Gentleman's Daughter*, p. 285, and Fletcher, *Gender, Sex and Subordination*, p. 172.

57 Vickery, *Gentleman's Daughter*, pp. 73–7.

58 Criminal Conversation action was illegal in Scotland. For further information on wife sales, see E. P. Thompson, 'The sale of wives', in E. P. Thompson, *Customs in Common*, Harmondsworth, 1993. It is not thought that the practice was widespread. In his extensive study of wife sales in British history, S. P. Menefee found evidence of 400: S. P. Menefee, *Wives for Sale: An Ethnographic Study of British Popular Divorce*, Oxford, 1981.

59 Domestic violence against wealthy women went virtually unrecorded. A. Clark, *The Struggle for the Breeches; Gender and the Making of the British Working Class*, Berkeley, CA, 1995, p. 64.

60 Ibid. pp. 7, 64, 219, 264.

61 See J. Burnett, *Destiny Obscure: Autobiographies of Childhood, Education and Family from the 1820s to the 1920s*, Harmondsworth, 1984, p. 258.

62 M. Thale, *The Autobiography of Francis Place; 1771–1854*, Cambridge, 1972, p. 109.

63 *The Times*, 10 Jan. 1785, as cited in Clark, *Struggle for the Breeches*, p. 83.

64 Hunt, 'Wives and marital "rights" in the Court of Exchequer', in P. Griffiths and M. Jenner (eds), *Londonopolis*, Manchester, 2000, pp. 118–21. See also Alexandra Shepard, *Meanings of Manhood in Early Modern England*, Oxford, 2003, pp. 80–6.

65 M. Hunt, 'Wife beating', pp. 10–33 and S. D'Cruze, *Crimes of Outrage: Sex, Violence and Victorian Working Women*, London, 1998, p. 67.

66 R. Jones, 'Women, community and collective action: the "ceffyl pren" tradition' in John (ed.), *Our Mother's Land*, p. 25.

67 B. Taylor, *Eve and the New Jerusalem: Socialism and Feminism in the Nineteenth Century*, London, 1993, Chapter 6.

68 J. Perkins, *Women and Marriage in Nineteenth-Century England*, London, 1989, p. 128.

69 A. J. Hammerto, *Cruelty and Companionship: Conflict in Nineteenth-Century Married Life*, London, 1992, pp. 5–6, 39, 149. M. Lyndon Stanley, *Feminism, Marriage and the Law in Victorian England, 1850–1895*, London, 1989, p. 22.

70 Vickery, *Gentleman's Daughter*, p. 73.

71 Stone, *Road to Divorce*, p. 357.

72 Lyndon Stanley, *Feminism*, pp. 9, 36. In Scotland, divorces were much cheaper to obtain. This meant that men and women of humble means could resort to them. See Stone, *Road to Divorce*, p. 357.

73 P. Laslett, 'Mean household size in England since the sixteenth century', in P. Laslett and R. Wall (eds), *Household and Family in Past Times*, Cambridge, 1972, pp. 77–8.

74 P. Sharpe, 'Marital separation in the eighteenth and early nineteenth centuries', *Local Population Studies*, 1990, vol. 45, pp. 66–70; K. Snell, *Annals of the Labouring Poor*, Cambridge, 1985, p. 360; and J. Gillis, 'Servants, sexual relations, and the risks of illegitimacy in London, 1801–1900', *Feminist Studies*, 1979, vol. 5, pp. 140–73.

75 Guildhall Library, London /MS2676/20, May 1794.

76 D. Defoe, *Roxana*, London, 1964, p. 12.

77 Hufton, ' "Women without men": widows and spinsters in Britain and France in the eighteenth century', *Journal of Family History*, 1984, vol. 9, p. 356.

78 Bennett and Froide, *Singlewomen in the European Past*, p. 2.

79 H. Whitbread, *I Know My Own Heart: The Diaries of Anne Lister, 1791–1840*, London, 1988. In 1778, to the outrage of their Irish aristocratic families, Eleanor Butler and Sarah Ponsonby eloped and escaped to set up home in North Wales, see E. Mavor, *A Year with the Ladies of Llangollen*, Harmondsworth, 1986.

80 A. Froide, 'Marital status as a category of difference: single women and widows in early modern England', in Bennett and Froide, *Singlewomen in the European Past*.

81 Finlay and Shearer, 'Population growth', p. 51.

82 Hufton, "Women without men", p. 361.

83 P. Crawford, 'The construction and experience of maternity in seventeenth-century England', in V. Fildes (eds), *Women as Mothers in Pre-Industrial England*, London, 1990, pp. 3–29.

84 A few historians have argued that contraceptive knowledge and practice was widespread among the poor. See J. Riddle, 'Contraception and abortion in the Middle Ages', in V. L. Brundage and J. A. Brundage (eds), *Handbook of Medieval Sexuality*, London, 1996 and A. McClaren, *Reproductive Rituals: The Perception of Fertility in England from the Sixteenth Century to the Nineteenth Century*, London,

1984, pp. 58–85. There is some evidence of women's desire to learn how to control their reproduction. See Crawford, 'The construction and experience of maternity', pp. 16, 20.

85 R. Houlbrooke, *The English Family, 1450–1700*, London, 1984, p. 135.

86 P. Ariès, *Centuries of Childhood*, Harmondsworth, 1962.

87 E. Badinter, *The Myth of Motherhood: An Historical View of the Maternal Instinct*, London, 1981.

88 On the rate, see D. George, *London Life in the Eighteenth Century*, Harmondsworth, 1976, p. 26.

89 Shorter, *Making of the Modern Family*, p. 195; Stone, *Family, Sex and Marriage*, pp. 296–7.

90 J. Lewis, *In the Family Way: Childbearing in the British Aristocracy, 1760–1860*, New Brunswick, 1986, pp. 209–12.

91 R. Perry, '"Colonising the breast": sexuality and maternity in eighteenth-century England', *Journal of the History of Sexuality*, 1991, vol. 2, pp. 204–34. See also, F. Nussbaum, *Torrid Zones: Maternity, Sexuality, and Empire in Eighteenth-Century English Narratives*, Baltimore, MD, 1995.

92 J. Locke, *Two Treatises of Government: II, section 58–61*, in J. Yolton, *The Locke Reader*, Cambridge, 1977.

93 For France, see S. Woolf, 'The société charité maternelle, 1788–1815', in J. Barry and C. Jones (eds), *Medicine and Charity Before the Welfare State*, London, 1991; for Germany, see M. Lindemann, 'Maternal politics: the principles and practices of maternity care in eighteenth-century Hamburg', *Journal of Family History*, 1984, pp. 44–61. For Britain, see V. Fildes, *Breasts, Bottles and Babies: A History of Infant Feeding*, Edinburgh, 1986, p. 115; Perry, "Colonising the breast", pp. 206–7.

94 D. Andrew, *Philanthropy and Police: London Charity in the Eighteenth Century*, Princeton, NJ, 1989; L. Forman Cody, 'The politics of reproduction: from midwives' alternative public sphere to the public spectacle of man-midwifery', *Eighteenth-Century Studies*, 1999, vol. 32, p. 484; M. C. Versluysen, 'Midwives, medical men and "poor women of labouring child": lying-in hospitals in eighteenth-century London', in H. Roberts (ed.), *Women, Health, and Reproduction*, London, 1981; on the Edinburgh Lying-in Hospital, see Marshall, *Virgins and Viragos*, p. 226.

95 T. Bowers, *The Politics of Motherhood, British Writing and Culture, 1680–1760*, Cambridge, 1996.

96 Robert B. Shoemaker, *Gender in English Society 1650–1850*, Harlow, 1998, pp. 127–8. Ruth Perry has suggested that the increase in the expression of maternal sentiment during the eighteenth century was rooted in the emergence of print culture during this period and the popularity of diary-keeping: see her, "Colonising the breast", p. 205, n. 1.

97 O. Hufton, *The Prospect Before Her: A History of Women in Western Europe: I: 1500–1800*, London, 1997, p. 191; P. Crawford, '"The sucking child": adult attitudes to child care in the first year of life in seventeenth-century England', *Continuity and Change*, 1986, vol. 1, p. 41.

98 Houlbrooke, *English Family*, p. 136 and H. Cunningham, *Children and Childhood in Western Society since 1500*, Harlow, 1995, p. 52.

99 L. Pollack, *Forgotten Children: Parent–Child Relations from 1500–1900*, Cambridge, 1983, p. 268; also L. Pollack, *A Lasting Relationship: Parents and Children over Three Centuries*, London, 1987, pp. 12–13; see also Crawford, "The sucking child", p. 41.

100 See T. Evans, *Unfortunate Objects: Lone Mothers in Eighteenth-Century London*, Basingstoke, 2005.
101 L. Gowing 'Ordering the body: illegitimacy and female authority in seventeenth-century England', in M. Braddick and J. Walter (eds), *Negotiating Power in Early Modern Society: Order, Hierarchy, and Subordination in Britain and Ireland*, Cambridge, 2001, pp. 44–62.
102 Crawford, 'The construction and experience of maternity', p. 22; and L. Pollock, 'Embarking on a rough passage', in Fildes (ed.), *Women as Mothers*, p. 47.
103 Wrigley and Schofield, *Population History*, pp. 308, 319.
104 Vickery, *Gentleman's Daughter*, p. 98.
105 Stone, *Family, Sex and Marriage*, p. 286.
106 Tillyard, *Aristocrats*, p. 62; Jenkins, *Making of a Ruling Class*, pp. 260–2.
107 Vickery, *Gentleman's Daughter*, pp. 113, 115.
108 Davidoff and Hall, *Family Fortunes*.
109 Shoemaker, *Gender in English Society*, pp. 32–3.
110 Davidoff and Hall, *Family Fortunes*, p. 183.

Chapter Four

 masculine

Sexuality and the body

Karen Harvey

In 1773, the Manchester Conversation Society met at the Angel Inn in the Market-Place to debate the question: 'Whether are the more difficult to bear, the Passions of the Mind, or the Maladies of the Body?' The Society concluded that 'The maladies of the body' were the greater burden.[1] Arguably, the flesh has been a greater burden for women than for men. From well before 1700, women's bodies were considered responsible for conditions of both a physiological and psychological nature. An English midwife wrote in 1671: 'There is a great agreement between the womb and the brain'.[2] And, even after 1850, the female body was still seen as determining not just women's state of mind, but the activities deemed suitable for them to perform. One physician wrote in 1870: 'While woman preserves her sex, she will necessarily be feebler than man, and having her special bodily and mental characters, will have, to a certain extent, her own sphere of activity.'[3]

While the body has always been regarded as a key factor in determining people's experiences, ideas about how bodies work have varied over time. The body is not simply (if at all) a biological given; it is culturally constructed or 'discursively constituted'.[4] Ideas about bodies have changed over time, and examining these ideas can tell us about other, often unspoken or unarticulated, ideas about women and gender. For example, even scientific ideas about bodies, which are presented as 'true' and 'factual', are never simple descriptions. Rather, they veil customary and conventional beliefs.[5] Some writers have reversed the old adage that sex produces gender, and have instead claimed that understandings of bodies are produced by ideas about gender. Joan Scott has argued that 'gender is the knowledge that establishes meanings for bodily differences'.[6] In other words, what is presented as the female body is the result of pre-existing ideas about what and who women and men should be. We can go further and say that, because bodies are on one level cultural constructions, the processes of building these constructions can tell us about power relations. The shaping of the categories 'male' and 'female', and the process of defining a female body – how it should look, move, and function – takes place in a specific context, and that context will be reflected in or reinforced by these ideas about bodies. What is defined as 'the female body', what is included in this category and what is excluded, is a political act.

For some historians, the period 1700–1850 witnessed massive trans-formations in ideas about bodies. For Thomas Laqueur, whose book *Making Sex: Body and Gender from the Greeks to Freud* (1990) was a key statement in this field, these changes can be observed in English and European works of science and medicine. The changes were purposeful: a political act designed to withhold formal public power from women. As such, they were integral to the nature of women's economic, social, and cultural experiences during this period. Several women's and gender historians of England in particular have situated transformations in ideas about the female body at the heart of their arguments about modern gender roles. Indeed, most evidence is drawn from London. Work on sexual behaviour in Ireland and Scotland concerns primarily the late nineteenth century, while the history of sexuality in Wales is chronically underdeveloped.[7] For this reason, this chapter will necessarily focus largely on England, beginning with the dominant vision of change in views of the female body, before moving on to reconsider this narrative by asking about other kinds of ideas about bodies and by exploring women's own writings and experiences. While these later sections will include some discussion of specifically Irish, Scottish, and Welsh examples, it is also worth pointing out from the outset that, unlike economic practices and social organization, ideas are not easily contained by geographical boundaries. Books published in London were read widely and – indeed – London itself was in large part a British, rather than an English, city.

The body

In thinking about the construction of the female body and sexuality in the past, historians have focused heavily on medical ideas. The period 1700 to 1850 saw great changes in medical understandings of bodies. At the beginning of our period, the classical works of Aristotle, Hippocrates, and Galen were still very important to theories of how the body worked, but changes were afoot which were lessening their relevance, and also the efficacy of the ancient humoral model which had been key to the under-standing of human physiology. This system saw the body consisting of four humours or fluids: blood, choler, black bile, and phlegm. And each humour was related to two qualities – hot or cold and moist or dry – of which the most perfect was hot and dry. This was a model of fungible fluids, which allowed for great variety and mutability within and between bodies, rather than simply absolutes. It was also a system that was highly susceptible to disruption and therefore required constant vigilance in order to keep things in balance. In terms of the relationship between male and female bodies, what mattered was not anatomy but the balance of the humours. Essentially, male and female bodies were based on the same model of physiology. For example, in trying to maintain a balance of the humours, they purged excess fluids in very similar ways. Women had an excess of blood, purged by menstruation; and, in some places, men were thought to purge excess blood through haemorrhoids.[8] Similarly, excess fluid could be purged through ejaculation. Indeed, according to the Hippocratic and Galenic two-seed theories, both women and men were believed to emit seed and excess fluid at the point of orgasm. This is not to say that women and men were the same. Differences did exist, but these originated from the different balance of the humours in male and female bodies. Women were always dominated by cold and moist humours, men by hot and dry humours. As the most perfect body was hot and dry, women were imperfect versions of men. This was a vertical system of sexual difference, then, in which women and men were on the same scale, but men occupied a higher place than women.

This essentially physiological model determined how bodies were built. Men's and women's genitals were structurally and functionally the same, and the same vocabulary was used for many body parts. For example, the word 'testicle' was used for the organs which contained the seed in both women and men: 'Women have *testicles* or *stones*, as have the men', wrote John Marten in 1708.[9] The only difference between male and female reproductive organs was their location. Their greater heat allowed men to push their genitals outside; correspondingly, women lacked this heat and their genitals remained on the inside. Illustrations of women's reproductive organs presented the uterus and vagina as one long and enclosed sheath, which looked remarkably similar to depictions of the penis.[10]

Using élite scientific and medical texts, Thomas Laqueur suggested that prior to the eighteenth century, women and men were placed on a vertical, hierarchical axis, their bodies seen as two comparable variants of one kind. Bodies were placed on a continuum and it was possible for there to be gradations of sexual difference. Laqueur has called this model – where women and men shared essentially the same kind of body – the 'one-sex model' of sexual difference.[11] One of the important aspects of this model for the construction of female bodies was the dominant theory of conception. In the one-sex model, both women and men were thought to produce seed crucial for conception, so both male and female ejaculation was required: 'both sexes experienced a violent pleasure during intercourse that was intimately connected with successful generation; both generally emitted something'.[12] Representations of women in the one-sex model therefore valued women's sexual pleasure and discussed it openly. Indeed, in this model women were seen as lusty and voracious.[13]

'In the late seventeenth and eighteenth centuries', however, 'science fleshed out . . . the categories "male" and "female" as opposite and incommensurable biological sexes'.[14] The drive for this was not new discoveries, but politics. In a world where the emerging Enlightened languages of 'natural rights' might apply to any one, the one-sex model threatened to lend support to demands for women's rights. Women and men were therefore defined as opposite sexes, in order that women's disenfranchisement could be sustained.[15] Londa Schiebinger argues:

> '[N]atural rights could be countered only by proof of natural inequalities. There were endless new struggles for power and position in the enormously enlarged public sphere of the eighteenth and particularly the nineteenth centuries: between and among women and men; between and among feminists and antifeminists'.[16]

In this context, the body was used as the evidence that difference was immutable and permanent: 'the battleground of gender roles shifted to nature, to biological sex'.[17] These changes began at the end of the seventeenth century and, by the nineteenth century, the one-sex model had ceded to a 'two-sex model'. Women and men were no longer variants of the same sex, but were defined as two opposite sexes. The humoral system declined in popularity and anatomical sexual differences were stressed.

That things were changing is perhaps best illustrated by the descriptions of reproductive organs. From 1700, the term 'vagina' was used in vernacular medical texts to describe the cavity that had previously not had its own name; later in the eighteenth century, the term 'ovary' appeared.[18] Women's reproductive organs were no longer seen as men's organs inside out, but were now seen as distinctive. When depicted visually, the uterus and vagina were often splayed open, lessening the parallel with the penis; sometimes the vagina – the organ that often closely resembled the penis in early visual depictions – was not shown at all.[19] But the new sexual difference infused the entire body in the form of the gendered skeleton. All images of skeletons had once been based on male corpses, but images of female skeletons began to emerge in England, France, and Germany between 1730 and 1790. The female skeleton was depicted with a narrower ribcage, wider pelvis, and smaller skull. The skeletons from which these drawings were made reflected the assumptions these men of medicine had about women's bodies. These images reflected not the nature of all female skeletons, then, but the pre-existing ideas about gender.[20]

Late-eighteenth-century wax models demonstrate how other anatomical and physiological attributes were deeply gendered. Muscles were shown using male models, nerves using female models: the musculature was masculinized, and the nervous system was feminized, implying the weakness and fragility of women.[21] In addition, these models of women featured several visual signs of femininity: they often displayed flowing hair and pearl necklaces, and reclined in passive poses.[22] Gender differences had always been thought to exist, but throughout the eighteenth century these differences were increasingly portrayed as 'natural' facets of the physical body. Biological 'sex' replaced cultural 'gender' as the origin of difference.[23] Well into the nineteenth century the power of this new medical thinking was palpable. Sex differences were understood to be the cause of gender roles; they, therefore, could not be tampered with. One vision of difference was grounded in theories about the different rates of cell metabolism, arrived at by comparing sperm and ovum: the sperm was a hungry, active cell, which dispelled energy; the ovum a quiescent cell, which stored energy.[24] In *The Evolution of Sex* (1889), proponents of this view, Patrick Geddes and J. Arthur Thomson, wrote: 'What was decided among the prehistoric Protozoa, cannot be annulled by an act of parliament.'[25] A woman was, therefore, 'an overgrown ovum'.[26]

The Laqueurian narrative is central to many histories of gender in England covering the period 1700 to 1850.[27] Anthony Fletcher sees the emergence of a new basis for gender relations in the eighteenth century, constituted partly on new understandings of male and female bodies as opposites.[28] Robert B. Shoemaker has linked these notions of opposite sexes with 'the distinct sexual roles of women and men' increasingly valued during this period.[29] Randolph Trumbach outlines a sexual revolution which produced a third gender of 'new effeminate adult sodomites' and was facilitated in part by the emergence of two opposite sexes.[30] Perhaps most dramatically, Tim Hitchcock has integrated the move from the one-sex to the two-sex model into a case for a sexual revolution in England in the second half of the eighteenth century, a revolution that consisted in changes in the sexual practices engaged in by women and men. In the earlier period, Hitchcock argues, sex was often characterized by mutual touching and fondling which did not necessarily led to other kinds of sex; in the later period, particularly in urban areas, as male sperm was increasingly valued as the active element in conception, sexual encounters between women and men were much more likely to involve vaginal penetration.[31]

Representations of the body strongly underpin many of the narratives of gender change in this period, yet knowledge about the body and sexuality was not only represented by élite medical texts; there were also more popular and less specialist forms of printed literature, and some of these cast doubt on Laqueur's narrative of change. Popular literature seems to have retained the vision of male and female genital homology for some time, for example. While recognizing there were some key anatomical differences between women and men, the 1725 edition of *Aristotle's Compleat Master-Piece* provided a very clear rendition of the one-sex model:

> Thus I the Women's Secrets have survey'd,
> And let them see how curiously they're made;
> And that, tho' they of different Sexes be,
> Yet in the Whole they are the same as we:
> For those that have the strictest Searchers been,
> Find Women are but Men turn'd Out-side-in;
>
> And Men, if they but cast their Eyes about,
> May find they're Women, with their In side-out.[32]

This book also spoke of the 'Testicles in Women', long after the word ovary was in usage in élite works.[33] Significantly, versions of this popular medical book were published well into the nineteenth century.[34]

Eighteenth-century erotica also presented older ideas about bodies long after élite medical texts had begun to excise them. Indeed, this material did not present bodies in terms of models at all, but rather chopped and changed rapidly, seeing male and female as the same kind of body on one page and speaking of their absolute differences on the next. On the topic of conception, for example, erotic authors claimed simultaneously that women and men provided sperm, that women provided eggs, and that women provided nothing more than the fertile ground for men's seed.[35] On the issue of genital homology, one mid-eighteenth-century erotica writer wrote that between the male and female genitals there was, 'the greatest Sympathy between this tree and the Shrub, *They are, . . . of the same Genus, and do best in the same Bed; the* Vulvaria *itself being no other than a Female* Arbor Vitae'.[36] This seems to be a straightforward presentation of the Galenic view of male and female genital homology, in which the male and female are of the same kind. But a tree is not a shrub and this distinction also allowed erotic authors to represent what they clearly considered to be stark and deep differences between male and female: differences of size, structure, and physiology.[37]

Desire and sexuality

Critical to Laqueur's argument is his view that in the élite scientific and medical discourses of the late eighteenth century, the female orgasm was relegated 'to the periphery of human physiology': women were reimagined as sexually passive.[38] While there was no new knowledge about female orgasm during this period, by the early nineteenth century, insists Laqueur, there was an 'erasure of women's orgasm from accounts of generation'.[39] Following the observation of spontaneous ovulation in dogs in 1843, 'the old physiology of pleasure and the old anatomy of sexual homologies were definitely dead'.[40] Late Victorian writers 'construed women as less passionate and hence morally more adept than men'.[41] Laqueur's argument about women's passionlessness is not new; the stereotype of the frigid Victorian woman is of considerable vintage, stretching back in women's history to at least the 1970s. Nancy Cott argued that after 1790 an ideology of 'passionlessness' existed which maintained that 'women lacked sexual aggressiveness, that their sexual appetites contributed a very minor part (if any at all) to their motivations, that lustfulness was simply uncharacteristic'.[42] This passionlessness was tied to the rise of Evangelical religion between 1790 and 1830.[43] More recent historians have argued that this desexualization of women began earlier in the eighteenth century, as the lusty and desiring early-modern woman was replaced by the passive and asexual female character. This was a powerful image of women, not necessarily at odds with the idea that women did, in reality, enjoy sex and experience sexual pleasure. But, at the level of ideas, historians tend to agree that 'the maternal succeeded, supplanted, and repressed the sexual definition of women, who began to be reimagined as nurturing rather than desiring'.[44]

The desexualization of women changed the way that women's engagement in sexual activity was viewed. In England there arose a 'cult of seduction', which saw women's pre-marital sexual activity as a 'fall' prompted by the dishonest, manipulative, or abusive behaviour of men. No longer were women sexual agents, rather they were now passive in the face of masculine action.[45] Towards the end of the eighteenth century, the periodical press began to feature stories that affirmed these stereotypes. In 1775, *The Lady's Magazine* warned women of 'the most abandoned, complicated villainy', the 'ungenerous, unjust, unmanly, and cowardly, but even cruel' practice of seduction. Men disguised their true motivations and misled 'innocent, unsuspecting, inexperienced, illiterate, giddy females', boasting about their 'victory over virtue'.[46] In 1797, *The Leeds Mercury* carried a warning under the headline 'Seduction', in which women were characterized as vulnerable, passive, and weak, while men were fraudulent, predatory, and rampant. 'The seducer practises the same stratagems to draw a woman's person into his power, that a swindler does', the author wrote.[47] Twenty years later, in September 1817, a case that was widely reported and heard at the Lancashire Assizes involved the seduction of the 17-year-old Miss Sarah Ingram by a Mr Fogg, who was in his mid-twenties. While Sarah was presented as a studious, obedient, and careful young girl, reporters discussed Fogg's drinking and his deceit in using the language of love and promises of marriage.[48] Other women were also affected by these ideas. It was argued that women were forced into prostitution by the tragic circumstances of seduction, and this is why from the middle of the eighteenth century, social policy-makers characterized prostitutes as victims rather than sinners or criminals. This had a profound effect on the way in which prostitutes were treated in England.[49]

In Scotland, legal differences produced a different perspective on seduction. While Hardwicke's Marriage Act of 1753 had outlawed informal marriage in England, Wales, and Ireland, the Act was not in force in Scotland. As a result, Scottish law recognized a verbal undertaking consummated by sexual intercourse as a form of marriage. When a man then denied agreeing to marry after sex, a woman was entitled to sue for damages in Scotland's national consistory court. Hence, Leah Leneham argued: 'Scottish law allowed women more autonomy and was more favourable to them.'[50] However, while women in these cases recounted standard seduction narratives, the men were required to demonstrate that the women were unchaste prior to the encounter. Alongside these seduction narratives were told more traditional tales of women being lusty and 'of easy virtue'. The legal situation in Scotland meant that stories of both men *and* women as seducers were taken extremely seriously throughout this period.[51]

There were also important cultural differences between England and Scotland. Scottish norms regarding sex appear to have been stricter than in England, and in part this was because of a Scottish church that 'displayed extreme distaste for physical intimacy between the sexes'. Later, this was compounded by a particularly well-developed middle-class morality of chastity and respectability.[52] The Scots had long regarded themselves as the moral superiors of the English, but this self-perception was dented in the middle of the nineteenth century by the discovery that Scotland's illegitimacy rate was higher than England's.[53] Intensified efforts to rid Scotland of sexual immorality ensued. The middle classes vigorously sought to impose their morality on the rural poor, although the latter resisted these attempts, particularly in the north-east.[54] Attempts to reform the female urban poor were more successful. Working-class women whose behaviour was regarded as lewd were singled out in attempts to rid the streets of prostitution. In this programme of reform, early Victorian 'wayward sexuality' was clearly associated with individuals of a particular sex and class.[55] A similar process can be seen at work in Ireland. By the end of this period, 'fallen' working-class women were housed in very restrictive and punitive Magdalen asylums run by nuns and sustained by a new middle-class Catholic morality bent on eradicating the sexuality of lower-class women and girls.[56]

Indeed, the evidence suggests that across Britain by 1850 'desexualization' was a peculiarly middle-class concern and many historians have claimed that it was middle-class women in particular who were redefined. This was part of a much wider construction of a new ideal of domesticated woman that emerged in the middle-class print culture of the eighteenth and nineteenth centuries. She was frugal and modest, and her sexuality – though not erased – was quietened.[57] The narrative we have of the emergence of a new type of female body might instead be replaced by a narrative of the bifurcation along class lines of traditional but contrasting views of women as chaste and modest. As purity, modesty, and chastity were increasingly associated with middle-class women, working-class women were characterized as sexual, loose, and often depraved.

From across Britain, then, there is some persuasive evidence for the desexualization of some women – at least in representation – during this period. Yet we need to be aware of the limits of this process and be attuned to what 'desexualization' might actually mean. Certainly, writers did begin to question the idea of female ejaculation in the early eighteenth century, but this did not necessarily go hand-in-hand with the discrediting of female pleasure. In 1718, Giles Jacob wrote of lascivious women who took considerable pleasure in sexual activity and were 'capable of every action belonging to a man, but that of ejaculation'.[58] The questioning of female orgasm did not inevitably mean that female desire was undermined: the myth of 'woman as a sexually insatiable creature' remained powerful throughout the eighteenth century.[59] Whether or not women could ejaculate, the clitoris was recognized as women's 'Seat of Lust'.[60] There is some evidence that, by the mid-nineteenth century, the clitoris was being undermined in medical thought. The few attempts at clitoridectomy, though rare, began in 1851. But, as Ornella Moscucci has pointed out, this was not evidence of 'the suppression of female sexuality'; rather, it was about the elevation of the vagina in constructions of female pleasure and therefore can be placed in the context of 'the enforcement of hetero-sexuality and the maintenance of gender boundaries'.[61] As Laqueur stresses, prior to 1905 when Sigmund Freud 'invented' the vaginal orgasm in the third of his *Three Essays on the Theory of Sexuality*, there was only one kind of female orgasm, a clitoral one.[62] But Victorian doctors clearly held that women felt strong and healthy sexual desire. 'That female passion exists', wrote one doctor in 1870, 'is as obvious as that the sun shines.'[63]

Throughout this period, it is easy to find images which admitted women's sexual desires. Erotic literature that retained older images of women as terrifying creatures with raging sexual appetites were being published well into the nineteenth century. *The Why and the Wherefore* (1765) depicted a giant vulva called 'Ingulpha' that reduced penises to a trembling mass, because they feared 'she would swallow them all'.[64] Erotica could also present female sexual desire in positive terms. As one author explained: 'Nature, in its Distribution of the Pleasurable Sensation to the two Sexes, has been far from illiberal to the Fair. It is even pretended that their Allotment is greater than ours.'[65] The early-modern sexually voracious woman was alive and well in this literature. At the same time, women were represented as inert stretches of land in which the male farmer might 'labour and toil', or as 'lands, tenements, &c.', to be bought and sold.[66] In fact, erotica featured both the early-modern sexually ravenous woman and the desexualized, domesticated woman that supposedly took her place. Similarly, the sexual and the maternal co-existed. The breast has been regarded as the exemplar of the new female gender role of the later eighteenth century, seen as increasingly desexualized, domesticated, and maternal over the period,[67] but, in erotic texts breasts are simultaneously objects of desire, linked to women's fertility, and expressions of their maternity. The author of one erotic book, *A New Description of Merryland* (1741), metaphorically described breasts 'as an Appendage' to women's reproductive organs, commenting that they produce 'a very wholesome Liquor much esteemed, especially by the younger sort of People', which appeared immediately after birth.[68] *The Man-Plant* presented the breasts as objects of sensual pleasure, describing them as round, tender, snow-white, and very pleasant to touch, before going on to mention their production of milk for breastfeeding.[69] These authors admired the beauty of breasts, but this was not separate from their role in breastfeeding. Maternity and sexuality were inextricably linked.

It is not difficult to find evidence of the growing restriction and the emerging prudishness for which the Victorians have been famous. Towards the end of the eighteenth century, women were called upon to cover up their bodies. In *The Lady's Magazine* in 1775 'a Bachelor' complained about 'men seducers'. He had visited a museum and had been distracted from the display when a young lady entered the room. She was 'the most capital structure' in the room and, because he was relatively innocent and 'just *fresh imported* on the stage of this world', he was deeply affected by sight of her:

> but what was my surprise, when, on its growing warm, she laid aside her cloak and discovered one of the finest bosoms nature ever formed? – This was too much!
>
> If girls are so imprudent as to commit such depredations on our sex, they are certainly, in a great measure, the authors of their *own* misfortune.[70]

It is likely that this young woman was wearing a low-cut dress, with a sheer kerchief tied across her chest to cover her breasts, but, whatever the coverage, the writer considered it to be too revealing. Female readers of *The Lady's Magazine* in 1791 were counselled that simply kissing a man put them in grave danger: 'It is an introduction to something more capital; it is the first page of the preface to seduction and adultery.'[71] A news story in 1817 told of a Sheffield man who was targeting women who wore revealing dresses by lightly stamping their skin with the words, 'Naked, but not ashamed'. Whether or not this story was true, the newspaper issued an 'IMPORTANT CAUTION TO THE LADIES'.[72] Rather than see these examples as evidence of a belief in women's sexual passivity, we might instead see them as revealing anxieties about women's seductive powers. After all, with their slightly alarmist tone, these stories present themselves as responses to hoards of women publicly expressing their sexuality. Indeed, in literature, if not in élite medical texts, female sexuality was not erased by the mid-nineteenth century. It has recently been argued, for example, that the novels of George Eliot – *Adam Bede* (1859) and *The Mill on the Floss* (1860) – actually unite 'the sexual woman with the angelic and proper middle-class ideal'.[73] Such a combination was reflected in changes in women's dress over this period. The popularity of the Renaissance voluptuous and rotund, 'fertile, bell-centered body' was in decline in during the eighteenth century, and was gradually replaced by a shape which emphasized breasts, buttocks and thighs. The looser neo-classical style of the Regency period was replaced by the hour-glass shape of the high Victorian period, with a nipped-in waist, full skirt and often a high neck line. Following the introduction of the metal eyelet in 1828, which allowed corsets to be more tightly laced, this new, sexualized female shape that emphasized women's reproductive capacity became popular.[74] Such changes represent more a shift in the expression of sexuality, than a growing prudishness.

Printed sources that seem closely related to actual practice certainly suggest that the narrative of women's desexualization pertains to ideas rather than to lived experience. The 'female problem' of unwanted pregnancies was raised in what might be the most 'public' of publications: newspapers. Expectant mothers wanting 'Care, tenderness . . . and Secrecy' were offered a temporary safe haven 'in a genteel House in an airy pleasant Part' of Manchester.[75] They would be attended by a man-midwife and midwife, and their children would be put out to a wet-nurse.[76] In the case of 'concealed Pregnancy', women were also offered pills 'to remove all Obstructions or Irregularities'.[77] It seems that women could scour the newspapers for information on where to go to have their babies in secret and on where to find things necessary to induce abortion. Not all women behaved in accordance with the ideals of the chaste and desexualized woman.

Women's knowledge and experience

So far this chapter has discussed some of the ways in which the Laqueurian narrative might be limited. One additional way that we might develop an alternative view is by considering the possibility that women had their own, female-centred knowledge about the body. This is a grossly undeveloped area of historiography – the historical association of women with certain kinds of bodily knowledge as healers is significant, yet, given that this knowledge was part of an oral culture, it is a difficult area to research. Gentlewomen in the Scottish highlands were considered 'guardians' of this type of knowledge, for example, but did not write it down.[78] In a series of works, however, Patricia Crawford has used written sources to suggest that women had distinct views of their bodily processes. She has argued, for example, that at the beginning of the eighteenth century women's views towards menstruation and pregnancy differed from those of men: 'While men saw in menstruation evidence of women's ambiguous position – a position of both weakness and power – women saw menstruation as a normal part of their lives.'[79] More recently, she has made the broader claim that all sexual knowledge was gendered: books written for women, and women's own ideas, were very different from books written for, or ideas held by, men.[80] Certainly, the printing industry distinguished between male and female audiences, catering to notions of women's greater frailty, ignorance, and civility. The author of the 1725 edition of the popular sex manual, *Aristotle's Compleat Master-Piece*, frankly describes 'the Instruments of Generation in Man', but then turns to 'the Secret Parts in Women', noting that he will describe these 'with as much Modesty and Sobriety, as will consist with our speaking intelligibly'.[81] Similar differences emerge in personal writings. The letters and diaries of women in England and Wales, for instance, illustrate the different notions of social decency circulating among groups of women and men.[82]

Yet, while tone may differ, material specifically aimed at a female audience did not offer radically different views on the body and sexuality. One key virtue of women propounded in a range of materials written by men and women, for example, was modesty. Women's magazines urged their female readers to be patient, chaste, and virtuous, and reproduced classic statements on modesty.[83] These statements were often veiled discussions of female sexuality, advising women that to over-expose one's attractions would make them less desirable. Modesty made women more attractive, not less; it was a form of seduction in which practices of concealment rendered women more alluring.[84] As a bishop wrote to his daughter in Dublin in 1751, 'Modesty, My Dear, is the great Ornament of your Sex.'[85] Not unlike much conduct literature written by men, women's magazines made it clear that modest behaviour earned women considerable power. One poem, 'On female power', stressed that because of women's beauty, 'ev'ry man is born to be a slave'.[86] Magazines for women advanced widely circulating notions of appropriate female behaviour.

At the same time, these magazines, published in the second half of the eighteenth century, also told exciting fictional stories about women's illicit encounters with men, stories in which women enjoyed heady love affairs. In doing so, they built on amatory fiction written earlier in the century. This was a form of erotic writing by women, full of desiring women wanting and enjoying sex. Mary Delarivier Manley's *New Atalantis* (1709) was typical in this regard. One female protagonist was 'blinded' by her desires and thrust herself on her young male lover:

> giving her eyes time to wander over beauties so inviting, and which increased her flame, with an amorous sigh she gently threw her self on the bed, close to the desiring youth; the ribbon of his shirt-neck not tied, the bosom (adorned with the finest lace) was open, upon which she fixed her charming mouth.[87]

Amatory fiction was firmly embedded in contemporary culture and its strictures on female behaviour. The sexual incidents were an opportunity to engage in serious discussions of the morality of men's and women's interactions.[88] This was packaged for a female audience and catered to some dominant ideas about chastity and morality, but there was considerable excitement and pleasure along the way. Amatory fiction was female-centred and it expressed female sexuality along with women's power and agency.[89] Current scholarship is divided over whether female authorship produced fresh ways of representing sexual activity and gender relations,[90] or simply replicated patriarchal visions,[91] but it seems that there was something distinctive about the approach to desire and sexuality in amatory fiction: this was the relishing of erotic pleasure in the context of serious moral arguments regarding men's and women's interactions.

Researching what women felt about the body and sexuality is difficult, but some women's memoirs seem to echo the candidness about sex that we find in amatory fiction. Laetitia Pilkington, the poet, was born in Dublin in 1712. Despite the public humiliation of being divorced from Matthew Pilkington, chaplain to the Lord Mayor of London, on the grounds of adultery, Pilkington launched into print with what were widely regarded as her scandalous *Memoirs*, published in 1748. Although the *Memoirs* are actually thin on the detail of any sexual adventuring, she did play on the possibility of sexual disclosure in her story. For example, Pilkington denied she had committed adultery, protesting that she and the man had merely read a book together late one night in her bedchamber.[92] Given the prevailing anxieties about the risks to women's virtue posed by the dangers of reading, this was an extremely provocative line of defence.[93] In addition,

Pilkington used the scenario of prostitution to describe her literary career. She described numerous encounters with men who offered her money for sex, and, while she claimed that she declined these offers, she admitted to taking the money as donations to her writing.[94] The same allusion was used in her poems, where there is deliberate confusion about whether the skills for which Pilkington wants remuneration are literary or sexual. In 'To the Hon. Colonel D-NC-BE', she enquires:

> Since so oft to the great of my favours you boast,
> When, you know, you enjoy'd but some kisses at most;
> And those, as you say, never ought to be sold,
> For love's too divine, to be barter'd for gold.
> Since this is your maxim, I beg a receipt,
> To know, how without it a lover can eat.[95]

In both fiction and autobiography, certainly prior to the mid-eighteenth century, some women eschewed powerful notions of feminine modesty and propriety and cultivated or exploited the frisson of women's private sexual lives.

We certainly need to explore female writings in more much detail in order assess what women knew and felt about the body and sex. This is a difficult task, because women rarely left writings that discussed the body or sex in any detail. The study of women in Scotland is plagued with a dire lack of sources, particularly before 1750, a period for which we have no diaries, recollections, novels, or other literature by women.[96] And while English gentry women's letters from the eighteenth century – rich on many topics – discuss the symptoms of pregnancy and the experience of childbirth, they do not explore the workings of the menstrual cycle and conception.[97] So it is that much of Crawford's evidence of women's attitudes towards menstruation is drawn from the printed medical works of men, and that historians have been tempted to use the diaries of men in order to learn about women's feelings about bodily events such as pregnancy.[98] Occasionally, we catch a glimpse of a woman caught up in her desires. One such woman is Gertrude Savile (1697–1758), the daughter of an affluent MP, who at the age of 24 fell in love:

> He had (or my wishes would have it so) the agreeableness of a soldier, the verassity of a gentleman, the faithfulness of a friend and the softness of a lover. A soldier's person, a gentleman's behaviour, a friend's soul and a lover's heart.[99]

Later, her heart skips with the memory of first meeting her beau, while at the same time she fears that she will never see him again:

> How did my heart flutter when I came into the place where I had first seen and left Captain Stanhope? How did it dance with the possibility of seeing him here again? but how much more ach with the improbability that I shoud . . . I was unwilling to be convinced but still kept some hopes alive until I went to a Ball.[100]

Such testimony is rare, though it is suggestive of a female world of strong desire and powerful emotion.

We know too little to say whether such hopes and fears were shared by other women, but it seems that women were by no means agreed on the place a woman's body should hold in her life. Savile, for example, yearned for men's appreciation and admitted in her diary that 'a young woman's chief felicity [is] the gratification of vanity'. Her favourite suitor was singled out for 'above all, jealous looks'. Here was a woman who liked to be looked at, one who appreciated that, in her world, beauty in a woman counted for a great deal.[101] While the importance placed on women's looks was a constant in this period, other women were more critical. Lady Mary Wortley Montagu (1689–1762), the wife of an ambassador, resisted views in England. Writing to a female friend from Vienna in 1716, she praised Austrian society for the way in which it accepted female sexuality in women of all ages. 'I can assure you', she explained, 'that wrinkles, or a small stoop in the shoulders, nay, even grey hair itself, is no objection to the making of new conquests.' Moreover, Montagu admired the easy way in which all women could express their sexuality without a concern about being denounced as either too prudish or too liberal: 'what you'll think very odd, the two sects that divide our whole nation of petticoats, are utterly unknown. Here are neither coquettes nor prudes.'[102] Such criticism was articulated in a more sustained way by feminist writers. A repeated complaint was that women were trapped in their bodies, that their destinies were dictated by the flesh. At the turn of the eighteenth century, Mary Astell exhorted women

> not to entertain such a degrading thought of our own *worth*, as to imagine that our Souls were given us only for the service of our Bodies, and that the best improvement we can make of these, is to attract the Eyes of Men.[103]

One hundred years later, Mary Wollstonecraft voiced similar concerns, asserting that women's sexuality was merely a learned response to men's wishes.[104] 'Why must the female mind be tainted by coquettish arts to gratify the sensualist?', she asked.[105] Such visions had no patience for the yearnings of Gertrude Savile.

The existence of such differences between women make it difficult to argue for a female subculture of knowledge about the body and sexuality. Certainly, being a body can produce a particular understanding of how that body works but, once we move away from this level of direct experience, understandings of bodies – and indeed the understanding of experiencing a body itself – are determined by cultural factors. Women may have had access to a female culture of sexual knowledge, but each woman would have also been part of a literate/illiterate, rich/poor, urban/rural culture that would have affected what she thought and felt. Nevertheless, we lack a good understanding of how gender affected an individual's knowledge and experience of the body and sexuality. There is a need to explore the languages used by women when discussing the body and sexuality, and in particular the ways that women expressed love, passion, and desire. Women's fictional writings seem to have offered a distinctive approach to desire and sexuality, but they do not equate with a subculture of knowledge about the body and its workings.

Conclusion

Laqueur did not argue for an overnight shift in the way sexual difference was understood. He was, instead, cautiously vague about timing: the transformation took place 'in or about the late eighteenth century'.[106] Indeed, 'one sex . . .', Laqueur urged, 'did not die'.[107] Yet his work has been used to bolster a story of momentous change – change in representations of women's bodies, in the relationship between women and men, and thus in the experiences of women in a range of arenas. We need to be very cautious about making claims for transformative change on this scale. Over time, there was a diversification of print culture and in ideas about the body. There were new theories and some types of publication – and therefore knowledge – did see considerable shifts during this period. At the same time, traditional ideas persisted in some genres and were often combined with the new. Ideas about the body and sexuality issued not simply from élite medical texts, but from popular guides to health, prose fiction and poetry, and newspapers and magazines. There existed a number of different sources for ideas about female bodies and a number of competing discourses. Changes were more pronounced in some forms of writing than others, therefore; and while it seems that professional science and medicine moved quickly, popular writing and fictional writing reproduced traditional ideas for decades.

The move from the one-sex to the two-sex model has been seen as part of a modernizing process where 'the foundations of the old social order were shaken once and for all'. The birth of the modern, opposite sexes took place alongside other developments:

the rise of evangelical religion, Enlightenment political theory, the development of new sorts of public spaces in the eighteenth century,

93

> Lockean ideas of marriage as a contract, the cataclysmic possibilities for social change wrought by the French Revolution, postrevolutionary conservatism, postrevolutionary feminism, the factory system with its restructuring of the sexual division of labor, the rise of a free market economy in services of commodities, [and] the birth of classes.[108]

But the patterns of change observable in work practices and the urban environment are not the same as those seen in the cultural categories of sex and gender. Élite medical works may have been increasingly constructing women and men as opposites, but the vision of these male medics was not all-encompassing. There were areas of print culture where different female bodies could be found and there were certainly areas of practice in which women failed to conform to the ideals of women as passive and desexualized. Even by the middle of the nineteenth century, there is evidence that women resisted the silencing of their sexuality, particularly among the working classes. Furthermore, the desexualized woman was not the only role available to middle-class women in 1850. Indeed, there are tantalizing hints that some women had their own ideas about the nature of woman and her difference.

Acknowledgements

I would like to thank Hannah Barker, Mike Braddick and Elaine Chalus for their helpful comments on this chapter.

Notes

1 *Manchester Mercury*, 2, 9 February 1773.
2 Jane Sharp, *The Midwives' Book*, London, 1671, p. 126.
3 Henry Maudsley, *Body and Mind: An Inquiry into Their Connection and Mutual Influence, Specially in Reference to Mental Disorders*, London, 1870, p. 32, as quoted in Ornella Moscucci, *The Science of Woman: Gynaecology and Gender in England, 1800–1929*, Cambridge, 1993, p. 40.
4 Thomas Laqueur, *Making Sex: Body and Gender from the Greeks to Freud*, Cambridge, MA, 1990, p. 15.
5 Ludmilla Jordanova, *Sexual Visions: Images of Gender in Science and Medicine Between the Eighteenth and Nineteenth Centuries*, Basingstoke, 1989, especially pp. 1–6.
6 Joan Wallach Scott, *Gender and the Politics of History*, New York, 1988, p. 2.
7 For example, a recent review article demonstrates that there is little on sexuality in Ireland before the Victorians: Richard Dunphy, 'Gender and sexuality in Ireland', *Irish Historical Studies*, 1999, vol. 31, no. 124, pp. 549–57. The bibliography for 'The body, health and sexuality', in Michael Roberts and Simone Clarke (eds), *Women and Gender in Early Modern Wales*, Cardiff, 2000, p. 295, is extremely

short and contains nothing that discusses women or gender in this period. Due to limitations of space and current historiographical emphasis, the focus of this chapter is unfortunately heterosexual; however, there is a growing literature on intimate relations between women. For a recent engagement with much of this work, see Sarah Toulalan, 'Extraordinary satisfactions: lesbian visibility in seventeenth-century pornography in England', *Gender and History*, 2003, vol. 15, pp. 50–68.

8 Barbara Duden, *The Woman Beneath the Skin: A Doctor's Patients in Eighteenth Century Germany*, Cambridge, MA, 1991, pp. 115–16.

9 John Marten, *A Treatise of All the Degrees and Symptoms of the Venereal Disease* (1708), as quoted in Ian McCormick (ed.), *Secret Sexualities: A Sourcebook of 17th and 18th Century Writing*, London, 1997, p. 17.

10 Laqueur, *Making Sex*, p. 26. See pp. 23–35 for a detailed account of this parity

11 Ibid., pp. 25–62.

12 Ibid., p. 46.

13 Angus McLaren, 'The pleasures of procreation: traditional and biomedical theories of conception', in W. F. Bynum and Roy Porter (eds), *William Hunter and the Eighteenth-Century Medical World*, Cambridge, 1985, p. 340. See also Luisa Accati, 'The spirit of fornication: virtue of the soul and virtue of the body in Friuli, 1600–1800', in E. Muir and G. Ruggiero (eds), *Sex and Gender in Historical Perspective*, Baltimore, MD, 1990; Kimberly Crouch, 'The public life of actresses: prostitutes or ladies?', in Hannah Barker and Elaine Chalus (eds), *Gender in Eighteenth-Century England: Roles, Representations and Responsibilities*, Harlow, 1997, pp. 58–78; Carolyn Merchant, *The Death of Nature: Women, Ecology, and the Scientific Revolution*, London, 1982; Londa Schiebinger, 'Gender and natural history', in N. Jardine, J. A. Secord and E. C. Spary (eds), *Cultures of Natural History*, Cambridge, 1996, p. 163.

14 Laqueur, *Making Sex*, p. 154.

15 Ibid., pp. 194–207.

16 Londa Schiebinger, *Nature's Body: Gender in the Making of Modern Science*, Berkeley, CA, 1993, p. 143. See also Londa Schiebinger, *The Mind Has No Sex? Women in the Origins of Modern Science*, Cambridge, MA, 1989, p. 216.

17 Laqueur, *Making Sex*, p. 152.

18 Ibid., pp. 159–61.

19 Compare the illustrations of genitals on pp. 82, 84, and 88 of Laqueur's *Making Sex*, with those on pp. 158, 159, and 160.

20 Londa Schiebinger, 'Skeletons in the closet: the first illustrations of the female skeleton in eighteenth-century anatomy', in C. Gallagher and T. Laqueur (eds), *The Making of the Modern Body: Sexuality and Society in the Nineteenth Century*, Berkeley, CA, 1987, pp. 58–9.

21 Jordanova, *Sexual Visions*, p. 58.

22 Ibid., pp. 44–5.

23 Laqueur, *Making Sex*, pp. 8, 149–54.

24 J. Conway, 'Stereotypes of femininity in a theory of sexual evolution', in Martha Vicinus (ed.), *Suffer and Be Still: Women in the Victorian Age*, Bloomington, IN, 1972, p. 144.

25 Quoted in ibid., p. 141.

26 C. E. Russett, *Sexual Science: The Victorian Construction of Womanhood*, Cambridge, MA, 1989, p. 102.

27 See, for example, Kathleen Brown, '"Changed . . . into the Fashion of a Man": the

politics of sexual difference in a seventeenth-century Anglo-American settlement', *Journal of the History of Sexuality*, 1995, vol. 6, p. 173; Anthony Fletcher, *Gender, Sex and Subordination in England, 1500–1800*, New Haven, CT, 1995, pp. 291, 402, 407; Tim Hitchcock, 'Redefining sex in eighteenth-century England', *History Workshop Journal*, 1996, vol. 41, pp. 73–90; Michael McKeon, 'Historicising patriarchy: the emergence of gender difference in England, 1660–1760', *Eighteenth-Century Studies*, 1995, vol. 28, pp. 300–1; Robert B. Shoemaker, *Gender in English Society, 1650–1850: The Emergence of Separate Spheres?*, Harlow, 1998, pp. 31–5, 85, 313–14; Randolph Trumbach, *Sex and the Gender Revolution: I: Heterosexuality and the Third Gender in Enlightenment London*, Chicago, 1998, pp. 1–11. For a more detailed discussion of the place of the body in work on gender, see Karen Harvey, 'The century of sex? Gender, bodies and sexuality in the long eighteenth century', *The Historical Journal*, 2002, vol. 45, pp. 899–916, and Karen Harvey, *Reading Sex: Bodies and Gender in Eighteenth-Century English Erotica*, Cambridge, forthcoming 2004, Chapter 2.

28 Fletcher, *Gender, Sex and Subordination*, 407. For bodies, see pp. xvii–xvii, 291, 402.

29 Shoemaker, *Gender in English Society*, p. 85. See also pp. 31–5, 313–14.

30 Trumbach, *Sex and the Gender Revolution*, p. 9.

31 Hitchcock, 'Redefining sex, 73–90; Tim Hitchcock, *English Sexualities, 1700–1800*, Basingstoke, 1997, p. 111, *passim*.

32 *Aristotle's Compleat Master-Piece: In Three Parts: Displaying the Secrets of Nature in the Generation of Man*, 11th edn, London [1725], p. 14.

33 Ibid., p. 17.

34 See Roy Porter, '"The secrets of generation display'd": Aristotle's *Master-piece*', in Robert Purks Maccubbin (ed.), *'Tis Nature's Fault: Unauthorized Sexuality during the Enlightenment*, Cambridge, 1987, pp. 1–21; Roy Porter, 'The literature of sexual advice before 1800', in Roy Porter and Mikulás Teich (eds), *Sexual Knowledge, Sexual Science: The History of Attitudes to Sexuality*, Cambridge, 1994, pp. 134–57; and Roy Porter and Lesley Hall, *The Facts of Life: The Creation of Sexual Knowledge in Britain, 1650–1950*, New Haven, CT, 1995.

35 Harvey, *Reading Sex*, Chapter 2.

36 *Arbor Vitae: Or, the Natural History of the Tree of Life*, London, 1741, pp. 2–3, 5.

37 Karen Harvey, 'The substance of sexual difference: change and persistence in eighteenth-century representations of the body', *Gender and History*, 2002, vol. 14, pp. 202–23.

38 Thomas Laqueur, 'Orgasm, generation, and the politics of reproductive biology', *Representations*, 1986, vol. 14, p. 1.

39 Laqueur, *Making Sex*, p. 188.

40 Laqueur, 'Orgasm, generation', p. 27.

41 Ibid., p. 23.

42 Nancy Cott, 'Passionlessness: an interpretation of Victorian sexual ideology, 1790–1850', *Signs*, 1978, vol. 4, p. 220.

43 Ibid., pp. 221–4.

44 Ruth Perry, 'Colonising the breast: sexuality and maternity in eighteenth-century England', in John C. Fout (ed.), *Forbidden History: The State, Society, and the Regulation of Sexuality in Modern Europe*, Chicago, 1992, p. 116.

45 Hitchcock, *English Sexualities*, pp. 99–100.

46 *The Lady's Magazine*, April 1775, pp. 198–9.

47 *The Leeds Mercury*, 19 August 1797.

48 *Sheffield Mercury*, 13 September 1817; *The Leeds Mercury*, 6 September 1817.

49 *The Lady's Magazine*, April 1775, p. 198; *The Leeds Mercury*, 19 August 1797; Hitchcock, *English Sexualities*, pp. 105–6.

50 Leah Leneman, 'Seduction in eighteenth and early nineteenth-century Scotland', *Scottish Historical Review*, 1999, vol. 78, p. 59.

51 Ibid., pp. 55, 57. There were also significant legal differences between England and Wales, which manifested in cases of abduction in the early modern period. See Garthine Walker, ' "Strange kind of stealing": abduction in early modern Wales', in Roberts and Clarke, *Women and Gender in Early Modern Wales*, pp. 50–74.

52 Rosalind Mitchison and Leah Leneman, *Sexuality and Social Control: Scotland, 1660–1780*, Oxford, 1989, p. 9.

53 Ibid., p. 9; J. A. D. Blaikie, 'The country and the city: sexuality and social class in Victorian Scotland', in Gerry Kearns and C. W. J. Withers (eds), *Urbanising Britain: Essays on Class and Community in the Nineteenth Century*, Cambridge, 1991, p. 83.

54 Blaikie, 'Country and the city', p. 101, *passim*.

55 Barbara Littlewood and Linda Mahood, 'Prostitutes, magdalenes and wayward girls: dangerous sexualities of working class women in Victorian Scotland', *Gender and History*, 1991, vol. 3, pp. 160–75.

56 Maria Luddy, ' "Abandoned women and bad characters": prostitution in nineteenth-century Ireland', *Women's History Review*, 1997, vol. 6, pp. 485–503.

57 Nancy Armstrong, *Desire and Domestic Fiction: A Political History of the Novel*, Oxford, 1987, pp. 66–8, 71–3, *passim*.

58 Giles Jacob, *Tractatus de Hermaphrodites: Or, a Treatise of Hermaphrodites* (1718), as quoted in McCormick, *Secret Sexualities*, p. 21.

59 Paul-Gabriel Boucé, 'Some sexual beliefs and myths in eighteenth-century Britain', in Paul-Gabriel Boucé (ed.), *Sexuality in Eighteenth-Century Britain*, Manchester, 1982, pp. 41, 43.

60 *Aristotle's Compleat Master-Piece*, p. 9.

61 Ornella Moscucci, 'Clitoridectomy, circumcision, and the politics of sexual pleasure in mid-Victorian Britain', in Andrew H. Miller and James Eli Adams (eds), *Sexualities in Victorian Britain*, Bloomington, IN, 1996, pp. 61, 72.

62 Laqueur, *Making Sex*, pp. 233–4.

63 Carl Degler, 'What ought to be and what was', *American Historical Review*, 1974, vol. 79, p. 1469.

64 *The Why and the Wherefore: Or, the Lady's Two Questions Resolved*, London, 1765, p. 76.

65 Vincent Miller [pseud.], *The Man-Plant: Or, a Scheme for Increasing and Improving the British Breed*, London: 1752, pp. 2–3.

66 Roger Pheuquewell [pseud., Thomas Stretser], *A New Description of Merryland: Containing a Topographical, Geographical, and Natural History of that Country*, 7th edn, Bath, 1741, p. 12; *The Polite Road to an Estate: Or, Fornication, one Great Source of Wealth and Pleasure*, London, 1759, p. 21.

67 Perry, Ruth, 'Colonising the breast', pp. 107–37; Londa Schiebinger, 'Mammals, primatology and sexology', in Porter and Teich (eds), *Sexual Knowledge, Sexual Science*, pp. 184–209.

68 Pheuquewell [Stretser], *New Description of Merryland*, pp. 28–9.

69 *Man-Plant*, p. 11.

70 *The Lady's Magazine*, June 1775, p. 320.

71 Ibid., supplement to 1791, p. 721.

72 *Sheffield Mercury*, 20 July 1817.

73 Margaret Homans, 'Dinah's blush, Maggie's arms: class, gender, and sexuality in George Eliot's early novels', in Miller and Adams, *Sexualities in Victorian Britain*, p. 35.

74 Casey Finch, '"Hooked and buttoned together": Victorian underwear and representations of the female body', *Victorian Studies*, 1991, vol. 34, pp. 341, 343.

75 *Manchester Mercury*, 2 March 1773.

76 *Sheffield Register*, Saturday 21 July 1787.

77 *Manchester Mercury*, 29 January 1788.

78 Stana Nenadic, 'Experience and expectations in the transformation of the highland gentlewoman, 1680 to 1820', *Scottish Historical Review*, 2001, vol. 80, p. 204.

79 Patricia Crawford, 'Attitudes to menstruation in seventeenth-century England', *Past and Present*, 1981, no. 91, pp. 71–2. See also Patricia Crawford, 'Attitudes to pregnancy from a woman's spiritual diary, 1687–8', *Local Population Studies*, 1978, vol. 21, pp. 43–5.

80 Patricia Crawford, 'Sexual knowledge in England, 1500–1750', in Porter and Teich, *Sexual Knowledge, Sexual Science*, pp. 82–106.

81 *Aristotle's Compleat Master-Piece*, pp. 3, 8.

82 Simone Clarke, 'Visions of community: Elizabeth Baker and late eighteenth-century Merioneth', in Roberts and Clarke (eds), *Women and Gender in Early Modern Wales*, pp. 251–2.

83 *The Lady's Magazine*, June, 1775, pp. 320–1; July 1773, p. 376; January 1791, pp. 62–3; November 1783, pp. 587–9.

84 Ruth Bernard Yeazell, *Fictions of Modesty: Women and Courtship in the English Novel*, Chicago, 1991, *passim*, especially pp. 3–11.

85 'Bishop Edward Syngem to his daughter Alicia, 31 May 1751', in Angela Bourke *et al.* (eds), *The Field Day Anthology of Irish Writing: V: Irish Women's Writing and Traditions*, Cork, 2002, p. 630.

86 *The Lady's Magazine*, January 1784, p. 47.

87 Mary Delarivier Manley, *Secret Memoirs and Manners of Several Persons of Quality, of Both Sexes: From the New Atalantis, an Island in the Mediterranean*, ed. Ros Ballaster, London, 1991, p. 21.

88 'Introduction', in Harvey, *Reading Sex*.

89 Ros Ballaster, *Seductive Forms: Women's Amatory Fiction from 1684 to 1740*, Oxford, 1992, pp. 34–5.

90 Ros Ballaster, 'Seizing the means of seduction: fiction and feminine identity in Aphra Behn and Delarivier Manley', in Isobel Grundy and Susan Wiseman (eds), *Women, Writing, History*, London, 1992, pp. 93–108; Alison Conway, 'The Protestant cause and a Protestant whore: Aphra Behn's *Love-Letters*', *Eighteenth-Century Life*, 2001, vol. 25, pp. 1–19; Paula McDowell, *The Women of Grub Street: Press, Politics, and Gender in the London Literary Marketplace, 1678–1730*, Oxford, 1998, pp. 262–3.

91 Toni O'Shaughnessy Bowers, 'Sex, lies and invisibility: amatory fiction from the Restoration to mid-century', in John Richetti (ed.), *The Columbia History of the British Novel*, New York, 1994, p. 59.

92 Lynda M. Thompson, *The 'Scandalous Memoirists': Constantia Phillips, Laetitia Pilkington and the Shame of 'Publick Fame'*, Manchester, 2000, pp. 91–4.

93 See, for example, Jacqueline Pearson, *Women's Reading in Britain, 1750–1835: A Dangerous Recreation*, Cambridge, 1999.

94 Ibid., p. 93.

95 'Laetitia Pilkington to the Hon. Colonel D-NC-BE', in Bourke *et al.* (eds), *Field Day Anthology*, p. 794.

96 Nenadic, 'Experience and expectations', p. 203.

97 Amanda Vickery, *The Gentleman's Daughter: Women's Lives in Georgian England*, New Haven, CT, 1998, pp. 97–106.

98 Crawford, 'Attitudes to menstruation', pp. 65–2; Adrian Wilson, 'The perils of early modern procreation: childbirth with or without fear?', *British Journal for Eighteenth-Century Studies*, 1993, vol. 16, pp. 1–19. Wilson accesses Jane Josselin's feelings about pregnancy through the diary of Ralph Josselin, her husband.

99 *Secret Comment: The Diaries of Gertrude Savile, 1721–1757*, ed. Alan Savile assisted by Marjorie Penn, Loddiswell: Thoroton Society Record Ser., xli, 1997, p. 3.

100 Ibid., p. 32.

101 Ibid., p. 3.

102 *Lady Mary Wortley Montagu: The Turkish Embassy Letters*, ed. Anita Desai, London, 1993, pp. 71, 72.

103 Mary Astell, *A Serious Proposal to the Ladies for the Advancement of the True and Greatest Interest*, 2nd edn, London, 1695, p. 13.

104 Mary Poovey, *The Proper Lady and the Woman Writer: Ideology as Style in the Works of Mary Wollstonecraft, Mary Shelley, and Jane Austen*, Chicago, 1984, pp. 71–4.

105 Mary Wollstonecraft, *A Vindication of the Rights of Woman*, Harmondsworth, 1985, p. 115.

106 Laqueur, *Making Sex*, p. 5.

107 Ibid., p. 154.

108 Ibid., p. 11.

Women and religion

Anne Stott

> The simple things she said seemed like novelties . . . the quiet depth of
> conviction with which she spoke seemed in itself an evidence for the truth
> of her message . . . The villagers had pressed nearer to her, and there was
> no longer anything but grave attention on all faces. She spoke slowly,
> though quite fluently . . . and when she came to the question "Will God take
> care of us when we die?" she uttered it in such a tone of plaintive appeal
> that the tears came into some of the hardest eyes . . . Her voice became
> deep and muffled, but there was still no gesture . . . She was not preaching
> as she heard others preach, but speaking directly from her own emotions,
> and under the influence of her own simple faith.[1]

George Eliot's depiction in *Adam Bede* (1859) of the Methodist preacher,
Dinah Morris, was based on her own aunt, Elizabeth (Betsey) Evans, né
Tomlinson (*c*.1776–1849). Her description was so admired by Queen
Victoria that she commissioned a painting of the scene, Edward Henry
Corbould's watercolour 'Dinah Morris Preaching on Hayslope Green'
(1861), which is in the Royal Collection.[2] The composition is modelled on
the traditional portrayal of the Madonna as *mater misericordiae*. Dressed
in simple, Quakerish clothes, and at the head of a triangular composition,
Dinah stands on a cart above her hearers – an old man in the attitude of
contemplation, a woman holding a baby, children of various sizes. Her
arms are outstretched to encompass and protect them, the expression on
her face is calm and benevolent. This feminine and maternal depiction of
Dinah follows Eliot's own description of her 'mild loving eyes', her small,
delicate features, and her direct, emotional style of preaching – so different
from the acquired techniques and authoritative delivery associated with
men. Dinah offers no challenge to gender stereotypes and poses no threat

to male dominance. At the end of the novel the reader is told that, since Conference has forbidden female preaching, Dinah has 'given it up, all but talking to the people a bit in their houses'.[3] She has abandoned preaching for the domestic world.

The fictional case-study of Dinah Morris can be seen as a model for the story of women and religion in this period: a window of opportunity provided by a religious revival which spawned a generation of charismatic women preachers; a closing of this window in the wake of industrialization, urbanization, the French Revolution, and the increasing prevalence of the doctrine of separate spheres; plebeian village evangelists supplanted by respectable middle-class philanthropists. It is the purpose of this chapter, however, to suggest a more ambiguous narrative of shifts, movements, and re-positionings – of dispiriting retreats on some fronts but steady advances on others. In the end, it is a matter of fine judgement whether religiously inclined women emerged gainers or losers from the transformations in the wider society.

Historical overview

It should be noted at the start that this discussion is confined to Christian women. The only non-Christian religious minority of any note were the Jews, who numbered 60,000 in 1850 – a mere 0.2 per cent of the total British population. Because the religion of Jewish women was essentially focused on the rituals of the home, there is no quantitive or statistical survey to assess their participation in the religious life of their community. The fact that in the 1902–3 census of London, they formed only 22 per cent of synagogue attendance does not necessarily indicate a low level of religious commitment.[4]

In 1700 there were two established and legally co-equal churches in Britain: the Church of England (Anglican), established in Wales and Ireland, as well as in England, and the Church of Scotland (Presbyterian) in Scotland. Neither church allowed women to be ordained, to preach, or, in the case of the Church of Scotland, to be elders. In England, Wales, and Ireland holders of civic offices had to take communion in the Church of England at least once a year, and students at Oxford, Cambridge, and Trinity College Dublin had to assent to the Thirty-Nine Articles before they matriculated. However, the Toleration Act of 1689 gave freedom of worship to the main Dissenting denominations (Presbyterians, Independents, Baptists, and Quakers), though the non-Trinitarian Unitarians had to wait until 1813 for legal recognition of their right to worship. Roman Catholics were expressly excluded from the Act. The following century and a half was to see the unstoppable development of religious pluralism in which Catholics and Dissenters challenged existing monopolies in all four countries.

The major eighteenth-century religious development was the Evangelical revival, which began in the 1730s. A second wave at the end of the century saw Methodism become a separate denomination and the Evangelical Anglican Clapham sect become prominent in the movement for the abolition of the slave trade.[5] In the nineteenth century, the High-Church Oxford Movement, also known as Tractarianism, re-energized the Church of England; Catholic emancipation helped end the marginalization of the Roman Catholic community and the Catholic hierarchy was re-established in 1850. Abroad, the growth of the British Empire opened new areas to Christian missionaries. All these developments had implications for women.[6]

Before, and indeed after, the deeply controversial publication of *Essays and Reviews* in 1860 – a series of essays by seven Anglican scholars, arguing that the Church needed to come to terms with recent discoveries in science and biblical criticism[7] – the Bible was often read uncritically. The Genesis account of creation which proclaimed woman's responsibility for the fall of man, and the New Testament prohibitions of women's preaching (I Corinthians 14:34 and I Timothy 2:9–15) were generally taken at face value, by women as well as men.[8] But if parts of the Bible condemned women to silence, submission, and even guilt, other texts (notably Galatians 3:28), asserted their spiritual equality As the preacher Catherine O'Bryan wrote:

> God doth his gifts and grace bestow,
> On Women too as well as men.[9]

The Bible also gave women a language to validate their callings. The title 'mother in Israel' was given to the Old Testament prophetess, Deborah (Judges 5:7), and in the eighteenth and nineteenth centuries it was regularly bestowed on women of exceptional courage and devotion – preachers, Sunday-School teachers, women who opened their homes to their fellow-believers. With its layered meanings of refuge, authority, and motherhood, the title provided a vindication for those women who sought a public role or assumed positions of leadership.[10] To put this in perspective, it should be remembered that no woman could be a Member of Parliament or a justice of the peace, or enter a university; it was only towards the end of the period that they could train to be nurses or teachers. Religion therefore provided women with opportunities denied them in secular society.

Some historians have claimed that Christianity become increasingly feminized in this period – and not only because women outnumbered men in many denominations.[11] The eighteenth-century fusion of Methodist enthusiasm with the secular cult of sensibility privileged deeply felt personal experience above academic rationality. The new religion of the heart was exemplified in the vivid language of the Methodist servant, Mary Barnard: 'I think the Lord has washed my soul as clean as the stones in the brook.'[12] William Wilberforce believed that 'the female sex' possessed a 'more favourable disposition to religion', which made women 'the medium of our intercourse with the heavenly world, the faithful repositories of the religious principle, for the benefit both of the present and of the rising generation'.[13] Many men were prepared to concede women's spiritual superiority at the same time as they denied them political or intellectual equality.

This double-edged compliment was reinforced by the increasing separation (in theory at least) of the worlds of work and home. Among the middle classes and some of the 'respectable' working classes, it increasingly became a matter of pride to a man that his income enabled him to support his wife and protect her from the grubbiness of the outside world.[14] However, the ideology of domesticity worked both ways. The middle-class daughter, kept at home while her brothers enter the world of work, is a familiar figure from Victorian novels and feminist autobiographies. On the other hand, many devout, energetic, and competent women – mainly middle class, though some, like the Norfolk prison visitor, Sarah Martin (1791–1843),[15] working class – engaged in a variety of good works, which could be justified as extensions of their caring roles as wives and mothers. Unwittingly in many cases, philanthropic women crossed and re-crossed the boundaries between the 'masculine' public and the 'feminine' private spheres, and, in doing so, they set up what might be described as a 'third sphere' of creative and flexible interaction between the domestic hearth and the world of business and politics.[16]

From the beginning of the eighteenth century, religion played a pivotal role in the development of proto-feminism. Mary Astell (1661–1731), now recognized as the first English feminist, derived her inspiration from a fusion of the philosophy of Descartes, the spirituality of high Anglicanism, and Christian Platonism. In her *Serious Proposal to the Ladies* (1694–7), she argued that women should be taken seriously as rational beings, and, in an anticipation of feminist separatism, envisaged a 'Protestant nunnery' – an independent space where they could cultivate their intellects as well as their souls.[17] Her contemporary, Susanna Wesley (1670–1742), mother of John and Charles, used her position as a clerical wife to carve out a niche for herself. During her husband's prolonged absences in 1710–12, she decided that 'though I am not a man, nor a minister of the gospel, and so cannot be engaged in such worthy employment as they were, yet . . . I might do something more than I do'.[18] Accordingly, she began holding meetings in her house for prayer and sermon-reading, which were attended by several hundred local townspeople. Recognizing her success, her husband over-rode the objections of his curate and allowed her to continue with her meetings.

In the 1730s, the first Moravians arrived in England, escaping persecution in the Habsburg Empire; it was at a Moravian chapel in Aldersgate in 1738 that John Wesley felt his heart 'strangely warmed'. Gender was central to Moravian identity. The most distinctive areas of their community life were their houses for single brethren and sisters; their resemblance to the monastic life delighted one Moravian woman, who confessed to 'secretly hankering after a cloister'.[19] Since Mary Astell's vision had never been realized, this was something denied women in mainstream Protestantism.

Of all the dissenting sects, the Society of Friends gave the greatest scope for female participation, and the high literacy rate among Quaker women is a tribute to their status in the movement.[20] Its founder, George Fox, had allowed women to preach, but for the majority of Quaker women it was the Women's Yearly Meeting, set up as a properly constituted Meeting in 1784, which gave them their most important role in the Society. Although it had only a very limited authority, no other religious denomination provided its female members with this kind of space. Another vital female contribution to the Society of Friends lay in the practice of hospitality, as they opened their homes to travelling ministers and maintained the family networks which were so vital to Quakerism: a pattern of specifically female service that can also be seen in early Methodism.

The Rational Dissenters and their successors, the Unitarians, were committed to liberalizing society, expanding education, and freeing the mind from the shackles of religious doctrine. In spite of the patriarchal attitudes of many mainstream Unitarians, the denomination provided a fertile environment for feminism.[21] The writer and educator, Anna Barbauld (1743–1825), represented the conservative strand of Rational Dissent, Mary Wollstonecraft (1759–97), the more radical. Though she later moved away from all brands of Christianity into an eroticized pantheism, Wollstonecraft learned her politics from Richard Price, the minister at Newington Green; her works were published by Joseph Johnson, the official publisher of the Rational Dissenters. The best-known mid-nineteenth century Unitarian was Elizabeth Gaskell (1810–65), wife of the minister of Cross Street Chapel in Manchester, whose disturbingly topical novel, *Mary Barton* (1848), alerted comfortable middle-class readers to the dark underside of industrial life.[22] Cultivated, educated women were not a Unitarian monopoly. In the 1820s the sisters, Mary and Rebecca Franklin, the daughters of a Baptist minister, ran a girls' school in Coventry that was intellectually stimulating enough to satisfy their most promising pupil, Mary Anne Evans, the future George Eliot (1819–80).

Nonconformists as a body were growing in numbers and in confidence, with the Methodists, who had broken from the Church of England in the 1790s, enjoying the most rapid expansion. With the repeal of the Test and Corporation Acts in 1828, Protestant Dissenters were allowed to stand for Parliament without taking Anglican communion or securing a special indemnity. The Anglican monopoly was further undermined by an Act of 1836 that allowed Dissenting chapels to be registered as places for marriages; no longer would couples like the Revd William Gaskell and Elizabeth Stevenson face the indignity of being forced by law to marry in their parish church. Nonconformists in England and Wales received a further boost when the religious census of 1851 recorded almost as many attendees at their chapels as at Anglican churches.[23] The many methodological flaws in the way the information was compiled could not disguise the scale of the Nonconformist advance. The less complete Scottish census, however, reflected a different religious situation, with the great majority of the population attending some form of Presbyterian worship, either the established Church of Scotland or the Free Church (the 'wee Frees') formed after the Great Disruption of 1843.[24] Ireland presented another picture again, and a striking anomaly: in an overwhelmingly Catholic nation, the Anglican Church of Ireland remained the established Church with all the attendant privileges, though it commanded the allegiance of a mere 10 per cent of the population. The word 'chapel', which in England and Wales denoted a Dissenting church, in Ireland applied (and still does) to a Catholic place of worship.[25]

On the British mainland, the census figures revealed that, thanks largely to the influx of Irish immigration, the number of Catholics had increased to about 750,000, an approximately tenfold increase in eighty years.[26] Their legal position had improved out of all recognition since 1700. Two emancipatory measures of 1778 and 1791 were followed by the Act of 1829 which enabled them to enter Parliament.[27] Then, in 1850, Pope Pius IX restored the Catholic hierarchy, a move that sparked a short-lived hysteria among outraged Protestants. These huge changes impacted on the position of women in the Catholic community. Post-Reformation 'seigneurial' Catholicism had been a household religion, largely dominated by propertied women, whose homes provided a secure base for priests. One such was Ann Fenwick (1724–77), the daughter of a Lancaster attorney and the widow of a leading landowner. Under an Act of 1700 she was not allowed to inherit her husband's property, which was transferred instead to her Protestant brother-in-law. When he failed to keep to his agreement to make her an allowance, she was forced to take him to court in a well-publicized suit that highlighted Catholic disabilities in a country that prided itself on its civil liberties. The result was a private bill, passed in 1772, which made over to her a substantial sum of money in compensation. Six years later, partly in response to her case, the first Catholic Relief Act enabled Catholics to inherit property even if their close relatives were Protestants. In spite of her financial difficulties, in 1762 she installed a priest at her home, Hornby Hall, for the seventy-eight Catholic families in the area. She also set up charitable schemes for the poor.[28] Although women such as Fenwick, born into the Catholic gentry or middle classes, continued to be important in the life of their church, their influence was lessening. As Catholicism assumed a greater role in national life, the clergy gained in importance. By 1850, the Catholic Church in the British Isles was more male- and clerical-dominated than at any time since the Reformation. This, however, did not mean that all Catholic women were doomed to marginalization.

No summary of the religious situation in Britain between 1700 and 1850 can do justice to the complexity of a situation in which four separate nations with differing histories and religious traditions all saw major changes and developments: challenges to the Anglican monopoly in England, Wales, and Ireland; the fracturing of Scottish Presbyterianism; the growth of Evangelicalism and Tractarianism; and the demographic advance of both Nonconformity and Roman Catholicism in mainland Britain. Throughout these changes, the main religious decisions were made by men, whether as legislators, clergy, or officeholders within their respective denominations. But, far from being passive onlookers, meekly acquiescing in the decisions made by their menfolk, religious women showed themselves remarkably ingenious and adaptable. If few of them mounted a direct challenge to male supremacy, they were nevertheless able to show that British Christianity could not function without their efforts. As the (not always silent) majority of church attenders, they were adept at finding strategies that would enable their voices to be heard.

Women preachers

How was it that Dinah Morris and her real-life counterpart, Elizabeth Evans, were able to defy St Paul's prohibitions and assume the role of preachers? The sociologist, Max Weber, famously noted that new religions have their beginnings in outbursts of charismatic energy when many of the normal restraints break down and women – along with other marginalized groups – assume prophetic roles.[29] This is particularly true of the early Methodists. Their classes and bands were segregated according to sex and marital status rather than occupation or social class, and in the ensuing atmosphere of emotional warmth, women gained significantly in self-confidence. In 1767, John Wesley gave Sarah Crosby (1729–1804) permission to 'properly intermix short exhortations with prayer', but warned her to 'keep as far from what is called preaching as you can'.[30] However, on 17 September 1776, her friend, Mary Bosanquet (1739–1814), went further when she preached at Goker in Yorkshire before a congregation of 2,000. 'I do not believe every woman is called to speak publicly', she had told Wesley in 1771, 'no more than every man to be a Methodist preacher, yet some have an extraordinary call to it, and woe be to them if they obey it not.' By this time, Wesley had come to believe that 'the whole work of God termed

Methodism is an extraordinary dispensation of his providence. Therefore, I do not wonder if several things occur therein which do not fall under ordinary rules of discipline.'[31] Accordingly, he allowed Bosanquet to continue her ministry.

But the doctrine of the extraordinary call was vulnerable to changes in the Connexion and in the wider society that came about during the conservative reaction to the French Revolution. In 1803, responding to the prevailing mood of quietism and respectability, a ruling of the Methodist Conference imposed a ban on women preachers, with one exception: that if a woman felt an extraordinary call, 'she should in general address her own sex, and those only'.[32] Though some women, including Betsey Evans, defied the ban, most submitted, and female preaching remained a dead issue with the Wesleyans until the twentieth century. However, the sectarian Methodism of the early nineteenth century – a 'cottage' religion centred on the labouring household – allowed more scope for female agency than the increasingly middle-class Wesleyans.[33] Hugh Bourne, the founder of the Primitive Methodists, never abandoned the notion of the 'extraordinary' call, and in his *Remarks on the Ministry of Women* (1808) he justified his acceptance by citing the text from Acts 2:18: 'Your sons and your daughters shall prophesy'.[34]

Another new denomination, the Bible Christians, founded in Devon in 1815, wholeheartedly supported female preaching, and, for the next ten years women preachers were even more significant than their male colleagues.[35] No ban on preaching was imposed on Quaker women either, and they had never needed the doctrine of an extraordinary call to justify their ministry. In general, these preachers were well-to-do women from distinguished Quaker families, and the call to preach was often handed down the generations. In spite of family commitments, Abiah Darby (1716–93), wife of the Coalbrookdale industrialist Abraham Darby II, and her step-daughter-in-law, Deborah Darby (1754–1810), travelled extensively 'in the ministry'.[36] Even when the Society of Friends came under the influence of Evangelical biblicism, the number of women preachers continued to rise: by 1815 there were twice as many female ministers as male.[37]

Founding mothers

Though religion has notoriously reinforced the subordination of women, it has also granted them special privileges. They have been viewed as closer to the deity, more intuitive, and more in touch with spiritual reality than men. In classical times, the god Apollo communicated his messages through women – the prophetess Cassandra, the Oracle at Delphi, the Sybil at Cumae – while in the modern world most spiritualist mediums are women. It is also a fact that throughout recorded history there have been powerful and wealthy women whose position in society enabled them at times to transcend the disadvantages of their gender. These two kinds of power, the one charismatic, the other class-based, can be seen in the careers of two separate types of 'founding mothers', women who started religious movements and assumed leadership positions within them.

Chapter 12 of the Book of Revelation presents a mysterious picture of a woman clothed with the sun, who is pursued by a dragon into the wilderness, where she gives birth to a male child destined to rule the nations. In the millenarian enthusiasm of the late eighteenth century, this strange and compelling image was given new life when it was applied by their followers to three extraordinary women. One was the former mill-worker, Ann Lee (1736–84), who in 1774 left England for New York where she helped set up a 'Shaker' settlement committed to celibacy and simple living. Another was the Scotswoman Mrs Elspat, ('Luckie') Buchan (c.1738–91). With the former Presbyterian minister, Hugh White, she built a community at Irvine in Ayrshire and waited the Second Coming of Christ. The movement collapsed when Mrs Buchan (to the dismay of her followers) died a natural death and failed to return from the dead. The most celebrated millenarian prophetess was Joanna Southcott (1750–1814), a domestic servant and a tenant farmer's daughter from Devon. In 1792, supported by a few sympathetic Anglican clergymen, she proclaimed herself the woman of the Apocalypse and the mother of 'Shiloh', the new Messiah. By the time of her death there were around 20,000 'sealed' believers, with women outnumbering men by 63 to 36]per cent.[38]

The second category of founding mothers was made up wealthy patricians. They generally worked within the existing power structures, and their activities reinforced the aristocratic dominance of society. Selina, Countess of Huntingdon (1707–91), and Diana, Baroness Barford (1762–1823), founded their own Calvinist churches. Lady Huntingdon's Connexion was part of her mission to convert the aristocracy and her chapels were located in London and in spa towns such as Bath and Tunbridge Wells. She patronized 'worthy' clergy and founded her own college at Trevecca in Breconshire. 'Lady Barham's Connexion' had six chapels and several schools on the Gower peninsula, which she organized between 1814 and 1822.[39] Other aristocratic women stayed within the Anglican fold, but used their wealth to found chapels and schools and promote approved clergy. The Scottish peeresses, Willielma, Lady Glenorchy (1741–86) and Lady Henrietta Hope (c.1750–86), founded Hope Chapel at the fashionable Hotwells in Bristol. When they died, its administration was taken over by another Scottish aristocrat, Darcy, Lady Maxwell (c.1742–1810), and, because it was a proprietary chapel, she ran it without reference to the diocesan bishop.[40] In the early nineteenth century, Cecil Chetwynd Kerr (1808–77) founded a chapel at Jedburgh, which was consecrated in 1844. Denied a priestly role by her gender, she was never-theless able to use her position as the widow of the seventh Marquess of Lothian to play a major role in the establishment of Tractarianism in Scotland.[41]

Women in religious orders comprised a third category of founding mothers, with the Catholic Church leading the way. After two centuries of persecution, twelve houses of women religious had been established in Ireland by 1750, and the numbers of women religious in that country increased from approximately 120 in 1800 to 1,500 by 1850.[42] In 1794, in the wake of the French Revolution, nuns returned to England for the first time since the Reformation and paved the way for the growth and expansion of women's religious orders that followed the granting of Catholic emancipation. The American, Cornelia Connelly (1809–79), was installed as Superior-General of the Society of the Holy Child Jesus, founded in Derby in 1846, the first congregation to be set up in England since the Reformation. A forthright and capable woman, she had no use for contemporary cloying stereotypes of femininity and was able to stretch creatively the apparently deterministic categories of masculine and feminine: 'We have to learn to make strong women, who while they lose nothing of their sweetness and gentleness, have a masculine force of character and will.'[43] By 1855, her nuns were teaching in eight poor schools in central London and seven in Preston.

This trend was not confined to Roman Catholicism. In 1839 the Tractarian, Edward Bouverie Pusey, suggested the creation of Anglican sisterhoods for women which would 'give holy employment to many who yearn for something' and 'channel female religious zeal, which might otherwise go off in some irregular way, or go over to Rome'.[44] In 1841, Marian Hughes (1817–1912), the daughter of a Gloucestershire rector, dedicated herself to the religious life and in 1845 the first community was founded in Park Village West, near Regent's Park in London. Three years later, Priscilla Lydia Sellon (1821–76), the daughter of a naval officer, founded a community to serve the poor of Plymouth and Devonport. In 1849 the sisters nursed the victims of a cholera epidemic in the area and the following years were to see their work expand among orphans, delinquent boys, girls training for domestic service, and retired sailors. 'Mother Lydia' was a woman of exceptionally strong personality, resembling Florence Nightingale (1820–1910) in what her supporters saw as fearless energy and her enemies as bullying megalomania. Such was her notoriety that in 1852 the Evangelical *Christian Observer* – hostile in principle to sisterhoods – mounted a savage attack on her, citing among her many offences, her 'gross assumption . . . of the rights and powers which the language and still more the spirit of the Holy Scriptures seems to deny to the female sex'.[45]

This animosity needs to be set in context. In the mid-nineteenth century climate of anti-Catholicism and gender anxiety, the sisterhoods were accused both of being instruments of 'romanization' and of taking women away from their rightful sphere. From a more modern perspective, they can be seen as firmly rooted in the feminist tradition, sceptical of the all-embracing ideology of domesticity, committed to women-created organizations, and dedicated to improving the lives of working-class women and children.[46] In view of the patriarchalism of Anglo-Catholic theology, with its emphasis on priestly authority, this may be a somewhat rose-tinted assessment. Nevertheless, even though they were in theory always subordinate to the clergy, the sisters formed the vanguard of the Anglo-Catholic advance into the Victorian slums and gained skills in teaching, nursing, and social welfare before these became established as secular professions.[47]

Writers, philanthropists and missionaries

With the rise of literacy, especially female literacy in the eighteenth century, the growing acceptance of the female author, and the rapid expansion of a reading public, many religious women lost their inhibitions about going into print. Whereas the eighteenth-century Baptist hymn writer, Anne Steele (1717–78), had published anonymously, the popular poets, Anna Barbauld and Felicia Hemens (1794–1835) published under their own names. By the nineteenth century, following Ann (1782–1866) and Jane (1783–1824) Taylor's *Hymns for Infant Minds* (1810), the great majority of hymns for children were written by women. The best-known practitioner of this genre was Cecil Frances Alexander (1818–95), wife of the Anglican Bishop of Derry, whose *Hymns for Little Children* (1848) included perennial favourites such as 'Once in Royal David's City'. Hannah More (1745–1833) wrote for a triple readership: the wealthy genteel, artisans and farmers, and the poor. Her conduct books sold widely among the aristocracy and middle classes, and her Cheap Repository Tracts (1795–8), which disseminated loyalist politics and religious instruction to the poor, sold over two million copies in the first year of publication. Martha Mary Sherwood (1775–1851) wrote ghoulish, best-selling Evangelical novels. Another Evangelical, Charlotte Elizabeth Tonna (1790–1846), combined novel-writing and innovative social criticism with the editorship of the virulently anti-Catholic *Christian Lady's Magazine*.[48]

From the second half of the eighteenth century, women also began to corner the market in a range of philanthropic and missionary projects which provided them with 'almost the only alternative to an entirely domestic life'.[49] It is only possible to mention a few of their activities here.

Traditional accounts which credit Robert Raikes with founding the first Sunday School in 1780 ignore the pioneering work of the Methodist, Hannah Ball (1734–92), who set up her school in High Wycombe in 1769. Ball's example was followed by the High-Church Anglican, Sarah

Trimmer (1741–1810), who founded a Sunday School at Brentford, and the Evangelicals, Hannah and Patty More (1750–1819), who founded nine schools and two women's friendly societies in the isolated and impoverished Mendip area of Somerset.[50]

One of Hannah More's friends and supporters was Margaret Middleton (d. 1792), the wife of an Evangelical MP, and mother of Baroness Barham. According to one account, it was Lady Middleton who first urged Wilberforce to campaign to abolish the slave trade.[51] Women were involved in the abolition movement from the start, with Quakers, Evangelical Anglicans, and Rational Dissenters prominent among the lists of subscribers to the cause. Hannah More and Anna Barbauld published anti-slavery poetry that used the fashionable language of sensibility to help British women identify with the sufferings of African wives and mothers. From the 1790s boycotts of sugar became increasingly common, a form of protest directly linked to women's domestic responsibilities.[52]

Women were also active in the Society for Bettering the Condition of the Poor, founded in 1796, by the Evangelical Sir Thomas Bernard. In 1803 the Methodist-turned-Quaker, Hannah Kilham (1774–1832), became a member of the Sheffield branch of the society, which formed a committee of lady visitors who called upon poor women and dispensed blankets and moral advice in equal measure.[53] Such activities opened the eyes of middle-class women to the terrible conditions of the poor at a time of unprecedented social change. The British and Irish Ladies' Society extended this work to the women of rural Ireland. Their exhortations can be seen as a form of colonialism, an imposition of middle-class mores on their less privileged sisters; the same point can be made about the work of Hannah More and Priscilla Lydia Sellon. But their aim was to enable poor women to acquire new skills in order to help themselves and their families, and eventually make them less dependent on well-meaning maternalism.

At the beginning of the nineteenth century this philanthropic activism was potentially controversial, as the ideological turmoil thrown up by the French Revolution and Britain's war with France spawned an 'anti-Jacobin' panic, much of it focused upon the alleged misdeeds of prominent women. Mary Wollstonecraft's turbulent life made her an obvious target. A less predictable victim of the new climate was Hannah More, who, in the so-called Blagdon controversy, was subjected to a McCarthyite campaign of vilification in the right-wing press, where she was accused of sexual impropriety and political subversion.[54] Her troubles coincided with the Methodist Conference's ban on female preaching. In this increasingly nervous atmosphere, women had to tread carefully if they were to escape the charge of breaking gender conventions.

The Blagdon controversy marks the high-water mark of the anti-Jacobin panic and, with the ending of the threat of a French invasion after Trafalgar, much of the hysteria died down. The Quaker philanthropist, Elizabeth Fry

(1780–1845), was more likely to be accused of neglecting her large family than of political subversion. Following her religious conversion, Betsy Gurney, as she then was, set up a school on her father's Norfolk estate and, after her marriage, undertook the usual social projects of supplying the local poor with food, clothing, and medicine. In 1811, she was recorded as a Quaker minister, and two years later, in the arresting phrase of her biographer, she 'gate-crashed into public life', when she made her first visit to Newgate Prison.[55] 'None but a woman, and none but a quaker woman, *could* have ventured, or if venturing could have succeeded', Hannah More, wrote wistfully. 'Their habits of public speaking have taken away that fear of men which would have intimidated one of *us*.'[56] In 1821, Elizabeth Fry founded the British Ladies' Society for Promoting the Reformation of Female Prisoners; by 1827, there were thirty-four associations in Britain and Ireland, all playing a significant role in the debate on penal reform.

Throughout the eighteenth century the Society for the Propagation of Christian Knowledge (SPCK), founded in 1698, had supplied religious literature, in particular for the poor and for charity-school children. From the outset, women had been prominent in the Society as subscribers, managers, trustees, and teachers.[57] But the SPCK was exclusively Anglican, a fact that did not work in its favour at a time when the numbers of Dissenting congregations were outstripping the growth of the population as a whole. In 1804, the British and Foreign Bible Society was founded on interdenominational lines, its remit to disseminate cheap Bibles throughout Britain, Europe, and the Empire. The Committee of the Bible Society was exclusively male, but women of all denominations entered enthusiastically into the grassroots work. In 1811, the first Ladies' Association was set up in Westminster and, by 1820, 180 of these associations were in existence, raising money and distributing Bibles, so that, as the Society's historian has noted, 'the whole system of Bible Associations began gradually to pass in a great measure into the hands of the female workers.'[58] This development aroused atavistic male anxieties – that the women would not be able to add up the collections, or that they would separate from their husbands rather than leave their associations. 'With the zeal and spirit, the forwardness and intrusive boldness of an active member of a Ladies' Bible Association', a Liverpool pamphleteer fretted, 'how is it possible to retain the softened diffidence and virgin modesty which form the great charm of the female bosom?'[59]

The Bible Society women learned organizational skills that could be transferred to other causes. In 1825, the Birmingham clergyman's wife, Lucy Townsend, who was already active in her local association, established the first women's anti-slavery society in Britain. Seventy-two imitators followed – largely English and urban-based, though with a few located in Scotland, Wales, and Ireland – all of them vital and articulate participants in the anti-slavery campaign of 1823–33.[60] These societies promoted anxieties similar to those already aroused by the Bible Society associations. William Wilberforce, in particular, was alarmed at the licence this gave for women 'to meet, to publish, to go from house to house stirring up petitions', thinking such activities 'unsuited to the female character as delineated in Scripture'.[61] The anti-slavery women were in the forefront of a significant policy change. In 1824, the Leicester Quaker, Elizabeth Heyrick (1769–1831), published a pamphlet, *Immediate, Not Gradual Abolition*, a critique of the caution of the male-dominated abolitionist establishment. Over the next few years, the majority of the ladies' associations were won over to the cause of immediate abolition. In response to sustained pressure, the national Anti-Slavery Society changed its policy in May 1830, and, as one Irish member admitted, it was the women who had led the way.[62]

In the earlier campaign to abolish the slave trade, women had played significant roles 'as runaways, as subscribers, as writers, and as abstainers'.[63] But the new anti-slavery networks involved a greater number of women (about 10,000 were members of ladies' associations) and a more impressive organization. On 14 May 1833, the day the Whig government introduced its Emancipation Bill, the national female petition, a huge document bearing 187,157 signatures, was presented to Parliament. In that year, more than 400,000 women signed anti-slavery petitions, making up a third of all the signatories. A second wave of petitioning crested later in the decade, this time against the near slavery of West Indian apprentice-ship. In 1838 three national addresses were presented to the new Queen, signed by an unprecedented number of women: nearly 500,000 in England and Wales, 135,083 in Scotland, and 77,000 in Ireland; the total of 700,000 women was around two-thirds the total number of signatures to anti-apprenticeship petitions.[64] Women were mobilized as never before, sometimes in opposition to the views of male relatives; inspired by Christian humanitarianism, well-meaning lady philanthropists had trans-formed themselves into quasi-political campaigners.

Anti-slavery campaigning was largely conducted from middle-class homes. An increasing number of women, however, were travelling abroad. The late eighteenth and early nineteenth centuries witnessed the rapid growth of missionary work, with the foundation of the Baptist, London, and Church Missionary Societies. Until the second half of the nineteenth century, the great majority of women involved in this work went overseas as the wives of missionaries; this would have been Jane Eyre's role if she had married St John Rivers. The Church of England societies forbade unaccompanied women to travel to the mission field, but other women were able to act independently. One of the pioneers was the widowed Hannah Kilham, who visited the Gambia in 1823 and the freed slave colony of Sierra Leone in 1827–8 and 1830–2. In India it soon became obvious that only women could reach the secluded women of the *zenanas* and the

Society for Promoting Female Education in the East was set up to promote *zenana* education. Mary Anne Cook (later Wilson) (*c.*1795–1861) was a member and by 1836 she was supervising thirty schools attended by nearly 600 girls.[65]

Women and spirituality

It is relatively easy to chart the activities of religious women; it is more difficult to assess the inner world of their spirituality. Did the doctrines and imagery of Christianity have an especial appeal for them? Do they help to account for the numerical preponderance of females in most denominations?

The millenarian prophetesses made much use of the erotic image of divine marriage found in the Song of Solomon. More mainstream women also found this image a source of power: in 1763 the Quaker preacher, Abiah Darby, dreamed that Christ was transformed into her second husband.[66] Such language was part of a mystical tradition, in which the believer of either sex assumed the female persona and adopted an attitude of loving submission and ecstatic devotion to the Bridegroom (Christ). This ancient imagery was part of the distinctive womb-like Moravian (and, to a lesser extent, Methodist) spirituality which focused on Christ's blood and wounds, particularly the 'side-hole', and used a secret language laced with terms of passionate endearment.[67] Though distasteful to many modern sensibilities, the imagery held a particular appeal for some women, for whom the language of blood, holes, and wombs was no mere abstraction. It provided a semi-erotic identification with a suffering saviour, a symbolic linking of blood and sexuality, a spiritualization of the agonies of the body in an age of primitive medicine.[68]

This identification can be seen in the hymns written by women described dismissively as 'sickly spinsters' – for instance, chronic invalids and depressives such as Charlotte Elliott (1789–1871), compiler of the *Invalid's Hymn Book* (1834) and author of *Hours of Sorrow* (1836):[69]

> Though dark my path and sad my lot,
> Let me 'be still' and murmur not;
> Or breathe the prayer divinely taught
> > 'Thy will be done!'
> . . .
> Though thou hast call'd me to resign
> What I most priz'd, it ne'er was mine:
> I have but yielded what was thine: –
> > 'Thy will be done!'[70]

Elliott's voice can seem abject and self-punishing, but her hymns clearly spoke to the condition of her numerous readers. She and many of her fellow women hymn-writers found in Christianity the valorization of their sufferings and frustrations, physical and mental. 'They became expert at describing pain and suffering, the impotence of having to sit with folded hands.'[71]

Unlike their Protestant sisters, Catholics were able to appropriate the Virgin Mary in defining their spirituality. Cornelia Connelly's devotion to the Mother of Sorrows arose from the agonizing death of her 2-year-old son. In 1842, the Irish Dominican teacher, Sister Margaret Hallahan (1803–68), arrived in Coventry from Belgium. There, she encouraged the Vicar-Apostolic, William Bernard Ullathorne, to promote the Rosary, a form of devotion that focused on the joys, sorrows, and glorification of the Madonna. In 1844, Sister Margaret devised a Catholic response to the Lady Godiva processions: an image of the Virgin, decked with flowers and surrounded by young girls in white, was fixed in a cart and pulled around the church in a rival procession.[72]

Both Catholics and Protestants were agreed on the importance of making a good death. Here, women, accustomed as they so often were to submit to unavoidable suffering, frequently had the advantage over men. In the last hours of their lives, the prescriptions to be silent and submissive were put aside. They were allowed to pray aloud, to exhort, and their dying words were often carefully recorded. For the first – and last – times in their lives, masculine language could be applied to them. For example, Susannah Rudge, who died in 1716, gave 'the last Admonitions and Blessings' to her family 'with the Majesty of an ancient *Patriarch*'. Wilberforce's cousin, Harriet Bird (d. 1792), a 'remarkably diffident and timid' young woman died in 'a truly heroic and pious' manner, showing 'a sort of righteous courage, an animated manner, and a ready eloquence which were all used as a means for awakening and striking others'.[73]

1850: loss and gain

Not all religious women, of course, experienced such elevating deaths; many died expressing anguished regret at leaving their loved ones; others were mercifully stupefied with laudanum. Only a small minority of women could be nuns, missionaries, or writers. For the rest, gender roles had become more sharply defined and the norms of respectability more oppressive. Even in the radical sects, the climate had chilled. The preacher, Ann Mason (1791–1826), left the Bible Christians in 1824 in protest at the Society's growing authoritarianism, and the last of the women travelling preachers of the Primitive Methodists retired in 1860.[74] The much-trumpeted expansion of philanthropy often took place with male permission and under male control. The influential writings of Sarah Stickney Ellis (d. 1872) and the sermons of her fellow Congregationalist, John Angell James (1785–1859) reinforced rather than challenged patriarchal Christianity.[75] George Eliot's Dorothea Brooke, a modern Saint Teresa, yearns in vain for a wider and more exalted sphere of action. So, for many years, did Florence Nightingale, who complained bitterly that the Church of England 'gave me no training . . . neither work to do for her nor education for it'.[76]

How had this come about? The closing of opportunities is a classic example of Max Weber's 'routinization of charisma', the process whereby a radical movement loses its initial energies, is institutionalized into a denomination with the attendant power structures, and, as a by-product, the roles of women are diminished.[77] In the secular world, this institutionalization was reflected in the growth of male-only professions and the relegation of women's work to the informal, the amateur, and the unpaid.[78] Part of the rationale for this development was provided by the ideology of separate spheres and the gendered culture of private domestic woman and public economic man.[79] As a result of these changes, the mother in Israel became the angel in the house of Coventry Patmore's poem (1845–62), the moral pivot of the family, its guardian and protector – but also its prisoner.

Yet in spite of this, it is difficult to argue that women were less important and influential in Christianity in 1850 than they had been 150 years previously. Though some avenues might have closed, others were opening. For all its limitations, religiously sanctioned domestic ideology legitimized many new outlets to the wider world. If Dorothea Brook had been a real rather than a fictional character, she might have found her mission any number of philanthropic projects. Dickens's grotesque Mrs Jellyby of *Bleak House*, more interested in Africa than her home or family, provides a telling reflection of masculine anxiety. To her immense frustration, Elizabeth Fry found her recommendations undermined by male professionals and by a growing lack of sympathy for penal reform; but when she gave evidence to Parliamentary committees, she did so as an expert witness, a professional woman *avant la lettre*. It was partly because of the undoubted expertise of Fry and other philanthropic women that women's lack of formal power came to seem increasingly unjust and anomalous.

The decades after 1850 saw an opening up of women's work. Members of the nursing sisterhoods, both Anglican and Catholic, went out to the Crimea in 1854. The order of deaconesses was set up in the Church of England in 1862. A new denomination – the Salvation Army – encouraged women's preaching. Ellen Ranyard's (1810–75) mission gave new opportunities to working-class 'Bible women'. Catherine Marsh's (1819–1912) work among the railway navvies was a daring extension of women's roles. A growing number of women went overseas as missionaries in their own right. The Bristol Unitarian, Mary Carpenter (1807–77), overcame her initial nervousness and began to give papers at conferences on juvenile delinquency; like Elizabeth Fry, she had become an expert.[80] Such developments were only possible because the ground had been prepared in a period often seen as a time of contraction and the closing down of opportunities.

Conclusion

It is no longer so common for historians of religion and historians of women and gender to operate in parallel universes, reluctant to acknowledge the existence, let alone the interdependence, of the others' area of study. Women's history is now far less likely to be written from an entirely secular perspective, which inevitably downgrades the religious experiences of women.[81] Gail Malmgreen's plea for feminist historians to try to understand 'the mental universe of the no doubt substantial majority of women who were believers' is being heeded, and serious attention is paid to David Hempton and Myrtle Hill's assertion that Evangelicalism was more significant than feminism in expanding women's horizons.[82] But why should this generalization be confined to Evangelicalism, when Catholic nuns and Anglican sisters were becoming more numerous and active? The truth is that a large proportion of eighteenth- and nineteenth-century feminists, from Mary Astell to Josephine Butler (1828–1906), were convinced Christians, while a far greater number, who would never have thought of themselves as propounding women's rights, found in their relationship with God a validation of their separate identity and integrity.

However, it would be misleading to lump all women together in a Whiggish story of progress and advancement towards the sunlight uplands of religious (though not political) equality. Like men, women were divided by denomination, ideology, temperament, and class. Anglicans and Non-conformists, Catholics and Protestants were frequently in bitter opposition to each other. Traditionally minded women were often discomfited by those more assertive women who seemed to be transgressing gender boundaries. Aristocratic and middle-class 'ladies' could insensitively impose their values on working-class 'women'; in convents, plebeian lay-sisters acted as servants to the middle- and upper-class nuns. Given the kaleidoscope of separate and sometimes conflicting stories, perspectives, and representations, it is impossible to construct a single narrative that encompasses the experiences of all women in this period. The Bible reinforced ancient notions of women's inferiority, yet gave them permission to operate in an expanding sphere of philanthropy, humanitarian campaigning, and missionary endeavour. It exhorted women to silence and submission, but also gave them role models of activators and leaders. Religion provided an opportunity for self-fulfilment and self-expression. It dispensed consolation and sometimes legitimated protest. It empowered and liberated at the same time as it constrained and suppressed. Feminist historians and historians of religion have somehow to construct their narratives within these polarities.

Notes

1 G. Eliot, *Adam Bede*, Oxford, 1998, pp. 27–8.
2 K. Hughes, *George Eliot: The Last Victorian*, London, 1998, pp. 288–9. For Elizabeth Evans, see D. Valenze, *Prophetic Sons and Daughters: Female Preaching and Popular Religion in Industrial England*, Princeton, NJ, 1985, pp. 64–73.
3 Eliot, *Adam Bede*, p. 539.
4 H. McLeod, *Religion and Society in England, 1850–1914*, Basingstoke, 1996, pp. 12, 45–7, 67.
5 J. Walsh, 'Origins of the Evangelical revival', in J. D. Walsh and G. V. Bennett (eds), *Essays in Modern English Church History*, London, 1966, pp. 132–62; I. Bradley, *The Call to Seriousness: The Evangelical Impact on the Victorians*, London, 1976; E. Jay, *The Religion of the Heart: Anglican Evangelicalism and the Nineteenth-Century Novel*, Oxford, 1979; D. W. Bebbington, *Evangelicalism in Modern Britain: A History from the 1730s to the 1980s*, London, 1989; W. R. Ward, 'The Evangelical revival in eighteenth-century Britain', in S. Gilley and W. J. Sheils (eds), *A History of Religion in Britain: Practice and Belief from Pre-Roman Times to the Present*, Oxford, 1994, pp. 252–72; M. A. Noll, D. W. Bebbington and G. A. Rawlyk (eds), *Evangelicalism: Comparative Studies of Popular Protestantism in North America, the British Isles, and Beyond, 1700–1900*, Oxford, 1994.
6 See J. Rendall, *The Origins of Modern Feminism: Women in Britain, France and the United States, 1780–1860*, London, 1985; Valenze, *Prophetic Sons and Daughters*; L. Davidoff and C. Hall, *Family Fortunes: Men and Women of the English Middle Class, 1780–1850*, London, 1987; C. Field, 'Adam and Eve: gender in the English Free Church constituency, 1650–1980', *Journal of Ecclesiastical History*, 1993, vol. 44, pp. 63–79; S. Gill, *Women and the Church of England: From the Eighteenth Century to the Present*, London, 1994; P. Mack, 'Religious Dissenters in Enlightenment England', *History Workshop Journal*, 2000, vol. 47, pp. 1–23; S. Morgan (ed.), *Women, Religion and Feminism in Britain, 1750–1900*, Basingstoke, 2000.
7 See *Essays and Reviews*, 2nd edn, London, 1860, as cited in O. Chadwick, *The Victorian Church*, 2 vols, London, 1970, vol. ii, pp. 75–90; G. Parsons (ed.), *Religion in Victorian Britain*, III: *Controversies*, Manchester, 1988, *passim*.
8 See J. Murray, 'Gender attitudes and the contribution of women to evangelism and ministry in the nineteenth century', in J. Wolffe (ed.), *Evangelical Faith and Public Zeal: Evangelicals and Society in Britain, 1780–1980*, London, 1995, p. 100.
9 As quoted in Valenze, *Prophetic Sons and Daughters*, p. 150.
10 Ibid., pp. 35–7. It was applied, for example, to the Countess of Huntingdon both as a compliment and a rebuke. In 1748, the Methodist, George Whitefield, pronounced her to be 'indeed a mother in Israel', though twenty years later an exasperated John Berridge admonished his autocratic patron: 'You threaten me, Madam, like a Pope, not like a Mother in Israel.' As quoted in B. Stanley Schlenther, *Queen of the Methodists: The Countess of Huntingdon and the Eighteenth-Century Crisis of Faith and Society*, Bishop Aukland, 1997, pp. 39, 102.

11 G. Malmgreen, 'Domestic discords: women and the family in east Cheshire Methodism, 1750–1830', in J. Obelkevich, L. Roper and R. Samuel (eds), *Disciplines of Faith: Studies in Religion, Politics and Patriarchy*, London, 1987; H. McLeod, *Religion and Society in England*, pp. 156–68; H. McLeod, *Religion and the People of Western Europe, 1789–1989*, Oxford, 1997, pp. 33–5; C. G. Brown, *The Death of Christian Britain: Understanding Secularisation, 1800–2000*, London, 2001, pp. 58–87; B. Taylor, *Mary Wollstonecraft and the Feminist Imagination*, Cambridge, 2003, pp. 99–102.

12 As quoted in M. P. Jones, 'From "The State of my Soul" to "Exalted Piety": women's voices in the *Arminian/Methodist Magazine*', in R. N. Swanson (ed.), *Gender and the Christian Religion, Studies in Church History*, vol. 34, 1998, p. 282.

13 W. Wilberforce, *A Practical View of the Prevailing Religious System of Professed Christians in the Higher and Middle Classes . . . Contrasted with Real Christianity*, London, 1797, p. 434.

14 Davidoff and Hall, *Family Fortunes*; A. Clark, *The Struggle for the Breeches: Gender and the Making of the British Working Class*, Berkeley, CA, 1995.

15 For Sarah Martin, see F. K. Prochaska, *Women and Philanthropy in Nineteenth-Century England*, Oxford, 1980, pp. 164–8.

16 L. Wilson, *Constrained by Zeal: Female Spirituality Amongst Nonconformists, 1825–75*, London, 2000, p. 1; Morgan, *Women, Religion and Feminism*, pp. 15–16.

17 R. Perry, *The Celebrated Mary Astell: An Early English Feminist*, Chicago, 1986.

18 Quoted in P. Wesley Chilcote, *John Wesley and the Women Preachers of Early Methodism*, Metuchen, NJ, 1991, p. 19.

19 C. Podmore, *The Moravian Church in England, 1728–1760*, Oxford, 1998, p. 4.

20 For the Quakers, see A. Davies, *The Quakers in English Society, 1655–1725*, Oxford, 2000; S. Wright, *Friends in York: The Dynamics of Quaker Revival, 1780–1860*, Keele, 1995.

21 See K. Gleadle, *The Early Feminists: Radical Unitarians and the Emergence of the Women's Rights Movement, 1831–51*, New York, 1995; K. Gleadle, 'British women and radical politics in the late nonconformist Enlightenment, *c.*1780–1830', in A. Vickery (ed.), *Women, Privilege, and Power: British Politics, 1750 to the Present*, Stanford, CA, 2001, pp. 146–9; R. Watts, *Gender, Power and the Unitarians in England, 1760–1860*, London, 1998; R. Watts, 'Rational religion and feminism: the challenge of Unitarianism in the nineteenth century', in Morgan (ed.), *Women, Religion and Feminism*, pp. 39–52.

22 For Elizabeth Gaskell, see J. Uglow, *Elizabeth Gaskell: A Habit of Stories*, London, 1993.

23 Out of a total population of nearly 18 million in England and Wales in 1851, 3.53 million (19.7 per cent) attended Anglican services and 3.479 million (19.4 per cent) attended the main Protestant dissenting churches on 'Census Sunday' (30 March 1851): see E. Evans, *The Forging of the Modern State: Early Industrial Britain, 1783–1870*, London, 2001, p. 536.

24 Out of a Scottish population of nearly 2.9 million, 351,000 attended Church of Scotland worship on the morning of Census Sunday and 292,000 worshipped with the Free Church. For the circumstances surrounding the Disruption, see S. J. Brown, *Thomas Chalmers and the Godly Commonwealth in Scotland*, Oxford, 1982.

25 There was no official religious census in Ireland but it has been estimated that in 1834 membership of the Church of Ireland was a mere 850,000 or 10.7 per cent of

a population of nearly 8 million: R. Currie, A. Gilbert and L. Horsley, *Churches and Churchgoers: Patterns of Church Growth in the British Isles since 1700*, Oxford, 1977, pp. 219–21.

26 In England and Wales 383,630 Roman Catholics attended mass on Census Sunday, the great majority of them Irish immigrants.

27 The Roman Catholic Relief Act (1778) allowed Catholics to own property legally, gave them access to the armed forces and abolished some of the penal legislation against priests. The Act of 1791 licensed Catholic worship. Three further Acts applied to Ireland. The Act of 1778 allowed Catholics to take 999-year leases and to inherit lands on the same terms as Protestants did. The Act of 1782 allowed Catholics who took the oath of allegiance to buy and lease freehold land, and relaxed laws concerning the registration of priests, the carrying of arms and education. The Act of 1793 gave the vote to Catholic tenants and allowed Catholics to occupy most civil and military posts. For the Catholic community, see M. A. Mullett, *Catholics in Britain and Ireland, 1558–1829*, Basingstoke, 1998; J. Bossy, *The English Catholic Community, 1570–1850*, London, 1975; E. Norman, *The English Catholic Church in the Nineteenth Century*, Oxford, 1984.

28 B. C. Foley, 'Ann Fenwick né Benson (1724–1777) heiress, foundress of Hornby Mission', in B. C. Foley (ed.) *Some People of the Penal Times*, Lancaster, 1991; Mullett, *Catholics in Britain and Ireland*, pp. 141–2. I am grateful to Professor Mullett for sending me a photocopy of Bishop Foley's booklet.

29 M. Weber, *The Sociology of Religion*, trans. E. Fischoff, London, 1965, pp. 104–5.

30 As quoted in J. Burge, *Women Preachers in Community: Sarah Ryan, Sarah Crosby, Mary Bosanquet*, Peterborough, 1996, p. 18.

31 Ibid., pp. 19–20.

32 As quoted in Chilcote, *John Wesley*, p. 236.

33 Valenze, *Prophetic Sons and Daughters*.

34 Ibid., p. 97. Bourne went on to justify women's preaching by citing I Corinthians 1:27: 'God hath chosen the foolish things of the world to confound the wise.' It is not clear whether this reflected a traditionalist view of women's capacities or was a rhetorical strategy designed to disarm his opponents on their own territory.

35 Ibid., pp. 140–58; D. Shorney, ' "Women may preach but men must govern"; gender roles in the growth and development of the Bible Christian denomination', in Swanson (ed.), *Gender and the Christian Religion*, pp. 309–22.

36 See R. Labouchere, *Deborah Darby of Coalbrookdale, 1754–1810*, York, 1993; R. Labouchere, *Abiah Darby of Coalbrookdale, 1716–1793*, York, 1998.

37 Chadwick, *The Victorian Church*, vol. 1, p. 423.

38 See C. Garrett, *Spirit Possession and Popular Religion: From the Camisards to the Shakers*, Baltimore, MD, 1987, pp. 160–241; T. J. Wenger, 'Female Christ and feminist foremother: the many lives of Ann Lee', *Journal of Feminist Studies in Religion*, Fall 2002, vol. 18, pp. 5–32; J. K. Hopkins, *A Woman to Deliver Her People: Joanna Southcott and English Millenarianism in an Era of Revolution*, Austin, TX, 1982.

39 Carter, *Anglican Evangelicals*, p. 315.

40 E. Kent Brown (ed.), *Studies in Women and Religion: Women of Mr Wesley's Methodism* (special issue), 1983, vol. 11, pp. 131–2; H. M. Jones, 'A spiritual aristocracy: female patrons of religion in eighteenth-century Britain', in D. W. Lovegrove (ed.), *The Rise of the Laity in Evangelical Protestantism*, London, 2002, pp. 85–94.

41 R. Strong, 'Coronets and altars: aristocratic women and men's support for the

Oxford Movement in Scotland during the 1840s', in Swanson (ed.), *Gender and the Christian Religion*, pp. 391–403.

42 M. Peckham Magray, *The Transforming Power of the Nuns: Women, Religion, and Cultural Change in Ireland, 1750–1900*, New York, 1998, pp. 6–9.

43 As quoted in S. O'Brien, '*Terra Incognita*: the nun in nineteenth-century England', *Past and Present*, 1988, no. 121, pp. 136, 138.

44 As quoted in Gill, *Women and the Church*, p. 148.

45 Ibid., p. 159. For Priscilla Seddon, see T. J. Williams, *Priscilla Lydia Sellon: The Restorer after Three Centuries of the Religious Life in the Church of England*, London, 1965; S. Gill, 'The power of Christian ladyhood: Priscilla Lydia Sellon and the creation of Anglican sisterhoods', in S. Mews (ed.), *Modern Religious Rebels: Presented to John Kent*, London,1993, pp. 144–65.

46 S. Mumm, *Stolen Daughters, Virgin Mothers: Anglican Sisterhoods in Victorian Britain*, Leicester, 1999, p. xi; J. Shelton Reed, *Glorious Battle: The Cultural Politics of Victorian Anglo-Catholicism*, Nashville, TN, 1996.

47 The first hospital trained nurses in Britain came from the sisterhood of St John's House in London in 1848: C. Helmstadter, 'Building a nursing service: respectability and efficiency in Victorian England', *Albion*, 2004, vol. 35, pp. 590–621.

48 For Tonna, see C. L. Krueger, *The Reader's Repentance: Women Preachers, Women Writers, and Nineteenth-Century Social Discourse*, Chicago, 1992.

49 McLeod, *Religion and Society in England*, p. 22. For female philanthropy, see Prochaska, *Women and Philanthropy*; E. Janes Yeo, *The Contest for Social Science: Relations and Representations of Gender and Class*, London, 1996.

50 See T. W. Laqueur, *Religion and Respectability: Sunday Schools and Working-Class Culture, 1780–1850*, New Haven, CT, 1976, pp. 24–5; W. Keutsch, 'Teaching the poor: Sarah Trimmer, God's own handmaid', *Bulletin of the John Rylands University Library of Manchester*, 1994, vol. 76, no. 3, 43–57; A. Stott, *Hannah More: The First Victorian*, Oxford, 2003, Chapter 5, *passim*.

51 J. Pollock, *Wilberforce*, London, 1977, p. 53.

52 K. Corfield, 'Eliza Heyrick: radical Quaker', in G. Malmgreen (ed.), *Religion in the Lives of English Women, 1760–1930*, London, 1986, pp. 41–67; L. Billington and R. Billington, '"A burning zeal for righteousness": women in the British anti-slavery movement, 1820–1860', in J. Rendall (ed.), *Equal or Different: Women's Politics, 1800–1914*, Oxford, 1987, pp. 82–111; C. Midgley, *Women Against Slavery: The British Campaigns, 1780–1870*, London, 1992; M. Ferguson, *Subject to Others: British Women Writers and Colonial Slavery, 1670–1834*, London, 1992.

53 See A. Twells, '"Let us begin well at home": class, ethnicity and Christian motherhood in the writing of Hannah Kilham, 1774–1832', in E. Janes Yeo (ed.), *Radical Femininity: Women's Self-Representation in the Public Sphere*, Manchester, 1998, pp. 34–40.

54 A. Stott, 'Hannah More and the Blagdon controversy, 1799–1802', *Journal of Ecclesiastical History*, 2000, vol. 51, pp. 319–46; Stott, *Hannah More*, Chapter 11.

55 'Prologue' [unpaginated], in J. Rose, *Elizabeth Fry: A Biography*, London, 1980. See also A. Summers, *Female Lives, Moral States: Women, Religion, and Public Life in Britain, 1800–1930*, Newbury, 2000, Chapter 2; A. van Drenth and F. de Haan, *The Rise of Caring Power: Elizabeth Fry and Josephine Butler in Britain and the Netherlands*, Amsterdam, 1999.

56 As quoted in Stott, *Hannah More*, p. 323.

57 Gill, *Women and the Church of England*, pp. 46–7.

58 W. Canton, *A History of the British and Foreign Bible Society*, London, 1904, p. 61. For the ladies' associations in Ireland, see D. Hempton and M. Hill, *Evangelical Protestantism in Ulster Society, 1740–1890*, London, 1992, pp. 138–9.

59 As quoted in R. H. Martin, *Evangelicals United: Ecumenical Stirrings in Pre-Victorian Britain, 1795–1830*, Metuchen, NJ, 1983, p. 82. See also Prochaska, *Women and Philanthropy*, pp. 25–8.

60 Midgley, *Women Against Slavery*, Chapter 3.

61 R. I. and S. Wilberforce, *The Life of William Wilberforce*, 5 vols, London, 1838, vol. 5, pp. 264–5.

62 Midgley, *Women Against Slavery*, pp. 103–18.

63 Ibid., p. 40.

64 Ibid., pp. 65–71.

65 See V. Cunningham, '"God and nature intended you for a missionary's wife": Mary Hill, Jane Eyre, and other missionary women in the 1840s', in F. Bowle, D. Kirkwood, and S. Aredner (eds), *Women and Missions: Past and Present. Anthropological and Historical Perceptions*, Oxford, 1993; Murray, 'Gender Attitudes', pp. 97–113; Twells, '"Let us begin well at home"', pp. 42–5; S. Thorne, *Congregational Missions and the Making of an Imperial Culture in Nineteenth-Century England*, Stanford, CA, 1999.

66 Labouchere, *Abiah Darby of Coalbrookdale*, p. xi.

67 Podmore, *Moravian Church*, pp. 128–34.

68 B. Taylor, 'Religion, radicalism, and fantasy', *History Workshop Journal*, 1995, vol. 39, pp. 102–12; P. Mack, 'Religious dissenters in Enlightenment England', *History Workshop Journal*, 2000, vol. 47, pp. 1–23.

69 I. Bradley, *Abide with Me: The World of Victorian Hymns*, London, 1997, p. 90. See also J. R. Watson, 'Quiet angels: some women hymn writers', in A. Hogan and A. Bradstock (eds), *Women of Faith in Victorian Culture: Reassessing the Angel in the House*, Basingstoke, 1998, pp. 128–44; M. Maison, '"Thine, Only Thine!" women hymn writers in Britain, 1760–1835', in Malmgreen, *Religion in the Lives of English Women*, pp. 20–36.

70 *Hours of Sorrow: or Thoughts in Verse*, London, 1836, p. 130.

71 Watson, 'Quiet angels', p. 131.

72 *The Life of Mother Margaret Mary Hallahan*, London, 1869, pp. 73–7, 111–14; E. Norman, *The English Catholic Church in the Nineteenth Century*, Oxford, 1984, pp. 163–4. For the cult of the Virgin, see C. M. Engelhardt, 'The paradigmatic angel in the house: the Virgin Mary and Victorian Anglicans', in Hogan and Bradstock (eds), *Women of Faith in Victorian Culture*, pp. 159–71; McLeod, *Religion and Society*, pp. 44–5; J. Singleton, 'The Virgin Mary and religious conflict in Victorian Britain', *Journal of Ecclesiastical History*, 1992, vol. 43, 16–34.

73 As quoted in R. Houlbrooke, *Death, Religion and the Family in England, 1480–1750*, Oxford, 2000, p. 186; W. Roberts, *Memoirs of the Life and Correspondence of Mrs Hannah More*, 4 vols, London, 1834, vol. 2, pp. 326–7.

74 Valenze, *Prophetic Sons and Daughters*, pp. 150–8; McLeod, *Religion and Society*, p. 163.

75 For Ellis, see H. Twycross Martin, 'The drunkard, the brute, and the paterfamilias: the temperance fiction of the early Victorian writer Sarah Stickney Ellis', in Hogan and Bradstock (eds), *Women of Faith in Victorian Culture*, pp. 6–30; for James, see Davidoff and Hall, *Family Fortunes, passim*.

76 As quoted in J. Daggers, 'The Victorian female civilising mission and women's aspirations towards priesthood in the Church of England', *Women's History Review*, 2001, vol. 10, p. 651.

77 M. Weber, *The Theory of Social and Economic Organization*, trans. A. R. Henderson and T. Parsons, London, 1947, pp. 334–42; Weber, *Sociology of Religion*, p. 104.

78 P. Corfield, *Power and the Professions in Britain, 1700–1850*, London, 1995; Summers, *Female Lives*, pp. 7–18.

79 See, for example, C. Hall, 'The early formation of Victorian domestic ideology', in S. Burman (ed.), *Fit Work for Women*, London, 1979, pp. 15–32; Davidoff and Hall, *Family Fortunes*; M. Dresser, 'Sisters and brethren: power, propriety, and gender among the Bristol Moravians, 1746–1833', *Social History*, 1996, vol. 21, pp. 304–29. For a counter-argument, see A. Vickery, 'Golden age to separate spheres? A review of the categories and chronology of English women's history', *Historical Journal*, 1993, no. 36, pp. 383–414.

80 Watts, 'Rational religion and feminism', pp. 39–52.

81 But see the lack of a chapter on religion in the otherwise excellent J. Purvis (ed.), *Women's History: Britain, 1850–1945*, London, 1995. For a recent example of the incorporation of religious insights into feminist historiography, see H. Mathers, 'The Evangelical spirituality of a Victorian feminist: Josephine Butler, 1828–1906', *Journal of Ecclesiastical History*, 2001, vol. 25, pp. 282–312.

82 Malmgreen, *Religion in the Lives of English Women*, p. 3; Hempton and Hill, *Evangelical Protestantism*, p. 130.

Chapter Six

 è❧

Women and work

Hannah Barker

Women's work is not an easy topic for historical research. The low status of female labour, coupled with the generally humble origins of women workers, mean that they are poorly recorded in historical sources. This was true even at the end of our period, when the census promised to record the occupation of every member of the population. In reality, women's labour often went unnoticed, as census returns were completed by male heads of household who tended to describe their womenfolk as dependants rather than workers.[1] The situation is further complicated as women's work was more likely to be seasonal than men's and often involved more than one occupation.[2] In rural Aberdeenshire during the eighteenth century, for example, women would work as weavers and knitters at the same time that they earned money from dulse-gathering, kelp-making, fish-selling, peat-digging, and the annual harvest.[3]

Not only is uncovering evidence of women's work difficult, but defining what constituted work is also problematic.[4] This chapter, not uncontroversially, assumes it to mean work that generated income: a definition which excludes some forms of women's work, such as housework. This distinction makes it hard to measure women's work in family enterprises, since these were often based in the home.[5] In such circumstances it is difficult to say where 'home' work stopped and work for the market began. Focusing only on paid work (for monetary reward or in kind) arguably undervalues women's work as a whole. Yet this is a distinction that we are used to drawing in modern-day society, and one which eighteenth- and nineteenth-century contemporaries would have found familiar. Moreover, despite the fact that most women in Britain during our period would have engaged in numerous unpaid domestic tasks, most did work for monetary income as well, and thus were 'visible' as women workers, even if this view of their working lives is a partial one.

Continuity and change

Arguments that the eighteenth century witnessed the demise of a 'golden age' of women's work have rightly received short shrift in recent years. As Amanda Vickery has pointed out, there is little evidence that early modern capitalism robbed women of the work opportunities and public liberties formerly enjoyed under a 'wholesome family economy'. Such a model of decline and fall, she states, 'rests on the dubious assumption of a lost egalitarian Eden, which has proved elusive to empirical research'.[6] This point was made convincingly by the medieval historian, Judith Bennett, who argued that women's work was low in status, skill, and pay from the thirteenth century to the present day.[7]

Few modern historians still maintain that the 'pre-capitalist' economy was any sort of economic idyll for women. However, the idea that the period 1700–1850 witnessed both a significant narrowing in opportunities for women's work and a lowering in its status is still widely held. Bridget Hill, for example, mourned the decline of the family economy in the eighteenth century and argued that women were both economically and socially marginalized by industrial development.[8] Deborah Valenze has also claimed that industrialization progressively side-lined women workers,[9] while Katrina Honeyman and Jordan Goodman have suggested that the mid-nineteenth century witnessed a period of 'gender conflict' when male workers acted to exclude women from the workplace following a period of female advance.[10] Others have linked nineteenth- and twentieth-century capitalism with patriarchy, describing them as dual structures in the creation of women's oppression. It has been claimed that the industrial revolution helped to promote separate spheres ideology, and with it such developments as restrictive labour practices and campaigns for the family wage, which served to redefine and revitalize patriarchal forces.[11]

As such arguments suggest, many accounts of women's work between 1700 and 1850 are dominated by discussions of the emergence of modern capitalism, specifically in the shape of the agricultural and industrial revolutions. Yet we should be wary of assuming that women's work in Britain was transformed in any sudden or uniform way. Indeed, many economic historians argue that this period was marked as much by continuity as by revolutionary change, so that the very use of the term 'revolution' is called into question. It appears that both the commercialization of agriculture and the process of industrialization which this period witnessed were more gradual and less uniform in impact than the term 'revolution' suggests. Instead, the changes that took place differed greatly between regions, industries, and over time,[12] while working patterns altered in diverse ways across the country. The industrial revolution did not result in the propulsion of the bulk of the workforce into factories,[13] nor did changes in agriculture mean that all farming was subject to vast increases in productivity and narrow regional specialization within a matter of years.

But this is not the same as saying that little altered, and that, as a consequence, a model of continuity and of slow, almost imperceptible change is the best way of describing women's work in this period. During the past few years, the work of Maxine Berg and Pat Hudson has done much to force a reconsideration of the 'gradualist' approach towards the industrial revolution. They have argued that the current orthodoxy underplays economic and social transformation during this period, and that the aggregate quantitative indicators used by historians ignore the very real transformation apparent in certain sectors of the economy and in particular regions.[14] Moreover, Berg has suggested that the emphasis placed by economic historians on continuity might have serious implications, specifically in terms of the history of women's work. She argues that the indices used to measure economic change have ignored the impact of women's labour and wages, and, as such, may well exclude many of the high-productivity industries that experienced the greatest transformations in terms of technical processes or organization, since these largely employed women and children.[15] Berg's examination of women in factories suggests that, at certain times and in certain industries, changes during the eighteenth and nineteenth centuries actually increased women's opportunities in the workplace.

In terms of agricultural change, whenever one dates any revolution or revolutions, it is clear that agriculture on a national level showed a significant increase in output after about 1700, and that it was able to sustain that output in the face of ever-increasing demand. At the same time, fewer people worked in this sector, so that one must assume huge leaps in the productivity of labour. The commercialization of agriculture was marked in particular regions: the Midlands and the South-east of England, East Anglia, and central and southern Scotland, during the eighteenth century; and, by the end of our period, other regions, such as north-eastern Scotland, had also experienced great change.[16] As we shall see, it does seem that some developments – such as crop specialization and the enclosure of common land – had a greater impact on women than men.[17]

The need to recognize the diversity of women's experiences, over time and between different regions and industries – in both rural and urban contexts – is brought out most clearly in the work of Pamela Sharpe on eighteenth- and early nineteenth-century Essex. She argues that here the development of capitalism had contradictory effects on working women in the county: with expanding niches of economic opportunity in the fashion trades, some areas of agriculture, and in service, but contracting opportunities in the wool trade and in the majority of agricultural work.[18]

Work in the countryside

Agricultural work

Farm labour in Britain has traditionally been divided into men's and women's work, with women who laboured for pay typically receiving one-third to one-half of a male wage: suggesting a long-standing presumption that female work was less valuable than men's.[19] There was, however, overlap between male and female work, and women would perform 'men's' tasks particularly when labour was in short supply, while what work men and women did was subject to a good deal of regional variation. By and large, men were primarily concerned with ploughing, reaping, and mowing, and caring for horses and oxen. Women performed a wider range of tasks, including planting seeds, controlling the dairy, keeping chickens and pigs, running cottage gardens, organizing the home, and, in the case of wealthier women, managing servants. Both men and women traditionally took part in the harvest. In Scotland, women were described by an Elgin farmer as, 'our neatest cutters', and they were regularly claimed to be better and quicker than men.[20] Finally, in coastal and marsh areas, women were also involved in fishing. Although they did not tend to go on boats, their labour was crucial to fishing communities throughout our period. The range of their activities becomes clear in a report from nineteenth-century Banffshire:

> The fisher wives . . . assist in dragging the boats on the beach, and in launching them. They sometimes, in frosty weather, and at unseasonable hours, carry their husbands on board, to keep them dry. They receive fish from the boats, carry them, fresh or after salting to their customers, and to market at the distance, sometimes of many miles.[21]

These Banffshire women worked as part of family teams, processing and selling their catch in a manner that would have changed little since the seventeenth century. In other parts of Britain, working practices changed radically, however. The eighteenth and nineteenth centuries witnessed a significant rise in the numbers of landless and wage-dependent rural workers. The second half of the eighteenth century may have also witnessed a decline in the employment of agricultural servants. According to Ann Kussmaul, this began in the south and east of England and spread later to the west.[22] These developments affected men and women in different ways, but the changes brought about by the commercialization of agriculture did not profoundly affect the traditional gendered division of labour and women continued to work as servants, wage labourers, and on family farms.

Most research on women's agricultural work in England has focused on the south and east. In his examination of this region, Keith Snell depicts the marginalization of female labour.[23] His findings, based on settlement examinations, suggest that growing specialization in farming, and a focus on grain production in particular, led women's work to become less important and increasingly seasonal from around the mid-eighteenth century. As men began to dominate harvesting, women were restricted in spring and summer to jobs such as weeding and haymaking, and to subsidiary roles at harvest, as gatherers, tyers, and gleaners. According to Snell, these developments were particularly marked in the South-east of England; he argues that in the west, where pastoral farming predominated, women's work did not become marginalized to the same extent. A similar tale is told by Michael Roberts, who describes how the growing use of the scythe in England to mow wheat and rye from the late eighteenth century further contributed to the marginalization of women's work. Whereas women had previously worked as reapers using sickles, the heavier scythe became the tool of strong men. Women were restricted to acting as followers and rakers – jobs demanding less skill and receiving lower pay.[24]

Nicola Verdon has recently suggested a very different vision of early nineteenth-century women's employment in agriculture, based on a study of 1834 Poor Law Reports. Unlike Snell, she has found evidence for women's continued involvement in farming in areas of the South-east, such as Sussex and Kent, which included harvesting. Female involvement was highest, she claims, in the north and east of England. For Verdon, who did not detect markedly higher levels of female employment in agriculture in the South-west, neither Snell's north–south divide, nor the split between west and east, were as clear.[25] Her conclusions echo those of other historians. Sharpe, for instance, has found little evidence for a shift in the sexual division of labour in Essex agriculture during the eighteenth century. Although there were changes in the opportunities for farm work open to women – most notably in the decline of hop growing – she argues that the greatest change for rural women was the decline in spinning as a form of employment.[26] Ivy Pinchbeck noted that women in the north of England were commonly employed in agricultural work under the bondage system, whereas in eastern counties they were increasingly employed in the nineteenth century as day labourers in agricultural gangs. In Northumberland, where men were increasingly involved in heavy industry that offered few jobs for women, women engaged in heavy farm work until the end of the nineteenth century.[27] Wage books from the county confirm that women were frequently employed as reapers and, in 1796, George Cully noted, 'our girls are all employed in agriculture, hoeing, haymaking and reaping etc.'[28]

Women agricultural out-workers, or bondagers, were a feature of the farm workforce not only in Northumberland, but also in south-east

Scotland, where women also worked in agriculture as part of family teams.[29] In Scotland, much of the population was engaged in farming during our period – often farming of a less commercialized nature than that found in parts of England. Women were particularly prominent in agricultural work in south-east Scotland. In the mid-nineteenth century, perhaps 26 per cent of the total permanent workforce in this sector was female, as compared to only 6 per cent in England.[30] During the late eighteenth century, it appears that women's opportunities to engage in agricultural work increased in Scotland. Improved crop rotations created new work peaks, which helped to offset periods of traditional seasonal unemployment, while specialist dairy production in the west-central lowlands also brought more jobs for women.[31] In the nineteenth century, R. A. Houston has argued (following Roberts) that while changes in agricultural technology may have meant that women became more marginalized in Scottish agriculture, as men came to dominate newer agricultural practices such as the use of the scythe and the two-horse plough,[32] women and young girls were prominent among highland seasonal workers from the 1790s onward, and constituted the majority of migrant harvesters who trekked to the south of the country to work for cash wages and support their highland crofting families. Despite the competition from Irish harvesters from the 1820s, William Howatson claims the number of highland workers involved in the 'hairst', or harvest, continued to increase to the mid-nineteenth century.[33]

In Wales, too, David Howell notes that female field labourers were common until the late nineteenth century, especially in the south.[34] Here, it was noted by an English visitor in 1799, women continued to do all 'the most arduous exertions of husbandry, and they are very commonly seen either driving the horses affixed to the plough, or leading those which draw the harrow'.[35] A writer describing Cardinganshire in the 1790s recalled how 'strong women worked in the fields during the hay havest, &c for three-pence a day, finding their own breakfast and dinner'.[36] Women from parts of rural Wales, and Cardiganshire, in particular, travelled every spring and summer to London to seek employment in market gardens. This practice was well established by the mid-eighteenth century and did not die out until the 1840s. These women were driven both by poverty and the unpleasant nature of alternative employments closer to home, such as peat carrying.[37]

One development associated with the agricultural revolution that did affect rural women particularly harshly was the process by which common land was privatized or 'enclosed' during our period. Enclosure denied women the ability to 'glean' – a means by which they could contribute to the family economy by gathering wild fruit and nuts, collecting fallen grain and beans following harvest, and scavenging for wood and other natural resources. This could constitute substantial quantities of food and fuel.

King has estimated that as much as 13 per cent of an annual household income could be derived from this source. Gleaning was almost exclusively a female occupation and may have been more prevalent in central and southern England, and the border counties of Wales, than in northern England or Scotland.[38] Enclosure also denied the rural poor the right to graze their animals on common land. Since women were the primary exploiters of common rights, this affected them more than men, although the loss impacted on whole families.[39] The decline in gleaning was largely the result of government legislation, although in early nineteenth-century Glamorgan, women's customary access to glean in the harvested fields was usurped by male migratory workers from Cardiganshire.[40]

Valenze's work on the dairy industry has described an additional area where women's work was marginalized during our period. It has shown how increasing demands for dairy products led to the rise of cheese factors who interfered with the work of women in dairies. A new scientific discourse that stressed female irrationality and subservience to traditional practices led to claims that farmers' wives, who had traditionally managed dairy work, were unable to introduce proper scientific methods and, as a result, could not produce consistent or reliable products. The result of such changes was that women were less likely to run dairies, as male managers took over; they were, however, still found working in the far more menial roles of dairy-maids, as well as running the dairies of smaller family farms.[41] Leonore Davidoff and Catherine Hall have suggested that a general trend in agriculture to supersede craft training and experience, compounded with the exclusion of women from a more scientific culture, as described by Valenze, made women less likely to participate in other scientific farming advances, such as the use of new machinery, chemical fertilizers, and new methods of breeding.[42]

Mining

Like female agricultural workers, women miners appear to have offended middle-class sensibilities by virtue of their physical appearance and dress.[43] For much of our period, women commonly worked underground in mining, although their involvement differed widely from region to region and among the different branches of the mining industry. In coalmines, most women were employed as bearers, carrying coal from the face to the surface. In pits in Bo'ness in West Lothian during the 1760s, women outnumbered male workers 2 to 1. In the western Lowlands, however, female mine labour was less common, as men and boys were usually employed as bearers.[44] Most female mine-workers were employed as parts of family teams – labouring under the control of fathers and brothers. This was the case in Welsh lead mines[45] and in most coal and tin mines. During the early nineteenth century, women formed less than 5 per cent of the total mine-working population. Female mine labour was geographically concentrated, though, so that in certain areas they formed an important part of the workforce. In Pembrokeshire they comprised 30 per cent of mine workers, and 25 per cent in Midlothian and East Lothian.[46] Elsewhere, the number of women in this sector declined from the late eighteenth century.

Robert Shoemaker points out that, in contrast to other industries, expansion in mining was accompanied by a reduction in the number of women workers.[47] This was the case in North-east England and the Midlands.[48] It seems women left mining – with its fourteen-hour days and unpleasant and dangerous working conditions – if they had a choice of alternative employment.[49] It was also the result of the 1842 Mines Act that led to the direct exclusion of women working underground. The Act was largely pushed through by middle-class reformers who were horrified by the notion of women and children working in such physically, and, they believed, morally, dangerous conditions.[50] Jane Humphries has discussed the apparent paradox of male colliers supporting a piece of legislation that impacted on the family wage and meant that the men had to work harder and for longer hours.[51] Jane Mark-Lawson and Anne Witz have, on the other hand, concluded that in areas where the family-labour system operated, and female labour was employed, men did not in fact support exclusionary legislation. In eastern Scotland, for example, where women constituted 35 per cent of the workforce, a sub-commissioner informed the Parliamentary Committee that the legislation would be universally condemned.[52] Even after the Act came into force, women continued to work above ground. They remained a presence, albeit a reduced one, not only in coalmining, but also in tin and copper mining in Cornwall and Devon.[53]

Proto-industrialization

Proto-industrialization is a term used to describe the rapid expansion of domestic handicraft production in the early eighteenth century, stimulated by the development of a worldwide market for consumer goods.[54] Women and children were employed in this type of manufacturing in dispropor-tionate numbers since much of the production was organized under the 'putting-out system' by merchants who demanded infinitely expandable supplies of cheap labour. It frequently centred around textiles and involved women working as spinners, silk throwers, lace-makers, and framework knitters.[55] Proto-industrialization was a largely rural phenomenon. In areas where fewer women were found in agricultural work, participation in such activities was higher. Thus, a high proportion of women could be found in straw-plaiting and lace-making in the south Midlands.[56] In Scotland, female involvement in commercial spinning and woollen manufacture was high and, in the first half of the eighteenth century, centred on the east coast around Aberdeen and Fife, and in West Lothian. Later, production spread to more remote districts, such as Highland Perthshire, the Moray Firth, Ross, and Orkney.[57] In Wales, women in rural areas were central to the manufacture of woollens, mainly working in carding and spinning.[58]

Pay for such home-based work was low and subject to dramatic slumps in demand. Valenze has described how changes in fashion and fluctuations in foreign trade could affect women straw-plaiters, button-makers, and lace-makers.[59] Pinchbeck found that the same was true of glovemakers in the west of England,[60] while Whyte has noted how female textile workers in otherwise agricultural areas were especially vulnerable to periodic trade slumps in the late eighteenth century, citing the Aberdeenshire stocking knitters as an example.[61] A similar picture emerges from Sharpe's description of women working in lace-making, straw-plaiting, and tailoring in Essex.[62] Such slumps were periodic and cyclical in nature. In 1751, it was reported that a good spinner in Scotland, working twelve-hour days, 'can gain 15 and 16d a week; but the price of corn at 3d a sack leaves a woman 1d a week for clothing, firing house rents, etc. Therefore she must starve'.[63] Almost seventy years later, in 1818, James Haxwell complained to poor law officials in St Botolph's in Colchester that his wife and daughter both worked at needlework, but earned so little that they could not afford materials.[64]

Work in towns

During our period, women, particularly young women, migrated to towns in greater numbers than men.[65] Sharpe has argued that women's migration was driven not just by reduced work opportunities in some agricultural areas, but also by increasing demand for female labour in towns. Migration was, she claims, 'as often a positive move as a result of despair'.[66] Eighteenth-century Edinburgh witnessed women travelling ever-greater distances to find work in the town, as migrants increasingly came from the Highlands and northern Scotland. The daughters of agricultural families were more likely to travel significant distances to find work than their brothers, who more commonly stayed on the family farm.[67] Here, we see a symbiotic relationship emerging between town and country, with both work and workers overlapping, and urban employment helping to support rural families.

Industry and manufacturing

Changes in the way production was organized in the later eighteenth century often resulted in new employment opportunities for women. 'When we talk of industry in the eighteenth and early nineteenth centuries', claims Berg, 'we are talking of a largely female workforce.'[68] Much of this workforce was poorly paid and doing work deemed less skilled than men's.[69] The increased use of female labour was especially marked in textiles – an industry that held an increasingly dominant place in the British economy. In both Lancashire and Scotland, women continued to outnumber male workers in this sector throughout the late eighteenth and early nineteenth centuries.[70] This was most marked in early nineteenth-century Scotland, where contemporary estimates counted twice as many female employees as male.[71] Similar patterns of employment – in which new technology and new manufacturing processes led to the greater employment of women – can be found in the Leicester hosiery industry, the rolling mills of the Merthyr Tydfil iron industry, and in metal manufacture in the Midlands.[72] Although women's wages were generally significantly lower than men's, in 'new' industries women could earn more than the average male worker. This was the case in the Staffordshire potteries, and in calico production and jenny-spinning in Lancashire.[73] In cotton mills, too, women received higher wages than was normal in manufacturing. Unusually, they also worked alongside men as fellow operatives – despite their work still not being perceived as equal to men's in some important respects, particularly in terms of the level of skill that workers were assumed to possess.[74]

The expansion of women's work described for the early phase of industrialization appears to have been temporary in many areas, however, and there is evidence for the decline or marginalization of female labour in certain sectors over time. Despite the introduction of new technology such as the spinning jenny in the 1770s and 1780s, which allowed greater employment of women and girls, men were reasserting their dominance in the cotton mills by the 1790s. Machinery, such as the self-acting mule, was redesignated as 'skilled' and reserved for male workers.[75] Yet, in times of economic hardship, such as during the depression following the Napoleonic Wars, increasing numbers of women were still employed in the mills, suggesting the fluid nature of gender roles in relation to work in this period. Despite men taking most of the better-paid and higher status jobs brought about by industrialization, women were still participating in the labour force in great numbers.

There are signs that changing ideas about gender and the respectable occupations of men and women made working-class men increasingly eager to exclude women from the workplace, even if this meant disadvantaging the income of the family as a whole, at least in the short term. Thus, as the nineteenth century progressed, the use of female labour was contested by male trades unionists. Sonya Rose has argued that women were an easily identifiable and distinctive group of workers who were linked to cheap labour and could be seen as a threat to male workers and to their status as providers.[76] Despite the challenge that female workers might have posed to working-class masculine identity, the impact of action against them was limited. In Glasgow, a series of strikes between 1818 and 1830 by male trades unionists, protesting at women being employed as mule spinners failed to push women out of these jobs, as did similar action in Manchester. [77] Indeed, female employment in textile factories appears to have increased in the 1830s and 1840s, in spite of such actions and a Factory Act in 1844 which was pushed through by an alliance of middle-class reformers and working-class activists and limited the work of women and children largely on gendered moral grounds.[78] Male trades unionists also failed to keep women and other unskilled workers out of trades such as hatting, calico printing, tailoring, and framework knitting in this period.[79] They succeeded in protecting their interests in the London bookbinding and printing trades, perhaps because this sector commanded better wages and was less easy for untrained workers to infiltrate.[80] Organized action against women workers should not be dismissed lightly, though, as it could involve violence. In 1819, several unemployed male spinners attacked a group of women spinners newly employed at the Broomward cotton mills near Glasgow. When they broke into the houses of two women and their mothers, they beat them so severely that one woman died.[81]

From early in the eighteenth century, women had also been involved in industries where production processes were reduced to their component parts, so that the skill needed to complete each task was not the same as that need to produce the whole. The expansion of glovemaking in eighteenth-century Perth was organized in this manner, with men cutting pieces and shapes while a 'vast number' of women sewed them up.[82] This was also the way in which 'slop work' in the needle trades, shoe-making and fancy cabinet-making was organized in early nineteenth-century London.[83] Much of this new work was 'sweated', as its relatively unskilled nature meant high competition for jobs, which in turn pushed down wages, ensuring a largely female workforce. [84] As payment was made at piece rates, workers had to put in long hours in order to support themselves, often in cramped and unhealthy conditions. In 1747, R. Campbell called attention to the plight of poorly paid women working for milliners:

> who have vast Profits on every Article they deal in; yet give but poor, mean Wages to every Person they employ under them: Though a young woman can work neatly in all manner of Needle-Work, yet she

cannot earn more than Five or Six Shillings a Week, out of which she is to find herself in Board and Lodging.[85]

The situation had improved little a century later, when Henry Mayhew wrote of needlewomen in London: 'I could not have believed that there were human beings toiling so long and gaining so little, and starving so silently and heroically.'[86]

Service

Service occupations, and domestic service in particular, were dominated by women workers and were by far the greatest employers of women during our period. In addition to the most common form of domestic servant, who lived in her employer's house, many women also earned a living as charwomen or as domestic servants who lodged separately from their employers.[87] Relatively little research has been done on domestic service, in part because servants, though ubiquitous, left little historical record. We have already seen how agricultural servants became fewer in number during our period; however, it has been argued that the very opposite was true of domestic servants, particularly in urban areas. Rising standards of living and the rapid expansion of the middle classes are generally assumed to have increased demand for servants. Still, Leonard Schwarz has recently argued that the proportion of female servants in London in 1851 was not higher than in 1780 and, indeed, may have declined from the middle of the eighteenth century.[88] The four largest Scottish towns in the late seventeenth century – Edinburgh, Glasgow, Aberdeen, and Dundee – probably employed at least 12,000 female domestic servants, which constituted some 10 per cent of all girls and women in Scotland between the ages of 10 and 25. Many of these would have come to urban areas from the countryside.[89] In cities such as York, with a large number of wealthy inhabitants and little industry, perhaps as many as three-quarters of the female population were employed in domestic service during the early nineteenth century.[90] By the time of the 1851 census, almost half a million women were employed in this sector country-wide.[91]

Tim Meldrum has noted that the sexual division of labour for servants was striking from the late seventeenth century, with female and male servants often carrying out very different roles.[92] While large aristocratic houses might employ a number of both male and female servants, this was not typical. Most servants were not only female but they were also employed in middling households with only one or two servants.[93] Work in such households was both varied and arduous. The diaries of Hannah Cullwick detail her life as a domestic servant in the mid-nineteenth century. The daughter of a housemaid and a saddler, she began full-time work as a servant in 1841, at the age of 8. In 1847, she was working as a nursery maid at the vicarage of Ryton in Shropshire:

> I stopp'd here through the winter & had a deal of hard work to do, for there was eight children. I'd all their boots to clean & the large nurseries on my hands & knees, & a long passage & stairs, all their meals to get & our own . . . I'd all the water to carry up & down for their baths & coal for the fire, put all the children to bed & wash & dress of a morning by eight, & I wasn't in bed after 5.[94]

Peter Earle suggests that servants in early eighteenth-century London found jobs relatively easy to get, hence their high turnover: few stayed with the same employer for over three years.[95] A similar picture has emerged in a study of estates in Fife.[96] Servants in husbandry may have changed jobs even more frequently.[97] Women in domestic service were disproportionately young and many seem to have left service altogether in their twenties and thirties.[98] In 1736, the Merchant Company in Edinburgh, which attempted to regulate shopkeeping in the town, complained that 'a great many women servants . . . turning wearie of services, have, out of a principle of avarice and habit of laziness, taken up little shops, albeit they have no title to the privilege of trade in this city'.[99] Such remarks were not isolated and the eighteenth and early nineteenth centuries witnessed a rash of literature complaining about the behaviour of servants.[100]

Prostitution

Prostitution was generally entered into by young, poor women, and higher incidents of prostitution seem to have coincided with rising levels of unemployment.[101] For many women, prostitution seems not to have been their only source of income, but a way of making money when times were hard. Thus, women who worked as servants, needlewomen, and engaged in other casual work, often supplemented their income in this way. Estimating the number of women who were involved in prostitution – both as prostitutes and brothel-keepers – is notoriously difficult. As Michael Mason has pointed out, the fact that many contemporary estimates are extremely high had more to do with middle-class moral panic than accurate social measurements. Commentators on nineteenth-century London were particularly liable to exaggerate the situation during a period when prostitution rates were probably falling.[102]

Although prostitutes were sometimes portrayed by contemporaries as relatively wealthy (eager to spend their money on clothes and liquor), studies of prostitution, such as Frances Finnegan's examination of York, paint pictures of poverty, destitution, and disease.[103] Still, we should not overlook the possibility that prostitution was sometimes entered into by choice, as an easier alterative to other forms of even more demanding and demeaning work, as the account provided by 'Swindling Sal', a prostitute in nineteenth-century London, suggests:

> I was a servant gal away down in Birmingham. I got tired of workin' and slavin' to make a living, and getter a ——— bad one at that; what o' five pun' a year and yer grub, I'd sooner starve, I would. After a bit I went to Coventry, cut brummagem, as we calls it in those parts, and took up with soldiers as was quartered there. I soon got tired of them. Soldiers is good – soliders is – to walk with and that, but they don't pay: cos why they ain't got no money; so I says to myself, I'll go to Lunnon and I did. I soon found my level there.[104]

Trade

At a very different point on the social spectrum to most prostitutes – and, indeed, to most workers – were the middle-class women who engaged in trade. Contemporary literature suggests that middling women were expected to withdraw from the world of work as the eighteenth century progressed, and historians such as Davidoff and Hall, and Stana Nenadic have supported this picture of gradual retreat.[105] Yet quantitative research in this area remains patchy – and what there is often challenges this view. Peter Earle's research on London suggests that perhaps one-third of women of property ran a business in the early eighteenth century, which constituted some 5–10 per cent of all businesses in the capital at that time.[106] Similar percentages are found for women in Manchester, Leeds, and Sheffield between 1804 and 1828, at the end of our period.[107] This suggests, rather than a decline, some consistency in terms of middling women's involvement in the world of work.

Earle argues that there was little change in women's employment between 1700 and 1851 and that women were already clustered in 'feminine' trades by the late seventeenth century.[108] His analysis of fire-insurance records suggests that women in business were predominantly located in the areas of food and drink, textiles and clothing, pawnbroking and retailing: 'the typical business for a woman was exactly what might be expected: running a catering establishment selling food and drink, or running a shop selling food, textiles, clothing or such fancy goods as toys, glass, china or perfumes'.[109] Other historians have supported this broad view. Elizabeth Sanderson's examination of women's work in eighteenth-century Edinburgh, for example, focuses on retailing and on the 'community care' jobs of letting rooms, nursing, and the making of gravesclothes.[110]

While it is true that women were predominantly involved in 'feminine' trades, they were not restricted to them. Schwarz's examination of London between the late eighteenth and mid-nineteenth centuries suggests that this period witnessed increasing numbers of women trading as butchers, cabinetmakers, upholsterers, chandlers, grocers, drapers, tailors, and shoemakers.[111] The 'feminization' thesis is also strongly challenged by Nicola Pullin's research on middling women, most of whom were based in the capital. Her study of fire-insurance policies taken out by women between 1735 and 1845 revealed little evidence that women's work became more concentrated in 'feminine' trades, and found instead that over 40 per cent of her insured businesswomen were spread, albeit thinly, over a wide variety of trades other than those associated with food and drink, dress, and education.[112] The household records of Dunham Massey Hall, the home of the Grey family in Cheshire, reflect this diversity, as they illustrate the widespread use of a variety of women traders in the 1820s: Mary and Sarah Dean received payment for the supply of clothing, bedding, fabrics, and paper; Ann Sykes for chimney pots; Sarah Southern for leather skins; and Mary Allen for the repair of a thermometer, plus the supply of tobacco water and silver paper.[113]

Women's involvement in trade was not unskilled: if the necessary skills were not learnt in the familial setting – as daughters and wives – women could go into formal or informal apprenticeships,[114] and younger women would form partnerships with older ones on this basis.[115] Even in the nineteenth century, learning a trade was considered crucial for women of the lower middle classes.[116] In 1832, Robert Ayrey, a straw-hat-maker from Leeds, implored friends living abroad as missionaries to 'looke at your childrens wellfair [sic]' and send their daughter, Hannah, back to England to learn a trade since she was approaching the age of 12: 'the proper age to lern a business'. 'I will take care for her that she gets her business lernt', he promised.[117]

Women traditionally worked with their husbands in retailing, often focusing on the selling side of the business. James Lackington, the London bookseller, wrote of his second wife, Dorcas: 'my wife's attachment to books was a very fortunate circumstance to us both . . . Accordingly, when I was out on business, my shop was well attended. This constant attention, and good usage, procured me many customers.'[118] It was because women were used to working alongside their husbands that they often continued to run businesses after they were widowed. Although widows frequently professed to run businesses on behalf of their families, they were not necessarily acting as caretakers until a male relative, typically a son, was available to take over. Examples can be found in both the English and Scottish print trades of widows running businesses in partnership with adult sons who, in practice, appeared to hold subordinate positions to their mothers.[119]

Although women often ran businesses as a result of widowhood, they could also set up on their own. Margaret Cameron, for example, founded a successful millinery business in Edinburgh in 1826 with money borrowed from her mother.[120] Yet female involvement in trade was restricted in important ways. In some towns, and varying from region to region, guild structures and local custom prevented women from trading freely alongside men. In Scottish towns, middling women could inherit the right to trade from their burgess fathers. This freedom was not lost when they married and, indeed, a woman with the freedom to trade could pass this on to her husband if he was unfree. Married women could also obtain the freedom to trade from their burgess husbands, even if they were employed in different occupations.[121] In England, women could also be members of guilds, often taking on their husbands' membership upon his death. The power of the guild system in England was in decline throughout the eighteenth century, however, so its impact on women's work was increasingly limited. While there is evidence that local customs and regulations restricted women's involvement in trade in older market towns such as Oxford,[122] more recent research on London, the Midlands, and northern 'industrial' towns suggests that in faster growing and less regulated urban centres, women were able to exploit commercial opportunities with greater ease and for a longer period than in less dynamic settings.[123]

Businesswomen in England and Wales were subject to property laws that could severely restrict the rights of married women in particular. They were technically subject to coverture and had their legal identity subsumed into that of their husband, meaning that they could not own property, make contracts, sue or be sued. This legal inferiority could result in disaster for married women traders. In 1778, Mary Holl, a London milliner, wrote to one of her husband's creditors after her shop goods and fixtures were seized to pay his debts:

> Alas, Alas, why wou'd you not put some confidence in me, your not doing so has undone both you & my self, you I fear, in the loss of your debt, or a great part of it, & me in the everlasting anguish of mind, in not fulfilling my engagements, so very separate from Mr. Holl, that many of my Cred[itor]s did not even know I was a married woman, & it was upon my Industry & the punctuality of my payments that my Credit was founded.[124]

Pullin has pointed out that coverture did not prevent married women from trading and that, in some cases, it could offer them greater protection under the law than single women or male traders would have expected. This was particularly evident in the case of women being pursued for debt.[125] In Scotland, married women were technically freer (and more vulnerable). Although a wife's moveable property was under her husband's control, her herititable or immoveable property (such as land) could not be sold by a husband – at least in theory – without his wife's permission.[126]

Despite the apparently restrictive legal situation across much of Britain and the misfortunes of women such as Mary Holl, the reality of many women's lives was very different. As the preceding discussion has suggested, is clear that married women across Britain circumvented or ignored the law in order to trade independently, often claiming a type of legal independence as 'femme soles'.[127] Jane Butter, an Exeter bookseller, for instance, continued to run her late husband's shop under her own name despite her remarriage in 1723 to another bookseller, Daniel Pring.[128] In addition, pre-marital agreements concerning property were not uncommon and women fairly low down on the social scale – such as traders and small manufacturers – might have property in a 'separate estate' which was supposed to be immune to the laws of coverture and the grasp of greedy or penurious husbands.[129] Women operating as femme soles were in an anomalous legal position: not only were they more vulnerable to legal action from creditors, but also husbands could still take both goods and profits if familial relations broke down.[130] This was the fate of Elizabeth Greenwood, who in 1769 inherited her husband's painting and dealing business in Manchester. Soon after, in 1770, she remarried James Walton, one of her late husband's employees, who, despite signing a pre-nuptial agreement to protect her property, was accused in 1780 of illegally assuming control of the business and spending the profits on liquor. Walton, it was claimed, was not only 'in a habit of dissoluteness and dissipation', but threatened his wife with violence when she challenged his actions.[131] In contrast, Sanderson describes the Edinburgh widow, Helen Pettigrew, who in the mid-eighteenth century married her journeyman soon after the death of her first husband, but continued to run the smithing business she had been left, contracting with merchants, granting bills, receiving payments, and paying wages.[132]

The professions

The professions were male-dominated during our period, but women were not totally excluded from the professional ranks during the eighteenth and nineteenth centuries. Penelope Corfield notes that women were clustered in the 'nurturing' branches of the professions (predominantly as nurses and teachers). In 1851 they could also be found in small numbers in administrative roles in the church, as government officials, and as actors and musicians.[133] As Anne Stott shows in this volume, noncomformist religion could offer women a leading role in some activities, such as preaching. Women also earned money as authors and painters.[134] They were largely excluded from the the law and the church, and, other than a number of women who cross-dressed as men and served as soldiers or sailors, also from the army and navy.[135]

As Deborah Simonton suggests elsewhere in this volume, the education given to women rarely fitted them for professions such as medicine or law. Women did perform medical care for money, but this was often at the lower end of the medical hierarchy: as midwives, nurses, wet nurses, and druggists.[136] Pinchbeck also found examples of women operating as dentists, surgeons, and occulists in England until the late eighteenth century.[137] Increasingly, as medical practitioners became increasingly professionalized during our period, such women (with the exception of nurses and wet nurses) came under attack. As with women in the dairy industry, medical women were frequently depicted as irrational and unscientific.[138] In Edinburgh in 1726, the physician, Joseph Gibson, petitioned the city's magistrates to have midwives registered with 'at least one Doctor and one Chirurgeon' in order to avoid the 'many fatal conse-quences' which had befallen 'women in childbirth and to the Children thro' the Ignorance and unskillfullness of midwives in this Countrey and City'.[139] In the early eighteenth century, women dominated midwifery and many appear to have undergone a period of formal training by other midwives.[140] By the end of our period, female midwives in England had been almost entirely replaced by men, for all but the poor (although this still constituted a majority of births).[141] Women were generally still present at births as nurses and they helped mothers during their lying-in periods, but their roles in middling- and upper-class births were secondary to those of the man-midwife. Subject to similar assaults on their credibility, and frequently labelled as 'quacks', female medical practitioners did not die out completely, although their numbers declined during the eighteenth century.[142] During the 1790s, for example, Sarah Loveless, who worked as a healer in the Somerset village of Stogursey, cured a number of patients, including a man with an inflamed foot and two scalded children.[143]

Teaching was one of the few professions open to women that expanded between 1700 and 1850. Women's entry into teaching was made easier precisely because it was not regarded as a profession in our period, and as such was largely unregulated. Susan Skedd's work on female teachers in England during the eighteenth and nineteenth centuries has shown how the expansion of girls' schooling in this period brought a new source of employment for women.[144] The 1851 census suggests that over 67,000 women in England and Wales were counted as schoolmistresses, gover-nesses, and teachers, making teaching the fifth most common occupation for women. In Scotland, teaching was a less common profession for women, with only 4,415 women appearing in official statistics.[145] Running a school offered women a chance to manage their own business and achieve a degree of independence. Those women with the necessary financial backing, such as the More sisters of Bristol, enjoyed a comfortable and respectable lifestyle in this way.[146] Governesses too became increasingly popular among the upper classes, although the writer, Mary Wollstonecraft, who had bitter personal memories of such work, complained that 'when a superior education enables [women] to take charge of the education of children, as governesses, they are not treated like the tutors of sons'.[147]

The gendered division of labour

There is no doubt that ideas about gender and about what constituted 'men's work' and 'women's work' had a great impact on the female labour force during our period. Increasingly, male identity was shaped by work, while the feminine was associated with domesticity.[148] As we have seen, a gendered division of labour was clearly in operation, with women more likely to work in certain economic sectors, undertake particular jobs (which were generally more menial than men's and less well paid), and experience greater restrictions on economic opportunity than male workers. Yet it was not the case than men and women always performed separate jobs. Men's and women's work evidently overlapped in areas such as shopkeeping, weaving, and innkeeping, in towns with one dominant industry – such as the mill towns of Oldham and Bury – and at certain times, such as when labour was in short supply or during harvest in rural areas. Although women were increasingly associated with the domestic and the maternal in literary sources, the evidence that this constrained their working patterns is not conclusive. Women in mining and agriculture seem to have been affected in this way (although it is clear that for some, leaving such jobs – usually to work in service – was seen a positive decision), but in many areas of manufacturing, women were not excluded from work which was deemed 'unfeminine', even if attempts might have been made to feminize the nature of their work. As we have seen, this process of feminization often included an element of de-skilling, either in real terms – in that jobs were made easier – or because, once work was deemed 'women's work', it was often reclassified as unskilled. As Phillips and Taylor have pointed out, 'skill is often an ideological category imposed on certain types of work by virtue of the sex and power of the workers who perform it'.[149]

It is easier to describe how the gendered division of labour might have changed between 1700 and 1850 than to explain why it existed in the first place and developed in the ways that it did. Contemporaries would have cited biology as one reason: women were supposedly weaker than men, but were also deemed more dextrous and thus suited to jobs where smaller hands and a 'natural' aptitude for manual dexterity and fine motor skills were thought to be an advantage. Some jobs may also have required more strength than most women had.[150] Yet men worked as tailors, watchmakers, and jewellers,[151] at the same time that women shovelled coal, transported heavy goods, and carried out physically demanding farm labour. In addition, because women bore children and men did not, their working lives were affected by the upheavals of birth and childcare. But it is worth noting how many women appear to have continued working with small children. Indeed, from her study of middling women, Margaret Hunt has argued that women in eighteenth-century England were *more* likely to work outside the home during their prime child-bearing years. Pregnancy did not result in permanent incapacity for most women, while the easy availability of childcare meant this too was not a bar to women working.[152] The situation may have been different for poorer women and those who worked in factories, although combining factory work with pregnancy, breastfeeding, and childcare does not seem to have been uncommon, even if it was not pleasant,[153] and the research of Sara Horrell and Jane Humphries has uncovered evidence of relatively high proportions of married women working in all major economic sectors.[154]

Functionalist or biological assumptions about women's employment assume that all women married and had children, but, as Tanya Evan's chapter in this volume makes clear, this was often not the case.[155] Indeed, we should remember that at any one time very large numbers of women workers were single, either because they had not yet married, were widows, or because they had never married. Other more spurious ideas about gender difference, such as women's lack of rationality or natural 'delicacy', were also cited as reasons for women not to enter certain trades and professions. Differences in female education and in female apprenticeship, which was often shorter than that of boys and less likely to have involved a formal training in skilled work, may well have made women less suited to certain employments.[156] An example of this is provided by Freifeld, who claims that a breakdown in skills transmission among female workers in the cotton industry in the late eighteenth century meant less women could perform skilled spinning jobs.[157] Conversely, Berg argues that women were especially prominent in new technologies – such as the spinning jenny of the late eighteenth century or the foot-operated spring hammer, or 'oliver', of the early nineteenth – because their employment allowed employers to bypass traditional artisan customs and arrangements. Moreover, such innovations were better presented to the public in terms of the female and child labour they would employ, rather than the male labour they would save.[158]

The reasons behind the gendered division of labour are therefore complex and sometimes contradictory. A range of factors was generally involved, including the attitudes and actions of households, male and female workers, employers, the state and social movements, as well as the condition of the economy on both a local and national level. All of these were linked; all were subject to change over time; and all varied between regions and industries. Attitudes towards gender and work clearly had a profound impact on women's experiences of employment during our period; however, as the preceding discussion has suggested, factors such as social class, geography, and marital status, could be even more influential.

On the whole, the conditions and opportunities afforded to women workers trailed behind those of men, but this was not always the case. In particular industries, and at certain times, women workers were relatively well off when compared to men. Moreover, even when women were paid less than male workers, as they generally were, their labour was crucial to the economy as a whole and their earnings were vital to their household income – particularly in the 'newer' areas of factory work and out-work.[159] As William Wingell asserted to the parliamentary commissioner investigating the condition of framework knitters in 1845, 'I should not be able to live at all if it was not for the little that my wife gets'.[160]

Acknowledgements

I am grateful to Deborah Simonton for her comments on this chapter and to Nia Powell and Colin Phillips for references.

Notes

1 Edward Higgs, 'Women, occupations and work in the nineteenth-century censuses', *History Workshop Journal*, 1987, vol. 23.

2 Sally Alexander, 'Women's work in nineteenth-century London: a study of the years 1820–1850', in A. Oakley and J. Mitchell (eds), *The Rights and Wrongs of Women*, Harmondsworth, 1976.

3 R. E. Tyson, 'The rise and fall of manufacturing in rural Aberdeenshire', in J. S. Smith and D. Stevenson (eds), *Fermfolk and Fisherfolk: Rural Life in Northern Scotland in the Eighteenth and Nineteenth Centuries*, Aberdeen, 1989.

4 See T. Meldrum, *Domestic Service and Gender 1660–1750: Life and Work in the London Household*, Harlow, 2000, pp. 128–37; Deborah Simonton, *A History of European Woman's Work*, London, 1998, pp. 1–2.

5 Leonore Davidoff and Catherine Hall, *Family Fortunes: Men and Women of the English Middle Class, 1780–1850*, London, 1987, Chapter 6.

6 Amanda Vickery, 'Golden age to separate spheres? A review of the categories and chronology of English women's history', *Historical Journal*, 1993, no. 36, p. 402.

7 Judith Bennett, 'History that stands still: women's work in the European past', *Feminist Studies*, 1988, vol. 14.

8 Ivy Pinchbeck, *Women Workers and the Industrial Revolution, 1750–1850*, London, 1930; Bridget Hill, *Women, Work and Sexual Politics in Eighteenth-Century England*, Oxford, 1990.

9 Deborah Valenze, *The First Industrial Woman*, Oxford, 1995.

10 K. Honeyman and J. Goodman, 'Women's work, gender conflict and labour markets in Europe, 1500–1900', *Economic History Review*, 1991, vol. 44.

11 Catherine Hall, 'The early formation of Victorian domestic ideology', in S. Burman (ed.), *Fit Work for Women*, London, 1979; S. Walby, *Patriarchy at Work*, Cambridge, 1986; S. Dex, 'Issues in gender and employment', *Social History*, 1988, vol. 13.

12 See N. F. R. Crafts, *British Industrial Growth During the Industrial Revolution*, Oxford, 1985; E. A. Wrigley, *Continuity, Chance and Change: The Character of the Industrial Revolution in England*, Cambridge, 1989; Pat Hudson, *The Industrial Revolution*, London, 1992; Maxine Berg, *The Age of Manufactures, 1700–1820*, 2nd edn, London, 1994; Mark Overton, *The Agricultural Revolution, 1500–1850*, Cambridge, 1996.

13 Raphael Samuel, 'Workshop of the world: steam power and hand technology in mid-Victorian Britain', *History Workshop Journal*, 1977, vol. 3; John Stevenson, 'Social aspects of the industrial revolution', in Patrick O'Brien and Ronald Quinault (eds), *The Industrial Revolution and British Society*, Cambridge, 1993.

14 Maxine Berg and Pat Hudson, 'Rehabilitating the industrial revolution', *Economic History Review*, 1992, vol. 45.

15 Maxine Berg, 'What difference did women's work make to the Industrial Revolution?, *History Workshop Journal*, 1993, vol. 35.

16 G. E. Mingay (ed.), *The Agrarian History of England and Wales: VI: 1750–1850*, Cambridge, 1989; Malcolm Gray, 'Processes of agricultural change in the north-east, 1790–1870', in Leah Leneman and I. D. Whyte (eds), *Perspectives in Scottish Social History: Essays in Honour of Rosalind Mitchison*, Aberdeen, 1988.

17 Jane Humphries, 'Enclosures, common rights, and women: proletarianization of families in the late eighteenth and early nineteenth centuries', *Journal of Economic History*, 1990, vol. 50.

18 Pamela Sharpe, *Adapting to Capitalism: Working Women in the English Economy, 1700–1850*, Basingstoke, 1996.

19 Houston, 'Women in the economy and society of Scotland, 1500–1800', pp. 123–4.

20 Simonton, *History of European Women's Work*, p. 118.

21 Ibid., p. 126.

22 Ann Kussmaul, *Servants in Husbandry in Early Modern England*, Cambridge, 1981, pt 3; K. Snell, *Annals of the Labouring Poor: Social Change and Agrarian England, 1660–1900*, Cambridge, 1985, Chapter 2; see also, A. J. Gritt, 'The census and the servant: a reassessment of the decline and distribution of farm service in early nineteenth-century England', *Economic History Review*, 2000, vol. 53.

23 Snell, *Annals of the Labouring Poor*, Chapter 1.

24 Michael Roberts, 'Sickles and scythes: women's work and men's work at harvest time', *History Workshop Journal*, 1979, vol. 7.

25 Nicola Verdon, 'The rural labour market in the early nineteenth century: women's and children's employment, family income, and the 1834 Poor Law Report', *Economic History Review*, 2002, vol. 55.

26 Sharpe, *Adapting to Capitalism*, Chapter 4.

27 Elizabeth Roberts, *Women's Work, 1840–1940*, Basingstoke, 1988, p. 43.

28 Cited in Hill, *Women, Work and Sexual Politics*, p. 58.

29 Jane Long, *Conversations in Cold Rooms: Women, Work and Poverty in Nineteenth-Century Northumberland*, Woodbridge, 1999, Chapter 4; Barbara W. Robertson, 'In bondage: the female farm worker in south-east Scotland', in Eleanor Gordon and E. Breitenbach (eds), *The World is Ill Divided: Women and Work in Scotland, 1830–1940*, Edinburgh, 1990.

30 T. M. Devine, 'Women workers, 1850–1914', in T. M. Devine (ed.), *Farm Servants and Labour in Lowland Scotland, 1770–1914*, Edinburgh, 1984, pp. 98, 100.

31 Houston, 'Women in the economy and society of Scotland, 1500–1800', p. 121.

32 Ibid., p. 121.

33 William Howatson, 'The Scottish hairst and seasonal labour, 1600–1870', *Scottish Studies*, 1982, vol. 26.

34 David W. Powell, *Land and People in Nineteenth-Century Wales*, London, 1977, p. 97. See also L. J. Williams and Dot Jones, 'Women and work in nineteenth-century Wales', *Llafur*, 1982, vol. 3.

35 Cited in Lesley Davidson, 'Spinsters were doing it for themselves: independence and the single woman in early eighteenth-century rural Wales', in Michael Roberts and Simone Clarke (eds), *Women and Gender in Early Modern Wales*, Cardiff, 2000.

36 Michael Roberts, 'The empty ladder: work and its meanings in early modern Cardiganshire', *Llafur*, 1995, vol. 6, p. 21.

37 John Williams-Davies, '*Merched y gerddi*: a seasonal migration of female labour from rural Wales', *Folk Life*, 1977, vol. 15.

38 Peter King, 'Customary rights and women's earnings: the importance of gleaning to the labouring poor, 1750–1850', *Economic History Review*, 1991, vol. 44.

39 Humphries, 'Enclosures, common rights, and women'.

40 M. I. Williams, 'Seasonal migration of Cardiganshire harvest-gangs to the Vale of Glamorgan in the nineteenth century', *Ceredigion*, 1956–7, vol. 3.

41 Deborah Valenze, 'The art of women and the business of men: women's work and the dairy industry, c.1740–1840', *Past and Present*, 1991, no. 130; Pinchbeck, *Women Workers and the Industrial Revolution*, pp. 40–2.

42 Davidoff and Hall, *Family Fortunes*, pp. 274, 309.

43 Angela John, *By the Sweat of their Brow: Women Workers at Victorian Coal Mines*, London, 1980; Karen Sayer, *Women of the Fields: Representations of Rural Women in the Nineteenth Century*, Manchester, 1993.

44 Houston, 'Women in the economy and society of Scotland, 1500–1800', p. 121.

45 David Howell, *The Rural Poor in Eighteenth-Century Wales*, Cardiff, 2000, p. 79.

46 Angela John, *Coalmining Women: Victorian Lives and Campaigns*, Cambridge, 1984, p. 6.

47 Robert B. Shoemaker, *Gender in English Society, 1650–1850: The Emergence of Separate Spheres?* Harlow, 1998.

48 John, *By the Sweat of their Brow*, p. 21.

49 Ibid., p. 42.

50 Ibid.

51 Jane Humphries, 'Protective legislation, the capitalist state and working-class men: the case of the 1842 Mines Regulation Act', *Feminist Review*, 1981, vol. 7.

52 Jane Mark-Lawson and Anne Witz, 'From "family labour" to "family wage"? The case of women's labour in nineteenth-century coal-mining', *Social History*, 1988, vol. 13.

53 Gill Burke, 'The decline of the independent Bâl Maiden: the impact of change in the Cornish mining industry', in Angela John (ed.), *Unequal Opportunities: Women's Employment in England, 1800–1940*, London, 1986.

54 Proto-industrialization is not an uncontested concept, see P. Hudson, 'Proto-industrialisation: the case of the West Riding', *History Workshop Journal*, 1981, vol. 12; Berg, *Age of Manufactures*, pp. 66–72.

55 Berg, 'Women's work, mechanisation and the early phases of industrialisation in England', in P. Joyce (ed.), *Historical Meanings of Work*, Cambridge, 1987;

R. A. Houston, 'Marriage formation and domestic industry: occupational endogamy in Kilmarnock, Ayrshire 1697–1764', *Journal of Family History*, 1983, vol. 8; Sharpe, *Adapting to Capitalism*.

56 Verdon, 'The rural labour market in the early nineteenth century', p. 304.

57 Ian Whyte, 'Proto-industrialization in Scotland', in Pat Hudson (ed.), *Regions and Industries: A Perspective on the Industrial Revolution in Britain*, Cambridge, 1989, pp. 235–7.

58 Howell, *Rural Poor in Eighteenth-Century Wales*, p. 85.

59 Valenze, *First Industrial Woman*, Chapter 6. Also Verdon, 'Rural labour market in the early nineteenth century', p. 306.

60 Pinchbeck, *Women, Work and the Industrial Revolution*, pp. 222–6.

61 Whyte, 'Proto-industrialization in Scotland', p. 242.

62 Sharpe, *Adapting to Capitalism*, Chapter 3.

63 Cited in Berg, 'Women's work, mechanisation and the early phases of industrialisation in England', p. 79.

64 Sharpe, *Adapting to Capitalism*, p. 69.

65 Joyce Ellis, 'Regional and county centres 1700–1840', in Peter Clark (ed.), *Cambridge Urban History of Britain: II: 1540–1840*, Cambridge, 2000.

66 Pamela Sharpe, 'Population and society, 1700–1840', in ibid.

67 Ian D. Whyte and K. A. Whyte, 'The geographical mobility of women in early modern Scotland', in Leneman and Whyte (eds), *Perspectives in Scottish Social History*.

68 Berg, 'What difference did women's work make to the Industrial Revolution?', p. 29.

69 Nancy Grey Osterud, 'Gender divisions and the organisation of work in the Leicester hosiery industry', in John (ed.), *Unequal Opportunities*, pp. 47–52.

70 Berg, 'What difference did women's work make to the Industrial Revolution?', pp. 27–8; J. Lown, *Women and Industrialisation: Gender at Work in Nineteenth-Century England*, Cambridge, 1990.

71 C. A. Whatley, 'Women and the economic transformation of Scotland, *c.*1740–1830', *Scottish Economic and Social History*, 1994, vol. 14, p. 29.

72 Osterud, 'Gender divisions and the organisation of work in the Leicester hosiery industry'; C. Evans, *The Labyrinth of Flames: Work and Conflict in Early Industrial Merthyr Tydfil*, Cardiff, 1993, p. 51; Berg, *Age of Manufactures*, Chapter 12.

73 Berg, 'What difference did women's work make to the Industrial Revolution?', p. 32.

74 Sonya Rose, *Limited Livelihoods: Gender and Class in Nineteenth-Century England*, London, 1992, pp. 157–60.

75 Mary Freifeld, 'Technological change and the "self-acting" mule: a study of skill and the sexual division of labour', *Social History*, 1986, vol. 11.

76 Sonya Rose, 'Gender antagonism and class conflict: exclusionary strategies of male trade unionists in nineteenth-century Britain', *Social History*, 1988, vol. 13.

77 Freifeld, 'Technological change and the "self-acting" mule'.

78 Robert Gay, 'Factory legislation and the gendering of jobs in Britain, 1830–1860', *Gender and History*, 1993, vol. 5.

79 Anna Clark, *The Struggle for the Breeches: Gender and the Making of the British Working Class*, London, 1995, p. 120; L. D. Schwarz, *London in the Age of Industrialisation: Entrepreneurs, Labour Force and Living Conditions, 1700–1850*, Cambridge, 1992, p. 192.

80 Felicity Hunt, 'Opportunities lost and gained: mechanisation and women's work in the London bookbinding and printing trades', in John, *Unequal Opportunities*.

81 Clark, *Struggle for the Breeches*, p. 135.

82 Whatley, 'Women and the economic transformation of Scotland, *c.*1740–1830', p. 32.

83 Alexander, 'Women's work in nineteenth-century London', pp. 80–3.

84 Duncan Bythell, *The Sweated Trades: Outwork in Nineteenth-Century Britain*, Batsford, 1978, p. 145.

85 R. Campbell, *The London Tradesmen* (1747), cited in Schwarz, *London in the Age of Industrialisation*, p. 181.

86 Cited in Bythell, *The Sweated Trades*, p. 80.

87 L. D. Schwarz, 'English servants and their employers during the eighteenth and nineteenth centuries', *Economic History Review*, 1999, vol. 52, p. 239.

88 Ibid.

89 Ian Whyte, 'Urbanisation in early modern Scotland: a preliminary analysis', *Scottish Economic and Social History*, 1989, vol. 9.

90 Bridget Hill, *Servants: English Domestics in the Eighteenth Century*, Oxford, 1996, p. 15.

91 Higgs, 'Women, occupations and work in the nineteenth-century censuses', p. 75.

92 Meldrum, *Domestic Service and Gender 1660–1750*, Chapter 5. See also Hill, *Servants*, Chapter 2.

93 D. A. Kent, 'Ubiquitous but invisible: female domestic servants in mid-eighteenth century London', *History Workshop Journal*, 1989, vol. 28, pp. 119–20.

94 *The Diaries of Hannah Cullwick, Victorian Maidservant*, ed. Liz Stanley, London, 1984, p. 37.

95 Peter Earle, *A City Full of People: Men and Women of London, 1650–1750*, London, 1994, pp. 128–9.

96 Houston, 'Women in the economy and society of Scotland, 1500–1800', p. 126.

97 Kent, 'Ubiquitous but invisible', p. 121.

98 Schwarz, *London in the Age of Industrialisation*, pp. 46–7; Kent, 'Ubiquitous but invisible', pp. 115–17; Meldrum, *Domestic Service and Gender 1660–1750*, pp. 15–18; Deborah Simonton, 'Bringing up girls: work in pre-industrial Europe', in Christina Benninghaus, Mary Jo Maynes and Brigitte Söland (eds), *Secret Gardens, Satanic Mills: Placing Girls in Modern European History*, Bloomington, IN, 2004.

99 Elizabeth C. Sanderson, *Women and Work in Eighteenth-Century Edinburgh*, Basingstoke, 1996, p. 39.

100 Patricia Seleski, 'Women, work and cultural change in eighteenth and early nineteenth-century London', in Tim Harris (ed.), *Popular Culture in England, c.1500–1800*, Basingstoke, 1995.

101 Robert B. Shoemaker, *Prosecution and Punishment: Petty Crime and the Law in London and Rural Middlesex c.1660–1725*, Cambridge, 1991, pp. 184–6; Frances Finnegan, *Poverty and Prostitution: A Study of Victorian Prostitutes in York*, Cambridge, 1979; Tony Henderson, *Disorderly Women in Eighteenth-Century London: Prostitution and Control in the Metropolis*, London, 1999.

102 Michael Mason, *The Making of Victorian Sexuality*, Oxford, 1994, pp. 76–82.

103 Finnegan, *Poverty and Prostitution*.

104 Cited in Judith R. Walkowitz, *Prostitution and Victorian Society: Women, Class and the State*, Cambridge, 1980, p. 13.

105 Davidoff and Hall, *Family Fortunes*; Stana Nenadic, 'The rise of the urban middle class', in T. Devine and R. Mitchison (eds), *People and Society in Scotland, 1760–1830*, Edinburgh, 1988, pp. 110–11.

106 Peter Earle, *The Making of the English Middle Class: Business, Society and Family Life in London, 1660–1730*, London, 1989, pp. 166–74.

107 *Deans & Co.'s Manchester & Salford Directory*, Manchester, 1817; *The Manchester*

and Salford Directory, Manchester, 1828; *Sheffield General Directory*, Sheffield, 1817; *The Sheffield Directory and Guide*, Sheffield, 1828; *The Leeds Directory for 1809*, Leeds, 1809; *Directory, General and Commercial, of the Town & Borough of Leeds*, Leeds, 1817; *General & Commercial Directory of the Borough of Leeds*, Leeds, 1826.

108 Earle, *Making of the English Middle Class*, pp. 166–74. See also Schwarz, *London in the Age of Industrialisation*, pp. 14–22.

109 Earle, *Making of the English Middle Class*, p. 170.

110 Sanderson, *Women and Work in Eighteenth-Century Edinburgh*. See also Margaret R. Hunt, *The Middling Sort: Commerce, Gender and the Family in England, 1680–1780*, Berkeley, CA, 1996, pp. 132–4.

111 Schwarz, *London in the Age of Industrialisation*, p. 21.

112 Nicola Pullin, *Women in Business, 1700–1850*, Woodbridge, forthcoming, Chapter 6.

113 John Rylands Library, Manchester, EGR7/12/1–12, Papers of the Grey family.

114 Simonton, 'Bringing up girls'.

115 Hunt, *Middling Sort*, p. 127.

116 Cf. Debbi Simonton's chapter in this volume.

117 Leeds Central Library, SR 826.79 AY 74, MS letterbook of Robert Ayrey, 1832.

118 James Lackington, *Memoirs of the Life of James Lackington*, London, 1974, p. 326.

119 Hannah Barker, 'Women, work and the industrial revolution: female involvement in the English printing trades, *c.*1700–1840', in Hannah Barker and Elaine Chalus (eds), *Gender in Eighteenth-Century England: Roles, Representations and Responsibilities*, Harlow, 1997, pp. 97–8; Alastair J. Mann, 'Embroidery to enterprise: the role of women in the book trade of early modern Scotland', in Elizabeth Ewan and Maureen M. Meikle (eds), *Women in Scotland, c.1100–c.1750*, East Linton, 1999, p. 140.

120 Stana Nenadic, 'The social shaping of business behaviour in the nineteenth-century women's garment trades', *Journal of Social History*, 1998, vol. 32, p. 631.

121 Sanderson, *Women and Work in Eighteenth-Century Edinburgh*, p. 130.

122 Wendy Thwaites, 'Women in the marketplace: Oxfordshire, *c.*1690–1800', *Midland History*, 1984, vol. 9; Mary Prior, 'Women and the urban economy: Oxford 1500–1800', in Mary Prior (ed.), *Women in English Society, 1500–1800*, London, 1985.

123 Pullin, *Women in Business*; Penelope Lane, 'Women in the regional economy, the east Midlands, 1700–1830', PhD thesis, University of Warwick, 1999; Christine Wiskin, 'Women, finance and credit in England, *c.*1780–1826', PhD thesis, University of Warwick, 2000; Hannah Barker, *The Business of Women: Female Enterprise and Urban Development in Northern Towns, 1760–1830*, forthcoming.

124 Cited in Hunt, *Middling Sort*, p. 125.

125 Pullin, *Women in Business, 1700–1850*, Chapters 2–4.

126 G. C. H. Paton, 'Husband and wife: property rights and relationships', in *An Introduction to Scottish Legal History*, Edinburgh, 1958, pp. 99–106.

127 Sanderson, *Women and Work in Eighteenth-Century Edinburgh*, p. 39.

128 Barker, 'Women, work and the industrial revolution', p. 99.

129 Amy Erikson, 'Common law versus common practice: the use of marriage settlements in early modern England', *Economic History Review*, 1990, vol. 43; Susan Staves, *Married Women's Separate Property in England, 1660–1833*, Cambridge, MA, 1990; Maxine Berg, 'Women's property and the industrial revolution', *Journal of Interdisciplinary History*, 1993, vol. 24; Hunt, *Middling Sort*, pp. 157–62;

A. D. M. Forte, 'Some aspects of the law of marriage in Scotland', in E. M. Craik (ed.), *Marriage and Property*, Aberdeen, 1984, p. 110.

130 Hunt, *Middling Sort*, pp. 139–42; Pullin, *Women in Business, 1700–1850*, Chapters 3 and 4.

131 National Archives, Kew, E112/1527/1555.

132 Sanderson, *Women and Work in Eighteenth-Century Edinburgh*, p. 125.

133 P. J. Corfield, *Power and the Professions in Britain, 1700–1850*, London, 1999, pp. 33–6.

134 Janice Helland, *Professional Women Painters in Nineteenth-Century Scotland: Commitment, Friendship, Pleasure*, London, 2000.

135 Julie Wheelwright, *Amazons and Military Maids*, London, 1989; Diane Dugdaw, *Warrior Women and Popular Balladry, 1650–1850*, Cambridge, 1989; Bridget Hill, *Women Alone: Spinsters in England, 1660–1850*, London, 2001, pp. 136–40.

136 Earle, *City Full of People*, pp. 130–9; Houston, 'Women in the economy and society of Scotland, 1500–1800', p. 125; Rosalind Marshall, 'Wet-nursing in Scotland: 1500–1800', *Review of Scottish Culture*, 1984, vol. 1.

137 Pinchbeck, *Women, Work and the Industrial Revolution*, pp. 300–3.

138 A. L. Wyman, 'The surgeoness: the female practitioner of surgery, 1400–1800', *Medical History*, 1984, vol. 28; Roy Porter, *Health for Sale: Quackery in England, 1660–1850*, Manchester, 1989.

139 Sanderson, *Women and Work in Eighteenth-Century Edinburgh*, p. 56.

140 Earle, *City Full of People*, p. 134.

141 J. Donnison, *Midwives and Medical Men: A History of the Struggle for the Control of Childbirth*, London, 1988; Adrian Wilson, *The Making of Man-Midwifery: Childbirth in England, 1660–1770*, Cambridge, MA, 1995; Lesley Diack, '"A woman's greatest adventure": the development of maternity care in Aberdeen since the eighteenth century', in Terry Brotherstone and Donald J. Withrington, *The City and its Worlds: Aspects of Aberdeen History Since 1794*, Glasgow, 1996.

142 Porter, *Health for Sale*.

143 M. Fissell, *Patients, Power, and the Poor in Eighteenth-Century Bristol*, Cambridge, 1991, p. 65.

144 Susan Skedd, 'Women teachers and the expansion of girls' schooling in England, c. 1760–1820', in Barker and Chalus (eds), *Gender in Eighteenth-Century England*.

145 Corfield, *Power and the Professions*, p. 34.

146 See also Hill, *Women Alone*, p. 60.

147 Mary Wollstonecroft, *A Vindication of the Rights of Woman*, ed. Mary Marnock, London, 1985, p. 162.

148 Clark, *Struggle for the Breeches*; Davidoff and Hall, *Family Fortunes*, Chapter 5.

149 Anne Phillips and Barbara Taylor, 'Sex and skill', in *Feminist Review* (ed.), *Waged Work, A Reader*, London, 1986, p. 55.

150 Freifeld, 'Technological change and the "self-acting" mule', p. 334.

151 Berg, 'What difference did women's work make to the Industrial Revolution?', p. 33.

152 Hunt, *Middling Sort*, p. 136. See also Sanderson, *Women and Work in Eighteenth-Century Edinburgh*, p. 132.

153 Rose, *Limited Livelihoods*, pp. 90–100.

154 Sara Horrell and Jane Humphries, 'Women's labour force participation and the transition to the male-breadwinner family, 1790–1865', *Economic History Review*, 1995, vol. 48, pp. 96–100.

155 See also Hill, *Women Alone*.

156 Deborah Simonton, 'Apprenticeship: training and gender in eighteenth-century England', in M. Berg, *Markets and Manufacture in Early Industrial Europe*, London, 1991; Michael Roberts, 'Gender, work and socialization in Wales *c.*1450–1850', in Sandra Betts (ed.), *Our Daughter's Land, Past and Present*, Cardiff, 1996, pp. 31–2.

157 Freifeld, 'Technological change and the "self-acting" mule', pp. 337–9.

158 Berg, 'What difference did women's work make to the Industrial Revolution?', p. 35.

159 S. Horrell and J. Humphries, 'Old questions, new data, and alternative perspectives: families' living standards in the industrial revolution', *Journal of Economic History*, 1992, vol. 52, p. 850; Horrell and Humphries, 'Women's labour force participation and the transition to the male-breadwinner family', pp. 100–8.

160 Osterud, 'Gender divisions and the organisation of work in the Leicester hosiery industry', p. 53.

Chapter Seven

ॐ

Women and poverty

Alannah Tomkins

On 29 December 1833, Frances James was anxious about the whereabouts of her husband. She wrote from her home in Wharf Street, Leicester, to the parish officers of Uttoxeter in Staffordshire:

> inform me if my husband Philip James has come to his parish, as he left me on the 18th of this month for to come to you for assistance he well knowing the situation he left me with only three half pence & four children and myself to be supported I have had a lying in & buried two children within six months I have been obliged to pledge and sell almost everything we had or we must have starved for want I feel greatly distrest at not hearing from him I beg sir you will write immediately . . . if I dont have a answer this next week I shall be obligated to fall on this parish & leave my goods for the rent due which is two pounds & no prospect of paying it . . . I consider he has not used me as a husband or he would have wrote before this time let his situation be what ever it would.[1]

By her own account, Frances was living in acute poverty, with fewer half-pence than children. She had sold or pawned her possessions in order to fend off starvation and was desperately facing the prospect of surrendering her remaining goods in lieu of rent. In addition, her reproductive health was in the balance after her lying-in, as was the health of her children (two of whom having already died). Finally, she had not heard from her husband in ten days and her precarious situation prompted her to pen a few sharp words about his failings as a correspondent. Frances would have been justified in fearing that Philip had absconded, but, as it happened, he had not, and Frances did not have to wait much longer for news. Philip had been taken ill on the road, but, thanks to the good offices of a former employer, he was back at home by 3 January 1834.[2]

Still, temporary relief from suspense did not mean that Frances' troubles were over. Philip and Frances wrote at least another twelve letters to Uttoxeter before May 1837, supplying further details about their material and emotional circumstances. Philip was ill with a liver complaint for almost all of 1833–6 and was unable to work for months at a time. It is perhaps regrettable that he was still able to have sex, as Frances fell pregnant again. Despite these challenges, she tried to keep the family with her 'little tripe business', presumably a shop or stall, and, in doing so, was compelled to stretch family resources to the utmost to cater for her sick husband and her children. This included pawning her wedding ring and sending one of her sons out to work for 1s. 6d. per week. Above all, she remained in a state of distress. In writing to thank her parish officers for the money they had sent in November 1834, she admitted ruefully, 'I am aware how much we have already cost you but the berrden has been much more mine.' What is more, the Jameses found numerous people willing to support their story. At least three different surgeons endorsed the letters to confirm that Philip was indeed suffering from a serious illness which rendered him incapable of work. Thomas Pickering (probably one of the parish officers of Leicester) wrote independently to say, 'the woman is considered deserving and industrious', although he added more cagily, 'the man is no great things'.[3]

This catalogue of hardship and distress exemplifies the difficulties which women had to face between 1700 and 1850. The absence of a bread-winner (or, worse, the presence of a breadwinner who evolved into a dependant), the uncontrollable conception of children who themselves might sicken and die, financial penury, and the need to handle household income and assets creatively were all repetitive features of the experience of poverty.

In this period, women comprised a disproportionate section of the poor; for example, in Scotland between 1690 and 1820, there were twice as many women acknowledged to be poor as there were men.[4] This chapter will concentrate on the experiences of women who were so poor they could not subsist on their own earnings, but needed to turn to external sources of assistance just to survive. It will try to answer three key questions: what made women poor in this period? How could they attempt to make ends meet? And, to what extent did poor women express meaningful choices about their material survival? It will argue that many of the principal causes of female poverty remained constant, albeit that the context in which female poverty was played out changed over the period. The process of urbanization in particular made dramatic changes to the backdrop of poverty; furthermore, the range of options open to women to assist them in grappling with poverty ostensibly broadened, but the impact of technical changes in poor relief and charity administration was relatively minor. The real change for poor women was in attitudes. While the stance of the prosperous towards their poorer neighbours fluctuated and can at no point in the period be characterized as universal, attitudes were essentially much harsher in 1850 than they had been in 1700.

Historians have recently been eager to stress that poverty did not always equate to abject powerlessness. Poor women may have been materially impoverished, but they did not necessarily surrender control of their lives. They may well have conducted a continual series of finely tuned calculations about their available resources and have exerted meaningful choices over their own daily lives, their children's upbringing, and their family's collective efforts to secure a living. Poor women did have choices in the ways they presented their poverty to authorities; however, ultimately, women had only narrow room for manoeuvre and the extent of their agency can at best be aligned with the 'imperfect empowerment' delineated for the poor in this period by Edward Thompson.[5] In other words, the strategies employed by Frances James for her family's survival constituted 'more an expression of despair and communal failure than the triumph of individual ingenuity'.[6]

Economic causes of female poverty: wages, warfare and weather

Work and low pay were the most obvious financial causes of poverty. The issue of women's paid work is taken up elsewhere in this volume by Hannah Barker. Suffice it to say that women's work was regarded as lower in status and skill than men's, and that women were always paid less than men where they were undertaking the same sort of work. It has been estimated that women's earnings comprised only half or two-thirds of an equivalent male wage.[7] Therefore, daughters, wives, and mothers struggled to make a large contribution to household income, let alone support themselves entirely, from their own earnings.

The difficulties engendered by inadequate wages also had a greater impact on women than they did on men. Women had a traditional responsibility for the family economy by undertaking marketing and balancing the household budget, but were also dependent upon an assumption that male earnings would form a significant portion of a family's income.[8] This seems to have become a more firmly held belief over the course of the nineteenth century.[9] Therefore, women found their responsibility for running a household increasingly problematic, because there was declining acknowledgment that women might need to earn money for themselves.

In addition, women's employment, and that of male relations, could be seriously disrupted by trade depressions initiated or exacerbated by war. Disruptions to overseas trade and increased levies of taxes to pay for war could quickly lead to a falling demand for non-agricultural goods, throwing industrial workers into unemployment.[10] A declaration of war could have other negative consequences, too. For the most part, British women in this period did not have to contend with the direct consequences of wars fought on their doorsteps (with the occasional exception of Scottish women), but they did have to cope with the protracted or permanent loss of breadwinners when men were drawn into military or naval service. England was technically at war for at least 57 years between 1700 and 1815, so this was not a negligible problem. Unfortunately, demobilization at the end of war also typically created difficulties for the poor. Thousands of able-bodied men returned to the British labour market, driving down wages and squeezing out opportunities for women.

Bad weather was another crucial factor that could influence both women's income and the spending power of any wages earned. First, and most importantly, bad weather over the summer months could give rise to poor harvests, forcing the price of the staple foodstuff, usually bread, to shoot up. This meant that the quality of diets worsened, as working people had to buy cheaper quality bread and fewer or no additional foodstuffs, such as butter, cheese, or meat. Broadly speaking, harvests were adequate and grain prices reasonable in *most* years up to 1760, but thereafter prices rose steadily and at times dramatically, so that people went hungry but were unlikely to starve.[11] Incidentally, the Irish potato famine of the 1840s provides a grimly spectacular example of complete crop failure, albeit from blight rather than bad weather, and was the only occasion in this period when people in Britain starved to death *en masse*. Trade could also experience a slow-down after severe weather conditions and bad harvests, because labouring families had to devote a much larger proportion of their disposable income to buying food, leaving little or no money to spend on manufactured goods. Finally, weather could have other sorts of impact on the poorest people. Harsh winter weather drove up the price of fuel and made the misery of thin clothing, insufficient bedding and inadequate housing all the more painful.[12]

Bodily causes of female poverty: illness and the lifecycle

Illness has long been recognized as one of the chief causes of poverty.[13] Typhus, typhoid fever, influenza, and smallpox were all epidemic (and to some extent endemic) during the eighteenth century and their propensity to kill their victims depended on a variety of factors including gender, age, and nutritional health. The nineteenth century brought new terrors to densely populated urban areas in the form of cholera. Other maladies such as malaria and tuberculosis were chronic and could have a debilitating influence over months or years before they either killed the patient or were cured.[14] Women juggled the economic impact of the illness of bread-winners, the consequences of their own ailments, the problems posed by children's ill-health, which kept mothers away from work, and the new expenses imposed by illness itself. Medical attention, surgical procedures, medicines, and nursing might all have to be paid for at a time when families were least well placed to meet additional costs.

Life-cycle poverty, on the other hand, is a phrase that has been coined to characterize those factors which nudged people into hardship at predictable points during their lives. Poor girls had only one real chance to improve their life-chances for prosperity – via a canny marriage – and life became precarious if marriage plans went awry. An illegitimate pregnancy was a decisive step into a downward spiral of poverty.[15] The rate of technically illegitimate births rose from around 2 per cent in 1700 to 5 per cent or more in 1850, so the deprivations of single motherhood became experienced more widely over the period. These women lacked breadwinners and risked losing the goodwill and support of their families. The presence of a small child meant that finding or keeping waged work was difficult, unless the work was wet-nursing.[16] Furthermore, blame attributed to single mothers by parish authorities could turn an application for help into a punishment in itself. Unmarried mothers might be taken to a magistrate to identify the father of the baby; this practice ostensibly allowed the mother's and child's maintenance costs to be recouped from fathers, but in the process women could be subjected to humiliating interrogation. For example, in 1734 Catherine Price was compelled to reveal in her bastardy examination both the number of times and all of the locations where she had had sex with Richard Williamson (who she swore was the father of her illegitimate daughter).[17]

For married women, the period just after marriage and before the arrival of a first child could be a time of relative plenty but, as family sizes increased, women's earning power declined as family responsibilities rose. Married women's dependency on their husbands was also problematic. Men could not be compelled to share their earnings with their wives and might choose to spend the money in another way: for example, in 1731–3, in Hackney, Thomasin Wheeler's husband John repeatedly refused to assist her to maintain their two daughters (and additionally beat her and threatened to kill her), compelling Thomasin to resort repeatedly to a local magistrate for financial and legal redress.[18] Alternatively, male incapacity threw women back on to their own meagre resources, as was the case for Frances James, cited in the introduction. Married women might also be deprived of access to their husband's earnings if their husband absconded. Between 5 per cent and 15 per cent of marriages ended in desertion, since male desertion was *relatively* easy (with job opportunities for men in the merchant navy or in military service during times of war) and pursuit or detection was very difficult.[19]

Single women presumably did not have any access to a male breadwinner unless they secured and retained a place in the household of a father or brother. They were therefore more than usually dependent on their own work for their survival and, as such, disadvantaged by the lower wages accorded to women, unless they were disposed to group together to share domestic expenses, a phenomenon known as 'spinster clustering'.[20]

Widowhood was a very common experience for women. Men's life-expectancy was three years shorter than women's, and wives were often younger than husbands, meaning that women were much more likely to become widows than men were to become widowers (despite the health risks arising from childbirth).[21] Some calculations suggest there were more than twice as many widows in the population than widowers.[22] A husband's death represented economic disaster, since it frequently either initiated or exacerbated poverty. Remarriage was a route to economic survival, but the majority of widows found remarriage difficult because widowhood had rendered them too poor to be attractive in the marriage market. Only a quarter of widows remarried in the late seventeenth century.[23] Widows who lived quietly were one of the recognized groups of the 'deserving' poor and there is evidence that English widows received more generous allowances than other poor people.[24] The picture was more blurred in Scotland and Ireland in the eighteenth and nineteenth centuries, where elderly widows were recognized as a deserving group but, even so, 'meanness to widows was common'.[25]

Old age, and the consequential loss of physical strength and earning capacity, tipped women who were already in want deeper into poverty. The onset of old age was determined partly by numerical age but largely in terms of experience and consequential aging. People might have been regarded as old at 50 or less, if their life experiences had been harsh and their physical health not good.[26]

Numerous causes of poverty made some impact on both men and women but all of the causes recounted here fell more firmly on women. Furthermore, the basic factors underlying female poverty were not subject to significant change during these 150 years: low wages, some dependency on male earnings, subjection to childbearing capacity, and the sufferings of old age were as familiar in 1850 as they had been in 1700.

The context of female poverty: urbanization

The ways in which experiences of poverty changed in the period 1700–1850 depended on broader changes in British society which propelled poverty from a largely rural to a significant urban problem. In 1700, a maximum of a fifth of the English population lived in towns; by 1850, the proportion had grown to a half.[27] Urban growth was largely built upon industrial expansion. Therefore, while the 'average' poor woman of 1700 lived in a squalid country cottage and was employed in part-time agricultural work or textile piecework at home, her counterpart in 1850 was more likely to live in cramped city accommodation and to spend part of her working life prior to marriage in industrial production outside the home, *perhaps* in a factory. The factory was not a ubiquitous feature of the employment landscape, being much more familiar in the Lancashire cotton towns than elsewhere, but women and children comprised over 70 per cent of cotton-factory workers in 1835.[28]

The immediate impact of urbanization on the female experience of poverty can be discerned in declining urban standards of living, most readily observable in terms of living space. Families became crowded into fewer and smaller rooms as poor people, particularly those dependent on casual labour, strove to live very near to their place of work.[29] In the first half of the nineteenth century, 12–22 per cent of the population of Liverpool and Manchester were living in cellar dwellings – the worst form of urban accommodation – comprising one or at most two dark, damp, low-ceilinged rooms with poor ventilation.[30] By the 1840s, the term 'slum' had come into use to describe the housing of the poor.[31] Acute over-crowding had immediate implications for hygiene and health, as multiple families were compelled to share a single privy, tap, or overflowing ash-pit. Urban mortality rates remained higher than their rural equivalents from the late eighteenth to the late nineteenth century.[32]

Towns also rendered the experience of poverty more acute in that they largely deprived the labouring poor of access to their own land, or means to generate their own food. Over the eighteenth century, '[m]aintenance of smallholdings and livestock in the towns to supplement earnings was becoming less and less usual'.[33] Thus the poor were increasingly or exclusively reliant on food they could buy rather than grow or gather, and, in the first half of the nineteenth century, having to deal with high prices and food adulteration on an unprecedented scale. Deceptions ranged from the (relatively harmless) substitution of alum for flour in bread through to the use of literally poisonous mineral dyes in sweets. The poor, who were compelled to put price above most other considerations, were the main market for impure foodstuffs and nutritionally low-grade or worthless foods had a significant if incalculable impact on public health.[34]

This unequivocally pessimistic view of urbanization on the experience of the female poor applies *up to 1850*. In the second half of the nineteenth century, urban living conditions were eventually ameliorated by the advent of measures such as widely applicable building regulations and public health legislation, but in the period 1700–1850 the material conditions under which women experienced poverty, whether it originated in economic or lifecycle causes, were becoming more harsh.

Welfare for women: resources and strategies to tackle poverty

British women were able to turn to a variety of welfare sources when trying to cope with their difficulties. Poor Law provision has been the resource best advertised by historians (particularly in England), but there were also benefits to be derived from kinship support and charity. Furthermore, women developed more independent self-help strategies, such as borrowing and small-scale saving, or other strategies not examined in this chapter such as growing or gleaning food or fuel, or resorting to crimes like prostitution or theft.

The Old Poor Law

Women in England and Wales were subject to Poor Laws that were first put in place in the late sixteenth century and continued to operate until 1834. The Poor Law worked at a very local level. Each parish raised a tax and distributed the money collected to the poor who 'belonged' to that place. The question of how to define 'belonging' was resolved by a series of 'settlement' laws enacted between 1662 and 1698. The majority of English parishes were raising this tax by about 1660, but it took much longer for the practice to become established throughout Wales.[35] Parish relief was dispensed in a variety of ways. Usually, people who asked for help were given small sums of cash, either as a one-off payment in cases of temporary difficulty, or a regular weekly or monthly payment or 'pension'. Cash might also be spent on behalf of poor people by paying for goods such as fuel, food, clothes, or medicines. From 1696, some places acquired workhouses where numerous poor people might be housed and fed, sometimes in exchange for work. An Act of 1723 permitted parishes to refuse help to anyone who would not go into the workhouse, on the basis that anyone in dire need would accept help in whatever form it was offered. This strategy was designed to deter all but the most needy people from asking for help, but in practice not all parishes enforced the rule.[36] By 1776, there were around, 2000 workhouses in England but only nineteen workhouses in Wales.[37]

Adult women were the biggest group of recipients for parish pensions throughout the period 1700–1850. In the late eighteenth and early nineteenth centuries the gender distribution of poor-relief recipients became less imbalanced, as regular cash payments were increasingly made to men who were in work but could not afford to support their families by their wages alone. Even so, women remained the biggest group among the poor helped by parish funds. Pension payments to adult women could be made for years, or even decades. It was quite usual for women to receive payments that increased gradually, presumably as the ability to earn anything from work declined, and then increased dramatically just before death.[38] Parish funds also supplied occasional employment opportunities for poor women as midwives, nurses, foster parents, or carers for the elderly, and in laying out or sitting up with the dead.[39] But the potential range of poor relief did not give rise to a smooth, predictable flow of benefits to all women: 'overseers combined relative generosity to married or widowed females who had children and settlement with high-handed repressiveness against those without clear rights or a powerful protector'. There were also regional variations in the extent to which parishes were willing to help women.[40]

The New Poor Law

By the early nineteenth century the poor-relief system was struggling to cope with the demands being placed upon it, giving rise to the Poor Law Amendment Act in 1834. The immediate impact of the new law is debateable. In the past, historians have characterized 1834 as a watershed, signalling a radical break with earlier relief practices and a more stringent, penny-pinching approach to the disbursement of relief.[41] There were certainly some clauses in the new law which would have proved at best unpalatable and at worse oppressive to the poor requiring help for example, Poor Law authorities were to operate workhouses in line with a strict policy based upon the principle of 'less eligibility'. This required material conditions inside workhouses to be so unpleasant – for instance, in terms of diet – that life in the workhouse would be 'less eligible' than in the labourers' own homes. The ideal consequence of this policy for legislators was that the poor would make every effort to remain out of the workhouse and off poor relief, thus reducing the financial burden for taxpayers. The new law also stressed the importance of vigilant oversight of relief applications to deter the idle or fraudulent from obtaining more than their due, and to this end intended to impose a uniform system of relief across the country, predicated on recognizable categories of pauper.

Still, it was one thing to create a law and quite another to enforce it.[42] In practice, poor relief continued to be dispensed in a familiar way in many places, at least at first. Poor-relief policy under the old law had, in a number of places, been moving towards a harsher regime which was effectively relabelled as 'less eligibility' after 1834. Furthermore, resistance to implementation of the law and an inadequate number of enforcing commissioners meant that the stringent new laws were not applicable everywhere in England until about the 1850s. Where the idea of 'less eligibility' was adopted suddenly and immediately, it quickly proved to be unworkable. It was impossible to provide a less sufficient diet, for instance, than people could expect in their own homes without starving workhouse populations; consequently, harsh rules about diet were revised within a decade of the law being passed. Even the use of the workhouse as the centrepiece of the new welfare regime was relatively limited; by 1849 only 12.2 per cent of all paupers were being relieved in workhouses. [43]

The New Poor Law was constructed on a raft of preconceived notions which had little or no basis in the changing shape of poverty (propelled by urbanization) or the composition of the poor. It could be argued that gendered assumptions on the part of Poor Law administrators gave rise to a number of continuities between the old and new laws for poor female recipients. [44] The new law envisaged the able-bodied man as the main, problematic applicant for assistance and subsequent discussions tended to omit explicit consideration of women. [45] The most prominent treatment of poor women in the report of the Royal Commission (which formed the basis of the new law) was of single mothers, demonized for their alleged propensity to use their fertility to gain access to welfare. [46] Against the backdrop of this ideology, the prominence of women impoverished by the standard means – deserted wives or widows, with legitimate children – remained high: 40 per cent of paupers in 1840 were adult women while another 40 per cent were children. Their day-to-day treatment did not change radically. [47] Perhaps one of the most positive views of poor relief under the new law suggests that, until the 1870s, the elderly poor (comprised substantially of women) could look to parish relief as their main or only source of income and survive at a standard of living 80–100 per cent of that of non-elderly labouring adults. [48]

Poor relief in Scotland and Ireland operated in a more restrictive or even intermittent way. In Scotland in this period poor relief was controlled by Kirk sessions and by heritors (landowners). It was largely funded by voluntary collections at the Kirk door and by Kirk fines for disciplinary offences, since local taxes were not raised in all parishes in all years. This system of finance meant that money was usually in short supply. A small measure of relief, typically insufficient as a sole source of income, was given to the poor who were considered unable to help themselves, but may have been withheld from able-bodied men and women except in unusual circumstances. [49] Consequently, relief from the Edinburgh Kirk sessions was usually given to widows, orphans, or the sick and disabled. Adult women might be compelled to beg even for unpalatable forms of relief. Edinburgh women had to petition to obtain a place in the city's Orphan hospital for one or more of their children. [50] Nonetheless, Scottish towns gradually acquired more welfare institutions than were available in the countryside: 'workhouses' were established in Glasgow, Aberdeen and Edinburgh from 1733 onwards. [51] Scotland acquired a New Poor Law in 1845. In Ireland, by contrast, there was nothing resembling a national Poor Law for most of the period under consideration. Dublin acquired a workhouse that opened in 1706 but parish and community efforts at welfare for the poor were patchy.[52] The Irish Poor Law was only enacted in 1838.

Kinship assistance

Did poor women often turn to families for assistance? In the past, historians have characterized kinship connections in pre-industrial England as very limited, but this impression is now being challenged. David Cressy's research suggests that kinship, 'involved a range of possibilities rather than a set of concrete obligations', and extended from advice and emotional or political support through to financial help. He argues that kinship was in fact 'valuable, versatile and wide-ranging'.[53] F. K. Prochaska effectively concurs, claiming that, '[w]hatever one's trouble, whatever one's station, the first place to turn was the family'.[54] Determination of actual practice in families is, however, a knotty problem. Perhaps the least surprising channels of assistance arose from vertical kinship ties, particularly those from adult children to their elderly mothers and from parents and parents-in-law to adult children. Early eighteenth-century evidence suggests that poor parents gave adult children assistance in the form of advice, help in illness, and small gifts and loans, while grown-up children offered elderly parents residential visits during illness, advice on taking lodgers, and protection for mothers who had been robbed.[55] Help could also derive from lateral rather than vertical kin; in particular, women turned to their brothers or brothers-in-law. Indeed, recent research suggests that poor people lacking uncles and brothers were disproportionately likely to need parish relief.[56] Crucially, for the issue of development over the period, the process of urbanization did not seem to undermine kinship connectedness. Historians tend to play down the disruptive elements of migration, stressing that the 'individual who moved alone and speculatively over a long distance to an unfamiliar place in which they had not friends or relatives, and no previously arranged employment or accommodation, was relatively rare'.[57]

The kinship experiences of poor, elderly women have been investigated via a study of living arrangements, with a view to determining how far people altered their households in order to cope with poverty. Research suggests that in late eighteenth- and nineteenth-century England elderly spinsters and widows of all ages did not tend to live alone. They shared houses with parents (in the case of young widows) or adult children, and shared accommodation with non-relations, either by taking in lodgers or by becoming lodgers themselves.[58] Older widows were much more likely than younger widows to become financially dependent on a relative who lived in the same household.[59] Yet living with others cannot always be given a positive slant. The poorest elderly women were likely to become dependants in other people's homes and were also the least likely group to co-reside with close kin, so that they 'remained very vulnerable to isolation and dependence'.[60]

Charity

Charity, paid from voluntary alms rather than from a local tax, could derive from bequests made in wills, gifts during life, or collective funds gathered by subscription. Testamentary charity was administered by a bewildering variety of different groups including individuals, trustees, trade companies, town councils, parish vestries, and religious organizations. Many charities provided an annual distribution of cash or bread which was reallocated each year, meaning that poor recipients could not *rely* on it from week-to-week or even from year-to-year as a source of support. Some types of charity typically founded by wills made a more significant dent in poverty than others. Almshouse charities were designed to provide accommodation and some form of income or other benefits to inhabitants, and selected almshouse charities were very generous. Almshouse charities were also particularly pertinent for women; one estimate suggests that, even as late as *c.*1850, 5 per cent or more of all elderly women received free housing in almshouses, especially in old established urban settlements (the percentage in earlier years being even higher).[61] Almshouses were most likely to be founded in the sixteenth or seventeenth centuries, but such charities continued to operate throughout the eighteenth century, and beyond.[62]

By the start of this period, charity given in people's wills had passed its heyday. Prosperous people were increasingly beset by the nagging suspicion that, however stringently they tried to control a charity after their death, it was inevitably susceptible to a distortion of rules (and the relief of the 'wrong' sort of poverty).[63] Consequently, from the 1690s onwards, a new sort of charity became popular which relied on regular, often annual, subscriptions being paid into a collective charity fund. From 1698 to approximately 1730 this form of charity saw the founding of numerous schools throughout Britain, while the 1720s onward witnessed the establishment of subscription hospitals for the treatment of the sick poor in provincial England and Scotland.[64] The second half of the eighteenth century saw a positive explosion of subscription charity for a wide variety of causes; however, each charity was fairly narrowly defined – witness the Society for the Relief of the Ruptured Poor for those with hernias who needed trusses.

The extent to which women benefited from these new subscription charities was significantly limited. Charity schools were more often established for boys than for girls; co-educational schools admitted more boys than girls; even hospitals for the sick tended to admit more men than women.[65] From 1749, lying-in charities were set up to assist poor married women with the costs associated with giving birth to legitimate babies and their immediate needs (for a midwife, possibly some nursing care, and linen or clothing for the babies).[66] These charities undoubtedly assisted some women with emergency costs which arose inevitably from married life but help was limited because assistance stopped abruptly, usually when babies were a month old.

The nineteenth century heralded the development of an additional variety of charity, which depended on close acquaintance (or scrutiny) of the poor by the charitable benefactors. Charity volunteers would investigate the claims of needy families by means of a home visit to determine both how impoverished and how deserving each case might be. An early example of this form of charity were the Strangers' Friend Societies, first founded in the 1780s in provincial towns. The policing function of the home visit made it an enduring feature of nineteenth-century charities.[67]

The problem with all of these forms of charitable endeavour, from the point of view of the poor beneficiaries, was that charity was always administered according to the dictates of the donors rather than the concerns of the poor. 'Charity was not equivalent to poaching as a way of getting by' in that the poor could not simply take what they needed but had to negotiate their entitlement for benefits which did not exactly or even approximately match their needs.[68] Each charity redefined the notion of appropriate giving and it was up to poor women to determine how or whether that charity could slot into their struggles for survival.

Borrowing and saving

Borrowing could take the form either of an advance of cash against some kind of material security or of a delay between money being owed and its collection. Pawning is a good example of the first type of borrowing. Pawnbrokers' shops were numerous in London by 1700 and a common feature of provincial industrial regions in England by 1800. Scottish pawnbroking took longer to become established and perhaps as a consequence there was an extensive unofficial money-lending culture in some Scottish cities.[69] People could obtain a small sum of cash in exchange for a 'pledge', (a pledge comprised the physical deposit of possessions like clothes or household goods), and, if the loan and any accruing interest were repaid, then the goods could be redeemed. Women represented the vast majority of pawnbrokers' customers, which is unsurprising, given women's central role in managing household economies, and typically obtained very small loans to tide them over short periods of difficulty. Pawning was not necessarily seen as an attractive option, but women were apparently more keen to pawn their possessions than to apply for poor relief while the option of pawning remained open to them.[70]

The second sort of borrowing involved negotiating delayed payments to shopkeepers, landlords, or other creditors.[71] It is thought that up to half of all retail transactions involved the extension of credit.[72] The problem with both sorts of borrowing was the fact that, in order to be successful borrowers, women needed to maintain a pretence that they would be able to repay the loan eventually. Pawnbrokers and retailers alike were reluctant to extend credit if they thought repayment was unlikely, so if a borrower's dire poverty became obvious it is likely that access to credit would have been witheld.[73]

The natural opposite of borrowing is saving, and while it seems odd to raise the possibility of saving for women who could not make ends meet, facilities emerged in this period which allowed working women to consider saving during prosperity so that they could help meet their own needs in case of future adversity. Friendly Societies encouraged working people to make small, weekly, or monthly contributions to a general fund, which would then make payments to members if they were too sick to work or would be used to pay for their burial if they died. Friendly Societies flourished only during the second half of the period; there were relatively few such clubs in 1760, but by 1803 there were at least 9,672 societies.[74] The vast majority of societies recruited men, but in some places women also set up their own schemes, often in places with relatively high rates of female industrial employment. In Bristol in 1803, for example, fourteen women's societies contained 939 members, comprising around 3 per cent of all women in the city and a much higher proportion of working-age women.[75] Nonetheless, it has been argued that even women in full-time employment found it difficult to justify the necessary contributions to Friendly Societies, particularly if a male relation was already a member of a similar club.[76]

The context of welfare: attitudes to poverty

Poor relief, charity, and borrowing all imply that both the reputation of poor people and the attitudes of the prosperous rate-payers, benefactors or creditors could be vital in securing adequate assistance for survival. To some extent, women's economic standing was always interpreted via judgements about appropriate behaviour. Women had to prove they were morally irreproachable and then constantly live up to the ideal in order to be uncontroversially deserving; low morality in women was foremost a matter of sexual chastity or continence, but could also rest on more subtle indicators.

Attitudes towards the male *and* female poor changed markedly over the period 1700–1850. In 1700, the official (legislative) attitude to poverty was one of increasing stringency; for instance, an act of 1697 authorized parishes to compel the poor on relief to wear a badge which would advertize their impoverishment. The mood of the rate-paying and charity-giving public, however, was rather more relaxed. The old Poor Law had been in operation for more than a century and the principle of paying poor relief was not widely attacked. There was broad acknowledgement that certain groups of the poor were entirely deserving and, consequently, legislation was not always enforced with great rigor. Badging the poor, for example, was desultory rather than universal. Rather than taking issue with poverty itself, reformist energies were directed at specific ills. The Reformation of Manners movement, which was at its height in London and selected provincial towns between1698 and 1738, aimed to correct behavioural faults among the poor such as profanity, drunkenness, irreligion, and promiscuity; however, this was principally a metropolitan cause and lost impetus in the mid-1720s.[77]

The vigorous, reforming spirit was replaced by a more moderate attitude to poverty in the early to mid-eighteenth century which can be aligned with the contemporary rise of 'politeness'. Polite philanthropy was humanitarian, but with a self-interested streak; according to this discourse, welfare for the poor was both politically rational (since it guarded against oppression and consequential social unrest) and economically prudent. Healing the sick poor, for example, would see them return to work and independence. In the mid-eighteenth century a related concern emerged, that the population of the country was declining and that efforts should be directed at bolstering the national population to reinforce military strength – particularly by ensuring the survival of babies. It was these polite impulses which spurred the founding of the subscription hospitals and the lying-in charities in the second half of the eighteenth century.[78]

It is widely accepted that there was a hardening of attitude towards the poor by the early nineteenth century (credited with giving rise to the ostensibly punitive New Poor Law of 1834).[79] Some commentators in the 1840s took the view that the slum-like qualities of urban housing arose from the improvidence and vice of the poor rather than the pressures of low wages, insecure employment, and the flight from misery.[80] There is less agreement on how far back into the eighteenth century this brusque attitude emerged. Deborah Valenze finds that 'charitable sentiment was notably in eclipse' in the second half of the eighteenth century and characterizes a shift in sentiment from the 1750s.[81] In related work, she identifies an increasingly negative image of working women in this period and endorses the idea that a kind of underclass was emerging by the 1750s, which exercised the imaginations of the rich, even if it was not readily identifiable in the behaviour of the poor.[82] In the early 1750s there was brisk trade in pamphlets which surveyed the weaknesses of the poor law and sketched out alternative schemes for national relief; such publications were not new of course, but the arguments acquired a fresh urgency in this decade.[83]

In contrast, Lynn Hollen-Lees emphasizes that the legal right to poor relief was persistently asserted by the poor throughout the eighteenth century and that the right was accepted with more-or-less good grace by local authorities and taxpayers. She positions a significant hardening of attitude around 1800, but not earlier than 1780, suggesting at least a grudging mutual agreement which was recognizable throughout England before that date.[84] The 1780s have also been identified as a period when a new strand of philanthropic thought emerged: charity-givers were becoming anxious that the poor were being conditioned to become dependent on welfare and were not sufficiently well motivated to work hard for their own maintenance.[85]

It seems likely that the harsh attitude of the 1840s had deep roots, put down in the 1750s and growing in the 1780s, but not really flourishing until the 1790s or later. In other words, moral assessments of the women who asked for assistance were likely to be most judgmental (and therefore more likely to govern access to help) in the years around 1700 and again from approximately 1810 onwards. Moral stringency became more exacting in the nineteenth century, when, 'to discuss women and their experiences without reference to morality was virtually impossible'.[86] Wherever women were regarded with suspicion, subjected to close and discouraging enquiry about their neediness, and only granted help with grudging agreement, then the miseries of the poor acquired an added, burdensome dimension.

The question that remains unanswered is how far the poor women felt seriously stigmatized by such attitudes. The traditional assumption, driven by attitudes among the poor to pauper burial in the nineteenth century, has been that recourse to the poor law was anathema.[87] Recently though, Llyn Lees has judged that, 'the stigma of relief operated more powerfully in the minds of poor law officials than in those of their clients', and Jane Long has revised this subtly with reference to the north-east by stressing the 'gendered stigma' of institutions for women.[88] For many historians, the jury is still out on the stigma of welfare.

Dependent or autonomous?

To what extent did poor women emphasize their dependency and how far did they secure a measure of agency in their quest to make ends meet? Pauper letters like the one from Frances James at the start of this chapter provide another means for assessing the balance of power between the female parish poor and the men who administered the poor laws.[89] Taken at face value, women's pauper letters reinforce the judgment that women were weak, dependent creatures. Women from all over England employed the phrase 'out of my power' to stress their inability to alleviate their own poverty.[90] Female letter-writers also made use of emotive language which pointed up their vulnerability. It was commonplace for women like Frances James to emphasize their 'distress'. Yet these letters were written by women who were asking for something and therefore were bound to reiterate their powerlessness to maximize both the sympathy of their readers and their claim to assistance.

The recent emphasis of historiography has been to restore a sense of agency to groups previously supposed to have been relatively powerless. Marcia Schmidt Blaine juxtaposes theoretical female powerlessness with practical female achievement in the context of eighteenth-century New Hampshire.[91] Responsibility for domestic life validated women's attempts to shore up that life when their endeavours took them into the public sphere.[92] Groups of women who were sporadically involved with the anti-poor law movement after 1834 justified their participation as 'defence of the family'.[93] As a consequence, some historians play down poor women's claims of powerlessness. Pam Sharpe has described widows' letters changing over time to become increasingly firm, more inclined to stress their legal right and their moral entitlement to relief. She has adopted Scott's 'weapons of the weak' to describe such letters.[94]

Female letter-writers could undoubtedly make vigorous and skilled attempts to make ends meet and assert their own preferences, but describing the actions of very poor women in order to survive as conscious choice, particularly where the available options may all have seemed to be objectionable to some degree, could be inaccurate and unjust. It is entirely plausible that the decision to enter a workhouse or engage in negotiations for charity took place in such a severe social and economic context that the cosy implication of 'choice' is entirely misleading. Clearly, we should guard against 'an over-determined concept of agency (a formula in which action equals autonomy and resistance)'.[95] Power was not shared equally between male parish officers and the needy women they encountered, but was instead tipped substantially in favour of the former. Poor women had the power to be manipulative or even disruptive, but they could not be confident that their efforts would secure their own preferred outcomes.

Conclusion

The poor were never a homogeneous group, but this chapter has aimed to draw together those experiences which poor women had in common. The routes down into poverty were well-worn, and causes could be gradual (via low wages or other long-term problems which gradually degraded women's ability to make ends meet) or sudden (via abrupt shocks like widowhood). Routes out of poverty were much more uncertain. The English Poor Law has been characterized as underpinning the labouring poor, providing them with a safety net in times of difficulty, and essentially insulating them from the worst consequences of poverty (death from starvation or exposure); however, the reach of the Scottish and Irish versions was much more restricted, and the extent to which poor relief anywhere in Britain could do more than just keep people alive is debateable. Some commentators characterize English relief as a systematic and relatively generous resource which provided for people adequately, if not comfortably; others are much more bleak in their judgement of parish provision, and stress instead the alternative sources of income as vital for the survival of the poor. [96]

Women were in a particularly invidious position as the people most likely to need assistance at all times between 1700 and 1850, but, also as the group most likely to be overlooked by any nationwide considerations of poverty. Able-bodied men were regarded as the most problematic paupers in England and women received secondary consideration, or none at all. In Scotland, women were frequently the chief beneficiaries of relief, but in the context of scanty resources, whereas in Ireland, vagrants and orphans attracted legislative interest and community action, but other groups seem to have been relatively neglected.[97]

How did individual women operate in this context? Where women turned to parish officers for help, they consciously stressed personal attributes which would recommend them for assistance such as powerlessness and emotional fragility. A closer reading of women's pauper letters can reveal a more robust picture of correspondents, but the extent to which this leverage can be positively talked up as 'agency' is uncertain; ultimately women were at the mercy of parish officers and vestries, who had the *duty* to dispense relief, but the *power* to minimize its content and offer it in unpalatable formats. Poor women were not just short of money; they were also short of influence. Their frequent creativity in making ends meet, like that exerted by Frances James in the 1830s, can be construed as testimony to the harsh constraints they faced in their everyday lives.

Notes

1 The letters of Philip and Frances James are in the Staffordshire Record Office, D. 3891/6/98–105, correspondence 1829–40: D. 3891/6/100, Frances James to overseers of Uttoxeter, 29 December 1833.

2 S.R.O., D. 3891/6/102, Philip James to overseers of Uttoxeter, 3 January 1834.

3 S.R.O., D. 3891/6/103, Thomas Pickering to overseers of Uttoxeter, 16 February 1836.

4 R. Mitchison, 'Who were the poor in Scotland?', in R. Mitchison and P. Roebuck (eds), *Economy and Society in Scotland and Ireland, 1500–1939*, Edinburgh, 1988, pp. 141, 145.

5 E. P. Thompson, *Customs in Common*, London, 1993; D. Eastwood, 'History, politics and reputation: E. P. Thompson reconsidered', *History*, 2000, vol. 85, p. 650.

6 S. King, 'Making the most of opportunity: the economy of makeshifts in the early modern north', A. Tomkins and S. King (eds), *The Poor in England, 1700–1850: An Economy of Makeshifts*, Manchester, 2003, p. 251.

7 M. Berg, 'What difference did women's work make to the industrial revolution?', *History Workshop Journal*, vol. 35, 1993, p. 31.

8 A. Kidd, *State, Society and the Poor in Nineteenth-Century England*, Basingstoke, 1999, pp. 146–7.

9 S. Horrell and J. Humphries, 'Women's labour force participation and the transition to the male-breadwinner family, 1790–1865', in P. Sharpe (ed.), *Women's Work: The English Experience, 1650–1914*, London, 1998.

10 T. S. Ashton, *Economic Fluctuations in England, 1700–1800*, Oxford, 1959, chapter 3.

11 P. Langford, *A Polite and Commercial People: England, 1727–1783*, Oxford, 1992, pp. 442–3.

12 R. Jutte, *Poverty and Deviance in Early Modern Europe*, Cambridge, 1994, p. 31; Ashton, *Economic Fluctuations*, pp. 35–6.

13 Jutte, *Poverty*, pp. 21–5.

14 A. Lawrence, *Women in England, 1500–1760*, London, 1994, pp. 95–8.

15 P. Sharpe, 'Literally spinsters: a new interpretation of local economy and demography in Colyton in the seventeenth and eighteenth centuries', *Economic History Review*, 1991, vol. 44, pp. 56–8.

16 See G. Debrisay, 'Wet nurses and unwed mothers in seventeeth-century Aberdeen', in E. Ewan and M. M. Meikle (eds), *Women in Scotland, c.1100–1750*, East Linton, 1999.

17 T. Hitchcock and J. Black (eds), *Chelsea Settlement and Bastardy Examinations, 1733–1766*, London, London Record Society, 1999, vol. 33, p. 4.

18 R. Paley (ed.), *Justice in Eighteenth-Century Hackney: The Justicing Notebook of Henry Norris and the Hackney Petty Sessions Book*, London, London Record Society, vol. 28, 1991, pp. 2, 12, 21, 26–7, 100, 118; S. Rose, *Limited Livelihoods: Gender and Class in Nineteenth-Century England*, London, 1992, p. 89.

19 Lawrence, *Women in England*, pp. 53–4.

20 O. Hufton, *The Prospect Before Her, 1500–1800: A History of Women in Western Europe*, London, 1995, pp. 255–6.

21 P. Thane, *Old Age in English History*, Oxford, 2000, p. 479.

22 P. Laslett, *Family Life and Illicit Love in Earlier Generations: Essays in Historical Sociology*, Cambridge, 1977, p. 198.

23 B. J. Todd, 'The remarrying widow: a stereotype reconsidered', in M. Prior (ed.), *Women in English Society, 1500–1800*, London, 1985.

24 P. Sharpe, 'Survival strategies and stories: poor widows and widowers in early industrial England', in S. Cavallo and L. Warner (eds), *Widowhood in Medieval and Early Modern Europe*, Harlow, 1999, pp. 224–9.

25 D. Dickson, 'In search of the old Irish poor law', in Mitchison and Roebuck (eds), *Economy and Society in Scotland and Ireland*, p. 152; R. Mitchison, *The Old Poor Law in Scotland: The Experience of Poverty, 1574–1845*, Edinburgh, 2000, p. 201.

26 J. Roebuck, 'When does old age begin? The evolution of the English definition', *Journal of Social History*, 1979, vol. 12.

27 Langford, *Polite and Commercial People*, p. 418; R. Rodger, *Housing in Urban Britain, 1780–1914*, Cambridge, 1989, p. 7.

28 P. Deane and W. A. Cole, *British Economic Growth, 1688–1959*, Cambridge, 1962, p. 294.

29 Rodger, *Housing in Urban Britain*, p. 12.

30 J. Burnett, *A Social History of Housing, 1815–1970*, Newton Abbot, 1978, pp. 58–61.

31 H. J. Dyos, 'The slums of Victorian London', *Victorian Studies*, 1967, vol. 11, p. 8.

32 P. Hudson, *The Industrial Revolution*, London, 1992, p. 155.

33 P. Corfield, *The Impact of English Towns, 1700–1800*, Oxford, 1982, pp. 135–6.

34 J. Burnett, *Plenty and Want: A Social History of Diet in England from 1815 to the Present Day*, London, 1979, Chapter 5.

35 P. Slack, *Poverty and Policy in Tudor and Stuart England*, Harlow, 1988, pp. 184–5; A. Teale, 'The battle against poverty in north Flintshire, *c.*1660–1714', *Flintshire Historical Society Journal* 1983–4, vol. 31, pp. 92–3, claims that rates were adopted early in selected Welsh parishes.

36 For a useful summary, see S. King, *Poverty and Welfare in England, 1700–1850*, Manchester, 2000, pp. 272–4, 'A legal chronology of the poor laws'.

37 J. S. Taylor, 'The unreformed workhouse, 1776–1834', in E. W. Martin (ed.), *Comparative Development in Social Welfare*, London, 1972, p. 61.

38 T. Wales, 'Poverty, Poor Relief and life-cycle: some evidence from seventeenth century Norfolk', in R. M. Smith (ed.), *Land, Kinship and Lifecycle*, Cambridge, 1984, pp. 362–3.

39 Sharpe, 'Literally spinsters', pp. 60–1.

40 L. H. Lees, *The Solidarities of Strangers: The English Poor Laws and the People, 1700–1948*, Cambridge, 1998, pp. 57, 202.

41 K. Snell, *Annals of the Labouring Poor: Social Change and Agrarian England, 1660–1900*, Cambridge, 1985, pp. 114–37.

42 J. H. Treble, *Urban Poverty in Britain 1830–1914*, London, 1979, p. 140.

43 King, *Poverty and Welfare*, pp. 65–70, 227–33; N. Edsall, *The Anti-Poor Law Movement, 1833–44*, Manchester, 1971; V. J. Johnson, *Diets in Workhouses and Prisons, 1835–1895*, New York, 1985, Chapter 5.

44 Kidd, *State, Society and the Poor*, pp. 37–9.

45 P. Thane, ' Women and the poor law in Victorian and Edwardian England', *History Workshop Journal*, 1978, vol. 6, pp. 29–32.

46 J. Long, *Conversations in Cold Rooms: Women, Work and Poverty in Nineteenth-Century Northumberland*, Woodbridge, 1999, pp. 134–6.

47 King, *Poverty and Welfare*, pp. 237, 249.

48 D. Thompson, 'The decline of social welfare: falling state support for the elderly since early Victorian times', *Ageing and Society*, vol. 4, 1984.

49 R. Mitchison, 'The making of the old Scottish poor law', *Past and Present*, 1974, no. 63.

50 E. C. Sanderson, *Women and Work in Eighteenth-Century Edinburgh*, Basingstoke, 1996, pp. 137, 163–4.

51 R. A. Cage, 'Debate: the making of the Scottish old poor law', *Past and Present* 1975, no. 69, p. 117.

52 Dickson, 'In search of the old Irish poor law'.

53 D. Cressy, 'Kinship and kin interaction in early modern England', *Past and Present*, 1986, no. 113, pp. 44, 49, 53.

54 F. K. Prochaska, 'Philanthropy', in F. M. L. Thompson (ed.), *The Cambridge Social History of Britain, 1750–1950: III: Social Agencies and Institutions*, Cambridge, 1993, p. 361.

55 I. K. Ben-Amos, 'Gifts and favors: informal support in early modern England', *Journal of Modern History*, 2000, vol. 72, pp. 302, 304.

56 S. Barrett, 'Kinship, poor relief and the welfare process in early modern England', in A. Tomkins and S. King (eds), *The Poor in England, 1700–1850: An Economy of Makeshifts*, Manchester, 2003, p. 215.

57 C. Pooley and J. Turnbull, *Migration and Mobility in Britain since the 18th century*, London, 1998, pp. 304, 306. See also Ben-Amos, 'Gifts and favors', pp. 307–9.

58 T. Sokoll, 'The household position of elderly widows in poverty', in J. Henderson and R. Wall (eds), *Poor Women and Children in the European Past*, London, 1994; S. Rose, 'Widowhood and poverty in nineteenth-century Nottinghamshire', in J. Henderson and R. Wall (eds), *Poor Women and Children in the European Past*, London, 1994, p. 273.

59 Thane, *Old Age*, p. 145; Rose, 'Widowhood', p. 281.

60 S. Otttaway, 'The old woman's home in eighteenth-century England', in L. Botelho and P. Thane (eds), *Women and Ageing in British Society since 1500*, Harlow, 2001, p. 131.

61 D. Thompson, 'Welfare and the historians', in L. Bonfield, R. M. Smith, and K. Wrightson (eds), *The World We Have Gained: Histories of Population and Social Structure*, Oxford, 1986, p. 369.

62 W. K. Jordan, *Philanthropy in England, 1480–1660*, New York, 1959, Chapter 7.

63 D. Andrew, *Philanthropy and Police: London Charity in the Eighteenth Century*. Princeton, NJ, 1989, pp. 19, 48.

64 M. G. Jones, *The Charity School Movement: A Study of Eighteenth Century Puritanism in Action*, Cambridge, 1938; J. Woodward, *To Do the Sick No Harm: A Study of the British Voluntary Hospital System to 1875*, London, 1978.

65 D. Simonton, 'Schooling the poor: gender and class in eighteenth-century England', *British Journal for Eighteenth-Century Studies*, 2000, 23, pp. 190–1; A. Borsay, *Medicine and Charity in Georgian Bath: A Social History of the General Infirmary, c.1739–1830*, Aldershot, 1999, pp. 224–30.

66 Andrew, *Philanthropy and Police*, pp. 65–9.

67 Kidd, *State and Society*, pp. 76–7, 79–84.

68 S. Lloyd, 'Agents in their own concerns? Charity and the economy of makeshifts in eighteenth-century Britain', in Tomkins and King (eds), *The Poor in England*, pp. 118–21.

69 M. Tebbutt, *Making Ends Meet: Pawnbroking and Working-Class Credit*, Leicester, 1983, pp. 2, 14, 107, 122–5; Sanderson, *Women and Work*, pp. 150–1.

70 A. Tomkins, 'Pawnbroking and the survival strategies of the urban poor in 1770s York', in Tomkins and King (eds), *The Poor in England*; Tebbutt, *Making Ends Meet*, Chapter 2.

71 Ben-Amos, 'Gifts and favors', pp. 312, 328–31.

72 P. H. Haagen, 'Eighteenth-century English society and the debt law', in S. Cohen and A. Scull (eds), *Social Control and the State*, Oxford, 1983, p. 229.

73 Treble, *Urban Poverty*, pp. 130–6.

74 P. H. J. H. Gosden, *Self Help: Voluntary Associations in the 19th Century*, London, 1973, pp. 9, 12, 13, 74.

75 M. Gorsky, *Patterns of Philanthropy: Charity and Society in Nineteenth-Century Bristol*, Woodbridge, 1999, p. 166.

76 Thane, 'Women and the poor law', pp. 34–5.

77 R. B. Shoemaker, 'Reforming the city: the Reformation of Manners campaign in London, 1690–1738', in L. Davison *et al.* (eds), *Stilling the Grumbling Hive: The Response to Social and Economic Problems in England, 1689–1750*, Stroud, 1992.

78 For a full consideration of changing charitable motivations 1680–1790, see Andrew, *Philanthropy and Police*.

79 Kidd, *State, Society and the Poor*, pp. 19–29.

80 Rodger, *Housing in Urban Britain*, pp. 2–3.

81 D. Valenze, 'Charity, custom and humanity: changing attitudes towards the poor in eighteenth-century England', in J. Garnett and C. Matthew (eds), *Revival and Religion Since 1700*, London, 1993, pp. 61–2.

82 D. Valenze, *The First Industrial Woman*, Oxford, 1995, pp. 25–7.

83 J. Innes, 'The mixed economy of welfare'in early modern England: assessments of the options from Hale to Malthus (*c.*1683–1803)', in M. Daunton (ed.), *Charity, Self-Interest and Welfare in the English Past*, London, 1996, p. 157, and *passim*.

84 Lees, *Solidarities of Strangers*, Chapter 3 and pp. 19, 77–9.

85 Andrew, *Philanthropy and Police*, pp. 141, 169–70.

86 Long, *Conversations in Cold Rooms*, pp. 139, 141.

87 R. Richardson, *Death, Dissection and the Destitute*, London, 1987,

88 Lees, 'Survival of the unfit', p. 88; Long, *Conversations in Cold Rooms*, pp. 158–9.

89 For a detailed discussion of this type of source, see T. Sokoll, *Essex Pauper Letters 1731–1837*, Oxford, 2001.

90 See, for example, Long, *Conversations in Cold Rooms*, p. 127; Sokoll, *Essex Pauper Letters*, pp. 274, 590, 598.

91 M. S. Blaine, 'The power of petitions: women and the New Hampshire provincial government, 1695–1770', *International Review of Social History*, 2001, vol. 46, p. 59.

92 L. Colley, *Britons: Forging the Nation, 1707–1837*, New Haven, CT, 1992, pp. 263–8.

93 Robert B. Shoemaker, *Gender in English Society, 1650–1850*, Harlow, 1998, p. 261.

94 Sharpe, 'Survival strategies', pp. 230, 233, 235–6; J. C. Scott, *'Weapons of the Weak': Everyday Forms of Peasant Resistance*, New Haven, CT, 1985.

95 Lloyd, 'Agents in their own concerns', p. 130.

96 S. King, 'Poor relief and English economic development reappraised', *Economic History Review*, 1997, L 2; P. Solar, 'Poor relief and English economic development: a renewed plea for comparative history', *Economic History Review*, 1997, L 2.

97 Dickson, 'In search of the old Irish poor law', pp. 149–50.

Chapter Eight

❧

Women and crime

Anne-Marie Kilday

Urbanization, industrialization, and key political changes, such as the Union of England and Scotland in 1707, meant that the physical, ideological, and political landscape of the constituent countries of Britain were wholly transformed between 1700 and 1850. These developments had implications for the would-be criminal. The law became far more centralized during the eighteenth century, especially north of the Tweed, and many customary practices that had previously been an accepted part of everyday life were now criminalized under a new and arguably tougher criminal code. At the same time as the statute book increased, the introduction of summary trials quickened the judicial process, and this, coupled with more intensified policing and greater public vigilance, meant that the number of criminals brought before the courts accelerated over a relatively short period of time.[1] It is no surprise, therefore, that crime has been the subject of a good deal of recent historical research on eighteenth- and nineteenth-century Britain.[2]

Studies of female criminality, however, have been rather thinner on the ground. Moreover, in contrast to the general trend of rising crime levels between 1700 and 1850, work has tended to depict a decline in women's criminal activity between 1700 and 1850. A survey carried out by Malcolm Feeley and Deborah Little, based on Old Bailey indictments between 1687 and 1912, concluded that the female offender all but 'vanished' from the criminal process in terms of serious felonies from the end of the eighteenth century.[3] Although their work has yet to be challenged, augmented, or substantiated by other studies of long-term trends in female criminality (on a regional or national basis), Feeley and Little convincingly explained the reduction of women's involvement in serious crime in their study as the result of a redefinition of women's roles in society, the family, and the economy.[4] Other research has also described the relative unimportance of female crime during this period, not only due to its apparently static or declining incidence after 1800, but more significantly because of the consistent lack of women brought before the courts in comparison to men – a trend clearly in evidence since medieval times.[5] Studies that do examine women criminals tend to emphasize what might be termed 'traditional' acts of female deviance, such as infanticide or prostitution,[6] while perceptions of women's involvement in criminal activity has been dominated by their role as the victim rather than the perpetrator of crime.

In common with other accounts of women and crime in this period, this chapter will argue that female participation in crime differed substantially from that of men in terms of the types of crime committed, the ways it was carried out, and the rationale behind it. However, it also offers some challenges to more familiar models of female criminality between 1700 and 1850. Most importantly, it argues that, while women might have been less likely than men to commit crime, especially violent crime, women were not adverse to using extreme violence in certain situations. Strangulation, drowning, battery, slashing with razors, gouging with knives, 'dashing brains out' with pokers and cudgels, hacking with axes, stabbing with pitchforks, and stoning were all methods used throughout the eighteenth- and early nineteenth-century by criminal women in Britain. Elizabeth Gratrix, from St Martins in the Fields for example, smashed her dining companion's skull to pieces with a pewter pot after an argument in 1710; Jane Churn from Middlesex bludgeoned her spouse to death with an iron poker during a heated argument in 1796; and Elizabeth Middleton from Whitechapel battered her 9-year-old adopted daughter to death with a cane and a rod, both stiffened in brine, in 1842.[7]

Cases such as these illustrate that women could be just as shocking and brutal in their criminal behaviour as men. Such violent women acted in a manner that we rarely associate with women from the period. Aggression was certainly not one of the celebrated traits of the 'fairer sex', yet its existence suggests that ideals of femininity could be – and were – challenged, particularly by women of the lower orders. As we shall see, women's crimes, violent or otherwise, have much to tell us about the lives and experiences of those who perpetrated them. Women's instincts to protect themselves, their interests, or their families were the main reason why they committed criminal acts. They often had clearer and more precise motives than men, and female criminal behaviour was usually – although not always – associated with practical needs rather than irrational, spontaneous displays of aggression. This, again, was often in contrast to male criminal behaviour. Reactions to female criminality, particularly by the law courts and wider, 'respectable' society, suggest that the 'disorderly' lower-class woman was increasingly under attack as efforts increased to control both women's behaviour and that of the poor and working-classes.

Women, the courts, and 'respectable' society

The attitude of the legal system in eighteenth- and nineteenth-century Britain towards crime and criminals was both highly gendered and classed. The vast majority of women who appeared before the courts were from the poor and labouring classes, and most female criminals were considered far less threatening and problematic than men. However, this had not always been the case. In the early modern period, for instance, the violence of women and, particularly, the violence of wives was a real cause for concern, perceived to be a threat both to domestic harmony and public order. Anxieties regarding the threat to society from violent women were publicized in ballads and pamphlet literature during the sixteenth and early seventeenth centuries.[8] However, by the end of the 1600s, attitudes had changed. With the elevation of domesticity and the reconfiguration of notions of patriarchy which took place during the eighteenth century, and were widely accepted by Victorian era, law and society no longer perceived women to be a threat to society, but rather as 'creatures' in need of protection. Conversely, it was their male counterparts who came to be depicted as dangerous, belligerent, and at times out of control.[9] Consequently, from the eighteenth century onward, women came to be associated with offences such as insult and defamation, rather than any of the more serious felonies. A powerful and idealized image of the virtuous woman underwrote the law and the attitudes of those élite men who created and directed the legal process. This image was, of course, well established prior to the beginning of the eighteenth century and continued to be highly influential well after 1850.

As a consequence, when women *did* commit crimes between 1700 and 1850, the authorities tended to regard them with pity rather than with disdain. It was widely believed that women could not be criminal in their own right or by their own nature, but that they must have been influenced by men or by severe personal circumstances, such as poverty or domestic abuse. As a result, women were more likely to receive lenient treatment from the courts than men.[10] Indeed, in England, married women could expect 'extra' protection from the courts due to the application of the legal principle of *coverture*, whereby a wife was not deemed responsible for a criminal act if her husband was present at the time.[11] This gendered leniency was limited, however; those women who presented a serious challenge to accepted notions of femininity and to idealized understanding of womanliness could expect harsher treatment from the authorities. For instance, when 53-year-old Elizabeth Barber brutally stabbed her lover, John Daly, in the breast with a knife at Greenwich in 1804, as part of a domestic dispute, she was discovered sitting beside the victim's body 'smoking her pipe unconcernedly' and claiming that her lover had stabbed himself in the heart by accident. Her nonchalance, as well as the violence of the crime itself (the complete antithesis to contemporary gendered notions of femininity), left the authorities with little choice: she was executed on Pennenden Heath on 25 March 1805.[12]

Women who were convicted of violent offences, in particular, were considered abnormal, unnatural, and animalistic. They regularly received epithets such as 'monster' or 'beast' in indictment returns, pamphlet literature, and press reports. Such cases attracted exemplary punishment.[13] The Newgate Calendar, based on eighteenth- and nineteenth-century broadsheets and chapbooks, cites one well publicized example dating from 1726, when Catherine Hayes of Birmingham was indicted for the murder of her husband, John. Described at various stages in the account as 'wretched', 'infamous', 'wicked', and 'diabolical', Catherine had coerced her lover and a son conceived from an earlier relationship, through black-mail and the granting of sexual favours, to murder her husband. John Hayes was first plied with drink and then set upon with a hatchet. He was decapitated (at his wife's recommendation) and his body was dismembered to facilitate burial. Although Catherine Hayes did not take part in the actual murder of her husband, her instigation of the crime and her 'bloody' involvement in the post-mortem butchering of her husband's body resulted in her conviction. Both she and the men were sentenced to death; however, unlike her lover and son, Catherine was found guilty of petty treason, because she had murdered her husband. According to the custom in English law up to 1790, she was therefore sentenced to be burnt at the stake, rather than hung on a gibbet. Normally, to ease suffering, the executioner strangled the convict before lighting the flames, but this did not happen in Hayes's case, as the executioner lit the fire too soon. It took more than three hours for Hayes's body to be wholly reduced to ashes.[14]

In the eighteenth and nineteenth centuries, women who threatened the stereotype of femininity through violence or aggression were not tolerated by society or the law. This was especially true for women like Catherine Hayes who killed their husbands, as their behaviour inverted the 'normal' power hierarchy of the household. Ultimately however, such acts and the punishments they attracted were rare, and, by and large, it was understood that women had little part to play in serious crime. The strength of response to these exceptions in women's behaviour and to the overstepping of boundaries, particularly in terms of violent crime, are important, though, for what they reveal about both the law and notions of gender and femininity in our period.

Property crime

As we shall see, while British women were both willing and able to participate in crimes against the person between 1700 and 1850, they were more likely to be indicted for property crime.[15] As J. M. Beattie has noted, '[f]or women even more than for men, it was theft and its related offences that most often brought them into trouble with the law'.[16] Crimes such as theft – for both men and women – were generally easy to commit; they were likely to bring some form of material or personal gain; and they were less likely to be reported than other types of crime, since the cost of bringing a prosecution often meant that legal action was not worthwhile. Despite the numbers of property crimes that went unprosecuted, this type of crime still dominated the business of British courts during the period. As Michael Weisser has argued, stealing was 'an activity so common as to be nothing less than banal'.[17]

Traditionally, women have been associated with less daring acts of theft.[18] Certainly, they were rarely involved in animal theft (such as sheep- or cattle-stealing), but contrary to conventional expectations, women *were* more commonly involved in substantial larcenies, especially when stealing from bleach-fields or breaking into shops or houses.[19] In Edinburgh in 1789, for example, Isobel McNeil and Catherine McVicar were indicted at the High Court of Justiciary after they had made a hole in the roof of a local provost's house, climbed inside, and stolen six pairs of sheets, five bolster slips, six pairs of pillow slips, nine shifts, four dozen table napkins, three table cloths, one dozen towels, four double blankets, ten pounds of flax, a muslin bonnet, a hank of green worsted yarn, the whole contents of a barrel of salted beef, two crocks of butter, six gallons of spirits, six salted tongues, three stone of candles, and about twenty pounds of hard soap.[20] Unfortunately, after having provided such a tantalizing list of the spoils of their activities, the indictment does not detail how the women managed to make off such a sizeable amount of booty. In 1835, Ann Lloyd and three other Welsh women broke into a victualler's shop in Llansadwrn. While inside, they dined on salmon and bread, and then proceeded to steal pans, tallow, and candlesticks from various rooms in the adjoining house.[21] These types of thefts must have involved a fair degree of planning and preparation, and the extent and range of items stolen suggest that, rather than being stolen for immediate use, the goods were commonly sold on to black marketeers for profit.[22] Receiving stolen goods, or fencing, was a crime strongly associated with female felons, partly because, as Hannah Barker has argued elsewhere in this volume, pawn-broking was a traditionally female occupation.[23] In lowland Scotland during the eighteenth century, women receivers outnumbered men by more than four to one.[24]

Thefts on a smaller scale were likely to have been more opportunistic in nature. Historians know less about this type of crime, since petty thefts played little part in the cases brought before the higher courts of Britain. They were prosecuted instead in the local courts, which have been less studied.[25] Moreover, as has been noted, such crimes often went unprose-cuted. It was usually only when offenders were known recidivists –

typically pickpockets and 'grab-and-dash' thieves – that they were brought
to trial. According to Garthine Walker, in cases of minor theft, women
generally stole goods 'which concerned them in the normal run of
things'.[26] Food and household items were, she has argued, the spoils most
sought after by female thieves, as they were the objects most needed in
their daily lives and the ones that could be put to immediate use. Certainly,
there were a number of women who stole items that reflected the requirements and preoccupations of their domestic lives: items such as crockery,
cutlery, bread, and bed linen were commonly stolen. But there were also
a large proportion of women who took items which were totally unrelated
to the necessities of home life: snuff boxes, stomachers, wigs, watches, and
church altar pieces, and so on.[27]

In fact, the goods stolen by British women were diverse in character and
reflected the opportunistic nature of the majority of small-scale larcenies.
Although historians have written at length about the relationship between
destitution and the incidence of theft (violent and otherwise),[28] only a small
proportion of women who were charged with such crimes stole to provide
immediate or instant relief from their destitution. It was far more common
for women to steal items which would bring them profit in the longer term.
It is worth noting that less than 15 per cent of the women indicted for theft
in Garthine Walker's study of early modern Cheshire had been indicted for
stealing food;[29] similarly, in eighteenth- and nineteenth-century Scotland,
the figure was less than 10 per cent.[30] Clothing, linen, jewellery, silver
plate, and other goods which could be sold on for substantial profit, were
more commonly taken by British women between 1700 and 1850.[31] For
the majority of female criminals, the motivation for robbery, theft, and the
receipt of stolen goods, appears to have been long-term profit rather than
short-term remediation from intolerable poverty. The time it would have
taken to plan, perpetrate, and then eventually generate money from the
theft of non-consumable, non-usable goods is testimony to the foresight,
premeditation, and patience of female thieves. It could, of course. be
argued that, as the higher courts were more likely to deal with more
'serious' instances of theft, indictment evidence is skewed to portray
women's thefts as being more calculated and profit-minded than they
actually were. A recent study of petty thefts brought before Oxfordshire
Quarter Sessions in the late eighteenth century, however, shows that, in
common with the more serious episodes of theft, women preferred to steal
items of 'greed', which could generate profit, whereas men were more
likely to steal items of 'need', which could be used immediately – either
food which could be eaten or fuel which could be burnt.[32]

The gender disparity in evidence suggests that men regularly stole out
of desperation, whereas women commonly did so with substantial lucre in
mind. Perhaps this difference is simply a reflection of the 'accepted' roles
of men and women in the households of the period, with men commonly

perceived as providers for the family and women regarded as keepers or controllers of the family purse. Another tentative conclusion which could be drawn from the evidence is that, for women, a theft had to be financially worthwhile before they would be persuaded to risk breaking the law. For men, on the other hand, the need for basic sustenance seems to have been more of a consideration. This hypothesis suggests that women criminals may have taken bigger 'risks' in their criminal endeavours in comparison to their male counterparts. Certainly, if it could be proven that women *did* favour more lucrative theft rather than petty misdemeanours, the belief that women merely acted as decoys and look-outs in property crimes during the period could no longer be sustained. Further research into the factors which motivated men and women to commit theft is clearly required, before any of these suggestions can be fully substantiated.

On the whole, property crimes in Britain between 1700 and 1850 did not involve the use of violence. Robbery was an important exception. Despite widespread anxiety about the threat of robbery,[33] it does not appear to have been a particularly common crime. Female participation in acts of robbery has always been regarded as rare, a belief that is supported by the relative scarcity of women robbers in indictment evidence.[34] However, as Beattie and Jim Sharpe have suggested, it should not be assumed that those women who took part in robberies were only indirectly involved, did not confront their victims, or that they did not behave violently.[35] There were few highwaywomen during our period, it is true, probably due to the fact that lower-class women were less likely to ride and have the skill with firearms that was required. Perhaps because they were more likely to work on foot rather than on horseback, women robbers used significant force and, commonly, some sort of weapon to incapacitate their victims. In Stepney in 1718, Sarah Brown attacked Nathanial Asser with a brick, which she used to beat him violently about the face and legs. She then robbed him of a purse, ten guineas, and two gold rings.[36] In 1766, three women were indicted for the robbery of Hugh Craig in Ayrshire. They beat him over the head with a pistol and repeatedly stabbed him in the legs with a pitchfork before carrying off his saddle-bags which contained 'items of silk finery'.[37] In Glasgow in 1780, Elizabeth Barron was accused of robbing Robert McNish by holding a knife to his throat, biting and striking him several times in the face, and threatening to 'knock out his brains' while stealing his wallet.[38] In 1788, Agnes Walker and Mary Robieson were indicted for a robbery in Wigtown, in south-west Scotland, where they attacked the postmistress, set her hair alight, cut off her nose with a razor, and attempted to slice off both of her ears. They then made off with several envelopes containing bank notes.[39] At Whitechapel in 1795, Mary Brown was charged with the robbery of William Whitnell, whom she had attacked ferociously with an iron shovel, after first grabbing hold of his hair and stealing a hat and other articles from his person.[40] Martha Davis was sentenced to death for robbing a foot-boy at St Giles in London in 1810. She dragged the boy by his hair from the highway into a room, where she viciously beat him about the head until he surrendered his hat and 2s. 6d.[41] Amelia Roberts was similarly executed for robbery in the nineteenth-century England. In 1827, she and her sweetheart, Patrick Riley, robbed and assaulted one Mr Austin of Red Lion Street, Clerkenwell, in his own house, where Amelia worked as a cook. After brutally battering Austin, they stole over £400 and made off into the night. Once apprehended, they were convicted and hung at Newgate.[42]

Violence in the home

While men committed the majority of violent crimes between 1700 and 1850 – women accounted for less than one-third of those indicted for assault throughout Britain as a whole – there were notable regional variations. Scottish women appeared to be more likely to resort to violence than women in Wales, whereas women in England were the least violent of all.[43] Murderesses were not common anywhere, but Beattie's study of Surrey between 1663 and 1802 revealed that 13 per cent of murder charges were brought against women.[44] In the Welsh assize courts between 1730 and 1800, 16 per cent of those charged with unlawful killing were women, while in lowland Scotland, during the eighteenth century, they made up 19 per cent of homicide indictments.[45] Preliminary studies of female homicide in the nineteenth century have shown that few women were indicted at the Old Bailey during that period.[46] While this is mirrored by a lessening in women's involvement in crime in general after 1815,[47] the Old Bailey indictments have not yet been fully explained or substantiated for any other part of Britain during the same period. What *is* clear from the available evidence, is that women were far more likely than men to get involved in a violent encounter with someone they knew, such as a relative, employer, or acquaintance. Unlike men, they were rarely involved in disputes with strangers. Historians have explained this gendered disparity in terms of women's limited social activity: they neither travelled as regularly to taverns as men, nor did they get involved in brawls or drunken disputes. In addition, women's work environment was far more controlled than men's, especially in rural areas.[48] The latter can explain in part why the majority of homicides, and indeed much of the violent crime committed by women, was carried out in the town rather than the countryside.[49] However, contrary to common perceptions, which link women's crime to the home, the higher incidence of female criminality in towns also suggests that women in urban settings were more likely to be active *outside* the home and to have mixed with significantly larger groups of people. The impact of town-dwelling on levels of female crime suggests that the ongoing process of urbanization increased the likelihood of this occurring.

The association of women with home-life in the eighteenth and early nineteenth centuries has meant that studies of female criminality have regularly centred on the domestic sphere. Contemporaries also tended to associate women with certain types of violent crime, specifically poisoning and infanticide. These 'feminine' murders were thought to fit well with women's abhorrence of bloodshed, their lack of physical strength, and their propensity to be devious. The association of poisoning with women was partly the result of the ease with which they could administer drugs in their domestic roles, as the preparers of food or nurse-maids. As the symptoms of poisoning are not unlike those for diseases such as cholera, which were common in our period, the actual act of murder was often hidden.[50] Poisoning showed a clear degree of premeditation, and in the British courts in the early-modern period it was 'detested because it tapped a profound male fear of female deviousness, it was the ultimate horror even to conceive of the possibility that the polite yet secretive female might harbour dark homicidal urges under the mask of gentility'.[51]

Despite the popular perception of poisoning as a woman's crime, relatively few female murders (or attempted murders) seem to have used this method between 1700 and 1850. Indeed, contrary to popular belief, most women who murdered did so using far more overt and brutal forms of violence, not unlike their male counterparts. In Scotland between 1750 and 1815, for instance, nearly two-thirds of the women indicted for murder used violent methods to kill their victims rather than poison.[52] In Surrey between 1663 and 1802, moreover, around 80 per cent of the women accused as principals in homicide cases had resorted to bloodshed.[53] Beatings with sticks, stones, household implements, and, to a lesser extent, attacks with knives and other instruments, both sharp and blunt, were common. Jene Buttery, for example, was indicted at the Old Bailey on 12 January 1711 for killing Mary Washenhoven by repeatedly battering her in the face and neck with an iron poker.[54] Dorothy Christian, who was indicted at the Old Bailey in 1743, was charged with viciously wounding and bruising her elderly mistress by beating her repeatedly with a brass ladle.[55] Jean Inglis was brought to the Scottish Justiciary Court for disembowelling her pregnant mistress with a broken bottle in 1755.[56] Mary Edmondson of Leeds was indicted in 1759 for slashing the throat of her aunt with a carving knife.[57] Agnes Dougall of Lanarkshire was charged in 1767 with murdering her daughter by cutting the 8-year-old's throat from ear to ear with a razor.[58] Elizabeth Richardson was indicted in London in 1768 for stabbing her lover through the heart with a pen-knife.[59] Mary Mitchell from Kirkcudbright attacked her brother with a pitchfork in 1812, and 'seeing him still awake, she preceded to attack him with a smoothing iron to the great effusion of his blood and danger of his life'.[60] At the

Newcastle Assizes in 1829 Jane Jameson, described by the local newspaper as 'an abominable jade' was convicted and sentenced to death for the brutal murder of her mother, Margaret. After a prolonged and heated argument, Jane had stabbed her mother in the heart with a red-hot poker, which she had grabbed from a nearby fireplace.[61] Then, in 1849, before a crowd of 30,000–50,000 people, Maria Manning and her husband Frederick were executed at Horsemonger Lane Gaol, convicted of the murder of Maria's erstwhile lover, Patrick O'Connor. Maria had shot Patrick in the head with a pistol at point-blank range at her home in Bermondsey and Frederick had battered him with a ripping chisel (crow bar). After burying Patrick's body in the garden, Maria went to O'Connor's residence and stole various items of value which had been in his possession.[62]

It is clear from this evidence that women could behave just as aggressively as men when committing acts of violence.[63] They were not hindered by a lack of physical strength, nor were they restrained by any notions of what was, or was not, appropriate or acceptable behaviour for women. It cannot be valid to argue, as Peter Spierenburg does, that women behaved violently in certain circumstances purely because they were imitating the actions of men.[64] It does, however, seem to be the case that the home provided the site of much female violence, with women most commonly attacking family members, and female servants assaulting their employers. Indeed, instances of such domestic acts of violence were probably far more common than the indictment evidence suggests, given that a degree of under-reporting seems likely in terms of assaults against both women and men. As Tanya Evans has argued elsewhere in this volume, familial relations in our period were often far from cordial and tensions and personal resentments could and did erupt into violence upon occasion. More commonly, women were the victims, as historians such as Shani D'Cruze and Anna Clark have demonstrated.[65] However, husbands could also fall foul of their wives. Elizabeth Fisher from Whitechapel was indicted at the Old Bailey in 1714, accused of stabbing her husband in the right breast with a large knife during a domestic dispute over a pair of boots.[66] In 1738, Susannah Hill of Surrey was charged with the assault of her husband, after having beaten him severely with a hammer and whip.[67] Agnes Keir was indicted in Glasgow in 1766 for attacking her husband with a chopping knife, which she embedded in his leg below the knee and 'fractured his bone to but splinters'.[68] Isobel McLean of Glasgow killed her husband in 1787 in a ferocious attack: he received forty stab wounds, including one which 'cut off his private member'.[69] Martha Alden was indicted at Norfolk in 1807 for the brutal murder of her husband – she had attempted to decapitate him with the aid of a bill-hook.[70] And Hannah Reed, the mother of four children, was executed at Leicester in 1825 for beating her husband, dragging him by the hair along a gravel path, and then pushing him into a canal, where he later drowned. Hannah, who was

36, had fallen in love with a 19-year-old boy and needed to get rid of her husband, in order to be with her 'new' lover.[71]

Infanticide (the murder of new-born children) was a type of assault commonly associated with women between 1700 and 1850. It was seen as an unnatural act that contradicted contemporary perceptions of femininity, particularly what were regarded as natural maternal feelings. Almost exclusively a women's crime, most commonly perpetrated by unmarried domestic servants desperate to keep their illegitimate pregnancies secret, the courts considered infanticide to be particularly serious. Women might be sentenced to death in the eighteenth century, solely on the grounds of concealing their pregnancies, regardless of whether there was any direct evidence to substantiate a subsequent charge of murder.[72] Charges of infanticide against women outnumbered those of homicide in our period.[73] Indeed, in lowland Scotland if the number of infanticides were added to those of homicides, the figures for killings committed by women between 1700 and 1850 would be substantially closer to those of men.[74]

According to Samuel Radbill, the 'methods used in infanticide have not changed much throughout history. Blood is rarely shed.'[75] Radbill's comments have been supported by others. Both Keith Wrightson's study of seventeenth-century England and J. Kelly's work on eighteenth-century Ireland, have contended that forms of asphyxia such as suffocation, drowning, or strangulation, predominated over more violent methods.[76] There appears, intriguingly, to have been a marked north–south divide in the level of violence used in cases of infanticide, with Scottish mothers behaving far more viciously than their English or Welsh counterparts. Although in lowland Scotland between 1720 and 1850, 19 per cent of infanticide cases revealed no discernible marks of violence on the body of the victim (6 per cent of the infants having been suffocated, 7 per cent strangled and 5 per cent drowned), 63 per cent of the indictments described blood being shed. Of these, with 48 per cent of the infants were killed by attacks with a sharp instrument and 15 per cent battered to death.[77] Thus, Anna Brown was found guilty at the High Court in Edinburgh in November 1720 of wilfully and repeatedly battering her newborn son with a stone before she threw him into the river; Sarah Quarrier was indicted in 1757 for slashing the throat of her child with a razor; Lilias Miligan was accused of 'dashing' her infant's skull of the ground in 1774; Hannah Main was brought to the Justiciary Court in 1793 charged with killing her new-born son with a hammer; and Catharine McDonald was accused in 1797 of using a spade to attack her child, leaving 'its left leg above the knee torn off . . . its right leg was disjointed and its nose flattened'. She then fed the child's remains to a neighbourhood dog.[78] Nineteenth-century examples include Mary Giffin from Bridgeton in Glasgow who was indicted for cutting the throat of her child with a bread knife in 1824; Margaret McInnis from Inverness-shire who had stamped upon her son until he was dead in 1832; and Elizabeth Stewart, a farm servant from Ayr, who was charged with concealing her pregnancy and then murdering her newborn son in 1845 by striking him repeatedly with an iron poker.[79]

Crimes of protest

While female acts of violence between 1700 and 1850 were often sited in the home, women were also represented in episodes of 'public' violence involving assaults against authority and forms of popular protest, such as rioting. Although these types of offences were carried out outside the home, the concerns which triggered them were often domestic ones, most commonly, the defence of family interests against what were perceived as aggressive acts on the part of the state, or individuals, such as merchants who drove up the price of food. The involvement of labouring communities in acts of defiance against authority during the eighteenth century has been described by E. P. Thompson as evidence of an alternative, plebeian, moral code. The moral economy of the lower orders differed in significant ways from that of the ruling élite and meant that many of the activities described as 'criminal' (including those which follow) would have appeared both fair and justified to those who perpetrated them.[80]

Assaults against authority usually involved an act of resistance against an officer of the law during the execution of his duty. This type of crime was usually regarded as extremely serious by the court authorities, as it encouraged behaviour that was seen to directly defy the King's authority. Given the gravity of such offences, it did not surprise Beattie to find that – in line with women's participation in other violent crimes in eighteenth-century England – less than one-fifth of those indicted for 'assaults on constables' were women.[81] By way of contrast, however, in lowland Scotland between 1750 and 1815, 181 cases of aggravated assault on state officials were brought against women, as compared to 180 brought against men.[82] Scottish women have consistently been at the forefront of resistance to authorized oppression. They were, for example, highly involved in resistance to the Highland Clearances, particularly at the height of the period known as 'The Land War' in the 1880s, where women regularly battled militia and troops to prevent forced evictions taking place.[83]

Both north and south of the border, the methods used to carry out attacks on authority figures were very similar. Sticks and stones were favourite weapons and, more often than not, women committing such offences tended to work in groups of three or four, rather than alone as was usual in other acts of 'domestic' violence. In 1735, Sarah How assaulted the night-watchman, Daniel Owen, who was trying to arrest her for disorderly conduct near St Paul's Cathedral in London. Sarah gave him 'two hearty knocks', which made his nose bleed, and she was subsequently indicted at the Old Bailey for aggravated assault of authority.[84] In Denbighshire in Wales in 1740, a high constable named Edward Parry was attacked by a mob of women who rescued his female prisoner (a woman from the local village) and then bludgeoned him repeatedly over the head with large sticks and stones until he had to be rescued by passing soldiers.[85] Rebecca Beecher from Sutton was indicted in 1751 for assaulting a constable who was trying to arrest her. She reportedly flew at the constable and beat him severely, punching him several times in the face.[86] Three women from Edinburgh were charged in 1758 for attacking an excise officer who had come to levy fines on them for selling liquor without a licence. The women set about the officer with sticks, rubbed manure in his hair, forced him to eat the warrants he had brought, tore his clothes from him, dragged him towards the sea in an attempt to drown him, and then, finally, one of the women sat on his face causing his nose to break.[87] Four more Scottish women were charged in 1781 with the assault of a Justice of the Peace named John McChlery, who was enquiring about a robbery said to have been committed by close relatives of the women. The women pinned McChlery to the ground and took it in turns to beat him. They poured hot candle wax in to his eyes and set his hair alight in an attempt to persuade him that his investigations would prove fruitless.[88] Similarly, in the early Victorian period, a Welshwoman, Grace Roberts, achieved notoriety in the press for habitually attacking constables and officers of the law and inciting others to prevent the authorities from carrying out their duties. She was eventually apprehended and arrested in Llanrwst.[89]

Women were also active in various types of riotous behaviour, including those associated with enclosure, patronage disputes, militia conscription, industrial and religious disputes, and political campaigns. Female rioting was most commonly associated with food shortages.[90] As Beattie has pointed out, women not only regularly took part in food riots, but they were also frequently 'their instigators and leaders, a reflection of the immediacy of their concern with the critical matter of the supply and price of food'.[91] Generally food-rioters either attempted to prevent the movement of foodstuffs out of a given area (as at Edinburgh in 1720, Lyme in the West of England in 1766, Tayside in Scotland in 1772, Comray in Wales in 1795 and Manchester in 1812), or, they tried to regulate the price of foodstuffs in the marketplace (as at Newcastle in 1740, Dumfries in Scotland in 1771, Delph in the north-west of England in 1795, Merthyr Tydfil in Wales in 1800 and Cornwall in 1847).[92]

According to John Stevenson, the most notable feature of food riots, 'was the element of discipline and restraint' exhibited by the rioters.[93] It seems that in England, the crowd rarely attacked individuals, preferring instead to direct any acts of violence towards property.[94] Scotland again appears to differ. Here, court testimony reflects a more aggressive attitude on the part of women rioters. Nearly 90 per cent of the women accused of rioting were also charged with aggravated assault.[95] Welsh women also appear to have been more aggressive than English women. Evidence suggests that they were overtly violent during food protests, attacking people as well as property and setting a precedent for the type of behaviour displayed in the rural-based anti-toll-gate protests known as the Rebecca Riots that took place throughout South Wales between 1839 and 1844.[96]

The reasons why women were more violent in Scotland and Wales have yet to be fully investigated. Perhaps economic conditions were worse in these areas and the force of necessity encouraged these women to behave in a desperate or aggressive way. Perhaps there was a long-standing social tradition among women of the 'Celtic fringe', where violence by and between women was normalized and considered acceptable. Or perhaps, the law, reinforced by the moral directives of the church in these areas was *less* accepting of women's violence and was therefore more likely to prosecute them than their 'sisters' in England.

Despite sporadic outbreaks of food rioting after the Napoleonic Wars, this type of popular protest, and women's involvement in it, was mostly restricted to the eighteenth-century. By the 1790s, particularly in the context of Revolution, food rioting came to be regarded as a threat to social order, even national security. As a consequence, the authorities became more aware of their social obligations to regulate the price, provision, and quality of food.[97] This paternalism, coupled with a reduction in prices by the end of the century meant that other forms of protest – industrial and political – overtook the food riot as the chief method for the populace to voice its discontent with local authorities and governments alike. New methods of defending living standards through strikes and trades-union activity became increasingly important.[98] Women eventually came to play a prominent part in these more 'modern' disputes, albeit in a more overt, but arguably less violent, way than their Scottish and Welsh food-rioting forbears.

Conclusion

This chapter has drawn heavily on High Court records as the most readily available and widely studied source for the study of women and crime between 1700 and 1850. In the future, the use of other types of primary source, such as prisoner records, confessions, and gallows speeches, as well as the records of courts of 'lesser' jurisdiction, and other types of testimony, such as those given by medical experts, should further illuminate the lives of female criminals in Britain and offer more concrete evidence about the attitudes and experiences of women involved in crime. Despite such limitations, this chapter has described the great range of women's criminal activities in Britain between 1700 and 1850. Women were less often indicted for serious felonies at courts than men, but they still committed the same kinds of crimes, and could, on occasion, be just as aggressive. This seems especially true of Scottish women, and, to a lesser extent, Welsh women, who were regularly more vicious than their English counterparts, particularly when perpetrating crimes such as infanticide or during instances of popular disturbance. The majority of women's violent activity occurred within the home and offences such as homicide and assault were largely directed against relatives, employers, and close acquaintances. However, women in towns seem to have been less restricted to the domestic sphere, suggesting that urbanization may have altered the traditional focus of female violence. Home and family still remained central to women's concerns, and, even when women committed crimes in 'public', domestic issues still predominated. Women most often participated in offences in defence of family interests or to bolster the family income and these motivations persisted throughout the period under review.

Notes

1 For further discussion, see J. Briggs, C. Harrison, A. McInnes, and D. Vincent, *Crime and Punishment in England: An Introductory History*, London, 1995, especially pp. 124–5; C. Emsley, 'Crime in nineteenth century Britain', *History Today*, April, 1988, pp. 40–6; D. Jones, *Crime, Protest, Community and Police in Nineteenth-Century Britain*, London, 1982, especially pp. 138–41.

2 See, for instance, J. M. Beattie, *Crime and the Courts in England, 1660–1800*, Oxford, 1986; F. McLynn, *Crime and Punishment in Eighteenth-Century England*, London, 1989; C. Emsley, *Crime and Society in England, 1750–1900*, London, 1996; G. Morgan and P. Rushton, *Rogues, Thieves and the Rule of Law: The Problem of Law Enforcement in North-East England, 1718–1800*, London, 1998; J. A. Sharpe, *Crime in Early Modern England, 1550–1750*, London, 1999; M. Gaskill, *Crime and Mentalities in Early-Modern England*, Cambridge, 2000; P. King, *Crime, Justice and Discretion in England, 1740–1820*, Oxford, 2000.

3 M. M. Feeley and D. L. Little, 'The vanishing female: the decline of women in the criminal process, 1687–1912', *Law and Society Review*, 1991, vol. 25, pp. 719–57.

4 Ibid.

5 See, for instance, the evidence presented in B. Hanawalt, 'The female felon in fourteenth-century England', *Viator – Medieval and Renaissance Studies*, 1974, vol. 5, pp. 251–73; J. M. Beattie, 'The criminality of women in eighteenth-century England', *Journal of Social History*, 1975, vol. 8, p. 81; D. J. V. Jones, *Crime in Nineteenth-Century Wales*, Cardiff, 1992, p. 171.

6 See, for example, M. Jackson, *New-born Child Murder: Women, Illegitimacy, and the Courts in Eighteenth Century England*, Manchester, 1996; T. Henderson, *Disorderly Women in Eighteenth Century London: Prostitution and Control in the Metropolis, 1730–1830*, London, 1999. There are few exceptions to the neglect of the study of female criminality in the period, the most important being Beattie,

'Criminality of women'; J. Kermode and G. Walker (eds), *Women, Crime and the Courts in Early-Modern England*, London, 1994; G. Walker, *Crime, Gender and Social Order in Early-Modern England*, Cambridge, 2003.

7 *The Proceedings of the Old Bailey*, case ref. no. Obt17100906–21, 6 September 1710; also case ref. no. Obt17960406–35, 6 April 1796; *The Complete Newgate Calendar*, London, 1926, vol. 5, p. 83.

8 See, for instance, F. E. Dolan, *Dangerous Familiars: Representations of Domestic Crime in England, 1550–1700*, New York, 1994.

9 J. Bailey, *Unquiet Lives: Marriage and Marriage Breakdown in England, 1660–1800*, Cambridge, 2003, pp. 110–11.

10 P. King, 'Gender, crime and justice in late eighteenth and early nineteenth-century England', in M. Arnot and C. Usborne (eds), *Gender and Crime in Modern Europe*, London, 1999, pp. 44–74; Morgan and Rushton, *Rogues, Thieves and the Rule of Law*, p. 118; Robert B. Shoemaker, *Gender in English Society, 1650–1850: The Emergence of Separate Spheres*, Harlow, 1998, p. 297. For further discussion of attitudes towards convict women and their treatment (in relation to the nineteenth century), see L. Zedner, *Women, Crime, and Custody in Victorian England*, Oxford, 1991; also, 'Women, crime and penal responses: a historical account', in M. Tonry (ed.), *Crime and Justice: A Review of Research*, Chicago, 1991, vol. 14.

11 For further discussion of *femme covert* and its applicability in England, see Shoemaker, *Gender in English Society*, p. 297; King, 'Gender, crime and justice', p. 64.

12 *Complete Newgate Calendar*, vol. 4, p. 297.

13 For similar conclusions, see King, 'Gender, crime and justice', pp. 61–2; Morgan and Rushton, *Rogues, Thieves and the Rule of Law*, pp. 118–22; Shoemaker, *Gender in English Society*, p. 298.

14 *Complete Newgate Calendar*, vol. 3, p. 30.

15 See my calculation on the evidence presented in Beattie, 'Criminality of women', p. 91; A.-M. Kilday, 'Women and crime in south-west Scotland: a study of the justiciary court records, 1750–1815', PhD thesis, University of Strathclyde, 1998, pp. 208–9.

16 Beattie, 'Criminality of women', p. 89.

17 M. Weisser, *Crime and Punishment in Early Modern Europe*, Hassocks, 1979, p. 16.

18 See, for instance, C. Z. Wiener, 'Sex roles in late Elizabethan Hertfordshire', *Journal of Social History*, 1975, vol. 8, p. 42; Sharpe, *Crime in Early Modern England*, p. 109; Beattie, 'Criminality of Women', p. 90; Beattie, *Crime and the Courts*, p. 238.

19 See G. Walker, 'Women, theft and the world of stolen goods', in Kermode and Walker (eds), *Women, Crime and the Courts*, p. 87; Kilday, 'Women and crime', pp. 219–20.

20 National Archives of Scotland (hereafter NAS), Justiciary Court Records (hereafter JC) 26/252.

21 Jones, *Crime in Nineteenth Wales*, pp. 118–19. For further information on female burglars in Wales, see D. Beddoe, 'Carmarthenshire women and criminal transportation to Australia, 1787–1852', *Carmarthenshire Antiquary*, 1997, vol. 13, p. 69; D. Howells, *The Rural Poor in Eighteenth-Century Wales*, Cardiff, 2000, pp. 227–36.

22 For further discussion, see Beattie, *Crime and the Courts*, p. 164; McLynn, *Crime and Punishment*, p. 88.

23 See Beattie, 'Criminality of women', p. 93; Walker, 'Women, theft and the world of stolen goods', p. 92; O. Pollak, *The Criminality of Women*, Philadelphia, PA, 1950, p. 87.

24 Kilday, 'Women and crime', p. 232.
25 Beattie only found fourteen women accused of this type of offence in the Home Counties during the eighteenth century: Beattie, 'Criminality of women', p. 91. Over the same period in lowland Scotland, fifteen women were indicted for petty theft: Kilday, 'Women and crime', p. 217. For further discussion, see C. Herrup, 'New shoes and mutton pies: investigative responses to theft in seventeenth-century East Sussex', *Historical Journal*, 1984, no. 27, pp. 811–30.
26 Walker, 'Women, theft and the world of stolen goods', p. 82.
27 See, for instance, Kilday, 'Women and crime', pp. 220–1; Walker, 'Women, theft and the world of stolen goods', p. 88.
28 For further discussion, see Beattie, 'Criminality of women', pp. 102–8; Beattie, *Crime and the Courts*, Chapter 5, especially pp. 199–237; McLynn, *Crime and Punishment*, p. 132; D. Hay, 'War, death and theft in the eighteenth century: the record of the English courts', *Past and Present*, 1982, no. 95, pp. 117–60; and, for the earlier period, P. Lawson, 'Property crime and hard times in England, 1559–1624', *Law and History Review*, 1986, vol. 4, pp. 95–127.
29 See Walker, 'Women, theft and the world of stolen goods', p. 88.
30 My calculation based on the data used to construct Chapter 5 of Kilday, 'Women and crime'.
31 See Walker, 'Women, theft and the world of stolen goods', p. 88; Kilday, 'Women and crime', pp. 220–9; B. Lemire, 'The theft of clothes and popular consumerism in early-modern England', *Journal of Social History*, 1990, vol. 24, pp. 255–76; also B. Lemire, 'Peddling fashion: salesmen, pawnbrokers, tailors, thieves and the second-hand clothes trade in England c.1700–1800', *Textile History*, 1991, vol. 22, pp. 67–82. For further discussion of the motives of women thieves in this period, see L. Mackay, 'Why they stole: women in the Old Bailey, 1779–1789', *Journal of Social History*, 1999, no. 32, pp. 623–39.
32 See A.-M. Kilday, 'Criminally poor? Investigating the link between crime and poverty in eighteenth-century England', in S. A. King and R. M. Smith (eds), *Poverty and Relief in England: From Monasticism to Modern Welfare*, Cambridge, forthcoming.
33 Beattie, *Crime and the Courts*, p. 148.
34 Beattie, 'Criminality of women', p. 91; Kilday, 'Women and crime', p. 167.
35 Beattie, 'Criminality of women', p. 90; also his, *Crime and the Courts*, p. 238; Sharpe, *Crime in Early Modern England*, p. 109.
36 *Proc. Old Bailey*, case ref. no. OBt17181015–21, 15 October 1718.
37 NAS, JC26/177.
38 NAS, JC13/22.
39 NAS, JC26/250.
40 *Proc. Old Bailey*, case ref. no. OBt17951202–38, 2 December 1795.
41 *Complete Newgate Calendar*, vol. 5, p. 76.
42 C. Hindley, *Curiosities of Street Literature*, London, 1871, p. 188.
43 In lowland Scotland 37 per cent of assault indictments were charged against women in the eighteenth century: Kilday, 'Women and crime', p. 35. In Surrey, the figure for that period was nearly 20 per cent: Beattie, 'Criminality of women', p. 85; and in the Welsh assize courts it was as low as 11 per cent between 1730 and 1800: Howell, *Rural Poor*, p. 219.
44 Beattie, 'Criminality of women', p. 85.
45 My calculation on the evidence presented in Howell, *Rural Poor*, p. 220; see also Kilday, 'Women and crime', p. 21.
46 See, for instance, Feeley and Little, 'Vanishing female', p. 725.

47 Ibid., pp. 738–9.

48 For further discussion, see Beattie, 'Criminality of women', p. 84; McLynn, *Crime and Punishment*, pp. 122–3; Shoemaker, *Gender in English Society*, pp. 299–300.

49 Beattie, 'Criminality of women', pp. 80–116; Jones, *Crime in Nineteenth Century Wales*, pp. 172–3.

50 For further discussion, see K. D. Watson, *Poisoned Lives: English Poisoners and their Victims* London, 2004; Pollak, *Criminality of Women*, pp. 17–18.

51 McLynn, *Crime and Punishment*, p. 119; C. Emsley, *Crime and Society*, p. 156.

52 Kilday, 'Women and crime', p. 26.

53 Beattie, 'Criminality of women', p. 83.

54 *Proc. Old Bailey*, case ref. no. OBt17110112–33, 12 January 1711.

55 Ibid., case ref. no. OBt17431012–35, 12 October 1743.

56 NAS, JC26/156.

57 *Complete Newgate Calendar*, vol. 3, p. 266.

58 NAS, JC26/180.

59 *Complete Newgate Calendar*, vol. 4, p. 63.

60 NAS, JC26/355.

61 *Newcastle Weekly Chronicle*, 7 March 1829.

62 Hindley, *Curiosities of Street Literature*, p. 198. For further detailed discussion of this case, see M. Alpert, *London 1849 – A Victorian Murder Story*, Harlow, 2004.

63 For corroboration that women could behave just as aggressively as men in the committal of violence, see O. Hufton, 'Women and violence in early modern Europe', in F. Dieteren and E. Kloek (eds), *Writing Women into History*, Amsterdam, 1990, p. 76; A. Finch, 'Women and violence in the later middle ages: the evidence of the officiality of Cerisy', *Continuity and Change*, 1992, vol. 7, p. 29.

64 See P. Spierenburg, 'How violent were women? Court cases in Amsterdam, 1650–1810', *Crime, History, and Societies*, 1997, vol. 1, pp. 9–28.

65 See, for example, S. D'Cruze, *Crimes of Outrage: Sex, Violence and Victorian Working Women*, London, 1998; also S. D'Cruze (ed.), *Everyday Violence in Britain, 1850–1950*, Harlow, 2000; A. Clark, *Women's Silence, Men's Violence: Sexual Assault in England, 1770–1845*, London, 1987; also A. Clark, *The Struggle for the Breeches: Gender and the Making of the British Working Class*, Berkeley, CA, 1997.

66 *Proc. Old Bailey*, case ref. no. OBt17140908–41, 8 September 1714.

67 Beattie, 'Criminality of women', p. 87.

68 NAS, JC26/177.

69 NAS, JC26/243.

70 *Complete Newgate Calendar*, vol. 5, p. 4.

71 For further discussion of this case, see M. Tanner, *Crime and Murder in Victorian Leicestershire*, Leicester, 1981.

72 Although infanticide remained a capital crime until the Infanticide Act of 1922, women could not be capitally convicted on the grounds of concealment alone after 1803. For further discussion of this crime and women's involvement in it, see Jackson, *New-born Child Murder*; R.W. Malcolmson, 'Infanticide in the eighteenth century', in J. S. Cockburn (ed.), *Crime in England, 1550–1800*, London, 1977; P. C. Hoffer and N. E. C. Hull, *Murdering Mothers: Infanticide in England and New England, 1558–1803*, New York, 1981; L. Rose, *The Massacre of the Innocents: Infanticide in Britain, 1800–1939*, London, 1986; A.-M. Kilday, 'Maternal monsters: murdering mothers in south-west Scotland, 1750–1815', in Y. G. Brown and R. Ferguson (eds), *Twisted Sisters: Women, Crime and Deviance in Scotland since 1400*, East Linton, 2002.

73 See, for instance, the evidence provided in Morgan and Rushton, *Rogues, Thieves and the Rule of Law*, p. 112; Beattie, 'Criminality of women', pp. 83–5.

74 In Scotland between 1720 and 1850, 462 men were indicted for murder. Only two men were indicted for the crime of infanticide over that period. Over the same period 116 Scottish women were accused of murder and 297 women were indicted for infanticide. In total, therefore, in terms of homicides, 464 men and 413 women were indicted for that offence in Scotland between 1720 and 1850. My calculations here are based on the evidence presented in Chapters 1 and 2 of Kilday, 'Women and crime', and from data collected from my current research project into trends in infanticide in Scotland, 1720–1850.

75 S. X. Radbill, 'A history of child abuse and infanticide', in R. E. Helfer and C. H. Kempe (eds), *The Battered Child*, Chicago, 1968, p. 9.

76 See K. Wrightson, 'Infanticide in earlier seventeenth-century England', *Local Population Studies*, 1975, no. 15, p. 15; J. Kelly, 'Infanticide in eighteenth century Ireland', *Irish Economic and Social History*, 1992, vol. 19, p. 18.

77 Statistics from Kilday, 'Women and crime', p. 92; data collected from my current research project into trends in infanticide in Scotland, 1720–1850.

78 See, in order of appearance, NAS, JC3/10; JC26/146; JC26/201; JC26/270; JC26/290.

79 See, in order of appearance, NAS, AD14/24/269; AD14/32/125; AD14/45/193.

80 E. P. Thompson, 'The moral economy of the English crowd in the eighteenth century', *Past and Present*, 1971, no. 50.

81 My calculation on the evidence presented in Beattie, 'Criminality of women', p. 85.

82 Kilday, 'Women and crime', p. 47.

83 For further information, see E. Richards, *A History of the Highland Clearances: II: Emigration, Protest, Reasons*, London, 1985.

84 *Proc. Old Bailey*, case ref. no. OBt17350522–33, 22 May 1735.

85 Howell, *Rural Poor*, pp. 207–8. For a fuller examination of violence in community disputes in Wales, see S. Clarke, 'Visions of community: Elizabeth Baker and late eighteenth-century Merioneth', in M. Roberts and S. Clarke, *Women and Gender in Early Modern Wales*, Cardiff, 2000, pp. 242–6.

86 Beattie, 'Criminality of women', p. 88.

87 NAS, JC26/161.

88 NAS, JC26/223.

89 See Jones, *Crime in Nineteenth Century Wales*, p. 89.

90 For further discussion of women's participation in riots, see J. Bohstedt, 'Gender, household and community politics: women in English riots, 1790–1810', *Past and Present*, 1988, no. 120, pp. 88–122; G. Rudé, *The Crowd in History, 1730–1848* London, 1981; J. Stevenson, *Popular Disturbances in England, 1700–1870*, London, 1992; D. Jones, *Before Rebecca: Popular Protests in Wales, 1793–1835*, London, 1973; J. E. Archer, *Social Unrest and Popular Protest in England, 1780–1840* Cambridge, 2000; C. A. Whatley, 'How tame were the Scottish lowlanders during the eighteenth century?', in T. M. Devine (ed.), *Conflict and Stability in Scottish Society, 1700–1850*, Edinburgh, 1990; K. J. Logue, *Popular Disturbances in Scotland, 1780–1815*, Edinburgh, 1979.

91 Beattie, 'Criminality of women', p. 88.

92 See n. 50.

93 Stevenson, *Popular Disturbances*, p. 105.

94 See, for instance, Rudé, *Crowd in History*, p. 257; Beattie, *Crime and the Courts*, p. 133.

95 Kilday, 'Women and crime', pp. 126–33.

96 Howell, *Rural Poor*, pp. 182–3. For further discussion of the nature of popular protest in Wales, see J. Bohstedt, *Riots and Community Politics in England and Wales, 1790–1810*, Harvard, MA, 1983; Jones, *Before Rebecca*; D. Williams, *The Rebecca Riots*, Cardiff, 1992; D. J. V. Jones, *Rebecca's Children: Study of Rural Society, Crime and Protest*, Oxford, 1989.

97 Stevenson, *Popular Disturbances in England*, p. 137; Whatley, 'How tame were the Scottish lowlanders?', especially pp. 17–21.

98 See Stevenson, *Popular Disturbances in England*, pp. 137–8.

Chapter Nine

ੲ☙

Women, consumption and taste

Helen Berry

An interest in the history of consumption has come to dominate social-science disciplines in recent decades, in contrast to previous economic histories of the Industrial Revolution, where a focus on supply rather than demand tended to dictate the interpretation of historical change.[1] As yet, however, the history of women's consumption during the transition from the early modern to the modern period has largely been confined to a limited number of case studies, with greater focus upon the better-off in society. Historians have used a range of contemporary sources to explore the acquisition, use, and disposal of goods from a gender perspective, including legal documents (such as wills and probate inventories), personal records (such as diaries and correspondence), and business records (including account books).[2] These provide evidence of the rapid social and economic changes that were taking place in women's lives at this time, although the nature of this evidence is often highly specific and localized.[3] This chapter sets out to synthesize the various social, economic, and cultural contexts in which British women acted as consumers, and to consider women's patterns of consumption from the eighteenth to the mid-nineteenth century. This subject is addressed in two stages: first, through consideration of the influence of a supposed feminine aesthetic, or 'female taste', in material goods (especially from the mid-eighteenth century onward, when the female consumer was targeted in everything from the literary style of the novel to the design of tableware); and, second, from the surviving evidence relating to women's personal consumption through the different stages of the life-cycle – the actual purchase of goods or services by women, or through their commission.

Contexts for consumption

From the late seventeenth century onwards, the middling sort in Britain grew rapidly in social, economic, and political influence.[4] During the Georgian era, in a process that economic historian, Jan de Vries, has called the 'industrious revolution', households became orientated more towards market-based economic activity than self-sufficiency, and wives in middle-class households began to assume a crucial responsibility for making consumer decisions for themselves and their families.[5] Further down the social scale, consumption among the most economically marginalized women, especially female servants and the poor, is a subject which has received less attention in the existing historiography for this period, although they made significant contributions to the development of specific markets in Georgian and Victorian Britain, notably for essential foodstuffs.[6] As Britain emerged as the leading industrial nation in the world, an increasingly wide range of women, including a now-substantial body of middle-class women, gained access to domestic markets for manufactured and imported goods.

Militating against women's economic independence, however, was their continuing subordination in law, which formally restricted a woman's ability to acquire and dispose of property without the sanction of her husband (or, in the case of unmarried women, a male relative). Until the Married Women's Property Act of 1882, for example, wives in theory could not own property independently of their husbands. Set against this overarching precept, there was a long-standing principle in common law that wives could undertake contractual obligations as agents of their husbands, the so-called 'law of necessaries', which encompassed the repeat-buys that were a vital part of feeding and clothing a family, and running a household.[7] There is also much evidence that wealthier women used legal arrangements such as prenuptial settlements to secure their own futures and dispose of inherited wealth as they wished.[8]

British women's consumption was thus proscribed according to the key variables of class, wealth, and level of personal regard for material goods, within a framework of legal and customary constraints. It was also shaped by factors such as religious conviction and ease of access to metropolitan or other urban centres of consumption. London, Europe's first and largest metropolis, had long exerted a magnetic attraction as a centre of British consumption among the ranks of English, Scottish, and Welsh gentle-women. Foreign visitors to Britain's capital city in the eighteenth century reported that its shops presented a dazzling array of imported and domestic goods.[9] Important provincial towns throughout Britain also exercised influence over wide geographical areas, notably ports or county towns that served as 'regional capitals'; Bristol manners and fashions, for example, permeated into Wales and South-west England.[10] The 'news revolution' also did much to stimulate consumer demand: from the early eighteenth century, the circulation of newspapers and periodicals multiplied both the speed and volume of information in circulation nationally about the latest fashions. One letter to *The Spectator* in 1711, from a correspondent in Exeter, complained that local ladies were crazy for the 'freshest Advices from *London*', and that they adorned themselves liberally with the latest fashion for 'Cherry-coloured Ribbon'.[11] Provincial shopkeepers soon found that they could make use of local newspapers to advertise that their goods were as diverse and of as high quality as any found in the shops in London.[12]

Improved communication and transport links brought many people greater access to urban markets from the mid-eighteenth century onwards: they also enabled the circulation of a wider range of goods than ever before. By 1770, 500 turnpike trusts had been set up, which oversaw the construction and maintenance of a national road network covering 15,000 miles, allowing movement of passenger and freight traffic to and from London and the regional capitals.[13] Increasingly during the eighteenth century, the British economy became geared towards imperialist expansion and the promotion of colonial trade, and the annual volume of imported luxury goods and commodities increased, with only relatively brief disruptions during periods of warfare. The East India Company and the Levant Company, plying trade routes with China, India, and the Middle East, imported commodities such as spices, tea, and coffee, and great quantities of luxury manufactured goods, including silks, china, paper goods, porcelain, and silverware. Fortunes were made in the exponential growth of the sugar trade, a commodity that brought wealth to English towns such as Bristol and Liverpool, but which was reliant upon African slave labour in the Caribbean and West Indies.[14] British manufacturers also became skilled at designing and producing luxury items for domestic and foreign markets in imitation of luxury Asian goods.[15] New fashions in domestic interior design and personal attire emerged in the eighteenth century through contact with far-distant cultures, stimulating demand for British imitations of Turkish carpets, chinoiserie, 'japanned' items (black lacquer designs made to look Japanese), and, later in the century, cotton cloth woven in northern industrial towns in imitation of Indian patterns.[16]

The century after 1750 was an era of 'nationalizing taste'. Across Britain there was much in common between what we might term the 'consumer opportunities' available to women in urban areas – whether Edinburgh, Newcastle, Bristol, or Cardiff – as compared to those in rural areas, such as the Scottish Highlands, Cardiganshire, Northumberland, or Cornwall.[17] In the changing environment of the town, where outward markers of status such as dress and deportment could be a passport to society, taste came to be seen as a defining characteristic of gentility or 'respectability'.[18] Whereas traditionally the hierarchy of British society had been founded upon lineage and ownership of land (and those whose status rested upon these elements proved to have a remarkably tenacious hold on power through to the nineteenth century), for the rest of society, the conditions of rapid urbanization and a developing market economy provided new opportunities after 1700 for social mobility and self-advancement. Through education and habituation, a consensus of taste emerged that distinguished one social group from another in an ongoing process of stratification. Taste was thus integral to the evolution of a consumer society in Britain, where culture came increasingly to be regarded as a commodity.[19]

Women and luxury

It was a long-standing idea that a gentleman ought to spend one-third of his income upon housekeeping, so that his lifestyle, and that of the female members of his household, would be in keeping with his status.[20] This principle was articulated at the end of the seventeenth century by Thomas Morgan of Tredegar in Glamorgan, who reasoned that he spent extravagantly on travel, clothes, and gambling 'to live according to my quality'.[21] The contemporary term 'decencies' encompassed essential items, as opposed those things that were 'desirable but not indispensable'.[22] It is, of course, difficult to define 'luxury' in relation to historically shifting ideas of 'necessity', but moral debates over what constituted luxury and whether the accumulation of material wealth was morally culpable were newly invigorated in the so-called 'luxury debates' of the eighteenth century.[23] In the face of new material temptations, these debates questioned the moral responsibility of both sexes in the realm of consumption. Controversially, the early eighteenth-century writer, Bernard Mandeville, proposed that 'private vice' was desirable, since greed, he argued, contributed towards 'public virtue' – the greater economic good of the nation.[24]

Mandeville was unusual in his outspoken defence of greed: many more voices warned of the ruinous consequences of profligacy, especially where insatiable female appetites were concerned. It was an oft-repeated maxim in eighteenth- and nineteenth-century public discourse, from plays to pulpit-lectures, that the 'fair sex' was especially prone to acquisitiveness and vanity. The iconic presence in literature and art of the acquisitive woman 'on the make' dates back almost as far as the historical record, but was certainly given new life in the Georgian and early Victorian periods.[25] In the era in which the novel was first popularized in Britain, the consuming woman took centre-stage as a social commentary upon the times. From Daniel Defoe's *Moll Flanders* (1722), who passes herself off as an heiress in order to marry a rich man (who was himself a fraudster), to William Makepeace Thackeray's shamelessly mercenary Becky Sharp, the anti-heroine of *Vanity Fair* (1847–8), female and male readers were provided with *memento mori* about what would happen to a woman who succumbed to greed. As the Revd James Hervey reflected cheerfully in his *Meditations among the Tombs* (1746–7): 'One night, *CORINNA* was all gaiety in her Spirits, all Finery in her apparel, at a magnificent Ball: The next Night, she lay pale and stiff, an extended Corpse.'[26] It was not just male writers who claimed that women's vanity led to the financial and moral ruin of men; novels by women at this time also feature women as actively embracing a dominant culture obsessed with consumption. In Fanny Burney's *Cecilia* (1782), the eponymous heroine's guardian, Mrs Harrel, is in thrall to luxury, which weakens her powers of reasoning and leads her virtually to extort money from her ward to pay off her debts, while Lydia Bennet in Jane Austen's *Pride and Prejudice* (1813) is 'extremely fond of lottery tickets', and brings near-ruin upon her family for the love of an officer's uniform.[27]

Contemporary literary critiques of consumption by moralists on this issue were aimed at men as well as women, although the female sex was certainly the target for some of the more lurid diatribes. For women, luxury was especially culpable, since upon their sex was heaped a whole host of other cultural expectations, such as chastity, piety, duty, and obedience.[28] In *The Rape of the Lock* (1714), Alexander Pope's air-headed society girl, Belinda, is surrounded by what Vivien Jones calls a 'chaos of commodities': 'Here Files of Pins extend their Shining Rows, / Puffs, Powders, Patches, Bibles, Billet-doux'.[29] John Brown reserved special opprobrium for consuming women in his *Estimate of the Manners and Principles of the Times* (1757), when he lamented 'the Character of the Manners of our Times . . . will probably appear to be that of a "*vain, luxurious,* and *selfish* EFFEMINACY"'.[30] The Scottish economist, Adam Smith, also observed the corrupting influence of luxury upon higher status women, whose bodies, he argued, were often rendered too feeble for childbearing: 'Luxury in the fair sex, while it enflames perhaps the passion for enjoyment, seems always to weaken, and frequently to destroy altogether the powers of generation.'[31] The stereotype of the consuming woman wracked by luxury was reiterated in print by some of the most influential male authors of the day, but also by ordinary, nameless men, such as the correspondent who wrote to his local newspaper in 1781 to complain that 'female hair-dressing' constituted a 'burthensome domestic tax', since it cost him more than 'land-tax, house-tax, window-tax, paving, cleaning and lighting the streets, scavengers and watch-rates, all put together'.[32] Many, though not all, male authors argued that female greed was a pernicious influence and censured women who were materially ambitious. By the late eighteenth century, the Evangelical revival had strengthened these ideas by presenting an ideal of womanhood and Christian charity that strongly favoured the abnegation of material wealth and sensual pleasure. The new importance placed upon family life in early Victorian Britain gave rise to the idea that house and home were expressions of morality as much in their material presentation as in the conduct of the family who lived there. As will become evident later in this chapter, this emphasis upon domestic propriety presented new responsibilities, and posed new problems, for the female consumer.

The acquisitive woman

During the eighteenth and nineteenth centuries, as today, certain sectors of society were regarded as fashionable icons and trend-setters. Royalty had traditionally provided a court-centred lead in the realm of the fine or 'ornamental' arts – painting, literature, music, architecture. With a shift of power from court to parliament after 1689, the nobility became the new focus of taste. Their penchant for undertaking Grand Tours to Italy and Greece inspired a vogue for estate improvements and patronage of the arts that was sponsored by the great landed families, including a number of well-known, flamboyant noblewomen. Lady Mary Wortley Montagu, for example, started a fashion in London for ladies to wear turbans and other forms of Turkish dress in the wake of the publication of her correspondence from her travels in the Middle East.[33] Élite style defined metropolitan standards of taste and was translated into popularized forms nationwide, partly through the migration of provincial gentry and nobility to and from London and spa towns like Bath. When they returned to their localities, they took with them the habits and styles of the capital and regional centres of sociability. For example, during the 1760s, the duchess of Northumberland set about 'improving' Alnwick Castle in Northumberland with the addition of gothic windows copied from Horace Walpole's Strawberry Hill mansion (a questionable endeavour which attracted criticism from the pioneer of gothic revival himself), and new interior decorations in the same style by Robert Adam.[34] An heiress in her own right, the duchess used her wealth and power to become a patron of the arts, travelling abroad to buy paintings, ivories, enamels, and miniatures.[35] At Bath during the season, leading society women were scrutinized by visiting gentlewomen, who then took their new styles home with them, a pattern of emulation which was exploited by the countess of Huntington in her campaign to make the new Methodist religion fashionable.[36] During the first half of the nineteenth century, the development of country estates continued under the direction of female aristocrats: Lady Louisa Thynne, daughter of the second Marquess of Bath of Longleat, married Henry, Viscount Lascelles in 1823, after which she supervised the refurbishments of Harewood House in Yorkshire and its extensive gardens in the 1840s. With thirteen children and the family nickname of the 'domestic oracle', Louisa exhibited the matronly qualities that were celebrated by the early Victorians. The material privileges enjoyed by the Lascelles family, however, far outstripped that of the vast majority of the British population at the time.[37]

One of the newest fashions to spread rapidly in society from the early 1700s and one which, in some senses, defined what it meant to be a female consumer, was the vogue for domestic sociability. The polite custom of visiting for tea, which was deemed appropriate to gender and status for women of the upper, and (later) middling sort, required the expense of fitting out a suitable parlour or salon. This new form of sociability stimulated the domestic and import markets for a wide range of accoutrements: silver spoons, china, tea caddies, delicate porcelain dishes, tongs, kettles, and mahogany tea-tables, not to mention suitable afternoon attire. In the early years of the eighteenth century, John Thomlinson, curate of Rothbury, recorded his parish visits in his diary, in which he also noted the expensive habits of his female relatives: 'Aunt would have 50*l.* to furnish her drawing room, *i.e.*, 20*l.* for silver tea-kettle, lamp and table; 5*l.* in glasses and sconces, 10 or 15*l.* in hangings, and the rest in chairs, cushions and curtains, etc.'[38] This was at a time when the typical curate's salary was about £60 per annum.[39] As the century progressed, form, design, and 'fitness' for purpose (that is, usefulness) were prized in enhancing the aesthetics of the tea table. Josiah Wedgwood's black basalt-ware, designed to imitate the design and form of Etruscan vases, by happy coincidence set off in relief the pale delicacy of the hostess' hands as she poured her tea.[40] A specific example of how domestic sociability stimulated consumer demand, and the centrality of women to this process, is recorded in the diaries of John Marsh, a gentleman musician and lawyer, who moved his household to Chichester in 1787. His wife's priority on this occasion was to refurbish their drawing room by ordering a new carpet, curtains, and chairs, which enabled the family 'to begin seeing Company'. Over three afternoons, they announced their arrival in the neighbourhood by receiving local polite society, mostly women.[41] Marsh's wife took centre-stage at these proceedings; a 'Miss Heron', Marsh recorded, 'sat each day with Mrs M. during this ceremony'.[42] The replication of afternoons such as these around the country raised the demand for sugar, tea, and chocolate in even the remoter parts of Britain. By the end of the eighteenth century, Robert's, a general shop in Penmarfon, a remote village some fifteen miles from Caenarvon on the hills above Tremadoc in Caenarvonshire, was supplying twenty customers with tea, the vast majority of whom were women.[43] Similarly, when James Boswell and Samuel Johnson toured the Highlands of Scotland in 1773, they visited the sociable Macleods of Raasay. The Macleods – with a family of ten daughters, of whom only the eldest, Flora, had been to Edinburgh – lived in a remote area, yet Boswell noted that they had adopted the custom of visiting with near neighbours and engaged every evening in activities such as guitar-playing, singing, and dancing.[44] By Victoria's accession, few parts of Britain were unaffected by the evolving consumer culture, even though social attitudes towards material goods, and their pattern of distribution, varied considerably.

Patterns of consumption

Women's patterns of consumption were shaped, as in so many other respects, by the female life-cycle. From early childhood, a variety of influences, both formal and informal, shaped girls' attitudes, tastes, and habits, but a consistent feature of female education across the social spectrum was a focus upon the domestic sphere. In the first phase of her adult life, a young single women of middling or upper status was usually supported by her parents, whose priority was to provide her with enough education to provide suitable accomplishments for the marriage market.[45] Household economy was one important feature of this training, something which girls most often learnt through observation of their mothers or other female relatives. Among the majority of British households, where money was not an unlimited resource, a reputation for prudence could improve a woman's chances of marriage. The necessity of economy was as true for middling households as for the labouring classes: John Thomlinson's uncles disagreed over which of two women would make their nephew, an impoverished clergyman, a better wife: the one 'a greater fortune and a genteeler woman'; the other a 'frugal woman' who could 'dress a dish of meat well'.[46]

In the vast majority of cases, marriage marked for girls the transition to adult womanhood. Part of the business of establishing a new household, if a man wished to enhance his own social status, would be to facilitate domestic sociability by providing his wife with a suitable home, furnishings, and a clothing allowance appropriate to his, and therefore her, rank in society. In George Eliot's *Middlemarch* (1871–2), set in a Midland town in 1830–2, the unfortunate Dr Lydgate discovers that the extravagance of his new wife, the sweet and apparently compliant Rosamund Vincy, is sufficient to bankrupt him.[47] In reality, and for the majority of law-abiding subjects, it was seldom the case that family fortunes among the middling and upper sort were ruined by a wife's poor management: women simply did not have ultimate control over the disposal of fixed assets, capital, and income, and their allocated portion of housekeeping money was largely directed towards maintaining children and home.[48] Historians who have studied legal documents relating to the transfer of property on marriage have found that the reverse was more common: it was husbands who often used their wives' dowries to refurbish their country houses and estates – as did Thomas Powell of Nanteos in Wales, when he married Mary Frederick, the daughter of a London merchant, in 1738.[49] The estate of the Ingram family at Temple Newsam, a mansion near Leeds, was enriched by £60,000 upon the marriage in 1758 of Frances Gibson Shepheard (1734–1807), an illegitimate heiress, to the ninth Viscount Irwin.[50] Although the most successful aristocrats and the emerging industrial magnates of the early- to mid-nineteenth century also generated wealth through other means (such as business speculation and property development), marriage remained an important means for long-established gentry families to consolidate their wealth and for rich self-made men to gain social prestige.[51]

Newlyweds acquired goods through a variety of means: while some were purchased new, others were acquired secondhand, or received as wedding gifts. Middle-class brides in eighteenth- and nineteenth-century Edinburgh and Glasgow were given a distinctive piece of furniture, a Scottish chest of drawers, which was deemed a 'vital symbol of respectable wifely status'.[52] In setting up their new households, young wives were more likely to have command over the movable and/or decorative items, which allowed them to express their individuality 'in distinctive materials and styles'.[53] Some entrepreneurs, like Josiah Wedgwood, deliberately appealed to the female consumer in the diverse and colourful wares they produced, and deployed female-friendly marketing strategies, such as elegant shops and polite sales assistants. Wedgwood, and his contemporary, Matthew Boulton, also manufactured pottery with appealingly prestigious 'brand' names, such as 'Queen's ware'.[54]

Marriage usually meant children, and the process of clothing and feeding a household (including servants) was the major channel of a wife's time and resources. It was a wife's responsibility to keep her family supplied with the necessities of life, such as regular meals, and to organize and regulate domestic labour, with or without the help of hired servants.[55] The second-hand clothing market was of particular importance to women, since they were usually charged with procuring cloth and making and mending clothes for their families.[56] Account-books kept by women of the middling sort and gentry indicate a meticulous attention to the minutiae of household expenditure. Mrs Inglebey of Settle in North Yorkshire, for example, started her housekeeping account-book in April, 1825. In it she kept regular monthly entries of the cost of running a middling household, detailing not inconsiderable monthly expenses of between £5 and £50 from 1828 until the end of 1839.[57] She was responsible for monitoring the purchase of small household items, such as candles (5s./5d.) and palm soap (2s./3d.), food and beverages, items of clothing, and servants' and tradesmen's bills.[58] She also kept track of her travel expenses to York, Leeds, and Lancaster, and her leisure costs, such as 2s. for a lecture, £2/1s. for a visit to the library and £1/5s. for a donation to the Bible Society.[59] The wealthier and more higher status the household, the more complex the level of organization required. In gentry households, cooks and house-keepers often kept their own account-books, although it was still not unusual for the lady of the house to keep a master copy of her own. The Durham gentlewoman, Judith Baker, started keeping a modest 'cash book' as a young bride in 1749; as a widow, she kept complex ledgers detailing the income and expenditure of her entire household and the management of the family's alum trade, even after her son had passed his twenty-first birthday. This arrangement changed only when he married.[60] In the 1780s, Mrs Baker was monitoring income and expenditure of over £200 per month and taking delivery of miscellaneous luxury 'chattels' from London, including fine silk, furniture, and imported foods.[61]

In an era when women's wages were scarce and erratic at all social levels, it was customary for husbands to provide their wives with 'pin money', an amount of disposable income in addition to housekeeping money, which they were free to spend at their discretion.[62] The amount that was paid varied considerably – from just a few shillings to £4,000 a year for the Duchess of Devonshire – and, as court records indicate, there were many disputes around non-payment of pin money.[63] There was also potential for marital conflict around what constituted 'necessary' household expenses and what constituted 'luxury' items that ought to have been paid with pin money. The fictional Betsy Thoughtless objected to her husband's insistence that she should buy coffee and chocolate out of her pin money, a reasonable enough protest if we consider these would have been ordinary items in household account-books by the mid-eighteenth century.[64] The sums of money available to married women, even those of higher status and wealth, were often limited according to whether their husbands approved of the expenditure. For most of our period, it was common to purchase goods on credit rather than for ready money, a situation which was necessitated in part by the lack of small-denomination coins. There were numerous advertisements in the eighteenth-century press in which husbands publicly disowned their wives, informing creditors that they would not pay their debts. In 1741, for example, Anne, the wife of Henry Brown of North Coulton in Yorkshire, was disowned by her husband in the local newspaper for having made off with 'two Cart-Loads of House-hold Furniture, and other Things, the Property of her said Husband'.[65] Deliberately running up bills, or even making off with the contents of the marital home, was a not uncommon strategy deployed by women, especially in situations where marriages had broken down. Historian Margot Finn has found that, right up to the Divorce Act of 1857, women used the 'law of necessaries' as a means of securing credit for themselves in their husbands' names in cases of informal marital separation. Lady Westmeath, for example, succeeded in having her estranged husband imprisoned in the King's Bench in the 1820s for failing to pay debts she had accrued for food, clothing, household purchases, and rent.[66] Further down the social scale, there is evidence that working-class women exploited the legal ambiguity of their status under *coverture* to gain credit when in difficult financial circumstances – a legal loophole which was exposed, rather than resolved, by the introduction of national county courts in 1846.[67]

Although by far the most common type of household was one centring upon a married couple, about 15 per cent of households in England at this time were headed by single women.[68] Their inventories record household linen more frequently than men's, an area of traditional female responsibility. Women's inventories also record more decorative items than men's: looking-glasses, for instance, may suggest that women had a concern for personal appearance and 'self-awareness', while their pictures were an outward expression of personal taste.[69] This evidence suggests that where a tradeswoman was the head of a household, she spent her money differently. This was not to say, however, that never-married or widowed women did not channel their consumption, like their married counterparts, towards their close family relatives. As Adrian Green has shown, the purchases of Betty Bowes, a spinster and eighteenth-century scion of the Bowes-Lyon family, were 'framed by family concerns and female sociability ... inextricably linked to the more individualized meanings of her material and print culture'.[70]

Historical records relating to the final stage of a woman's life-cycle, when her goods were distributed according to her wishes after her death, often reveal the meaning of goods with respect to a woman's affective ties and loyalties. In a study of eighteenth-century wills from Birmingham and Sheffield, Maxine Berg found that, for women more than men, clothes, light furnishings, table linen, tea-ware, and china were 'personal and expressive goods', passed on to relatives as a means of conveying 'identity, personality and fashion'.[71] Women used whatever possessions they had to create a sense of their own identity and to be remembered after their deaths by their families and friends. Since higher status women were not usually able to dispose of larger 'fixed' assets, such as estate, land, or capital, even their purchases were confined to moveable goods for their families (in particular, fabric to make clothing for their children), while their personal expenditure was limited to smaller items – trinkets and gifts for relatives and friends that conveyed personal affect. Using diary evidence, Amanda Vickery has highlighted the complex ways in which Lancashire gentlewomen left their possessions as legacies.[72] There is considerable evidence that these women regarded their possessions more as a means of constructing relationships between family members and within the wider community, such as the bequest of clothing from mistress to servant. Even the staging of a funeral entailed 'consumption' that could express something of the identity of the deceased. When John Bedford's wife died in 1756, her funeral *cortège* was preceded by five women in hoods of white Irish linen, and the coffin itself was carried by eight widows in hoods and scarves of the same fabric.[73] The dressing of this scene in white, and the active participation of female pall-bearers, conveyed powerful messages about the femininity and virtue of the departed woman. By 1850, funeral drapery had become big business. The trend for lavish displays of mourning, which is more usually associated with Queen Victoria's prolonged grief for Prince Albert, had already become entrenched in British culture with the death in 1810 of Princess Amelia, George III's favourite daughter, when twelve weeks of national mourning had been declared. Entire industries, from the 1820s onward, were devoted to the manufacture of black ribbon, 'dark Norwich crape', and the paraphernalia of grief, including black-edged stationery and black sealing wax.[74]

From cradle to grave, British women actively fuelled economic growth through their consumer choices. In some respects, it was ever thus, but from the late-eighteenth to the mid-nineteenth century, the difference was one of unprecedented scale and diversity of consumer goods and services on offer to expanding sectors of the population. Cash rather than credit came to dominate consumer transactions and women were targeted by manufacturers and retailers in an attempt to persuade them to spend money on their families and themselves through an increasingly sophisticated language of advertising.

Negotiating consumerism

We have seen how many male authors (and some female ones too) publicly lamented the decline of the nation into vanity and luxury. The Evangelical revival of the late eighteenth and nineteenth centuries emphasized charity over luxury and prudence over profligacy. It served only to raise the stakes in the debate – which had gained public attention in the early 1700s – between those who believed in profit and those who feared that acquisitiveness would have a debilitating, corrupting, and 'effeminizing' influence upon the nation. A new wave of late Georgian and Victorian social reformers, inspired by the Evangelical revival, campaigned for a check upon the luxury of the age. John Wesley at first even condemned taking sugar in tea, but later favoured moderate pleasures if enjoyed within the context of a godly household.[75] Nonconformist women had long curbed their consumption as a mark of their removal from the prevailing values of the society in which they lived. Quaker women in mid-eighteenth century Glamorgan, for example, resolved at their annual meeting that, 'no young women go to shop keeping or House-keeping without advice from the meeting they belong to'.[76] The Evangelical revival gave new voice and validation to this anti-consumer stance. At the end of the eighteenth century, publications like the *Lady's Museum* (1798) championed Hannah More, founder of the Religious Tract Society, as a female exemplar.[77]

From the last quarter of the eighteenth century, it was not only religious conviction, but also a heightened emphasis upon 'feeling' (the so-called 'culture of sensibility') that encouraged a more empathetic and spontaneously emotional response to life and art. In the first three decades of the nineteenth century, the provincial art market flourished, with woman as the primary consumers in this sphere. Respectable Edinburgh ladies commissioned the services of portrait painter, Sir Henry Raeburn, who contributed sentimental portraits featuring women and children to a national taste for domestic art collections.[78] The relationship between consumption, literary fashion, and female taste in the development of trade in Victorian Britain was no better demonstrated than in the Waverley novels of Sir Walter Scott: a new volume was published almost annually from 1814 to 1831. The Scottish Romantic movement started a craze for tartans and tweeds that did much to revive the ailing Galashiels weaving industry. Queen Victoria herself not only sported the new Balmoral plaid, but also had most of the interior of her Highland retreat decorated in Royal Stuart tartan. The vogue for Scottish manufactured goods had taken hold in London during the 1840s; Scott Adie's 'Royal Clan Tartan and Scotch Shawl Warehouse' in Regent Street received the ultimate accolade of the Queen's seal of approval and did a brisk trade in 'Ladies' Shetland Shawls and Veils, Scotch Hosiery'.[79]

Among female consumers, romanticism also inspired awareness of the injustice of slavery. The otherwise dedicated consumer, Sophie La Roche, was unimpressed by the sight of gold bars on display in the Bank of England, having spared a thought for 'the miserable plight of the blacks who extract it from the earth'.[80] Other women also made the connection between imperial wealth and the exploitation of African labour, and it was female consumers who led the way in boycotting sugar.[81] Continuing this trend, in the 1830s and 1840s, Chartist women employed the tactic of 'exclusive dealing', that is, boycotting shopkeepers who refused to support their cause. It would be another half-century, however, before the potential to use consumption as a political weapon was fully realized by British women of the Socialist movement.[82]

A growing number of periodicals and magazines appealed specifically to a female readership. These comprised of items of miscellaneous interest rather than current affairs, as the following advertisement, allegedly written '*by a* YOUNG LADY *at Mrs* ——'s BOARDING SCHOOL' illustrates:

If you would seek for taste refin'd,
Instruction and amusement join'd,
If you would pass the fleeting hours
In culling learning's choicest flowers;
If you desire, at small expence,
To purchase works of wit and sense:

All this you certainly will glean,
From Wheble's Lady's Magazine.[83]

The *Lady's Magazine* (1770–1832) was among the pioneering late eighteenth-century miscellanies that appealed to female readers. In the early nineteenth century, publications like *Ackerman's Repository* (1809–29) and the *Ladies Fashionable Repository* (1809–95) included plate illustrations to keep their female readers informed of the fashion trends in London and Paris. Middle-class Victorian women's magazines took an especial interest not only in fashion and gossip, but also in family and domestic concerns, household management and Christian piety. By the 1830s, the female consumer had her own magazines and fashion pages, and was bombarded with advertisements promising happiness through consumption, for herself and her children. From the eighteenth century onwards, certain shops selling female accoutrements such as hats, ribbons, and cosmetics had begun to advertise the fact that they were run by women, for women.[84] The development of a fully articulated language of advertising directed towards women as consumers accelerated from the 1840s onwards, when a truly 'mass media' emerged. It was especially pronounced in the growing number of advertisements for medicines for various women's ailments, especially nervous and hysterical diseases.[85] As Margaret Beetham has argued, the popular press increasingly came to feature women as readers and consumers, with a shift in emphasis over the period from 'aristocratic' reader to bourgeois consumer, especially after the tax on advertising was repealed in 1853.[86]

Changes in the customary use of domestic space from the 1820s also impacted upon women's influence in middle-class society. In Edinburgh and Glasgow, the dining-room became the new focus of conspicuous display, giving prominence to masculine sociability as the custom of female 'withdrawal' after dinner was widely adopted. Yet, the increasing presence of pianos in dining-rooms provided an opportunity for Scottish women to participate in social occasions by displaying their talents in performing upon an expensive instrument, a 'skill that was both expensive and time-consuming to acquire'.[87]

If there was broad continuity in the moral and religious instruction meted out to women regarding the perils of worldly goods over the 150 years in question, there was considerable change by the start of the nineteenth century in the methods of consumption available to the female consumer and the range of products on offer. One of the greatest changes that took place in the supply-side of the British economy at this time was the rise in the ready-made clothing industry, especially in the manufacture of clothes from cheap cotton fabrics, the price of which fell by about one-third from the 1770s to 1850.[88] This new development was of especial interest to female customers, who up until that point had taken primary responsibility for the repetitive and onerous task of making (or acquiring second-hand) the clothing for their entire households, including the servants. Shopping for 'ready money' rather than credit also opened up new possibilities during the Regency period.[89] Cash-only shops emerged that dealt in quick profit and faster turnover of goods. In 1831, a new 'Bazaar' had opened in King Street, Manchester, where the diverse businesses of 'Manufacturers, Artists, and Tradesmen' were housed under one roof for the convenience of shoppers, and (as the prospectus specified) 'to give employment to industrious Females'.[90] Arising out of the bazaar was another innovation – the modern department store.[91] In 1838, Emerson Bainbridge opened a drapery shop in Newcastle upon Tyne that diversified its wares, offering several product lines under one roof. This outlet offered variety and choice in commodious surroundings, with polite service and tea-rooms especially devised for female sociability.[92] Nationally, drapers were quick to diversify and expand their businesses along the lines established by Bainbridge's: in 1843, Marshall & Snelgrove opened a branch in Harcourt Place, Scarborough, during the season; they later opened another shop in the fashionable spa town of Harrogate.[93] Debenham, Pooley and Smith (the forerunner of modern-day Debenhams department store) traced its origins to a London drapery shop in 1778. By 1837, the business had diversified through a series of acquisitions and mergers into Debenham & Freebody's, with branches in Cheltenham and Harrogate.[94] During the course of the nineteenth century, department stores thus developed into 'a feminine universe *par excellence*'.[95]

Another momentous change was the railway, which provided greater mobility and access to urban markets that had hitherto been beyond the reach of the middling and lower sorts. The railway, with its first-, second- and third-class carriages, nurtured both tourism and trade across the social spectrum, especially after 1844, when government legislation introduced cheap travel, such as 'penny a mile' specials.[96]

Conclusion

By 1850, for perhaps the first time in British history, a growing number of ordinary people had access to an unprecedented level of domestic comfort. Bourgeois eighteenth-century homes had been furnished with valuable decorative items such as prints, carpets, silverware, mirrors, and clocks. Nineteenth-century domestic interiors became more cluttered still, with even modest households having access to 'non-essential' items by the mid-1800s, such as books, pottery, and cutlery. Some historians argue that this proliferation of material goods constituted a 'consumer revolution', which, although controversial, has sparked subsequent research into the development of modern consumer society.[97] The Georgian era was certainly one in which a socially constructed idea of 'feminine' taste proved to be highly influential and women were integral to the process of developing the demand-side of a new consumer culture.[98] Items such as clothing, china and porcelain, kitchen utensils, and furnishings designed for household use were often purchased by women and regarded as their peculiar domain (as evidenced by the fact that these were often handed down to female relatives by women in their wills).[99]

Overall, in theory at least, the undeniable rise of consumerism, whether it constituted a 'revolution', might not have been a bad thing for women. Who could deny the material comforts resulting from the 'decencies' of life, such as improvements to diet, health care, and overall standard of living that many women (and men) experienced as Britain entered the modern era? Some historians present a positive interpretation of the new opportunities that existed for women, starting in the Georgian period.[100] The pleasures associated with new types of leisure activity at this time seemed actively to court women's participation; indeed, the assemblies, balls, card parties, and pleasure gardens were characterized by hetero-sociability that paid particular deference to the women present.[101] 'In *Great-Britain'* commented John Potter in 1762, 'the ladies are as free as the gentlemen; and we have no diversions, or public amusements, in which the one may not appear, without any offence, as frankly as the other.'[102] This picture needs balancing, however, with the proviso that society in Georgian and Victorian Britain was riven by inequality, with a highly localized pattern of economic development, and with incidences of terrible urban poverty as well as social improvement. One Welsh historian reminds us that, while the goldsmiths and mercers of Cardiff were 'investing in silver tea-sets and linen napkins', in impoverished Cardigan-shire, even the gentry 'were still eating . . . out of cups and spoons of wood'.[103] Not all parts of Britain had a growing middle-class urban population and disposable wealth continued to be unevenly distributed by rank and gender, even if, theoretically, women and men could have a share in the prosperity associated with rapid industrialization. In the newly privatized world of Victorian domestic sociability, middle- and upper-class women proved they could adapt as social rituals changed.[104] However, economic dependence upon male relatives, followed by the transition to their own homes upon marriage and a new form of economic dependency, remained the most common means for women of all classes to obtain the accoutrements of a materially comfortable life. To the crushing effects of economic subordination was added the ongoing invisibility of working-class women in the sphere of cultural production and consumption. Though she tried to appropriate the books and cheap prints that were to hand for her own ends, Mary Ann Ashford, a London domestic servant with ambitions as an author, complained in 1842 that ordinary 'Mary Smith' and 'Susan Jones' never appeared in print unless it was to die, at the end of a novel, of lingering disease. Likewise, Ellen Johnson (b.1830) the 'Factory Girl' poet of Glasgow, found that other women of her class 'became jealous, and told falsehoods of me' when she talked of poetry.[105]

The exercise of female consumer autonomy and the ownership and disposal of property and earned income were issues around which the voices of early feminist writers had started to gather by the mid-nineteenth century, but it would be many decades before legal reform and increasing opportunities for women in the workplace, brought to fruition these basic rights of citizenship. Even then, it was primarily middle and upper-class women whose horizons of opportunity were first to broaden. Class, as well as gender, thus fundamentally determined who had access to both economic benefits and cultural capital as Britain moved towards a modern consumer-orientated society.

Acknowledgements

Research used in this chapter was made possible in part through the award of a Visiting Fellowship at the Huntington Library, San Marino, California, in July 2002. My thanks to Scott Ashley; to Richard Allen, Karen Atkinson, Karen Hunt, Stana Nenadic, and Diana Paton for assistance with references; and to Miss Irene Dunn for generous access to her private collection of household account books. I am also grateful to Michelle Dixon for her views on an early draft.

Notes

1 For a detailed summary of this historiographical trend, see Maxine Berg, 'Consumption in eighteenth- and early nineteenth-century Britain', in Roderick Floud and Paul Johnson (eds), *The Cambridge Economic History of Modern Britain: vol. I: Industrialisation, 1700–1860*, Cambridge, 2004, especially pp. 375–6; Sara Pennell, 'Consumption and consumerism in early modern England', *Historical Journal*, 1999, vol. 42, no. 2, pp. 549–64.

2 For examples of diaries and correspondence, see Elizabeth Shackleton and her peers in Amanda Vickery, *The Gentleman's Daughter: Women's Lives in Georgian England*, New Haven, CT, 1998, especially Chapters 4–5; Marcia Pointon, *Strategies for Showing: Women, Possession and Representation in English Visual Culture, 1665–1800*, Oxford, 1997, especially Chapter 1; for examples of the use of probate inventories and wills, see Lorna Weatherill, *Consumer Behaviour and Material Culture in Britain, 1660–1760*, 2nd edn, London, 1996; also Lorna Weatherill, 'The meaning of consumer behaviour in late seventeenth and early eighteenth-century England', in John Brewer and Roy Porter (eds), *Consumption and the World of Goods*, London, 1993.

3 A good starting point is three influential collections on consumption published in the 1990s: John Brewer and Roy Porter (eds), *Consumption and the World of*

Goods, London, 1993; John Brewer and Susan Staves (eds), *Early Modern Conceptions of Property*, London, 1994; Ann Bermingham and John Brewer (eds), *The Consumption of Culture, 1660–1800: Image, Object, Text*, London, 1995. These ground-breaking volumes explored the various aspects of eighteenth-century consumer society. Certain chapters focused in particular upon the subject of women and consumption, including those by James Grantham Turner (female entrepreneurs), Elizabeth Bennett Kubek (women and urban culture), Mary D. Sheriff (salons), Ann Bermingham (connoisseurs and the female body in art), and Richard Leppert (music). For these chapters, see Bermingham and Brewer (eds), *Consumption of Culture*, pt V.

4 The question of whether the middling sorts had greater disposable income, and when, has provoked much debate. As Ben Fine and Ellen Leopold point out in 'Consumerism and the Industrial Revolution', *Social History*, 1990, vol. 15, pp. 151–79, there must have been a concomitant rise in disposable income if people were to have been able to afford the goods on offer as a result of industrial development. E. A. Wrigley concluded from his study of wages and prices that it is extremely difficult to posit an exact fit between a rise in disposable income and the acceleration in the rate of industrialization. See E. A. Wrigley, 'Urban growth and agricultural change: England and the Continent in the early modern period', in E. A. Wrigley (ed.), *People, Cities and Wealth: The Transformation of Traditional Society*, Oxford, 1987, pp. 157–8, *passim*. By 1700, half of the households in the country (700,000 out of 1,400,000) could be defined as middling – this proportion continued to rise during the eighteenth century. See Weatherill, 'Meaning of consumer behaviour in late seventeenth and early eighteenth-century England', Brewer and Porter (eds), *Consumption and the World of Goods*, p. 210. Unlike other European countries, England had only a tiny élite group at the top of the social scale, comprising royalty and nobility. In 1801, there were still fewer than 300 peers and approximately 1,000 families in the upper gentry; by contrast, there were more than 10,000 upper-middling families, headed by military men, professionals, and richer merchants. Margaret R. Hunt, *The Middling Sort: Commerce, Gender and the Family in England, 1680–1780*, Berkeley, CA, 1996, p. 17.

5 Jan de Vries, 'Between purchasing power and the world of goods', in Brewer and Porter (eds), *Consumption and the World of Goods*, pp. 85–90, and *passim*.

6 The second-hand clothing market was a 'hidden' market to which middling and lower-status women made significant contributions. See Beverley Lemire, *Fashion's Favourite: The Cotton Trade and the Consumer in Britain, 1660–1800*, Oxford, 1991, pp. 96–114; see also Beverley Lemire, 'Consumerism in pre-industrial and early industrial England: the trade in secondhand clothes', *Journal of British Studies*, 1988, vol. 27, pp. 1–24. Certainly, the income and expenditure of poor families were shaped by the seasonal or sporadic nature of their employment and, universally, by their susceptibility to debt, especially in years of poor harvest. The impression of increasing wealth and consumer spending nationwide during this period is put into perspective if we consider that agricultural workers in England earned on average from 8–12*d.* a day: in Wales, the figure was 6–10*d.*, with lower wages in winter than in summer. Keith Wrightson, *Earthly Necessities: Economic Lives in Early Modern Britain*, New Haven, CT, 2000, p. 312.

7 Margot Finn, 'Women, consumption and coverture in England, *c.*1760–1860, *Historical Journal*, 1996, vol. 39, p. 707.

8 Ibid., p. 706.

9 See, for example, César de Saussure, *A Foreign View of England in 1725–29: The Letters of Monsieur César de Saussure to His Family*, trans. and ed. Mme Van Muyden, London, 1995, p. 134; Sophie La Roche, *Sophie in London, 1786: Being the Diary of Sophie V. La Roche*, trans. and ed. Clare Williams, London, 1933.

10 For the influence of Bristol fashions in Wales, see Philip Jenkins, *The Making of a Ruling Class: The Glamorgan Gentry, 1640–1790*, Cambridge, 1983, p. 245;

11 *The Spectator*, 20 September, 1711. Acquisitive men are also ridiculed for their love of 'Silver Hasps' on their coats.

12 See, for example, the *Newcastle Courant*, no. 5470, 4 August 1781.

13 Paul Langford, *Public Life and the Propertied Englishman, 1689–1798*, Oxford, p. 163.

14 For the quantitative value of sugar imports, see Woodruff D. Smith, *Consumption and the Making of Respectability, 1600–1800*, New York, 2002, Table 2, p. 300.

15 Maxine Berg, 'From imitation to invention: creating commodities in eighteenth-century Britain', *Economic History Review*, 2002, vol. 55, pp. 1–30; see also Carole Shammas, *The Pre-Industrial Consumer in England and America*, Oxford, 1990; John Brewer, *The Sinews of Power: War, Money and the English State, 1688–1783*, London, 1989.

16 John Styles, 'Product innovation in early modern London', *Past and Present*, 2000, no. 168, pp. 148–64.

17 Peter Borsay, *The English Urban Renaissance*, Oxford, 1989; Jonathan Barry, 'Provincial town culture, 1640–1780: urban or civic?', in J. H. Pittock and A. Wear (eds), *Interpretation and Cultural History*, Basingstoke, 1990; Joyce Ellis, 'Regional and county centres, c.1700–1840', in P. Clark (ed.), *Cambridge Urban History of Britain*, 3 vols, Cambridge, 2000, vol. 2, pp. 673–704.

18 Taste has been described as one of the primary means through which individuals differentiate themselves from others: see Pierre Bourdieu, *Distinction: A Social Critique of the Judgement of Taste*, trans. Richard Nice, London, 1984.

19 A process which Jean Baudrillard calls the 'industrial production of difference' in *The Consumer Society: Myths and Structures*, trans. La Société de Consommation, London, 1998, p. 88; see also John Brewer, ' "The most polite age and the most vicious": attitudes to culture as a commodity, 1660–1800', in Bermingham and Brewer (eds), *Consumption of Culture*, pp. 341–61.

20 Felicity Heal and Clive Holmes, *The Gentry in England and Wales, 1500–1700*, Basingstoke, 1994, pp. 288–9.

21 Ibid., p. 163.

22 Lorna Weatherill, 'Meaning of consumer behaviour', p. 207, and *passim*.

23 For a discussion of these debates, see John Sekora, *Luxury: The Concept in Western European Thought from Eden to Smollett*, Baltimore, MD, 1977; see also Christopher Berry, *The Idea of Luxury: A Conceptual and Historical Investigation*, Cambridge, 1994.

24 Bernard Mandeville, *The Fable of the Bees; Or, Private Vices, Publick Benefits*, London, 1714.

25 See, for example, the acquisitive and socially ambitious *hetaeras* (prostitutes) of ancient Greece in James Davison, *Courtesans and Fishcakes: The Consuming Passions of Classical Athens*, London, 1997.

26 Robert Dighton's *LIFE and DEATH contrasted – or, An ESSAY on WOMAN*, London, c.1784, is an artist's impression of this idea, an engraving depicting a fashionable figure, half woman–half skeleton. Death's arrow points to a funeral monument inscribed with Hervey's *memento mori*.

27 Fanny Burney, *Cecilia: Or Memoirs of an Heiress* (1782), ed. Peter Sabor and Margaret Anne Doody, Oxford, 1988, pp. 196–7; Jane Austen, *Pride and Prejudice* (1813), ed. Tony Tanner, Harmondsworth, 1972, p. 120.

28 Consumerism has always been 'heavily associated with the female, particularly in its early forms when tied to luxury, display and distinction'; Ben Fine and Ellen Leopold, *The World of Consumption*, London, 1993, p. 69; see also Maxine Berg and Elizabeth Eger, 'The rise and fall of the luxury debates', in Maxine Berg and Elizabeth Eger (eds), *Luxury in the Eighteenth Century: Debates, Desires and Delectable Goods*, Basingstoke, 2003, pp. 7–27.

29 Vivien Jones, 'Introduction', in Vivien Jones (ed.) *Women and Literature in Britain, 1700–1800*, Cambridge, 2000, p. 11.

30 Ibid., p. 10.

31 Adam Smith, *An Inquiry into the Nature and Causes of the Wealth of Nations* (1775–6), ed. R. H. Campbell and A. S. Skinner, Oxford, 1976, p. 97.

32 *Newcastle Courant*, no. 5470, 4 August 1781.

33 Lady Mary Wortley Montagu, *Letters of the Right Honourable Lady M[ar]y W[ortle]y M[ontagu]e: Written During Her TRAVELS in Europe, Asia and Africa*, first publ. 1724; new edn, 2 vols, London, 1784.

34 For her love of elaborate entertainments, feasts, and opulent furnishings, Walpole called the duchess 'junketaceous': Rachel Kennedy, 'The duke and duchess of Northumberland: aristocratic patrons', in Michael Snodin and John Styles (eds), *Design and the Decorative Arts: Britain, 1500–1900*, London, 2001, p. 218; see also Nikolaus Pevsner and Ian A. Richmond, *The Buildings of England: Northumberland*, Harmondsworth, 1957, p. 69; see also Rosemary Baird, *Mistress of the House: Great Ladies and Grand Houses, 1670–1830*, London, 2003.

35 Kennedy, 'Duke and duchess of Northumberland,', p. 218.

36 Jenkins, *Making of a Ruling Class*, p. 245.

37 Karen Lynch, 'Some Lascelles ladies', in Ruth M. Larsen (ed.), *Maids and Mistresses: Celebrating 300 Years of Women and the Yorkshire Country House*, York, 2004, pp. 59–60.

38 'The diary of the Rev. John Thomlinson, 16 October, 1717', in *Six North Country Diaries*, ed. J. C. Hodgson, Surtees Society, vol. cxviii, 1910, p. 85.

39 Peter Earle, *The Making of the English Middle Class: Business, Society and Family Life in London, 1660–1730*, London, 1989, p. 64.

40 Berg, 'From imitation to invention', p. 11; Elizabeth Kowaleski-Wallace, *Consuming Subjects: Women, Shopping and Business in the Eighteenth Century*, New York, 1997, p. 29.

41 Huntington Library, San Marino, California, HM54457/11, Diary of John Marsh, 3 June, 1787, p. 67: 'Mrs Frankland, Mrs Bull, Mrs Luxford & the Miss Jordans, the Lloyds Messrs Middleton (ye new Vicar) [and] Drew (ye Banker)'.

42 Ibid.

43 H. and L. Mui, *Shops and Shopkeeping in Eighteenth-Century England*, London, 1987, pp. 216–19.

44 Stana Nenadic, 'Experience and expectations in the transformation of the Highland gentlewoman, 1680–1820', *Scottish Historical Review*, 2001, vol. 80, p. 215.

45 Stana Nenadic, 'Middle-rank consumers and domestic culture in Edinburgh and Glasgow, 1720–1840', *Past and Present*, 1994, no. 145, p. 129.

46 'Diary of Rev. John Thomlinson, 9 November 1717', p. 90.

47 George Eliot, *Middlemarch: A Study of Provincial Life* (1871–2), introduction by R. M. Hewitt, Oxford, 1967. Lydgate ignores ominous early signs of his fiancée's

preoccupation with 'lace-edging and hosiery and petticoat-tucking . . . house linen and furniture', p. 375.

48 There were notorious examples of aristocratic women, such as Georgiana, Duchess of Devonshire, who disregarded this convention magnificently by squandering today's equivalent of millions of pounds: see Amanda Foreman, *Georgiana, Duchess of Devonshire*, London, 1998, p. 42.

49 Gerald Morgan, 'Dowries for daughters in West Wales, 1500–1700', *Welsh History Review*, 1995, vol. 17, pp. 536–7. Philip Jenkins estimates that 8 per cent of the eldest sons of Glamorgan gentry families married the daughters of wealthy Londoners: *Making of a Ruling Class*, p. 242.

50 James Lomax, 'Temple Newsam: a woman's domain', in Larsen (ed.), *Maids and Mistresses*, pp. 90–1.

51 For example, see David Cannadine, *Lords and Landlords: The Aristocracy and the Towns, 1774–1967*, Leicester, 1980, and *passim*.

52 Nenadic, 'Middle-rank consumers', p. 137.

53 Maxine Berg, 'Women's consumption and the industrial classes of eighteenth-century England', *Journal of Social History*, 1996, vol. 30, p. 429.

54 Berg, 'From imitation to invention', p. 17.

55 Caroline Davidson, *A Woman's Work is Never Done: A History of Housework in the British Isles, 1650–1950*, London, 1982, pp. 25–9.

56 Beverley Lemire, *Fashion's Favourite*; see also her, 'Consumerism in pre-industrial and early industrial England'.

57 MS Account-book, Mrs Inglebey of Settle, 15 April 1825–23 December 1839, courtesy of Miss Irene Dunn of Newcastle upon Tyne, private collection.

58 Ibid., 25 August 1832.

59 Ibid., 14 March 1833; 2 September 1833.

60 Palace Green Library [hereafter PGL], University of Durham, Baker papers, BB45/1. For a full account of Judith Baker's life, see H. Berry, 'Prudent luxury: the metropolitan tastes of Judith Baker, Durham gentlewoman', in P. Lane and R. Sweet (eds), *Women and Urban Life in Eighteenth-Century England: 'On the Town'* Aldershot, 2003, pp. 131–56.

61 PGL/BB45/25, 31 March 1773, for example, details the purchase of a Persian coat at £1 1*s.* from Jackson and Lucht's warehouse, Tavistock Street, Covent Garden.

62 Cf. Hannah Barker's chapter in this volume.

63 Ibid. See also Susan Staves, *Married Women's Separate Property in England, 1660–1833*, Cambridge, MA, 1990, Chapter 6.

64 Eliza Haywood, *The History of Miss Betsy Thoughtless*, ed. Christine Blough Toronto, 1998, pp. 498–501; Gillian Skinner, 'Women's status as legal and civic subjects: "A worse condition than slavery itself?"', in Jones (ed.), *Women and Literature in Britain*, pp. 95, 97.

65 *Newcastle Courant*, no. 2496, 10–17 October 1741.

66 Finn, 'Women, consumption and coverture', p. 711.

67 Ibid., pp. 714–19.

68 Weatherill, 'Meaning of consumer behaviour', p. 211.

69 Ibid.

70 Adrian Green, '"A clumsey countrey girl": the material and print culture of Betty Bowes', in H. Berry and J. Gregory (eds), *Creating and Consuming Culture in North-East England, 1660–1830*, Aldershot, 2004, pp. 72–97.

71 Berg, 'Women's consumption', p. 421. Elizabeth Kowaleski-Wallace suggests that, while men collected certain luxury goods, such as chinaware, women simply used them: see her *Consuming Subjects*, pp. 57–8.

72 Amanda Vickery, 'Women and the world of goods: a Lancashire consumer and her possessions, 1751–81', in Brewer and Porter (eds), *Consumption and the World of Goods*, pp. 274–301; also her, *Gentleman's Daughter*, especially Chapters 4–5.

73 'The Diary of Thomas Gyll, 26 June 1756', in *Six North Country Diaries*, ed. Hodgson, p. 199.

74 Alison Adburgham, *Shops and Shopping, 1800–1914: Where and in What Manner the Well-Dressed Englishwoman Bought her Clothes*, London, 1964, pp. 58–69.

75 Smith, *Consumption and the Making of Respectability*, p. 233.

76 Glamorgan Archive Service, D/DSF/382, Women's Yearly Meeting Minute Book, 1749–56, p. 1. I am extremely grateful to Richard Allen for this reference. For a more detailed exploration of this subject, see Richard C. Allen, 'An alternative community in north-east England: Quakers, morals and popular culture in the long eighteenth century', in Berry and Gregory (eds), *Creating and Consuming Culture*, pp. 98–119.

77 Margaret Beetham, *A Magazine of Her Own? Domesticity and Desire in the Woman's Magazine, 1800–1914*, London, 1996, p. 22.

78 Stana Nenadic, 'Romanticism and the urge to consume', in Berg and Clifford (eds), *Consumers and Luxury*, pp. 211–12.

79 Adburgham, *Shops and Shopping*, pp. 70–4.

80 *Sophie in London*, p. 164.

81 See Claire Midgley, 'Slave sugar boycotts, female activism and the domestic base of British anti-slavery culture', *Slavery and Abolition*, 1996, vol. 17, pp. 137–62.

82 June Hannam and Karen Hunt, *Socialist Women: Britain, 1880s to 1920s*, London, 2002, Chapter 6, 'Socialist women and a politics of consumption', pp. 136–7. I am grateful to Karen Hunt for this reference.

83 *Newcastle Courant*, no. 4955, 7 September 1771. See also Ros Ballaster *et al.*, *Women's Worlds: Ideology, Femininity and Women's Magazines*, London, 1991.

84 Mary and Anne Hogarth ran a shop selling 'Ready Made Frocks' by Little Britain gate in London and were fortunate enough to have trade cards designed by their artistically gifted brother, William: Jenny Uglow, *Hogarth: A Life and a World*, London, 1997, pp. 152–3.

85 Sally Shuttleworth, 'Female circulation: medical discourse and popular advertising in the mid-Victorian era', in M. Jacobus, E. Fox Keller, and S. Shuttleworth (eds), *Body/Politics: Women and the Discourses of Science*, New York, 1990; see also Roy Porter, *Health for Sale: Quackery in England, 1650–1850*, Manchester, 1989.

86 Beetham, *Magazine of Her Own*, p. 8. I would challenge Dr Beetham's notion of a rather ill-defined 'aristocratic' female readership, even in the early periodicals such as the *Female Spectator*. There was considerable 'status inflation', with middling-sort women flattered that they were buying into a *bona-fide* genteel publication, which may or may not have numbered noblewomen among their readers.

87 Nenadic, 'Middle-rank consumers', pp. 145–53.

88 Berg, 'Consumption in Britain', p. 379.

89 Berry, 'Polite consumption', pp. 392–3; see also Claire Walsh, 'The newness of the department store: a view from the eighteenth century', in G. Crossick and S. Jaumain (eds), *Cathedrals of Consumption: The European Department Store, 1850–1939*, Aldershot, 1999, pp. 63–8.

90 Adburgham, *Shops and Shopping*, pp. 19–20.

91 Bill Lancaster, *The Department Store: A Social History*, Leicester, 1995, *passim.* Berg highlights the fact that the seventeenth-century Royal Exchange was a sort of department store and therefore denies the Victorians credit for their invention, in 'Consumption in Britain', p. 385; this argument is explored in full by Claire Walsh

in 'Social meaning and social space in the shopping galleries of early modern London', in John Benson and Laura Ugolini (eds), *A Nation of Shopkeepers: Five Centuries of British Retailing*, London, 2003.

92 Oliver Lendrum, 'An integrated élite: Newcastle's economic development, 1840–1914', in Robert Colls and Bill Lancaster (eds), *Newcastle: A Modern History*, Chichester, 2000, pp. 37–8.

93 Adburgham, *Shops and Shopping*, pp. 45–8.

94 Ibid.

95 Geoffrey Crossick and Serge Jaumain, 'The world of the department store: distribution, culture and social change', in Crossick and Jaumain (eds), *Cathedrals of Consumption*, p. 2.

96 Jim Cheshire, 'The railways', in Snodin and Styles, *Design and the Decorative Arts*, pp. 424–5.

97 Neil McKendrick, John Brewer and J. H. Plumb (eds), *The Birth of a Consumer Society*, London, 1983. See, for example, the household goods depicted in William Redmore Bigg's, *A Cottage Interior* (1793), Victoria and Albert Museum (1799–1885), reproduced in Snodin and Styles (eds), *Design and the Decorative Arts*, p. 181; Stana Nenadic, 'Print collecting and popular culture in eighteenth-century Scotland', *History*, 1997, vol. 82, pp. 203–22; Leonore Davidoff and Catherine Hall, *Family Fortunes: Men and Women of the English Middle Class, 1780–1850*, London, 1987, pp. 356–7.

98 See Robert W. Jones, *Gender and the Formation of Taste in Eighteenth-Century Britain: The Analysis of Beauty*, Cambridge, 1998, and *passim*.

99 Pennell, 'Consumption and consumerism', pp. 554–5.

100 'If we often sigh over the "commodification of culture", we should recognize that such commodification gave women a chance they had lacked otherwise': Margaret Anne Doody, 'Women poets of the eighteenth century', in Jones (ed.), *Women and Literature*, p. 217.

101 On the range of public pleasures enjoyed by the Georgians, see Roy Porter, 'Material pleasures in the consumer society', in R. Porter and M. Mulvey Roberts (eds), *Pleasure in the Eighteenth Century*, Basingstoke, 1996, pp. 19–35.

102 John Potter, *Observations on the Present State of Music and Musicians* (1762), as quoted in John Brewer, *Pleasures of the Imagination: English Culture in the Eighteenth Century*, London, 1997, p. 77. One must certainly allow for hyperbole in this statement.

103 Jenkins, *Making of a Ruling Class*, p. 252.

104 This brings in the debate over whether a 'separate spheres' ideology was increasingly delineated in the nineteenth century, a subject discussed at length and with reference to the relevant and extensive historiography in Robert Shoemaker, *Gender in English Society, 1650–1850: The Emergence of Separate Spheres?* London, 1998, pp. 315–18, and *passim*. While Shoemaker is surely right to suggest that historians have neglected to consider continuities, such as the ongoing influence of the sexual double standard, he concedes that there were also changes in the ideological construction of gender in the Victorian period: 'women's opportunities increased, but the subjects of their concerns seem to have narrowed'. He concludes that women's public roles increasingly 'lay in areas where they could take advantage of the traditional feminine strengths of maternity, morality, religiosity, and philanthropy' (p. 316).

105 Jonathan Rose, *The Intellectual Life of the British Working Classes*, New Haven, CT, 2002, p. 20.

Chapter Ten

ಇಲ

Women and politics

Elaine Chalus and Fiona Montgomery

When, at the end of *Sybil* (1845), the eponymous heroine, the 'daughter of the people', marries her aristocratic lover, one of the 'natural leaders of the people', the marriage unites the Two Nations.[1] This ending is symbolic in uniting the two most important strands of female political involvement between 1700 and 1850. In Sybil, we have the new and growing politicization and participation of women of the lower and middling classes in increasingly formalized, issue-based popular politics; in her mother-in-law, Lady Deloraine – 'the only good woman the Tories have'[2] – we have the long-established traditional involvement of élite women in politics for familial, social, and party-political ends. What is missing from Disraeli's tableaux is anyone who represents the third strand of female political involvement, that nascent feminist political consciousness which would develop into the woman's movement and, in time, draw in women from each of the other female political traditions.

Between 1700 and 1850 there was both entrenched continuity and radical change in women's involvement in British politics. Attitudes changed slowly and unevenly over this period of 150 years – and for some individuals and groups, not at all. There is no neat, whiggish trajectory that can be traced for women and politics across this period, yet the distance between the 'parliament of women' satires of the seventeenth century, when the idea of enfranchised women was so outlandish that they could only be imagined satirically,[3] or Joseph Addison's numerous essays aimed to guide and keep in check the 'Race of Female-Patriots springing up in this Island' at the height of the Age of Party just prior to the passage of the Septennial Act (1716),[4] and the publication of Harriet Taylor Mill's essay advocating woman's suffrage in July 1851, is indeed vast. Publications like these must be read across the grain, however, for while they decry and trivialize women's political involvement, they simultaneously testify to its existence and its significance. Negative beliefs about women and politics had staying power and persisted throughout the period, but they existed alongside both the traditional political involvement of élite women and the developing women's movement.[5] Nor were all politicians unappreciative of the abilities of political women; thus, Charles James Fox, who owed much of his 1784 election success in Westminster to the outstanding efforts of the duchess of Devonshire and other female canvassers, paid tribute to them when speaking in favour of parliamentary reform as early as 26 May 1797:

> And yet, justly respecting, as we must do, the mental powers, the acquirements, the discrimination and the talents of the women of England, . . . knowing . . . that they have interests as dear and as important as our own, it must be the genuine feeling of every gentleman who hears me, that all the superior classes of the female sex of England must be more capable of exercising the elective suffrage with deliberation and propriety, than the uninformed individuals of the lowest class of men to whom the advocates of universal suffrage would extend it.[6]

While some individual eighteenth-century women may have seen themselves as politically competent and deserving of enfranchisement, the development of enfranchisement as a goal – and increasingly as the ultimate mark of individuation and public recognition of women – took place slowly in the nineteenth century and must be seen in context as emerging from a period of hotly contested parliamentary reforms, including the widening of the franchise for men in 1832. By the second quarter of the nineteenth century small groups of radical, non-conformist women were beginning to see themselves as potential voters, and in 1832 Matthew Davenport Hill, a radical Unitarian, openly gave his backing to woman's suffrage while electioneering successfully for a seat in Hull. Questions remained, however, as to which women should be enfranchised and what approach was necessary to secure the necessary parliamentary majority. If sex itself was not an absolute barrier to suffrage, then all women should be enfranchised; however, the concept of universal suffrage was not yet widely accepted in the mid-nineteenth century, even for men. Consequently, it is not surprising to find that the first petition for woman's suffrage, that of Mary Smith of Stanmore, presented to Parliament by Henry Hunt in August 1832, argued: 'every unmarried female, possessing the necessary pecuniary qualifications, should be entitled to vote for members of parliament'.[7] Thirty years later, when the Kensington Society voted in favour of enfranchising women, shortly after John Stuart Mill's election to Parliament in 1865 on a woman's suffrage platform, this property-based approach to enfranchisement still held sway, as Helen Taylor's (Mill's stepdaughter) advice to Barbara Leigh Smith Bodichon illustrates:

> No idea is so universally accepted and acceptable in England as that taxation and representation ought to go together, and people in general will be much more willing to listen to the assertion that single women and widows of property have been overlooked and left out from the privileges to which their property entitles them, than to the much more startling general proposition that sex is not a proper ground for distinction in political rights.[8]

Bodichon acted on her suggestion and within a month had gathered 1,499 women's signatures. John Stuart Mill presented this petition to Parliament on 7 June 1866; the question of woman's suffrage would thereafter become a perennial, if at times seemingly intractable, parliamentary problem.[9]

Women and the British polity

In order to understand the place of women in the British polity between 1700 and 1850, it is crucial to understand that the polity was resolutely imagined to be male – and that assumptions about women's nature were understood to render them constitutionally unfit for political responsibility.[10] While these beliefs changed slowly, a creative tension existed, however, between the pervasive rhetoric that politics was men's business alone and the reality which saw ongoing, significant, and growing – if widely varying and unconnected – female political involvement. As a result of birth, inheritance, necessity, or personal interest and commitment, women at all levels of society took part in politics: their activities ranged from the popular politics of food riots, machine-breaking, Chartist actions, protests against the New Poor Law or the repeal of the Corn Laws, through politically inflected humanitarian causes like the abolition of slavery, to various forms of social politics, patronage, and electoral involvement. Among the aristocracy and gentry, it was by no means unusual to find widows and dowagers managing estates and political interests, and controlling patronage, either in their own rights or for a minor, ordinarily their underage heirs. In Wales, at any point in time between 1640 and 1790, for example, 10 per cent of gentry families were experiencing a minority.[11] While unmarried, female landowners were more rare, they could be as political as their male counterparts: the diary of the dedicated Tory, Anne Lister of Halifax, records, for example, her success in canvassing her tenants and other men in the lead-up to the elections of 1835 and 1837.[12] On the whole, however, women's political participation was generally accepted as long as their activities could be interpreted in familial terms, growing out of traditional female roles, supportive of men who were family members, and/or motivated by duty to family or family interest. It was when women challenged male political hegemony by moving away from this familial model and, especially when they outperformed the men they were ostensibly supporting – as did, most famously, Georgiana, duchess of Devonshire in the 1784 Westminster election – that they rocked the gendered foundations of the polity and drew upon themselves the ire of satirists, moralists, and critics of all political hues.[13]

While this period saw Britain headed by two female monarchs, peeresses (*suo jure*) did not sit in the House of Lords and women did not, by custom, vote in parliamentary elections. Still, even when women's political involvement is narrowly delimited, in solely electoral terms, it cannot be entirely dismissed. Prior to the Representation of the People Act of 1832 (2 Will. IV, c. 45, better known as the Reform Act), which in England and Wales (not Scotland) legally defined voters as *male* persons,[14] those women who met the criteria set out in the various borough franchises technically had the right to vote. Indeed, as some late seventeenth-century controverted (challenged) election cases reveal, they occasionally had.[15] That they do not seem to have voted in eighteenth-century elections reflects the development of an electoral custom whereby single or widowed women, who were technically enfranchised, appointed proxies to vote in their stead; husbands voted in right of their wives.

Parliamentary rationalization and reform, through the Reform Act and the Municipal Corporations Act of 1835 (5 and 6 Will. IV, c. 76),[16] saw women in England and Wales lose their official electoral privileges as well as their ability to vote. For most of our period, though, women in the ninety-two freeman boroughs, who were the daughters or, in some cases, the widows of freemen, had the right to make their husbands freemen and voters. In cities such as Bristol or Wells, this process was straightforward; in others, it might be limited to the eldest daughters of freemen who had no sons – as at Hertford – or apply to men only while their wives were alive – as at Dover.[17] This ability to make votes gave the women status, added to their marriageability, and could provide them with substantial electoral influence. In the thirty-five burgage and freeholder boroughs, where the vote was based on property ownership, women who bought or inherited burgages or freeholds had the same right to vote as men.[18] While some of these were élite women, such as Frances, Lady Irwin, who in the early nineteenth century owned most of the burgages – and thus the votes – in Horsham, East Sussex, it also included less lofty women like Mrs Mary Somerset, who in 1788 sold her three messuages and garden in Horsham for exceptional price of £1,750.[19]

The importance attached to these privileges varied, but their removal after 1835 undoubtedly affected the daughters of freeman and small female property-holders more than it did élite women, who had other avenues of political involvement open to them. However, as late as 1845, it is possible to find Richard Cobden referring to them, as if they were still extant, in a speech on free trade at Covent Garden Theatre:

> There are many ladies present, I am happy to say; now, it is a very anomalous fact that they cannot vote themselves, and yet that they have a power of conferring votes upon other people. I wish they had the franchise, for they would often make much better use of it than their husbands.[20]

Nor did their elimination put paid to the belief that voters' womenfolk wielded political influence and needed to be won over. As Matthew Cragoe has demonstrated, nineteenth-century politicians continued to bestow kisses, compliments and cups of tea on voters' womenfolk, in their attempts to secure their support.[21]

Scotland operated under a different political system than England and Wales. Not only did it send a mere 45 Members (53 after 1832) and 16 representative peers to Parliament – out of a total of 558 Members (605 after 1832)[22] – but also, prior to 1832, only 15 Members came from the burghs: a full 30 of the 45 were county Members.[23] A higher real property qualification than that in England and Wales and a different borough structure ensured that the unreformed electorate in Scotland was tiny, comprised only of substantial landholders and those who held property directly from the Crown.[24] Sutherland was the exception. There, in recognition of the vast estates and overwhelming political control of the Sutherland family, land held from the earl of Sutherland or, from 1771 until her death in 1839, from the countess of Sutherland (*suo jure*; after 1833, the countess-duchess), also gave the right to vote.[25] Despite – in some ways, because – of this restricted electorate, Scottish landholders exercised greater power than their counterparts in England and Wales. While it has been argued that Scottish women as a group had less political power than women did south of the border,[26] Scottish female landholders, especially those who had the power to make superiorities, may have had more.

Although it was rare, women could be the patrons of burghs in Scotland in their own right – the countess-duchess of Sutherland was exceptional in controlling the Kirkwall burghs, as well as the county of Sutherland. Single women and widows who held estates directly from the Crown, which were valued at £400 Scots (c.£35 sterling) or more, could, like men, make votes on their estates by dividing them into £400 parcels, or 'superiorities'. Thus, in 1788, Miss Buchanan of Drumakiln could make two votes and Mrs Napier of Milliken could make six.[27] Superiorities could also be made on estates which met the financial criteria but were not held directly from the Crown, as long as the owner was willing to surrender her charter to the Crown. Once new charters had been granted for the superiorities and the electoral privilege obtained, the land could then be conveyed back to the original landholder.[28]

While there was no woman during this period who could rival the countess of Sutherland's personal control of twenty-two of the thirty-four votes in Sutherland,[29] there were always some women, such as Lady Hyndford who controlled four votes in Peebles, who could and did periodically control smaller numbers of county votes. In Scotland, as in England and Wales, although women could and did inherit property and political interests in their own rights, it was an early widowhood often combined with an underage heir that was most likely to place élite women in charge of family interests. Thus, Katharine, duchess of Gordon, who controlled the powerful Gordon family interest in Scotland for twelve years, 1752–64, until the fourth duke came of age,[30] was only one of many British women who found themselves in this position between 1700 and 1850. Isabella, Lady Irwin, not only brought two seats at Horsham, East Sussex, with her into her marriage in 1685, but also managed the family interest in Yorkshire and Sussex for five years after her husband's death, 1702–5, and remained a force to be contended with until her death, aged 94, in 1764. Similarly, Gertrude, duchess of Bedford, whose reputed influence over her husband's political decisions had occasionally provoked bitter denunciations from fellow politicians during his lifetime,[31] was in charge of the extensive family interest, scattered from Bedfordshire down through London to the south coast, for her grandson between 1771 and 1786. Élite women's political involvement through family and property continued into the nineteenth century as well: one need only consider involvement of the countess of Sutherland in Scotland or that of Louisa, Lady Sandwich, who maintained her son's interest in Huntingdonshire from 1818 until he came of age in 1832 (and stayed active thereafter), or that of the redoubtable Frances Anne, Lady Londonderry, in and around Durham before and after her widowhood in 1854, to realize that it was a woman's personality, ability, family, and circumstances, and not the Reform Act of 1832, that predicated her involvement.[32]

Familial and factional politics

Women have always been active and influential at the very top of the British political world, be it as members of the royal household, mistresses, daughters, mothers, wives, or as the monarchs themselves.[33] Not only does the period 1700–1850 open and close with female monarchs – Queen Anne (1702–14) and Queen Victoria (1837–1901) – membership of whose households provided a small group of élite women with unrivalled access to the monarch and, at least theoretically, the greatest potential for influence and access to patronage of all British women, but it is important to remember that women were also members of other royal households throughout the period. George II's daughters, Amelia and Caroline, were the first unmarried adult princesses in contemporary memory to have their own households, something that would later be replicated for George III's sister, Augusta, prior to her marriage in 1764,[34] if not for his six daughters.[35] There were also female households for four princesses of Wales – chronologically, later Queen Caroline, the politically astute consort of George II; Augusta, Princess Dowager of Wales, mother of George III and the head of the reversionary interest at Leicester House after her husband's death; Queen Caroline, the unloved consort of George IV, whose trial in 1820 split the political world into opposing camps; and Princess Charlotte of Wales – as well as two queen consorts (Charlotte and Adelaide), and several royal duchesses.

Court appointments were particularly useful as a means of increasing the portions and improving the marriage prospects of cash-poor daughters from large aristocratic families, but they were also political appointments in themselves. They were eagerly sought after and obtained through patronage and connexion. They placed women at the very centre of the political world, where they could develop useful networks of contacts and hone their socio-political skills. Of course, not all court women were politically active: the writer, Fanny Burney, seems only to have found her time at Queen Charlotte's court onerous and stultifying,[36] while Lady Augusta Bruce (later Stanley), who spent two decades between the households of the duchess of Kent and her daughter, Queen Victoria,[37] appears to have been interested primarily in religion and children. Other court women made more of their positions. Lady Cecilia Isabella Finch, Princess Amelia's trusted woman of the bedchamber, enjoyed being one of 'ye Court Ladies en *haut*'.[38] She handled financial affairs and business for the princess, dealing frequently on an even footing with leading politicians, and was acknowledged to have political influence over certain of her male friends.[39] While the overall power of the court did decline between 1700 and 1850, court appointments were a well-known way for women to forward personal or family interests, particularly through securing lucrative patronage for family members and clients. They also played a part in unifying the political élite, particularly after the Jacobite threat, by regularly including some women from loyal Scottish families. Lady Susan Stewart, later marchioness of Stafford, provides a case in point: as one of the thirteen children of the sixth earl of Galloway, her fortune was limited and her appointment to the household of George III's sister, Augusta, in 1761 when she was 16, appears to have been a reward for Galloways' support of Lord Bute. Instilled with the importance of duty to family interests from childhood, she used her position at court to develop extensive networks of personal contacts and seek and secure patronage for her brothers.[40] In later years, after her marriage in 1768 to Lord Gower (later Stafford), a leading courtier-cum-politician, she became an outstanding political wife, mother, and hostess, applying those same socio-political skills to forwarding her family's interests and those of a range of clients.[41]

While more needs to be known about the way that women operated at the points of transition between court and parliamentary culture, there was enough overlap that experienced female courtiers, such as Sarah, duchess of Marlborough, and her arch-rival Abigail, Lady Masham, could extend their activities successfully to the new parliamentary world that emerged in the Age of Party.[42] Where they and other women remained stymied, however, was in their attempts to direct policy. As the duchess of Marlborough learned to her disgust, neither her influence at court nor, later, her status as landowner with a recognized political interest gave her the ability to direct or implement policy: she was ultimately dependent upon, and frustrated by, men.[43]

Just as the rise of Parliament after 1688 involved more men more directly and more consistently than ever before in the political life of the nation, the personal and familial nature of politics that grew up in the eighteenth century incorporated more women in more ways. Women's resulting political activities can be loosely grouped into three interrelated areas: social politics, patronage, and electoral politics. The first half of the nineteenth century saw the political élite adapting gingerly to changes brought about by the French Revolution, parliamentary reform, emerging notions of meritocracy, stricter ideas of political respectability, and the gradual development of party politics. Women undoubtedly lost some opportunities for patronage and electoral management as a result. They also had to adapt to shifting boundaries of acceptable female political behaviour, but, as recent work by historians such as Kathryn Gleadle, Sarah Richardson, Matthew Cragoe, and Kim Reynolds has revealed, the basic shape of women's traditional political involvement remained largely unchanged in the first half of the nineteenth century.[44] Reynolds has suggested that, if there was a lull in aristocratic women's overt commitment to electoral politics, it was,

> broadly a generational one: those women who came to prominence before the 1830s – Ladies Jersey, Palmerston, Londonderry, the Duchess of Sutherland, and Lady Charlotte Guest, for example . . . Then in the late 1870s and 1880s, there appears to have been a resurgence of activity by aristocratic women such as Lady Derby, Lady Salisbury, Lady Randolph Churchill, and Louisa Athole.[45]

It must be remembered that nineteenth-century women also had more options than their eighteenth-century predecessors. The proliferation of issues-based campaigns, growing out of philanthropy, religion, moral causes, education, or empire attracted women who wanted to make a difference, women who might otherwise have focused more on parliamentary politics. The philanthropic work which Angela Burdett-Coutts, Baroness Coutts (*suo jure*) is a case in point. She set up schools and funded sanitation projects in London's East End, and built the church of St Stephen's in Westminster (of which she retained the patronage). In conjunction with the church, she also established a community structure which included working and friendly societies, as well as self-help associations. Such activities can only be categorized as apolitical, if politics is narrowly defined indeed.[46]

Women's use of the social arena and social contacts for political ends is a well-known aspect of their historical political involvement, but until recently it had received little serious attention.[47] Given a relatively small political élite, personal-cum-factional politics, and the development of the London Season in conjunction with the parliamentary year, there was considerable overlap between the social and political arenas. Men and women alike used social encounters politically. Walks, talks, and visits; tea tables and card tables; assemblies and balls; attendance at the theatre, the opera, or the court when in London, or at the annual racemeet, the assizes, or public days when in the country. Moreover, social activities were inevitably politicized during contested elections or periods of crisis.[48] Agneta Yorke's comment in 1789 – that there was 'no Subject of conversation but Politics'[49] – could stand as a refrain for any period of high political tension; it was as appropriate during the trial of Dr Sacheverell in 1710 as during that of Queen Caroline in 1820.

Politics provided the gossips of both sexes with essential conversation fodder for their inevitable rounds of visiting, but the 'news' that was gained socially could also be politically useful. 'I will now try to write upon common occurrences & worldly events', noted Betty, Lady Waldegrave, to her sister-in-law, Susan, Lady Gower, when introducing the subject of Lord North's problematic Administration in 1780:

> I still think our internal uneasyness & troubles are far from being settled & I fear that they only Subside, during the [good?] and the present attention of our rulers & I'm persuaded from the general Conversation of the World. that a discontent prevails. w$^{ch.}$ nothing but a Strengthening of Ad$^{n.}$ & w$^{ch.}$ seems most earnestly wish'd for, by all *good* People. can get the better of.[50]

Considering that her brother had resigned his position in North's ministry in 1779 and was known to want North replaced, the opinion of 'the World' – that is, political society in London – was more than just chitchat. Correctly gauging the political temperature could provide electoral advantage by foreshadowing dissolutions or ministerial changes. It could also be used to identify patronage opportunities and other potentials for advancement. What was learned was then disseminated, in person or by letter. While noteworthy local political news also fell into this category, particularly during heated elections, news from London generally took priority. Isabella Ramsden, writing to Frances Ingram (later Lady Irwin) in 1761, punctuated an ironic report of young MPs' attempts at public speaking with information about factional connexions and upcoming parliamentary business:

> Lord Middleton and Tommy Townshend talk nonsense without end. 'Tis said the latter has meetings at his house on an evening where young Bunbury and some others practise speaking before the glass. They expose themselves horridly, but Barry [Isaac Barré] is really clever with a great assurance and a vast deal of satire. Lord Shelburne is his patron and protector. Rigby likewise is very busy and is supposed the deliverer of Mr. Fox's sentiments. After the holidays the scheme for making the militia perpetual is to be brought in by Lord Strange, supported by Pitt and the Townshends. I hear Lord George Sackville has spoke very well upon the German affairs.[51]

Nearly eighty years later, Lady Palmerston's letters served up strikingly similar information for her correspondents. Writing to Mrs Husskisson in 1846, she predicted the imminent repeal of the Corn Laws and the future of Sir Robert Peel's government:

> all parties meet willingly in our House. I suppose the bill will be carried in the Lords as so many have turned round: but the numbers will be very near and after this bill is disposed of everybody expects Peel to be turned out on some motion made by the Whigs which the Protectionists out of revenge will join . . . Altogether the state of affairs he has brought us to is in my opinion very disagreeable, so much ill blood and squabbling in families and all parties in confusion.[52]

As the fora for heterosexual socializing expanded between 1700 and 1850 and women came to take a more dominant position in the social arena,[53] a small group of women emerged who were acknowledged by contemporaries to be the leading political hostesses of their day. Situated at the heart of the political world by birth and/or marriage, with convenient homes in London, these women had the means and the motivation, as well as the requisite charm or force of character, to entertain for factional or party ends. They provided like-minded individuals with a warm welcome, comfortable surroundings – preferably with food, drink, and some enter-tainment – convivial company and good conversation. Outstanding hostesses attracted young men, introduced them into political society, and worked to secure their future allegiance: in the mid-eighteenth century, the young Irish peer, Lord Charlemont, was introduced to Henry Fox through Lady Hervey and, in the mid-nineteenth, W. E. Gladstone made much-needed Whig connections with Lord Granville, the duke of Argyll, and the Cavendish family through Harriet, Duchess of Sutherland.[54] While the importance of the political hostess for the ruling faction or party should not be trivialized, the political hostess really came into her own when factions or parties were out of office. Without access to power or patronage, and lacking the formalized membership structures and activities that would later provide party cohesion, groups in Opposition needed the meeting space, the entertainments, and the sense of social exclusivity and belonging provided by political hostesses. Reynolds has argued that the apotheosis of the political hostess came in the mid-nineteenth century, before the advent of mass politics, with the development of the 'official' party hostesses – adepts such as Ladies Palmerston, Waldegrave, and Jersey.[55] Yet their lineage can readily be traced back to women such as the Duchesses of Shrewsbury and Marlborough whose competing socio-political entertainments emerged in the fierce political struggles spawned by Queen Anne's failing health and the heated party politics of the 1710s.[56]

Whether it was Lady Rockingham entertaining at Wentworth Woodhouse in Yorkshire in support of her husband in the mid-eighteenth century or Lady Waldegrave following her own political agenda at Strawberry Hill in Twickenham or Dudbrook House in Essex in the mid-nineteenth, women entertained politically in the country as well as the city. Eighteenth-century politically active aristocratic families often hosted Public Days in an effort to woo and secure the support of the local élite, and, throughout the period politicians' country houses were magnets for the like-minded. Extended country house visits of carefully select guests tended to reflect national rather than local political allegiances, but much local socializing could also carry a political edge. Maintaining a family's political presence in the locality meant, paradoxically, being open and hospitable, while also retaining a degree of grandeur. For women, it generally involved a certain amount of dutiful visiting, dining, and taking tea. At times, having an understanding of the pretensions of the local voters or the local gentry families was indispensable; even remembering whose daughters should be led first on to the dance floor by the male members of the family could be important. When Thomas Coke inherited the earldom of Leicester at the age of 22 in 1776, he was already a Member of Parliament for the county of Norfolk, but the widowed Lady Leicester was determined that he understood and appreciated the niceties due his new rank. Not only did she send him to the Assizes in Norwich in high style – in the state coach pulled by six horses, complete with postillions, outriders, and a large group of other servants – but she also quizzed him on his return, to find out with whom he had danced. Discovering that he had led out the beauty of the evening, a Miss Pratt, she chastised him accordingly: 'Sir, you should have led out no one of lower rank than Miss Walpole!'[57] While age or lack of inclination might have been behind Lady Leicester's decision not attend the Assizes herself, attendance was hardly an option for women from families that were actively working to create or maintain a political interest. Events which gathered the local community together and encouraged socializing, such as the Assizes and the annual racemeets, provided a range of social events (visits, teas, public breakfasts, assemblies, balls, and so on) which were readily politicized, especially as elections, or the threat of one, loomed. They were showcases for political families and racemeets, in particular, required both great attention to dress and jewellery, as well as physical endurance, from the women of the community's most political families.

Neither was this sort of socio-political activity limited to England and Wales. The selection of sixteen Scottish representative peers at every general election after 1707[58] made some ambitious Scottish aristocratic families as eager to take part in local social politics as their English and Welsh counterparts. The social whirl of the Scottish Marchmont family, as described by the newlywed Lady Polwarth in September 1772, would have sounded very familiar to her mother. Marchmont was a peer who took his politics seriously. Not only did he have one of the best records of attendance of all the Scots peers between 1760 and 1775 – over fifty days per session[59] – but he was also a loyal Administration man and, after 1764, Keeper of the Great Seal of Scotland (the most prestigious Scottish office in the gift of the Crown).[60] Politics was very much a family affair for the Marchmonts – everyone including the married children were involved in socializing when in the country – personal inclinations notwithstanding, as Lady Polwarth made clear when praising her mother-in-law's ability to perform all of her expected duties cheerfully, even though she would personally have preferred fewer public days and dining visits. But, as Lady Polwarth said, 'it would not do here'.[61]

The social arena was not used solely for electoral ends, however; it was often a prime location for making, or following up, patronage requests. Political patronage was only one aspect of a many-faceted phenomenon; it was as likely to be used for recruitment and advancement in the domestic, cultural, social, and economic domains, as in the political.[62] Political patronage requests can chiefly be categorized as attempts to secure any of the five 'Ps' of place, pension, preferment, parliament, and peerage. Even political patronage operated at multiple levels, in person and in writing, through many different patronage networks, from the independent country gentleman MP through to the First Lord; thus, quantifying women's overall involvement or success rate is impossible. While little work has been done on women and political patronage, an examination of requests in the

Newcastle Papers between 1754 and 1762, when he was First Lord, reveals that even at this highest level of politics and through only the surviving written requests, women formed about 10 per cent of the total.[63] In fact, women's involvement in patronage across the political spectrum and throughout the period suggests that, while their requests always formed a small proportion of the whole, they were consistently – sometimes insistently – involved. They took part for much the same reasons, in much the same ways, and with similar results, as their male counterparts. Nor were all women clients; some were brokers (intermediaries), and a small group were patrons. While opportunities for patronage rose throughout the period with the gradual growth of the state, specific incidents also provided patronage opportunities: the accession of a new monarch or the formation of a new royal household; an election landslide; a vindictive political action (for instance, the proscription of the Tories with the Hanoverian succession or the Massacre of the Pelhamite Innocents under George III); and, of course, war. In 'Roxana Or the Drawing room', Lady Mary Wortley Montagu turned her satirical insider's eye on the political élite, capturing them as they jostled for places at the new court of George I in 1714/15.[64]

Men's and women's requests in the eighteenth century were frequently cast in emotive language, stressing entitlement to patronage on personal and familial grounds, and drawing upon arguments of rank, lineage, honour, loyalty, and service to bolster claims. Some clients were able to approach patrons directly, but many needed intercessors and sought the 'protection' or 'favor' of brokers in forwarding their causes.[65] While it is not surprising to find that less women than men used the various patronage networks which existed, given how few patronage appointments they could hold directly, studies of their written requests which survive in politicians' correspondence reveal that they requested the same things (albeit often for male relatives or clients), in the same way, and for many of the same reasons, as men. Eighteenth-century women's involvement grew predominantly out their duty to forward their own or their family's interest and, in Harriett Lane's words, from a 'desire to Serve my friends'.[66]

Even by the mid-nineteenth century, when political reform and modern notions of professional, meritocratic public service were starting to make an impact, both public and private patronage remained important. Indeed, J. M. Bourne has argued that nineteenth-century patronage, while more covert than that of the eighteenth century and sometimes operating in different areas, remained varied, extensive, and highly unsystematic. This was most true of salaried patronage, which existed at the Court, in national and local government, the Church of England, the armed forces, and various commercial or quasi-commercial enterprises (especially the East India Company until at least 1858). The honours system was more clearly defined.[67] Moreover, as Bourne points out, '[p]rivate patronage centred on the country house . . . remained a socially significant phenomenon until the certainties of English upper-class life were overwhelmed in the aftermath of the Great War'.[68]

For women, patronage provided an ideal intermediate area of political involvement. It operated through networks of personal contacts and spider-webs of obligation and influence. It broke down the barriers between direct and indirect political participation, public and private life, and the political and social worlds. A patronage request written in the comfort of woman's bedroom was as political, and could be as important, as any made in a dining-room, ball-room, or assembly-room; or, of course, at a levée, in the parliamentary lobbies, or at a drawing-room at Court.

Most of the women involved in patronage were clients. Of the requests that women made for themselves, the majority were for pensions or places that would alleviate personal or family financial distress. When Hester Brook, the widow of the Dean of Chester, petitioned George II for a pension, 'Sufficient to Supply her and her Daughters with the Common Necessaries of Life', c. 1758, she based her claim on her family situation and her late husband's known attachment to the king. She emphasized that, although her four sons were self-supporting, they could not contribute to her upkeep or that of her two provisionless daughters. Four eminent men added their signatures to the petition and, as the duke of Newcastle's note on the cover of the petition indicates, she succeeded in securing a pension of £100 p.a.[69]

Maternal arguments had purchase, especially those of widows who portrayed themselves as struggling dutifully to protect their children's interests. While women did make requests for their daughters, more requests were understandably made for sons. Lady Margaret Macdonald took this approach when trying to secure, first, patronage for her son and then the Administration's support in a local power struggle against a rival clan chief who was allied with the leader of the military force on Skye.[70] Even when dealing with the latter, she was careful to couch her requests in terms of a mother's duty to her son: 'Your Grace will excuse this Complaints from a Mother, And a Guardian, for such severe hardships affecting the interests of a Son, too young to have offended in any shape.'[71] In 1754, she poured out her family history and her tribulations to Newcastle, countering accusations about both her child-rearing techniques and her efforts to preserve her son's interests on Skye.[72] She had, she maintained, given Sir James goat's milk to counter a tendency to consumption and, in his interest, she had erected a distillery and linen manufactory on Skye, and ensured that the rents were collected. Perceptively, given the Administration's lingering insecurity about the loyalty of the Highlands and Islands, she then turned her tale into a request for patronage that was sure to have some appeal for the politicians in London. While stressing her own loyalty, she claimed that she could not afford to send her eldest son, Sir

James, then aged 12, to be educated in England. If, however, the king would agree to sponsor his education, she would gladly bring him to London. On the very day that she was writing this letter in Edinburgh, Newcastle and his Lord Chancellor, Lord Hardwicke, courtesy undoubtedly of Newcastle's network of informants, were already discussing what response they should take to the forthcoming request. Hardwicke, who saw through Lady Margaret's financial scheming, felt that the request should be granted for political reasons:

> 'Tis certainly right & of consequence that Sir James Macdonald be educated in England . . . but I fear by the Proposition, that Lady Margaret wants the King to bear the expence of his education; & That may be worth while if the Young Gentleman can be secured by it.[73]

Young Sir James was accordingly sent to Eton at the king's expense and, when Lady Margaret's ongoing problems on Skye prompted her to send a memorial to the king the next year, she reminded Newcastle tartly that when the king had taken her son under his protection, 'His Majesty designed the Protection of his Estate as well as his Person'.[74]

The extent to which élite widows became involved in the interlaced concerns of estates and politics varied widely, but arguably none went further in fighting for the interests of young male family members than did the duchesses of Douglas and Hamilton in the famous Douglas Cause, 1761–9. Although the Douglas Cause was concerned with Scottish estates and political interests, it came to capture the attention of the political élite and, in its final stages, courtesy of the women involved, the questions it raised about the transmission of property, and the publications it spawned,[75] divided political society. Some of its appeal no doubt rested in the fact that it contained the elements of a classic eighteenth-century romantic novel: there was a reclusive, difficult, and childless duke; his sister's romantic elopement, resulting in irreconcilable family estrange-ment, her poverty, and eventually her death; the birth of potential heirs in mysterious circumstances on the Continent; and, with the duke's death, a disputed inheritance, followed by a hugely expensive and lengthy legal battle, all of which was fronted by two remarkable duchesses. Between 1762 and 1769, the Douglas Cause saw these two widows – Peggy, duchess of Douglas, a formidable Scot, and Elizabeth, duchess of Hamilton, one of the beautiful Anglo-Irish Gunning sisters and a Lady of the Bedchamber to the queen – use all of their influence and every legal avenue available, including a final appeal to the House of Lords, in order to gain control of the estates (reputedly worth more than £12,000 p.a.) and political interest of the late duke of Douglas, for a nephew and a son, respectively. The duchess of Douglas[76] championed Archibald Douglas (neé Stewart; he took the name Douglas once he became heir), whereas the duchess of

Hamilton[77] fought to secure what had been, until 1760, her eldest son's inheritance. The Douglas Cause sought to prove that Douglas was not the son of the duke's late sister, Lady Jane Stewart, but a French peasant child that Lady Jane had obtained and passed off as her own. Lady Jane had been over 50 when she had supposedly given birth to twins in France, of whom Archibald was the survivor. This, and other circumstances around Douglas' birth, proved questionable at best, as the Scottish Court of Session's judgment in favour of the Hamiltons acknowledged in July 1767; however, the Douglases appealed to the House of Lords. The Cause cost the two families upwards of £54,000 and saw both of the duchesses heavily involved. As Lady Mary Coke's journals indicate, by the beginning of 1769, the Cause had split élite society in London into opposing camps, with each of the duchesses drawing on her friends and connexions to secure the support of individual peers.[78] The peers' own interests in filiation, or birthright, and in directing property transmission, triumphed, however, and on 27 February 1769 the earlier judgment was overturned in Douglas' favour.[79]

Women's patronage requests for other kin or members of their extended networks of obligation varied widely, but surviving letters indicate that the more politically aware the woman, the more likely she was to know what was available. Whether it was Abigail Masham securing for her Tory brother the colonelship of a regiment of dragoons from Queen Anne in 1710 (and thus precipitating an ultimatum from the duke of Marlborough), the duchess of Portland in 1726 soliciting Newcastle for the post of governor of Bermuda for her nephew, or Louisa Perfect requesting from Lord North in 1774 a vacant landwaitership for her husband, knowledgeable women made requests to appropriate patrons for positions that were available, or likely to become available imminently.[80] When Frederick Lamb was seeking a larger pension in 1823, he used both male and female patronage networks; rather like Joseph Yorke in the 1750s whose sister, Lady Anson, also served as a useful additional broker,[81] Lamb sought the help of his sister, Lady Cowper, who, in turn, engaged her friend, Princess Lieven, to use her friendship with George IV and his mistress Lady Conyingham to Lamb's benefit.[82]

Patronage, while often decried as the foundation of Old Corruption, played an important part in maintaining the networks of obligation that held together the political system, particularly prior to Reform. The importance attached to electoral patronage is reflected in the attention it was given. In one letter to William Pitt in 1789, Mary Isabella, duchess of Rutland, who was managing the Rutland family interest for her son, thanked him for places awarded to some of her supporters in Scarborough and set out four separate patronage requests, all of which were 'material to my Interest at Cambridge'.[83]

Until 1832, there were always some women who were patrons in their own rights. While women could hold ecclesiastical patronage, which often had political implications, some women were also landowners, or had the necessary life interests in property, to make them electoral patrons. After the duke of Marlborough's death in 1722, his indomitable duchess – already a property-owner in her own right – retained her position as the head of the Marlborough family. With estates of her own, her birth family's electoral interest at St Albans, a life interest in Blenheim Park (with its pocket borough of Woodstock), and the threat of disinheritance wielded unsparingly over four grandsons who had or would have political interests when they came of age, she was rightly recognized by the Opposition as a political figure in her own right.[84] Fiercely anti-Walpolean, her letters to her grand-daughter Diana, duchess of Bedford in 1733–4, show her juggling boroughs to ensure that her grandson, John Spencer, obtained a seat:

> I might possibly succeed in setting up John for Surrey . . . but I can't think it is so proper to have him stand there or indeed anywhere as at Woodstock . . . But I will set John up at St. Albans too, where I have a natural right to recommend, and when I see I can [nominate?] him in both places, I can just before the election at St. Albans recommend a proper man to that town, instead of him.[85]

Having done this, she then directed his electioneering. By April 1734, she was commenting with asperity on news from Lady Carteret, who informed her that Marlborough and Bedford had had 'to buy Humphrey Monnoux and his interest for John' (by having Monnoux selected for Stockbridge), and casting a highly critical eye on Bedford's election prospects in Bedfordshire.[86] While the duchess of Marlborough's approach to politics, as to life in general, tended to be extreme, she was not alone in making the most of her electoral interest. Frances, Lady Irwin, maintained her hold upon the borough of Horsham in East Sussex from 1787 until her death in 1807, despite controverted elections, vast expense, and the concerted opposition from the duke of Norfolk;[87] similarly, Louisa, Lady Sandwich used the family interest in Huntingdonshire to support Palmerston in 1825 and to fight fiercely against Reform in the elections of 1831–2;[88] and, even after the Reform Act, Frances Anne, Lady Londonderry, managed her political interest with a tenacity that would have impressed the duchess of Marlborough. According to Reynolds, Lady Londonderry,

> treated her political interests in much the same way as she did her estates and industrial concerns . . . any Conservative, and sometimes Liberals also, wishing to stand for any of the county and borough seats in Durham would ritually seek her approval before continuing in his endeavour.[89]

While women like these could be important and were certainly recognized as political actors both in their localities and by the Administrations of their day, the number of female electoral patrons, like the number of vehemently committed female politicians, was always small. Elections in the long eighteenth century were not always contested to the poll, and, in the more placid boroughs, electioneering might require little more than careful (if sporadic) attention to the social politics and patronage that were part of the electoral process.[90] Most women from politically active families took part in any of an assortment of electioneering activities over the course of the period, including sponsoring or attending treats and entertainments, taking part in processions and parades, or formal and informal canvasses.[91] Occasionally, they were – like the duchess of Devonshire in Westminster in 1784 or Lady Antrim in Durham in 1813 – the butt of print and squib wars;[92] infrequently, like Lady Susan Keck in the 1750s, they contributed to them.[93] Women who electioneered the most often and openly usually did so for family members or kinsmen, but some women also campaigned for friends or lovers; in addition, there were always some women who campaigned out of conviction and whose political allegiances were factional or ideological. As recent publications have demonstrated, as long as they could be seen in a familial light, their activities were largely accepted.[94] Since country houses tended to be at the centre of election management, it is not surprising to find that women who were not otherwise involved in electioneering, had, at the very least, their routines affected and their correspondence infected by a heated election. Some women, like Lady Susan Keck, Lady Rockingham, or Dorothy, duchess of Portland, were much more engaged in the process, acting as managers and administrators, collecting and passing on information as necessary, and co-ordinating agents, candidates, patrons, and events to ensure that campaigns ran as smoothly as possible.[95] When families were involved in multiple elections, women might also become the family representatives in one borough while the men travelled around, or were based in, other boroughs. In some families, multiple political interests were divided among family members, leaving women to co-ordinate and run certain campaigns, as was the case with the Spencer family in the last half of the eighteenth century. Lady Spencer managed St Albans while her son managed the family's political interest in Northampton.[96]

Issues, protests, and campaigns

While there were always some women from outside the circle of the political élite who took part to varying degrees in the same kinds of political activities as élite women – soliciting (and obtaining) patronage, participating in election entertainments and activities, acting as witnesses in controverted election cases, expressing political opinions through their influence over the votes of their menfolk or their tenants, or even through their possession of electoral privileges – these women were more likely to participate in various forms of popular politics, including the politics of the street. Indeed, their political activity encompassed food riots, anti-militia riots, action against enclosure, trade unionism, and local and national politics. Increasingly during our period, as was the case with women of the élite, middle-class women involved themselves in issues-based, morally inflected campaigns such as slavery and the Anti-Corn Law movement, which stemmed from their wider involvement in philanthropy, religion, education, or empire, and were driven by a belief in women's 'special duty' to promote a more moral, Christian approach to the nation's affairs.

Food riots were the most common form of popular protest in England from the late sixteenth to the late eighteenth century. A mob would assemble, demand redress of a particular grievance and refuse to move until the grievance had been righted. As E. P. Thompson famously argued, this was not an objection to the existing system as such, rather to what was seen as exploitation;[97] consequently, it was not uncommon for the rioters to sell what they seized, at what they considered a fair price, and then give the money raised back to the original owners – often with the empty sacks of grain. Just such a riot found its way into the *Annual Register* in 1776: 'at Malmesbury they [rioters] seized all the corn; sold it at 5s. a bushel, and gave the money to the right owners'.[98]

It will always be difficult to determine the extent of women's involvement in food riots, not only because no official records were kept of the riots, so that what we know stems largely from any subsequent legal action, but also because there was a reluctance to prosecute women for an activity that went against contemporary ideas of womanly behaviour. Nevertheless, as the *Gentleman's Magazine* in 1753 recorded, there is no doubt that women at times did play a prominent role in food riots:[99]

> Taunton, Somersetshire, June 25. Several hundred women and a great number of men, assembled in this town, in a tumultuous manner, and proceeded to a large weir, call'd the Town Mills, when the women went briskly to work demolishing it, and that so as to prevent any corn being ground at the mills. The men all the while stood lookers on, giving the women many huzzas and commendations for their dexterity in the work. Their reason for it was a dislike they had to the manager of the mills, whom they charge with sending flour to other parts, whereby they apprehend corn was advanced to a higher price than otherwise it would have been.[100]

Nor were food riots limited to England. At Macduff in Scotland, on 2 January 1796, Margaret Gillon and Isabel Minto led a crowd and boarded a ship, declaring that they would not allow meal to be exported unless the magistrates provided it at 1/– (5p) a peck. Only the intervention of the local minister brought a temporary end to the riot when he pledged to provide 50 bolls of meal at the price that the women demanded.[101]

Contemporaries, such as the poet, Robert Southey, writing in 1807, attributed women's involvement in crowd actions in part to women's 'nature' and in part to their legal circumstances:

> women are more disposed to be mutinous; they stand less in fear of law, partly from ignorance, partly because they presume upon the privilege of their sex, and therefore in all public tumults they are foremost in violence and ferocity.[102]

Historians, however, have differed in their interpretations, both of women's roles in riots and of the extent to which they resorted to violence. Whereas the Hammonds and Thompson understood food riots to be female-dominated,[103] John Bohstedt has suggested instead they were only present as adjuncts to men.[104] What can be said is that where women did act, they were often successful in preventing the movement of grain and fixing what they believed to be a 'fair' price. Nor can it be denied that purchasing food for their households ensured that women had more face-to-face dealings with the market, daily, than men.[105] Their presence in food riots, as part of a community with ideas of what constituted 'fairness', is important and illustrative of the idea that women took action in defence of family interests.[106]

Shared familial and community interests were also at the heart of the enclosure riots in areas such as Northamptonshire and Wales. Women relied on access to common land to graze animals, which provided their families with milk and/or meat, and to collect firewood and herbs, the latter in particular being essential for medicines. When enclosure threatened these rights, they protested – sometimes, as in Wales, violently. Thus, in 1809 in Llanddeinlolen, a reward of five guineas (£5.25) was offered for the arrest of Margaret Owen, Jane Jones, Margaret Hughes, and Jane Evans, who, it was noted, were often violent, attacking bailiffs, constables, and other officials 'like a rolling torrent'.[107] Some idea of the nature of women's involvement in enclosure riots can be gleaned from this description of a protest in 1812 against the enclosure of 10,000 acres in the Llŷn Peninsula:

> We had not been there an hour before about forty persons, men and women and children, assembled and after reasoning with the men for some time and telling them the consequences of opposing the Surveyor I think they had made up their minds not to molest them, until a fresh set of women from the neighbourhood of Llithfaen came up who immediately abused the men for their supineness and

commenced a salute of sods upon the Commissioner and the Surveyor and the old women continued to do so until we came to the boundary of Nevin and Pistill when the action became general and the Commissioner, the Surveyor and myself were obliged to retreat.[108]

In Scotland, women participated not just in food riots but also in demonstrations against excise duties and the militia. According to C. A. Whately, crowds dominated by women appear to have been most common in Dumfries and Galloway between 1711 and 1718, with 'at least four major incidents involving virtually all-female crowds of 100 and up to 200 people'.[109] Seventeen women were tried at Dumfries for deforcing[110] customs officers, but, intriguingly, no one would identify them as having played such a role – evidence that suggests that they enjoyed the loyalty of the wider community. As Anne-Marie Kilday has argued elsewhere in this volume, women were not averse to using force; moreover, Whately maintains that Scottish women were more likely than their English counterparts to do so: in south-west Scotland, they were even often accused of aggravated assault. In the early eighteenth century, armed women attacked the Queen's warehouse and terrified the custom service at Dumfries and, at Edinburgh in 1740, a magistrate sought protection 'from the Women and most dangerous part of ye Mob . . . who called out to knock him down'. In 1757, four days of food rioting at Montrose led to the arrest and imprisonment of twelve women and, in 1773, women were certainly perceived as a threat when the Lord Provost of Perth was told 'to show that Sex gives no privilege to commit Mischief'.[111] Nor were Scottish women afraid of their social superiors. When Lord Findlater tried to move the weekly market from Old Keith to New Keith in 1726, his agents were beaten and forced to flee, 'by a very great Multitude of Women'. To add insult to injury, and to ensure ritual humiliation, the women even removed the agents' wigs.[112]

Women's tactics seemed to have been designed to throw the authorities into disarray; thus, a protest in Glasgow on 24 June 1727 consisted of, 'several Assemblies of riotous and Disorderly people consisting mostly of Women, & Boys running through the Streets and exclaiming against the Malt Tax'.[113] While women's protests against new or higher taxes can be understood in familial terms, as stemming from concerns about the impact upon family finances or interests, Scottish women did not confine their behaviour to disturbances related purely to familial interests. Logue found that 46.4 per cent of those charged with mobbing and rioting in patronage riots were women, although not all came to trial or were sentenced. The Patronage Act of 1712 gave landowners, the Crown, town councils, and the universities influence over the choice of a minister. Despite the fact that women had no formal role in the government of the Church of Scotland, they were committed members of congregations and resented having a minister foisted upon them. Women were prominent in resistance to the Act at Newburgh, Fife, in 1785; Salcoats, Ayrshire in 1790; and Assynt, Sutherland in 1813.[114]

Women's actions in disturbances against legislation such as the Militia Acts could, however, been seen as relating to family interests. When the militia was reorganized in England in 1757, the implementation of enforced conscription led to rioting. Because the government was too afraid of Jacobitism at the time to allow Scots to bear arms, the Act was not applied to Scotland. Interestingly enough, as soon as the Militia Act of 1797 was passed in Scotland, rioting occurred there as well. This Act was designed to secure the country in the event of an attack from France. It aimed to raise a force of 6,000 men who would serve for the duration of the war, plus a month. Teachers and constables had to draw up a list of those aged 19 to 23. There were a number of exceptions, including married men with two children, school masters, sailors, and apprentices. The lists were then forwarded to the Privy Council, who decided on a quota to be met by ballot. Each man was given three options: serve; find a substitute; or pay a £10 fine which would then be used to hire someone to take the original man's place. Not surprisingly, the Act was very unpopular, both with those men who were called on to serve and their womenfolk, who did not want to lose valuable manpower from their families. One of the most famous militia riots took place at Tranent in 1797 and resulted in twelve deaths and countless injuries. Troops were sent to ensure compliance, but, according to *The Times*, had little success:

> So formidable a body of military created much confusion and alarm in the street. The women, in particular, became exasperated, and began throwing stones at the window of *Glen's* [the constable] house. The Cinque Port cavalry, some of whom were struck by the stones became impatient; and the women continuing to throw stones, the cavalry were ordered to charge through the women in the streets; which they accordingly did . . . The women again threw stones, and seemed regardless of the dragoons on their horses; they even seized the horses by their bridles and held them. The Commanding Officer now gave orders . . . to fire. Isabel Rogers, a young women about 20 years of age, servant to Mr William Nelson, stocking-maker in Tranent, was the first who fell.[115]

This was not an isolated incident. In Bathgate in Scotland, 'a rabble of women said "there they go with their pensions and houses and lands; if it were not for those things it would not be so ill with us today"'.[116] The women who took part in these Scottish riots were defending the concerns of their communities in general, and their families in particular. In contrast, Bohstedt states that women were, 'strikingly absent from the wave of riots that swept villages from Lincolnshire to Cumberland to protest against balloting for the Supplementary Militia Act of 1796'.[117]

Women participated to a more limited degree in labour disputes and attacks on new machinery. They did, however, react when they felt their livelihoods were threatened. Again, their involvement reflected ideas of what constituted fair competition. Violence was directed against large machines which were felt to present an unfair advantage over hand-workers. At Spitalfields in 1720, for instance, women protested against the import of calicoes; in 1739, they burned looms at Macclesfield.[118] Women and men were present at outbreaks in Lancashire in 1776, 1779, and 1826, in Somerset in 1801,[119] and at Nottingham in June 1779, where framework knitters protested against an attempt to fix prices:

> In a few hours all was in a ferment, and the spacious market-place began gradually to fill with malcontents, when, about ten at night, the attack being begun by women and boys, they dashed up the numerous yards into Parliament-street, and broke every pane of glass in the house of Mr. James, an obnoxious hosier. . . .[120]

They continued to smash and demolish the houses of other employers. The authorities forbade the workers to assemble in groups. 'The women and children were ordered to obey the notice, as the law knew no distinction of age or sex.'[121] M. I. Thomis and J. Grimmett point out that women took a limited part in Luddism, as such, although they may have been part of the crowds: 'On the whole machine breaking appears to have been men's work.' Where they did play a role, as in the riots at Middleton in April 1812, there is evidence that this was linked to food rioting.[122]

There are also examples of women's involvement in political riots during the eighteenth century and early nineteenth centuries. Women were a very active component of the mob that created mayhem in London during the Gordon riots of 1780: 80 women were prosecuted as a result of their involvement; 24 were convicted; and 7 hanged.[123] Nor was this sort of mob action limited to London. At Trowbridge, when riots broke out in July 1819 in respect of the Wiltshire election, women played an active part:

> On Tuesday night, about 10 o'clock, an infuriated rabble, consisting of many females (to their disgrace be it spoken), with men and boys, assembled in this town, and proceeded to acts of violence, in destroy-ing the windows, window-frames, and shutters, of several of the inhabitants, whom they had previously marked out as the objects of their vengeance: at some houses not a pane of glass was left whole, and the desolation which the morning light presented was horrid. . . .[124]

Nevertheless, unlike their sisters in France, who formed their own clubs and debated political rights, British women did not – on the whole – take an active part in the new political radicalism of the 1790s.[125] Individual voices, like that of Mary Wollstonecraft debated political rights in print, but there is, for instance, no surviving evidence of women participating in the Corresponding societies which were established largely by artisans to campaign for manhood suffrage.[126] Women's involvement in radical protest emerged largely after 1815, when distress and discontent in the post-war economy led to renewed interest in radicalism. The radical, Samuel Bamford, with hindsight, even tried to take the credit for this:

> At one of these meetings . . . I in the course of an address, insisted on the right, and the propriety also, of females who were present at such assemblages, voting by show of hand, for, or against the resolutions. This was a new idea.[127]

The first female radical society appears to have been based in Blackburn. *The Times* for 13 July 1819 was hostile:

> With repugnance we mention that one novel and most disgusting scene took place – a Deputation from the Blackburn *Female* Reform Society mounted the stage, to present a cap of liberty and an address to the meeting. The latter was read, and in it the women composing the society, 'pledged themselves to instil into the minds of their children a hatred of (what they pleased to call) civil and religious tyranny!' These women then mixed with the orators, and remained on the hustings during the rest of the day. The public scarcely need be informed, that the females are women well known to be of the most abandoned of their sex.

When the Blackburn reformers visited Manchester, *The Times* criticized the them by obliquely referring to a woman's proper sphere: 'We are informed that at this meeting, Mrs I___, Mrs W___ and other Amazons harangued the audience on the usual topics at considerable length. Might not *women* be better employed?'[128]

Similar societies that met weekly and passed resolutions were soon established throughout Britain.[129] In 1819, the Stockport Female Union may have played to male egos by giving the impression that its members lacked confidence in their abilities:

> Ladies and Gentlemen, Before we proceed into the business of the evening, I desire that the gentlemen will withdraw; it is not done with a view to transact anything of a secret nature, for it is commonly said that women can keep no secrets, but merely with a view that if in our

debates (for it is something new for women to turn political orators,) we should for want of knowledge make any blunders, we should be laughed at, to prevent which we should prefer being by ourselves [Their male brethren immediately obeyed] and she proceeded on[130]

But the Union was in no doubt what its objects were and it was not afraid to state them boldly:

1. . . . every female on becoming a member, shall pay weekly to her collector *one penny* for the purpose of assisting our male friends in obtaining their object . . .

3. We collectively and individually pledge ourselves to instil into the minds of our children a thorough knowledge of their natural and inalienable rights, whereby they shall be able to form just and correct notions of those *legalized banditti of plunderers*, who now rob their parents of more than half the produce of their labour; [131]

These societies challenged accepted notions of a woman's place and were met with opprobrium from *The Times*. The newspaper's language itself is instructive. It referred to radical women as 'the most abandoned of their sex',[132] suggested they should know their place, and contrasted them with 'Females of respectability', who suffered 'Insults of the grossest description . . . by those of their own sex who were in the mob'.[133] Cartoonists and satirists drew upon well-established means of criticizing political women, concentrating on attacking their appearance, their manners and their morals.[134] Arguably, it was not until after the horrifying circumstances of the Peterloo 'massacre' captured public attention that representations changed. The women at Peterloo, in particular, were then subsequently represented in caricatures as the innocent victims being trampled underfoot by a corrupt and oppressive state. Peterloo was the name given to the huge open air rally at St Peter's Fields, Manchester, on 16 August 1819. Women appeared both in the platform party, among the audience, and two were subsequently killed when the local yeomanry charged upon the unarmed crowd.[135] As M. L. Bush has argued recently, women's involvement at Peterloo was important:

It represents the earliest expression of organized female activity in British politics. It also reveals that the driving force was predominantly working women. They had been suddenly transformed into a potent and disturbing political force not by the feminist message of Mary Wollstonecraft but by the process of industrialization. . . .[136]

These were confident women who demonstrated an understanding of the issues at stake. They were willing to invade what had previously been 'male' public space by taking a stand and speaking in public about issues that were not directly linked to familial concerns and – in common with male radicals – they were conversant with the symbolism of the French Revolution.[137] Caps of liberty abounded in 1819, not only in Manchester, but also in much smaller places, such as Galston, a weaving village in Ayrshire that had had a history of meal riots:

> On Saturday last, a meeting of Radical Reformers was held at Galston ... During the proceedings, the female Reformers from Galston, accompanied by a band of music arrived. When they came within 20 yards of the hustings, a vocal band sung, "*Scots Wha ha'e wi' Wallace bled*", and moving on "solemn and slow", to the music, a deputation of female Reformers mounted the hustings, and one of them placed a splendid cap of liberty on the head of the Chairman, and another presented a flag inscribed "Annual Parliaments, University Suffrage, Election by Ballot"; reverse, "Rise Britons and assert your rights:" and a third presented an address from the Galston Female Reform Society, consisting of 279 members. When the cap of liberty was placed upon the head of the Chairman, the meeting gave three cheers. Speeches of the usual kind were delivered. The people dispersed in an orderly manner.[138]

Radical women had a clear idea of how they could subvert their feminine roles in order to forward reform. They often concentrated on the role of mother-as-educator, as Mary Hallam of the Stockport radical society did in 1819:

> We hope the *Liverpool Courier* will not start from his seat when he reads the declaration and rules of the Female Union Society; which declares that WE WILL instil into the minds of our children *what he calls* revolutionary principles, but what we call principles which will safely carry them through the maze of political ignorance which now pervades the circle of the HIGHER ORDER.[139]

Women reformers rarely cast themselves in the role of passive victims; rather, they took the fight to their oppressors. While convention dictated against women speaking in public, individual women appear to have been quite content to do so. Susannah Wright, while awaiting sentencing at the King's Bench on a charge of publishing a blasphemous libel in the *Republican*, would not be silenced. Although *The Times* attempted to ridicule her by making a point of her inability to pronounce the word 'anomaly' – 'The defendant pronounced this word so imperfectly that the Court were obliged to ask her to repeat it, and at last were compelled to guess at its meaning' – she had the last word: 'Mrs Wright said she was there for the purpose of delivering her sentiments, and she would deliver them.' She went on to make her point a further ten times before ending, 'You may make what order you please – I will pay no attention to it.'[140]

Susannah Wright, along with other women, was prominent in the struggle for the unstamped press. Government taxes on newspapers rose constantly during the eighteenth and early nineteenth centuries, meaning that the price of 'stamped' or legally produced papers was out of the range of most of the working classes.[141] Radicals saw this as a 'tax on knowledge' and responded by producing a flood of cheap, unstamped newspapers, which espoused radical political ideas, including calls for the removal of stamp duty.[142] Women distributed and sold the papers (criminal offences in themselves). Richard Carlile's wife, Jane, was imprisoned as a result in February 1821, and his sister, Mary Anne, in June 1822.[143] At times, women even took over the actual running of individual papers while the male proprietors were in gaol, as Susannah Wright and Eliza Sharples did for Richard Carlile (editor of the *Republican*) in 1832. Women, once more acting in defence of the family, set up organizations such as the Friends of the Oppressed (1832) to support the families of those men who were imprisoned. Jane Hutson, secretary of the Friends of the Oppressed was described by *The Times* as 'a gigantic woman, "secretary of the Female Radical Society", and an occasional orator'.[144] Eliza Sharples, who came from a middle-class Bolton family, also secured a reputation for herself as an orator lecturing on the radical circuit:

I propose to speak . . . of superstition and of reason, of tyranny and of liberty, of morals and of politics. Of politics! Politics from a woman! some will exclaim. YES, I will set before my sex the example of asserting an equality for them with their present lords and masters and strive to teach all, yes ALL that the undue submission which constitutes slavery is honourable to none; while the mutual submission which leads to mutual good is to all alike dignified and honourable.[145]

In 1832 she took control of Carlile's enterprises, but she did not remain in his shadow. She published her own paper, *Isis*,[146] which was devoted to female emancipation and provided searing critiques of 'Old Corruption':

Whig tyranny is more atrocious than Tory tyranny, there is an apology in education, though not in morals and in politics. Whig tyranny has no apology but its hypocrisy. We have proof enough that the Whigs wish to keep every thing as near as possible to its present state: that is, they wish if possible, to collect the present revenue of fifty millions for the state and ten for the church. There is a very agreeable feeling associated with the fingering of large sums of money; as agreeable to dishonesty as to honesty. Whigs have this feeling as well as the Tories.

> They are not light-fingered gentry. The siftings of fifty millions through
> the various public offences is an onerous task and justifies *liberal*
> takings.[147]

Political education for women was also provided by the Owenite movement, a minority movement founded by Robert Owen (1771–1835), a
successful industrialist, who wanted to create a 'new moral world' based
on a commonwealth of co-operation and mutual interest, rather than the
competitive world of capitalism. His 'doctrine of circumstances' (people
become what they are through the conditioning of their environment)
provided the possibility for reviewing women's position within society.
During the 1820s and early 1830s, women from the working and lower
middle classes attended Owenite lectures, spoke at Owenite meetings, and
contributed to its journal, *New Moral World*. Owenite communities were
established, but, despite the supposed emphasis on equality within them,
women found that they were still expected to do domestic tasks. Very few
women ever served as branch officials.[148]

In the struggle leading up to the 1832 Reform Act, radical women
formed new female societies, such as the Female Radical Reform Society of
Manchester, which saw itself as a radical branch of the National Union
of the Working Classes; others were accepted into the male organizations,
such as the Birmingham Political Union.[149] When the Lords threw out
the Reform Bill on 7–8 October 1831, women in Bristol, for instance, took
part in the subsequent riots. Pro-Reform female activists also encouraged
women to engage in 'exclusive dealing', that is, to buy only from shopkeepers who supported the cause. They justified this by setting it within
the context of women's domestic responsibilities: 'The spending of money
(especially in domestic concerns) is the province of women, in it we can
act without the risk of being thought politicians.'[150]

Having been led by radicals to believe that reform of the political system
could result in improvements in all areas of life,[151] the 1830s were to prove
a great disappointment to the working classes. Attacks on unionism
and, especially, the passage of the Poor Law Amendment Act of 1834
were seen as being directly against their interests. The New Poor Law, in
particular, sparked hostility and spawned local anti-Poor Law associations
in Lancashire, the West Riding, and the south and east of England.[152] These
contained middle- and working-class men, and working-class women.[153]
For the latter, involvement combined issue-based politics with the defence
of family interests.[154] Taking people into the workhouse meant the
splitting up of homes and the selling of possessions. At Colne, for instance,
women 'declared their determination to petition themselves "before they'll
be parted fro ther children or ther lads"'.[155] At Elland in Yorkshire in
1838, they even resorted to direct action, as they rolled Thomas Power, the
Poor Law Commissioner, in the snow.[156] Women organized their own

associations, chaired meetings, and listened to female speakers. The anti-Poor Law movement, therefore, embodied women's domestic concerns and their growing political awareness and organized campaigning.

Women came to Chartism – as did the Chartist leader, Feargus O'Connor, himself – through their experiences in anti-Poor Law agitation. Chartism grew out of the feelings of disillusion resulting from the 1832 Reform Act's failure to give the vote to working men, compounded by the economic depression that began in 1837. It was essentially a working-class agitation designed to gain practical rights for the ordinary working man. The Charter had six aims: universal male suffrage, the ballot, no property qualifications for MPs, paid MPs, annual parliaments, and equal electoral districts. Chartist women were present from the beginning. They formed their own political unions, democratic societies, and Chartist associations. Their associations were well organized, with committees including President, Treasurer, and Secretary, and a weekly subscription. Members frequently built upon their anti-Poor Law experiences, attending demonstrations, petitioning, propagandizing, and raising funds.[157] The position of women within Chartism was ambiguous, however. The original Charter had included a provision for female enfranchisement, but this was dropped for fear of losing male support. Nevertheless, there were Chartist men who supported female suffrage, including the moral force leader, William Lovett, and men like Ernest Jones and J. R. Richardson, who advocated woman suffrage on the grounds of natural, civil, and political rights.[158] Moreover, despite the fact that the Charter would not enfranchise women, male Chartists regularly appealed to them, stressing the importance of the Charter to them and the need for their help.[159] In common with their male counterparts, Chartist women sought to defend family life against the onslaught of capitalism and industrialization; however, unlike male Chartists, it was this familial argument which lay at the heart of their political rhetoric:

> Fellow-Countrywomen, – We call upon you to join us and help our fathers, husbands, and brothers, to free themselves and us from political, physical, and mental bondage . . .
>
> We have been told that the province of woman is her home, and that the field of politics should be left to men; this we deny; the nature of things renders it impossible, and the conduct of those who give the advice is at variance with the principles they assert . . .
>
> For years we have struggled to maintain our homes in comfort, such as our hearts told us should greet our husbands after their fatiguing labours. Year after year has passed away, and even now our wishes have no prospect of being realised, our husbands are over wrought, out houses half furnished, our families ill-fed, our children uneducated – the fear of want hangs over our heads; the scorn of the rich is pointed

towards us; the brand of slavery is on our kindred, and we feel the degradation. We are a despised caste; our oppressors are not content with despising our feelings, but demand the control of our thoughts and wants! – want's bitter bondage binds us to their feet, we are oppressed because we are poor – the joys of life, the gladness of plenty, and the sympathies of nature, are not for us; the solace of our homes, the endearments of our children, and the sympathies of our kindred are denied us – and even in the grave our ashes are laid with disrespect.[160]

Chartist women worked hard to secure the male breadwinner wage that would enable them to be supported by their husbands.[161] They ran schools and youth clubs, and took part in Chartist churches and temperance associations. They were well aware of their role as educators and how essential this was to a changed world. The female political union in the Potteries made this clear:

the Chairwoman [Mrs Kay] descanted upon the influence that the women had in Society, and their right to use it for political purposes. She called upon every mother to educate her children in thorough Radical principles, and upon maids to marry none but Radicals.[162]

Despite their perceived importance, Chartist women did not sit on any National Committees or direct the movement. Chartism overwhelmingly made its appeal to skilled artisans on the basis of family and domesticity. Some women, however, were clearly starting to move beyond issue- and family-based politics to make political demands in their own rights. For women such as the contributor to the *Northern Star* who signed herself 'A working woman of Glasgow', in 1838, even the lack of a formal education was no barrier to enfranchisement:

Fellow Countrywomen – I address you as a plain working woman – a weaver of Glasgow. You cannot expect me to be grammatical in my expressions, as I did not get an education, like many other of my fellow women that I ought to have got, and which is the right of every human being . . . It is the right of every woman to have a vote in the legislation of her country and doubly more so now that we have got a woman at the head of our government.[163]

On the whole, working-class women grew in political awareness and confidence in the early nineteenth century and began to develop a sophisticated political analysis of their own. Middle-class women were also becoming increasingly politicized, but differently: their involvement in campaigns, including those against slavery (where they developed their own independent societies) and the Corn Laws, were strongly motivated by a sense of moral mission.

Women participated in the anti-slavery movement from the 1780s. The first women's anti-slavery society was founded in Birmingham in 1825 by Lucy Townsend and Mary Lloyd, and was quickly followed by many others. The Sheffield Anti-Slavery Society made the moral dimension of women's involvement clear:

> We would remind every lady in the United Kingdom that she has her own sphere of influence, in which she may usefully exert herself in this sacred cause; and the effect of that influence (even if it were quietly and unobtrusively confined to the family circle, or to the immediate neighbourhood) in awakening sympathy, in diffusing information, in imbuing the rising race with an abhorrence of slavery and in giving a right direction to the vices of those on whom, under Providence, hang the destinies of the wretched slaves.[164]

By 1833, there were seventy-three ladies' associations. They were a new development, in that they did not exist simply as adjuncts to the all-male local associations. Louis and Rosamund Billington, Karen Hadbersleben, and Clare Midgely have shown convincingly that they operated independently of men's societies.[165] The ladies' associations had a well-developed structure with a committee, Treasurer, and Secretary, and some, like the Birmingham Society, even had their own paid agents, although ironically these were all men. As well as contributing financially to the National Anti-Slavery Society, they directed fund-raising to what could be seen as specifically women's causes: female refuges, and relief and educational work. And they also urged women to boycott slave-produced sugar.

The ladies' associations developed their own propaganda, strategies, and networks. It was women, for example, who were responsible for organizing the three-nation petitions against slavery in 1833, 1838, and 1853. Prior to 1830, anti-slavery petitions had been considered the preserve of men. Elizabeth Heyrick, treasurer of the Birmingham Female Society, challenged the national leadership on its policy of gradual abolition in 1830 and, with the support of other ladies' associations, secured a change – a demand for immediate abolition. Women took a familial and moral stance on slavery. It was an evil which led to the disruption of family life: female slaves were sexually exploited by their owners; they were beaten when pregnant; they often had their children taken away from them; and they were usually not allowed to live with their husbands or partners. The anti-slavery movement was essentially middle class, motivated by Evangelical Christian and philanthropic commitment. The ladies' associations made use of working-class women when they were seen to be useful – for example, in petitioning – but on the whole, they did not consider them as equals, something that would cause resentment from the Chartists:

> when told of the oppression exercised upon the enslaved negroes in our colonies, we raised our voices in denunciation of their tyrants, and never rested until the dealers in human blood were compelled to abandon their hell-born traffic; but we have learned by bitter experience that slavery is not confined to colour or clime, and even in England cruel oppression reigns.[166]

There is evidence that some societies, such as that in Perth, had a more upper-working-class membership, but even the society in Glasgow, with its subscription of 2s. 6d. would have been out of the range of most of the working classes.[167]

There is no doubt that the anti-slavery movement saw middle-class women carving out a niche for themselves. It gave a political education to many who, like Barbara Leigh Smith Bodichon, would be found campaigning for women's rights in a wider sense after 1850. Nevertheless, in terms of members, it remained relatively small, at about 10,000.[168] Moreover, in the wake of the Abolition of Slavery Act of 1833, these independent societies were disbanded and the ambiguous position of women in the movement was highlighted when the World Anti-Slavery Convention, held in London in 1840, tried to ban women delegates. Arguably, this gave a boost to the women's movement in both Britain and the United States. Middle-class women had entered the political arena for what they saw as the moral good of the nation. The discourse of 'mission' secured them a way to participate in politics without being charged with having entered the masculine area of 'political debate'. [169]

Women's involvement in the Anti-Corn Law movement also took on moral overtones. The Corn Laws, which were passed in 1815, attempted unsuccessfully to protect the income of the landed interest and stabilize grain prices. They immediately came to be seen as creating poverty and causing distress by raising the price of bread and strangling trade.[170] Opposition, which grew in the 1820s, was spearheaded by the industrial and commercial classes working together. In 1838, the Anti-Corn Law League was founded in Manchester and associations soon spread across the country.[171] The League argued for the repeal of the Corn Laws and the introduction of free trade, in the belief that it would benefit the country by providing new markets for British manufactures, and thus more employment, and, by opening British agriculture to foreign competition, make it not only more effective and productive, while also lowering the price of bread. Free trade between nations would also, it was argued, help to promote international peace. The League spread its message through public meetings, lecture tours, publications, various fund-raising activities, and the promotion of pro-free-trade MPs. While middle-class women first became involved in Anti-Corn Law activities through their husbands – holding tea parties, bazaars, and fund-raising activities, socio-political activities which could be considered, on one level, simply as extensions of their domestics roles as hostesses – the League's dedication to free trade and international peace fed into the prevailing rhetoric of women's moral mission and opportunities for extending their political awareness and involvement. As Simon Morgan has argued, the League provided 'discursive and institutional spaces within which women could operate'.[172]

By 1850, therefore, both working-class and middle-class women were becoming increasingly politicized. Although it could be argued that women's issues-based campaigns of the early nineteenth century, which had grown out of familial concerns, had seen radical working-class women develop a level of politicization and experience which was more advanced than that of middle-class women, after 1850 it would be middle-class women, in the main, who would go on to campaign for women's rights. While working-class women's interest in reform diminished with the return of prosperity and the gradual adoption of pervasive ideals of domesticity, middle-class women would lead the way in the development of a personal and a feminist political consciousness which would become the driving force for the later nineteenth-century women's movement.

Conclusion

In tracing the political involvement of women in the 150 years prior to the rise of the woman's movement, this chapter has suggested that three interrelated strands of women's political involvement can be identified for the period. While the world of formal British politics in 1850 still operated according to the belief that the polity was male and that politics was man's business, this view was increasingly hard to maintain by the middle of the nineteenth century, as women from all levels of society gained varying amounts of political experience and confidence, and some women, at least, were beginning to see themselves as (potential) political actors in their own rights. Elite women's political involvement, based on family interests, duty, and personal networks, continued along broadly similar lines throughout the period; the majority changes and developments in women's political participation occurred with the growing politicization of women from middle and working classes. Drawing upon long-established traditions of protest and riot, the women of the late eighteenth and early nineteenth-century working classes moved beyond involvement in food riots and isolated political outbursts to play an increasingly sophisticated political role in movements such as Chartism and anti-Poor Law agitation – movements which intertwined familial concerns with political issues.

Similarly, middle-class women tended to find their way into political involvement through traditional female roles and moral issues. Their involvement in the anti-slavery campaign and the Anti-Corn Law League saw them drawing upon and subverting contemporary gendered assumptions about women's nature and women's mission to justify participation. The trajectory from familial or issue-based politics to personal and, increasingly, feminist politics was by no means direct or predetermined across this 150 year period, but, despite continuing unresolved tensions about the nature and extent of women's political participation, women's political involvement by the middle of the nineteenth century was not only remarkably more diverse than it had been in 1700, but it was also increasingly more personal.

Notes

1 Benjamin Disraeli, *Sybil*, London, 1995, pp. 238, 237.
2 Ibid., p. 177.
3 *The Parliament of Women: With the Merrie Lawes by them Newly Enacted*, London, 1646. For a further examination of some of these pamphlets and broadsides, see Gaby Mahlberg, 'The politics of patriarchialism in 17th century pamphlet literature', *Women's History Network Magazine*, 2004, vol. 46.
4 Joseph Addison, *The Freeholder*, ed. James Leheny, Oxford, 1979, p. 103; see the essays at pp. 51–4, 71–5, 87–90, 103–6, 135–8, 145–8, 181–5, 205–7.
5 Document 15: Harriet Taylor Mill, excerpt from 'Enfranchisement of Women', *Westminster Review*, July 1851, pp. 295–6, as reprinted in Ann P. Robson and John M. Robson (eds), *Sexual Equality: Writings by John Stuart Mill, Harriet Taylor Mill, and Helen Taylor*, Toronto, 1994, pp. 178–203.
6 Charles James Fox, as quoted in Erich Eyck, *Pitt versus Fox: Father & Son, 1735–1806*, London, 1950, p. 222.
7 Kathryn Gleadle, *The Early Feminists: Radical Unitarians and the Emergence of the Women's Rights Movement, 1831–51*, Basingstoke, 1995, p. 71.
8 Hansard, 3 August 1832, as quoted in Caroline Ashurst Biggs, 'Great Britain', in Elizabeth Cady Stanton, Susan B. Anthony, and Matilda Joslyn Gage (eds), *History of Woman Suffrage*: vol. 3: *1876–1885*, Rochester, NY, 1886, p. 835; Barbara McCrimmon Papers, The Women's Library, London Guildhall University, 7/BMC/B1: Helen Taylor to Barbara Leigh Smith Bodichon [London], 9 May 1866, as quoted in Pam Hirsch, *Barbara Leigh Smith Bodichon: Feminist, Artist and Rebel*, London, 1999, p. 217.
9 Ibid., p. 219.
10 This section draws upon, Elaine Chalus, 'Women, electoral privilege and practice in the eighteenth century', in Kathryn Gleadle and Sarah Richardson (eds), *Women in British Politics, 1760–1860: The Power of the Petticoat*, Basingstoke, 2000, pp. 19–38; see Elaine Chalus, *Elite Women in English Political Life, c.1754–90*, Oxford, 2005, Chapter 1; Hilda Smith, 'Introduction', in Hilda Smith (ed.), *Women Writers and the Early Modern British Political Tradition*, Cambridge, 1998, pp. 9–12.
11 Philip Jenkins, *The Making of a Ruling Class: The Glamorgan Gentry, 1640–1790*, Cambridge, 1983, p. 256.

12 See *Anne Lister's Journal*, 22 March 1834–29 February 1836, ed. Jill Liddington, 2003: http://www.historytoherstory.org.uk/index.php?nextcount=2&targetid=35, accessed 12 January 2005; ibid., 16–17 July 1837: http://www.historytoherstory.org. uk/index.php?targetid=44, accessed 12 January 2005.

13 For the most thorough examination of the duchess and her wide-ranging political activities, including the 1784 election, see Amanda Foreman, *Georgiana: Duchess of Devonshire*, London, 1997; for recent interpretations of the graphic satires the election generated, see Cindy McCreery, *The Satirical Gaze: Prints of Women in Late Eighteenth-Century England*, Oxford, 2004; Renata Lana, 'Women and Foxite strategy in the Westminster election of 1784', *Eighteenth-Century Life*, 2002, vol. 26, pp. 46–69. Peter Mandler also notes some men's discomfort with being the beneficiaries of female political influence, but attributes it to 'guilt' for having 'succumbed': Peter Mandler, 'From Almack's to Willis's: aristocratic women and politics, 1815–1867', in Amanda Vickery (ed.), *Women, Privilege and Power: British Politics, 1750 to the Present*, Stanford, CA, 2001, p. 156.

14 *The Law and Working of the Constitution: Documents, 1660–1914*, ed. W. C. Costin and J. Steven Watson, 2 vols, London, 1952, vol. 2, pp. 57, 59.

15 Derek Hirst, *The Representative of the People? Voters and Voting in England under the Early Stuarts*, Cambridge, 1975, pp. 18–19.

16 *Law and Working of the Constitution*, ed. Costin and Watson, vol. 2, pp. 79–91.

17 J. Cowley, *Orders and Resolutions of the House of Commons on Controverted Elections and Returns*, 2nd edn, London, 1736, pp. 23, 107–8, 159–60; Edward and Annie G. Porritt, *The Unreformed House of Commons: Parliamentary Representation before 1832*, 2 vols, Cambridge, 1903, vol. 1, p. 78.

18 Porritt and Porritt, *Unreformed House of Commons*, vol. 1, p. 41; John Brooke, *The House of Commons, 1754–1790: Introductory Survey*, London, 1968, p. 44; Sir Lewis Namier and John Brooke, *The House of Commons, 1754–1790*, 3 vols, 1964, vol. 1, p. 31.

19 Horsham Museum, Parliamentary elections, MS 3, no. 26: 'An account or rental of the burgages purchased by His Grace the Duke of Norfolk in the Borough of Horsham, 25 Dec. 1788'.

20 Richard Cobden, as quoted in Biggs, 'Great Britain', p. 836.

21 Matthew Cragoe, ' "Jenny rules the roost": women and electoral politics, 1832–68', in Gleadle and Richardson, *Women in British Politics*, pp. 153–68.

22 Michael Brock, *The Great Reform Act*, London, 1973, pp. 310–11.

23 Porritt and Porritt, *Unreformed House of Commons*, vol. 1, pp. 26, 28; Namier and Brooke, *House of Commons*, p. 54.

24 The county franchise in Scotland gave the vote to freeholders with land valued at 40*s*. 'of old extent', that is, according to the old medieval valuation, and to people who held land from the Crown rated at £400 Scots (approximately £35 sterling): Brooke, *House of Commons*, p. 55.

25 Ibid. See also Eric Richards, 'Gower, Elizabeth Leveson- , duchess of Sutherland and *suo jure* countess of Sutherland (1765–1839)', in *Oxford Dictionary of National Biography*, ed. H. C. G. Matthew and Brian Harrison, Oxford University Press, 2004: http://www.oxforddnb.com/view/article/42000: accessed 19 November 2004.

26 Porritt and Porritt, *Unreformed House of Commons*, vol. 1, p. 174.

27 Sir C. E. Adam, *View of the Political State of Scotland in the Last Century: A Confidential Report on the Political Opinions, Family Connections or Personal Circumstances of the 262 County Voters in 1788*, London, 1887, pp. 91, 291; Porritt and Porritt, *Unreformed House of Commons*, vol. 1, pp. 173–4; Judith S. Lewis,

Sacred to Female Patriotism: Gender, Class and Politics in Late Georgian Britain, London, 2003, p. 19.

28 Porritt and Porritt, *Unreformed House of Commons*, vol. 1, pp. 155–6; Brooke, *House of Commons*, pp. 55–6; Lewis, *Sacred to Female Patriotism*, p. 19.

29 Adam, *Political State of Scotland*, as quoted in Porritt and Porritt, *Unreformed House of Commons*, vol. 1, p. 172.

30 Chalus, *Elite Women in English Political Life*, Chapter 6; E. H. Chalus, 'Gordon, Katharine, duchess of Gordon (1718–1779)', in *Oxford Dictionary of National Biography*: http://www.oxforddnb.com/view/article/68359: accessed 19 November 2004.

31 *HMC. 28*, 12th Report, Appx, pt 10, *The Manuscripts and Correspondence of James, First Earl of Charlemont: I: 1745–1783*, London, 1891, p. 10.

32 K. D. Reynolds, *Aristocratic Women and Political Society in Victorian Britain*, Oxford, 1998, pp. 132–40, 147–8.

33 See Clarissa Campbell-Orr (ed.), *Queenship in Britain, 1660–1837: Royal Patronage, Court Culture, and Dynastic Politics*, Manchester, 2002.

34 For example, Lady Susan Stewart (later marchioness of Stafford) gained her appointment to Princess Augusta's household through Lord Bute in 1761: see E. H. Chalus, 'Gower, Susanna Leveson-, marchioness of Stafford (1742/3–1805)', in *Oxford Dictionary of National Biography*: http://www.oxforddnb.com/view/article/68366: accessed 9 January 2005.

35 A. W. Purdue, 'George III, daughters of (*act.* 1766–1857)', in *Oxford Dictionary of National Biography*: http://www.oxforddnb.com/view/article/59209: accessed 9 January 2005.

36 See Hester Davenport, *Faithful Handmaid: Fanny Burney at the Court of George III*, Stroud, 2000; Kate Chisholm, *Fanny Burney: 1752–1840*, London, 1999.

37 *Letters of Lady Augusta Stanley: A Young Lady at Court, 1840–1863*, ed. Albert Baillie and Hector Bolitho, London, 1927.

38 British Library (hereafter BL), Add Ms 32,862, fo.494v, Lady Isabella Finch to Newcastle, 14 February 1756.

39 See BL, Add. MS 32,955, fols. 56–7, Newcastle to Lady Bell Finch, Claremont, 4 January 1764; ibid., fols. 450–1, Lady Bell Finch to Newcastle [Berkeley Square, 12 February 1764]; Alan Hardy, 'The Duke of Newcastle and his Friends in Opposition, 1762–1765', MA thesis, University of Manchester, 1956, p. 182.

40 See for instance, Public Record Office (hereafter PRO) 30/29/4/3, no. 70, fol. 403, Galloway to Lady Susan Stewart, Galloway House, 19 June 1766.

41 Horace Walpole, who found assertive women unappealing and felt that his favourite niece had suffered socially at the hands of Lady Stafford, was unsurprisingly scathing about her and her use of the patronage system: Horace Walpole, *The Last Journals of Horace Walpole during the Reign of George III, from 1771–1783*, notes by Dr Doran, ed. A. Francis Steuart, 2 vols, London, 1910, vol. 1, p. 223.

42 See Linda Levy Peck, *Court Patronage and Corruption in Early Stuart England*, London, 1993.

43 See Frances Harris, *A Passion for Government: The Life of Sarah Duchess of Marlborough*, Oxford, 1991.

44 See Kathryn Gleadle and Sarah Richardson (eds), *Women in British Politics*; Reynolds, *Aristocratic Women and Political Society*.

45 Reynolds, *Aristocratic Women and Political Society*, p. 146.

46 Mandler, 'From Almack's to Willis's', pp. 160–7; Edna Healey, 'Coutts, Angela Georgina Burdett-, *suo jure* Baroness Burdett-Coutts (1814–1906)', in *Oxford*

Dictionary of National Biography: http://www.oxforddnb.com/view/article/32175: accessed 17 January 2005; F. K. Prochaska, *Women and Philanthropy in Nineteenth-Century England*, London, 1980.

47 Elaine Chalus, 'Elite women, social politics and the political world of late eighteenth-century England', *Historical Journal*, 2000, no. 43, pp. 669–97.

48 See, for example, Bedfordshire Record Office, Wrest Park (Lucas Papers) L30/9/17/125 Breadalbane to Marchioness Grey, Edinburgh, 10 November 1767.

49 BL, Add. MS 35,386, fol. 435v, Agneta Yorke to Philip Yorke, Sydney Farm [18 January 1789].

50 PRO 30/29/5/2, Granville Papers, no. 45, fol. 177v, Lady Waldegrave to Lady Gower, Whitehall, 29 June 1780.

51 'I[sabella] Ramsden to [Frances] Mrs. Charles Ingram, Charles Street, 17 December 1761', in *HMC, Var. Coll. VIII*, London, 1913, p. 180.

52 'Lady Palmerston to Mrs Huskisson, London, 19 March 1846', in *The Letters of Lady Palmerston*, ed. Tresham Lever, London, 1957, p. 273.

53 For women and the development of polite society, see Paul Langford, *A Polite and Commercial People: Britain, 1727–1783*, Oxford, 1989; for women as social arbiters by the early nineteenth century, see Leonore Davidoff, *The Best Circles: Society, Etiquette and the Season*, London, 1973.

54 BL, Add. MS 51,416, fol. 57, Henry Fox to Lady Caroline Fox, Pay Office, 28 Nov. 1758; Reynolds, *Aristocratic Women and Political Society*, p. 166.

55 Reynolds, *Aristocratic Women and Political Society*, p. 153.

56 R. O. Bucholz, ' "Nothing but Ceremony": Queen Anne and the limitations of royal ritual', *Journal of British Studies*, 1991, vol. 30, pp. 304, 309. Identifying women throughout the period who used their London homes politically, is not difficult. To name only a few: in the first half of the century, Lady Sundon, Lady Cowper, the duchess of Queensberry, the Jacobite Lady Primrose, and Lady Katherine Pelham; in the middle of the eighteenth century the duchesses of Bedford and Northumberland, Ladies Hervey and Rockingham; later, the Pittite duchesses of Rutland and Gordon, and Ladies Salisbury and Stafford, and Pitt's niece, Lady Hester Stanhope; and their Foxite counterparts, the duchess of Devonshire, Lady Melbourne, and Mrs Crewe; then, in the early nineteenth century, Ladies Liverpool and Holland.

57 As quoted in A. M. W. Stirling, *Coke of Norfolk and his Friends*, London, 1912, pp. 71, 62.

58 William C. Lowe, 'Bishops and Scottish representative peers in the House of Lords, 1760–1775', *Journal of British Studies*, 1978, vol. 18, p. 97.

59 Ibid., p. 99.

60 Ian Maitland Hume, 'Campbell, Hugh Hume, third earl of Marchmont (1708–1794)', in *Oxford Dictionary of National Biography*: http://www.oxforddnb.com/view/article/14143: accessed 21 January 2005.

61 Wrest Park (Lucas Papers), L30/9/60/3, Lady Polwarth to Lady Grey, n. pl., 3 September 1772.

62 Namier, *Structure of Politics*. Harold Perkin corroborates Namier's work in *Origins of Modern English Society*, London, 1991, pp. 44–5, 51. See also, J. H. Plumb, *The Growth of Political Stability in England, 1675–1725*, London, 1967; and his *The First Four Georges*, London, 1987, p. 78.

63 See Chalus, *Elite Women in English Political Life*, Chapters 4–5.

64 Isobel Grundy, *Lady Mary Wortley Montagu: Comet of the Enlightenment*, Oxford, 1999, p. 86.

65 See, for example, Lady Yonge, who seeks Newcastle's 'Compassion & Powerful Protection' in her request for a place for her son, following her husband's death: BL, Add. MS 32,859, fol. 14v, Lady Yonge to Newcastle, Escott, 6 September 1755; or, Lady Fawkener's request for Newcastle's 'favor & protection' in the cover letter to her petition to the Lords Commissioners of HM Treasury asking that she continue to receive the 'Salary and usual Advantages' of her late husband's position as Postmaster General until his successor is appointed: BL, Add. MS 32,890, fol. 380–1, Lady Fawkener to Newcastle [n. pl.], 27 April 1759; ibid., fol. 382–3, Lady Fawkener's Petition to the Rt. Hon. the Lords Commissioners of HM's Treasury [1759].

66 BL, Add. MS 32,735, fol. 380, Harriett Lane to Newcastle, Bingley House, June 4, 1754.

67 J. M. Bourne, *Patronage and Society in Nineteenth-Century England*, London, 1986, pp. 13–14.

68 Ibid., p. 29.

69 BL, Add. MS 32,876, fols 512–13, Petition of Mrs Hester Brooke [July 1758?]; Newcastle's note is on fol. 513v.

70 BL, Add. MS 32,736 fol. 107, Ed Edlin to Newcastle, 29 July 1754.

71 BL, Add. MS 32,855 fol. 248, Lady Margaret Macdonald to Newcastle, London, 29 May 1755.

72 BL, Add. MS 32, 736, fols 458–9, Lady Margaret Macdonald to Newcastle, Edinburgh, 7 September 1754.

73 BL, Add. MS 32, 736, fols 436v–7, Hardwicke to Newcastle, 7 September 1754. The widowed Duchess of Gordon would use the same tactic – successfully – for her eldest son as well.

74 BL, Add MS 32,861 fol. 529, A Memorial from Lady Margaret Macdonald and her son James to the Duke of Newcastle [1755]. Young Sir James, unfortunately, died in Rome at the age of 25. James Boswell was so touched by the high praise accorded him by his friend Lord Lyttelton that he transcribed the Lyttelton's inscription on Sir James's monument in the parish church of Slate. 'Sunday, 5 September 1773', in James Boswell, *The Journal of a Tour to the Hebrides with Samuel Johnson, LL.D.* (London, 1785): http://www.visionofbritain.org.uk/Travellers/chap_page.jsp?t_id= Boswell&c_ID=7&cpub_ID=0: accessed 29 January 2005.

75 See, for instance, the *Condescendance of Facts* . . . (Edinburgh, 1763), put together by the Hamilton side, or the voluminous *Memorials* published by each side later: Sir Ilay Campbell *et al.*, *Memorial for Archibald Douglas of Douglas, Esq; and for Margaret Dutchess of Douglas, and Charles Duke of Queensberry and Dover, his curators, defenders : against George-James Duke of Hamilton, Lord Douglas Hamilton, and their tutors, and Sir Hew Dalrymple of Northberwick, Baronet, pursuers*, [Edinburgh], 1766; James George Hamilton, 7th Duke of Hamilton *et al.*, *Memorial for G. J., Duke of Hamilton* . . ., *Lord D. Hamilton, and their tutors, and Sir H. Dalrymple of Northberwick, Baronet, persuers, against the person pretending to be A. Stewart, alias Douglas, only son now on life of the marriage between Colonel J. Stewart, afterwards Sir J. Stewart of Grandtully, and Lady J. Douglas, sister-german of Archibald, Duke of Douglas, . . . defender . . .*, [Edinburgh], 1767. In addition, James Boswell, then a young lawyer and an ardent Douglas supporter, devoted his pen to the Cause, writing broadsides, poems, newspaper articles, essays, and three books on the Cause.

76 See Hugh M. Milne, *Boswell's Edinburgh Journals, 1767–1786*, Edinburgh, 2003; Sir James Balfour Paul, *The Scots Peerage*, 9 vols, Edinburgh, 1904–14, vol. 9, p. 13.

77 Rosalind K. Marshall, 'Campbell, Elizabeth, duchess of Argyll and *suo jure* Baroness Hamilton of Hameldon [*other married name* Elizabeth Hamilton, duchess of Hamilton and Brandon] (*bap.* 1733, *d.* 1790)', in *Oxford Dictionary of National Biography*: http://www.oxforddnb.com/view/article/11744: accessed 31 December 2004.

78 Lady Mary Coke, who was jealous of the duchess of Hamilton and whose niece would later go on to marry Archibald Douglas, took a strongly pro-Douglas stance; her journals for the beginning of 1769, give a interesting, if decidedly catty, insight into the last weeks of the Cause and women's involvement therein: Lady Mary Coke, 'Journals (Jan.–Feb. 1969)', in *The Letters and Journals of Lady Mary Coke*, 4 vols, Edinburgh, 1889–96, vol. 3, pp. 2–33.

79 William C. Lowe, 'Douglas, Archibald James Edward, first Baron Douglas (1748–1827)', in *Oxford Dictionary of National Biography*: http://www.oxforddnb. com/view/article/7874: accessed 30 December 2004; Marshall, 'Campbell, Elizabeth, duchess of Argyll', ibid.

80 'Marlborough to Queen Anne [20 January 1710]', in Geoffrey Holmes and W. A. Speck, *The Divided Society: Party Conflict in England, 1694–1716*, London, 1970, p. 84; BL, Add. MS 32,687, fol. 190, duchess of Portland to Newcastle, 8 April 1726; BL, Add. MS 61,868, fols 199–200, Louisa Perfect to North, St Kitts, 28 March 1774.

81 See his correspondence with his sister, BL, Add. MS 35,388–9.

82 'Lady Cowper to Frederick Lamb, Panshanger, 19–20 January [1823]', in *Letters of Lady Palmerston*, ed. Lever, London, 1957, p. 119.

83 PRO, 30/8/174/2, fols 245v, duchess of Rutland to William Pitt, Albemarle Street, 4 November 1789.

84 Clyve Jones and Frances Harris, '"A Question . . . Carried by Bishops, Pensioners, Placemen, Idiots": Sarah, Duchess of Marlborough and the Lords' Division over the Spanish Convention, 1 March 1739', *Parliamentary History*, 1992, vol. 11, p. 256.

85 'Sarah, duchess of Marlborough to Diana, duchess of Bedford, September 1733', in *Letters of a Grandmother, 1732–1735*, ed. Gladys Scott Thompson, London, 1944, p. 95.

86 'Sarah, duchess of Marlborough to Diana, duchess of Bedford, 19 April 1734', ibid., pp. 112–15.

87 Elaine Chalus, 'Maintaining the Family Interest: Lady Irwin, 1778–1807', unpublished paper.

88 Reynolds, *Aristocratic Women and Political Society*, pp. 134–5.

89 Ibid., p. 141.

90 For a thorough overview of the electoral process in the long eighteenth century, see, Frank O'Gorman, *Voters, Patrons, and Parties: The Unreformed Electorate of Hanoverian England, 1734–1832*, Oxford, 1991.

91 For women's electoral involvement in more detail, see Sarah Richardson, 'The role of women in electoral politics in Yorkshire during the 1830s', *Northern History*, 1996, vol. 32; also essays by Chalus and Cragoe in Gleadle and Richardson (eds), *Women in British Politics*; Reynolds, *Aristocratic Women and Political Society*.

92 See J. Hartley *et al.*, *History of the Westminster Election, containing Every Material Occurrence, from its Commencement on the First of April, to the Final Close of the Poll, on the 17th of May*, London, 1784; *The Addresses Together with the Speeches, Hand Bills, and other Particulars, Relative to the Election of One Citizen to Serve in Parliament for the City of Durham, December 1813*.

93 Elaine Chalus, 'How Lady Susan Wooed the Voters', *BBC History Magazine*, 2001, vol. 2, pp. 44–6; also *Elite Women in English Political Life*, Chapter 7.

94 See Chalus, *Elite Women in English Political Life*.

95 Ibid., Chapters 6 and 7.

96 Ibid.

97 E. P. Thompson, 'The moral economy of the English crowd in the eighteenth-century,' *Past and Present*, 1971, no. 50, pp. 115–16.

98 'Chronicle 1776', in *Annual Register*, 1776, pp. 124–5, 137–40, as quoted in, G. D. H. Cole and A. W. Filson, *British Working Class Movements: Select Documents, 1789–1875*, London, 1967, p.21; see also J. L. and Barbara Hammond, *The Village Labourer*, 2 vols in 1, London, 1948, pp. 116–18.

99 For a full description of riots, see John Bohstedt, 'Gender, household and community politics: women in English riots, 1790–1810, *Past and Present*, 1988, no. 120, pp. 88–122.

100 *Gentlemen's Magazine*, 1753, p. 343, as quoted in Bridget Hill, *Eighteenth-Century Women: An Anthology*, London, 1987, p. 254.

101 K. J. Logue, *Popular Disturbances in Scotland, 1780–1815*, Edinburgh, 1979, p. 36.

102 *Letters from England*, London, 1814, vol. 2, p. 47, as quoted in Thompson, 'Moral economy of the English crowd', p. 116.

103 '1795, the year of what may be called the revolt of the housewives': Hammond and Hammond, *Village Labourer*, p. 116. 'Initiators of the [food] riots were, very often, the women': Thompson, 'Moral economy of the English crowd', pp. 115–16.

104 Bohstedt, 'Gender, household and community politics'.

105 Cf. Olwen Hufton: 'The woman had both to procure food and to cook it; all her husband had to do was eat what she had prepared and judge whether he was hungry or not': Olwen Hufton, 'Women in Revolution, 1789–96', in D. Johnson (ed.) *French Society and the Revolution*, Cambridge, 1976, pp. 161–2, as quoted in John Stevenson, *Popular Disturbances 1700–1817*, Harlow, 1979, pp. 101–2.

106 Robert B. Shoemaker, *Gender in English Society, 1650–1850*, Harlow, 1998, p. 234.

107 This account follows that of D. Jones, *Before Rebecca: Rural Protests in Wales, 1793–1835*, Allen Lane, 1973.

108 Jones, *Before Rebecca*, p. 47.

109 C. A. Whately, *Scottish Society, 1707–1830*, Manchester, 2000, p. 197. What follows relies on Whately.

110 A term under Scots Law meaning, to resist the execution of the law; to oppose by force, as an officer in the execution of his duty.

111 PKCA B 59 /26/78, William Nairne to Walter Miller, 26 January 1773, as quoted in Whately, *Scottish Society*, p. 199.

112 C. A. Whately, 'How tame were the Scottish lowlanders during the 18th Century', in T. M. Devine (ed.), *Conflict and Stability in Scottish Society, 1700–1850*, Edinburgh, 1990, p. 5.

113 Whately, *Scottish Society*, p. 197.

114 Logue, *Popular Disturbances in Scotland*, pp. 199–200; Whately, *Scottish Society*; W. Ferguson, *Scotland, 1689 to the Present*, rev. edn, Edinburgh, 1978.

115 *The Times*, 5 September 1797.

116 *Herald and Chronicle*, 9 October 1797, as quoted in Logue, *Popular Disturbances in Scotland*, p. 216.

117 Bohstedt, 'Gender, household and community politics', p. 114.

118 Nicholas Rogers, *Crowds, Culture and Politics in Georgian Britain*, Oxford, 1998, pp. 233–4.
119 Shoemaker, *Gender in English Society*, p. 235.
120 Gravenor Henson, *Henson's History of the Framework Knitters* (1831), introduction by Stanley D. Chapman, Newton Abbott, 1970, p. 401.
121 Ibid., p. 409.
122 M. I. Thomis and J. Grimmett, *Women in Protest, 1800–1850*, Croom Helm, 1982, pp. 47–8.
123 Rogers, *Crowds, Culture and Politics*, p. 226.
124 *The Times*, 26 July 1819.
125 Mary Thale (ed.), *Selection from the Papers of the London Corresponding Society, 1792–1799*, Cambridge, 1983.
126 H. Collins, 'The London Corresponding Society', in John Saville (ed.), *Democracy and the Labour Movement*, London, 1954.
127 Samuel Bamford, *Passages in the Life of a Radical* (1844), preface by Tim Hilton, London, 1967, p. 123.
128 *The Times*, 21 July 1819.
129 *The Times*, 26 July 1819, Rules of the West of England Female Union Society, 'the flame of liberty from the north has reached the west'.
130 *The Times*, 4 August 1819.
131 *The Times*, 21 July 1819.
132 *The Times*, 13 July 1819.
133 Account of a radical meeting at Rochdale 26 July 1819: *The Times*, 29 July 1819.
134 James Epstein, 'Understanding the cap of liberty: symbolic practice and social conflict in early nineteenth-century England', *Past & Present*, 1989, no. 122, p. 104.
135 Bamford, *Passages in the Life of a Radical*; D. Read, *Peterloo*, Manchester, 1958.
136 M. L. Bush, 'The women at Peterloo: the impact of female reform on the Manchester meeting of 16 August 1819', *History*, 2004, vol. 89, p. 210.
137 Epstein, 'Understanding the cap of liberty'.
138 *Glasgow Herald*, 28 October 1819, as quoted in *The Times*, 2 November 1819.
139 *The Times*, 26 July 1819.
140 *The Times*, 15 November 1822.
141 Hannah Barker, *Newspapers, Politics and English Society, 1695–1855*, Harlow, 2000, p. 39.
142 Patricia Hollis, *The Pauper Press: A Study in Working-Class Radicalism of the 1830s*, Oxford, 1970.
143 Phillip W. Martin, 'Carlile, Richard (1790–1843)', in *Oxford Dictionary of National Biography*: http://www.oxforddnb.com/view/article/4685: accessed 2 February 2005.
144 *The Times*, 13 December 1833.
145 *Isis*, 11 February 1832, as quoted in Jane Rendall, *The Origins of Modern Feminism: Women in Britain, France and the United States, 1780–1869*, Chicago, 1985, p. 237.
146 This folded at the end of December 1832 due to her lack of business skills.
147 *Isis*, 27 October 1832, as quoted in Edmund and Ruth Frow, *Political Women 1800–1850*, Introduction by Julie Swindell, London, 1989, p. 50.
148 J. F. C. Harrison, *Robert Owen and the Owenites in Britain and America: The Quest for the New Moral World*, London, 1969; Barbara Taylor, *Eve and the New Jerusalem: Socialism and Feminism in the Nineteenth Century*, London, 1983.

149 Rendall, *Origins of Modern Feminism*.
150 As quoted in Thomis and Grimmett, *Women in Protest*, p. 107. This peculiarly feminine tactic was to be taken up enthusiastically by the Chartists after the 1832 Act was passed.
151 Bronterre O'Brien made the point in 1839: 'Universal suffrage means meat and drink and clothing, good hours, and good beds, and good substantial furniture for every man and woman and child who will do a fair day's work', *Operative*, 17 March 1839, as quoted in Patricia Hollis (ed.), *Class and Conflict in Nineteenth-Century England, 1815–1850*, London, 1973, p. 216.
152 N. C. Edsall, *The Anti-Poor Law Movement, 1834–44*, Manchester, 1971.
153 The middle classes objected to the proposed degree of centralization.
154 A sentiment echoed by working men: 'They were met together to defend themselves, their wives, their little ones, and their relatives'. See, 'Anti-Poor Law Meeting, Bury, 2 January 1838', *The Times*, 9 January 1838.
155 *The Times*, 25 January 1838.
156 *Northern Star*, 24 February 1838.
157 Dorothy Thompson, *The Chartists: Popular Politics in the Industrial Revolution*, London, 1984, Chapter 7; Jutta Schwarzkopf, *Women in the Chartist Movement*, New York, 1991, Chapter 6.
158 R. J. Richardson, *The Rights of Woman* (1840), as quoted in Dorothy Thompson (ed.), *The Early Chartists*, London, 1971, p. 115.
159 Thomas Wheeler, 'Address from the London Delegate Council to the Male and Female Chartists of Great Britain and Ireland', *English Chartist Circular*, vol. 1, p. 133.
160 'Address of the Female Political Union of Newcastle upon Tyne to their Fellow Countrywomen', *Northern Star*, 2 February 1839, as quoted in Thompson (ed.), *Early Chartists*, pp. 128–9.
161 Such ideas, however, helped to give rise to differential rates of pay and, although never implemented, were ultimately detrimental to women's rates of pay.
162 *The Times*, 19 November 1838.
163 'A working woman of Glasgow', *Northern Star*, 23 June 1838, as quoted in Dorothy Thompson, 'Women in nineteenth-century radical politics: a lost dimension', in J. Mitchell and A. Oakley (eds), *The Rights and Wrongs of Women*, London, 1986, p. 123.
164 *Ladies' Anti-Slavery Associations* (n.d.), as quoted by James Walvin (ed.), *Slavery and British Society, 1776–1846*, Baton Rouge, LA, 1982, p. 62; Rendall, *Origins of Modern Feminism*, p. 246.
165 Louis and Rosamund Billington, ' "A burning zeal for righteousness": women in the British anti-slavery movement, 1820–1860', in Jane Rendall (ed.), *Equal or Different: Women's Politics, 1800–1914*, Basingstoke, 1985, pp. 82–111; Karen Irene Halbersleben, ' "She hath done what she could": women's participation in the British antislavery movement, 1825–1870', PhD thesis, State University of New York at Buffalo, 1987; Clare Midgely, *Women against Slavery: The British Campaigns, 1780–1870*, London, 1992.
166 'Address of the Female Political Union of Newcastle upon Tyne to their Fellow Countrywomen', in Thompson, *Early Chartists*, p. 128.
167 Midgley, *Women against Slavery*, p. 85.
168 Ibid., p. 83.
169 A. Tyrrell, ' "Woman's mission" and pressure group politics (1825–1860)', *Bulletin of the John Rylands University Library*, 1980, vol. 63, pp. 194–230.

170 For the popular response to the passage of the Corn Laws, see John Stevenson, *Popular Disturbances in England, 1700–1832*, pp. 235–8. See also, Boyd Hilton, *Corn, Cash, Commerce: The Economic Policies of the Tory Governments, 1815–30*, Oxford, 1977; F. A. Montgomery, 'Glasgow and the movement for Corn Law Repeal', *History*, 1979, vol. 64, pp. 363–79; N. McCord, *The Anti-Corn Law League, 1838–1846*, London, 1958.

171 For the connection between the Anti-Corn Law League, Chartism and Dissent, see Norman Gash, *Aristocracy and the People, 1815–1865*, London, 1992, pp. 208–9, 221–3.

172 Simon Morgan, 'Domestic economy and political agitation: women and the Anti-Corn Law League, 1839–46', in Gleadle and Richardson (eds), *Women in British Politics*, pp. 115–33.

Chapter Eleven

ϩ**

British women and empire

Kathleen Wilson

Charlotte Browne was not afraid of the French or the Indians. Instead, she sailed from England to America in 1754 as matron of the general hospital to be established for General Edward Braddock's troops in his campaign against Britain's enemies on the edge of the Ohio River Valley, on the eve of what would become the Seven Years War. Enduring the hardships and miseries of a transatlantic transport vessel with her reputation for good sense and strict chastity intact, she met with as civil a reception in America as the unpolished colonists could provide. The 'English Ladies' of Frederickstown, Maryland invited her to a Ball, where, according to Browne, the company was composed of 'Romans, Jews and Hereticks . . . Ladys danced without Stays or Hoops and it ended with a Jig from each Lady'. The strangeness of 'Englishness' in the American frontier did not lessen Brown's resourcefulness or deter her from her duty of ministering to wounded British and American soldiers, and their bereft partners, despite insect-infested beds, drenched camps, treacherous roads, her brother's passing, and news of her daughter's death in England. 'It is not possible to describe the distraction of the poor Women for their Husbands,' Browne recalled, following Braddock's defeat in the autumn of 1755.[1]

Browne's story, and those of the tens of thousands of other women who served, followed, and toiled for the British military in its long wars for empire, rarely figure prominently in the imperial saga. Yet, as scholars have come to recognize the varied and vital roles of eighteenth- and nineteenth-century women in British public, as well as private, life, they have also begun to appreciate their importance in 'forging the nation' and building an empire.[2] British women were intimately involved in imperial projects and aspirations, key figures in orchestrating the consumption or boycott of imperial goods, subsidizing or resisting imperial wars, and refashioning the empire through anti-slavery and missionary campaigns. They turned up in western Atlantic colonies and eastern trading outposts (Africa, India, Sumatra, and Australasian settlements) from all over the British Isles and in all conditions: as forced and indentured labourers; soldiers, sailors and officers' wives; teachers, actresses, nurses, sutlers, merchants, and prostitutes; the partners or daughters of religious pilgrims, naturalists, slavers, planters, and officials; and as slave traders, adventurers, and explorers themselves. This chapter will examine how women helped establish, maintain, and challenge British dominion in the period from 1700 to 1850. It will consider both general contexts for understanding women's roles in British networks of maritime, military, and commercial power, and the experiences of individual women within these systems of rule. In doing so, the horizons of Britishness will be expanded to include the contributions of the empire's extended territories and peoples to British culture and to the British understanding of national and gender difference.

Empire at home

To consider 'British women' in the 'empire' is to consider the historical practice and performance of Britishness and femininity in global settings across four oceans. It is also to take into consideration the changing and unstable nature of the empire and the nation themselves. Most histories divide the empire of the period from 1700 to 1850 into two distinct stages. The first stage, enabled by English political domination of Ireland and Union with Scotland, centred on British overseas settlements in North America and the West Indies (although including trading outposts in Asia, Africa, and the south Atlantic) and the establishment of British supremacy in the slave trade. The second stage, extending from the end of the Seven Years War in 1763 to the abolition of the slavery (1833) and its aftermath, was defined by a turn towards the East (especially in the wake of the revolt of the American colonies), a more authoritarian and extractive imperial apparatus, and the extension of British dominance over a proliferating range of peoples and territories in India, Asia, Australia, and Africa. Over the entire period, women were integral to colonizing hopes and projects, but the symbolic meanings and material realities of their roles considerably changed. What remained constant was the inextricable relationship between ideas about men and women's distinct capacities and activities, and the categories of national and imperial belonging forged by Britain's imperial adventures.

'Empire' must also be reconceptualized in relation to 'nation'. Empire did not happen 'out there', cordoned off from the psyches and daily lives of Britons in the British Isles. Rather, 'nation' and 'empire' were mutually constitutive concepts and territories, even as they comprised vast differences in local conditions and prospects. For despite a certain lack of coherence in central policy, the Georgian and early Victorian empires created a network that was remarkably efficient in allowing people, gossip, commodities and ideas to travel and be transformed. Empire was part of everyday life for most British people, who read about it in newspapers and novels, poured it out of their teapots, wore its shawls and muslins, enjoyed its images in theatre and painting, ogled its exotic plants and peoples, invested in its trade, and wrote to families and friends its expanse. British manufactures and capital contributed to African, East Indian, American, West Indian and, after 1768, South Pacific economies and power struggles. Women were integral to imperial networks and the social practices and rituals generated by them; debates over women's status and roles in national life were intertwined with those over the impact of empire and commerce, dominating public and private discussion, and spawning new forms of pleasure and representation.[3]

Finally, eighteenth-century British understanding of gender was intricately linked to the formulation and dissemination of other categories of difference produced by Enlightenment initiatives that proliferated across broad social terrains, largely in consequence of British colonial contacts and expansion. For example, categories such as nation, 'race', rank, geography, and religion, as well as degrees of civility, politeness, and 'stage' of civilization, were mulled over by British intellectuals and ordinary people in an effort to bring order to the marvellous cultural, linguistic, and physical multiplicity of the modern world. 'Nation' provided perhaps the most important category of difference of the period, combining older biblical and juridical concepts of a people located in fixed spatial and cultural terrain with emergent concepts of a political-territorial entity worthy of allegiance. Britons' vigorous explorations of self and world confirmed that different nations had different moral, social, and intellectual – as well as physical – characteristics, yet also remained fairly confident in the superiority and modernity of Britishness. 'Nation' provided, in other words, both a ground for social taxonomy and a way of imagining community that tied people together less by physical characteristics (although these played a significant role) than by customs, descent and 'blood' – that mysterious if 'common substance passed on through heterosexual relations and birth'.[4] In an age of slavery and revolution, who was British and who was not was a matter of utmost significance, and the social performances of nationality, freedom, gender, and rank – by men and women, slave and free – were acts of resounding political importance. Women were crucial actors in marking the boundaries of this constantly re-imagined national community.

We are now better placed to appreciate the complexities of women's roles within imperial systems of power. Britain's continuing struggles with the Bourbon monarchies on the Continent drew colonists and metro-politans of both genders and all ethnicities into the 'demands and meanings of Britishness',[5] while also underlining the importance for national prosperity of British colonies in the New and Old Worlds. Yet British women's imaginative, symbolic, and material participation in the imperial adventures of the day revealed the tensions between contending patriotic and gender ideals. Women were avid supporters of the opposition hero Admiral Vernon, whose defeat of the Spanish at Port Bello in 1739 crystallized the spectacular vision of the Atlantic empire as an extensive, homogenous polity bounded by freedom and guided by manly and virtuous leaders. Women sold ballads, garlands, or snuff, participated in street demonstrations or presided over tea tables that celebrated Vernon's victory and his status as a hero of empire. 'The women talk all day long of Conventions, Depredations and *Guarda* Costas', one observer in Newcastle upon Tyne complained at the outbreak of the war with Spain.[6] Throughout the period, middle- and upper-class women avidly read 'the prints' for the latest word on war, treaties, and politics, supplementing print culture with correspondence networks that passed on late-breaking news to friends.[7] As the example of Charlotte Brown suggests, women laboured for the national and imperial honour at the front, feeding, clothing, nursing, sexually servicing, and occasionally fighting with the men, as professionals or as unpaid workers. Mary Ludwig Hays, or 'Molly Pitcher', as she became known, carried buckets of water to the soldiers and manned an artillery piece for the Americans in the Battle of Monmouth (1778). Upper-class women too followed their husbands into battle. Lady Harriet Acland, six months pregnant, went on the march with her husband, Colonel John Acland, from Canada to New York as part of General Burgoyne's campaign against the Americans in 1776–7, valiantly retrieving her wounded spouse from the enemy camp. For this, she was immortalized as the incarnation of female patriotism in painting and prints. Even women's symbolic roles expanded. Although women's bodies had long served as symbols of national virtue, in the eighteenth century these images began to take on geographical and regional particularity: the most abstract iconographic prints tried to differentiate the physical as well as mental and moral features of the 'national character', as the growing ubiquity of the pale-skinned figure of Britannia in prints and paintings from the 1740s through the 1840s clearly demonstrate.

On the home front, women sewed uniforms; collected or donated money for the troops; attended military reviews and fast-day services; donned regimentals themselves, like the Duchess of Devonshire; and shouldered their absent men's work in the effort to keep their families intact or afloat. Naturally, many resented and some even rebelled against the additional burdens placed on them by imperial wars: women were prominent in anti-impressment riots, hid their sons or husbands from the press gangs or even staged rescue efforts to retrieve those taken; others opposed the wars on religious grounds. The Quaker Elizabeth Brown Wheeler and her family refused to observe fast days and illuminations during the American war, for which they had their windows broken.[8] In the divisive period of the French Revolution, women were active in loyalist and radical politics. Many roused their men to join volunteer forces for defence against invasion or associations to defend the nation against 'levellers and republicans'; some, like Hannah More, fought the war of ideas on the home front with her *Cheap Repository Tracts*, designed to convince the lower classes of the virtues of hearth, home, and English liberty over French tyranny, popery, and wooden shoes. Her ideas were contested by radical dissenting writers like Anna Laetitia Barbauld, Helen Maria Williams, Mary Hays, and Mary Wollstonecraft, who wrote polemical and imaginative works in favour of natural and women's rights, supported English Jacobin societies, and opposed the war on ethical as well as political grounds.

Such examples could be multiplied many times over. The point is this: British women in all social positions engaged in most aspects of the national struggles of war and empire-building – save the governmental. Equally important, however, and unfolding in tension with women's experiences, the long eighteenth-century wars had the effect of idealizing notions of the national character, particularly those 'manly' qualities necessary to military triumph and successful colonization – independence, fortitude, courage, daring, resourcefulness, strength, and paternalistic duty – and this composite of gendered national virtues would elide women's multifaceted roles in the extended polity of nation and empire.

For imperial conquest was held up by some as the antidote to the aristo-cratic 'effeminacy' and effeteness that was believed to plague the nation and threaten its courage, potency, and virtue. Particularly when Britain faced challenges from its purportedly effeminate enemy across the Channel, France, the corroding impact of effeminacy riled commentators and village shopkeepers alike. Effeminacy was a complex notion in this period, appearing in a range of political, cultural, and satirical, as well as sexual, discourses. Designated, according to Samuel Johnson's *Dictionary*, as both 'the admission of the qualities of a woman, softness, unmanly delicacy' and 'addiction to women', effeminates were men who resembled women, or who excessively desired them.[9] Civic humanists and other critics of the burgeoning consumer society had been quick to blame effeminacy on expanded commerce and empire, which had generated the webs of patronage, credit, and dependence, as well as inessential commodities that allowed the forces of luxury and moral turpitude to flourish. Women seemed emblematic and symptomatic of these forces of corruption, as primary purchasers of household and luxury goods and doyennes of social rituals based on colonial and foreign products. Patriotic

British women were accordingly urged to give up their natural inclinations towards effeminizing luxuries in order to promote the stoicism and love of country within the home that produced a manly fighting service at the front.[10]

In the 1740s and 1750s, effeminacy was blamed for undermining Britain's position in the world by relinquishing to France its place as 'Empire of the Seas.' The Revd John Brown of Newcastle most vividly summed up the problem when he declared that the 'ruling Character of the present times is that of a vain, *luxurious* and *selfish* Effeminacy', extinguishing love of country and the 'Spirit of National Defense' in Britain and her extended territories'.[11] But these concerns also agitated women, from bluestockings to village shopkeepers: Hannah Snell, famous female warrior who fought Britain's enemies on battlefields across the New and Old Worlds, explained that her call to arms rested largely on the need to rouse her country's men from the 'Effeminacy and Debauchery [that] have taken Place of the Love of Glory, and that noble Ardor after warlike Exploits'. Like other 'warrior women' who followed their lovers, Snell demonstrated that manliness and patriotism were not confined to biological males.[12]

Fears of effeminacy continued to have a wide currency for some time. Throughout the American war (1775–83), writers pilloried the empire as a source of 'luxury, effeminacy and tyranny' that corroded national mores and wreaked havoc with the gender order.[13] The French Revolutionary wars set off a similar panic, when concerns about the spread of 'levelling' principles and political and gender anarchy to Britain galvanized efforts to strengthen divisions between the feminine private and the masculine public spheres.[14] Significantly, Mary Wollstonecraft herself would also rail against the 'effeminacy' of women, albeit to a different end, exhorting them to become more 'manly', austere, forceful, disciplined, and self-directed in order to forge the virtuous polity that would vindicate their rights.[15] The discourses of effeminacy thus privileged the claims to political status of the white, trading, commercial or intellectual classes, while excluding a range of 'effeminate' others who threatened their supposedly distinctive goals: most women, Frenchmen, aristocrats, and non-white colonial subjects; the foppish, the irrational, the dependent, and the timid.

To be sure, other ideological and political currents contended with these views and revised the understanding of women's power and influence. By the 1770s, for example, women's role in empire and patriotism was represented as more beneficial if less direct than previously, as their capacity for domestic virtue was promoted as a source of moral authority in the broader imperial polity.[16] The rise of the cult of sensibility, which endowed women with the power to nurture the 'natural affections' and 'habitual sympathies' central to its ethical system of moral benevolence, had shifted somewhat the ideological grounds of women's position in the national polity.[17] Sensibility as a marker of civilization also was central to

Enlightenment social theory, which used examples culled from exploration and colonization to plot the progress of humanity through space and time, from its earliest 'savage' state (found most frequently in the torrid zones of the southern hemisphere) to its most advanced and polished 'commercial' state (typical of the temperate northern zone). From this progressive view of history emerged the belief that the character and position of women was the infallible sign of a society's progress. 'That women are indebted to the refinements of polished manners for a happy change in their state, is a point which can admit of no doubt', William Robertson asserted: 'To despise and to degrade the female sex, is the characteristic of the savage state in every part of the globe'.[18] European and especially British women were believed to have attained the highest levels of physical, mental, and moral refinement and chastity, a view widely disseminated by such popular writers as William Alexander and Hannah More.[19]

The political crisis wrought by the French Revolution combined with the moral fervour of evangelicalism to give such arguments an even higher purpose, for it exhorted men and women to join in a reformation of manners, at home and abroad, that would save heathen souls and advance Britain's imperial, commercial, and moral ascendancy in the world.[20] The order imposed by the British example of sensibility, bifurcated gender roles, and monogamous marriage were central to civilization's advance, and women's 'virtue' became defined less in terms of the capacity for polite and polished conversation than in terms of sexual chastity and innocence, which separate-sphere ideology and the evangelical emphasis on women's domestic nature both emphasized. These ideas were supported by new medical theories, which posited the incommensurability of men and women's bodies and rooted biological sex to gender in a new, absolutist way.[21]

In this guise, these constructions of virtuous womanhood could be deployed on behalf of imperial causes, as the anti-slavery campaigns aptly demonstrate. Between 1787 and 1792, led by the activities of former slaves in America and Britain, British women joined in the effort to abolish the slave trade, bringing their feminine compassion and sympathy to bear on the cruelties of slavery, and especially upon the sexual exploitation of black women and the break-up of black families. As the *Manchester Mercury* put it in 1787: 'A Female may meet, from the Pity of her own Sex, the assistance with the Inhumanity of the other [sex] may deny.'[22] Through the language of sensibility, evangelical and dissenting women – artisan, middle, and upper class, radical and loyalist – used their roles as consumers to put pressure on parliament, boycott plantation-produced goods, organize petition drives, attend public meetings, and speak and write against slavery and the slave trade. The connection they claimed with women across the empire through the language of universal womanhood enlarged their role, but it also produced images of enslaved Africans as victimized, passive, and silent – as savages living in immoral conditions who needed enlightened British women to lift them to freedom and civilization. After the abolition of the slave trade in 1807, anti-slavery regained force following slave revolts in Demerara (1823) and Jamaica (1831), becoming a badge of Britishness and British womanhood. The Birmingham Ladies Society for the Relief of Negro Slaves, founded by Anglican Lucy Townsend, Quaker Mary Lloyd, and Baptist Sophia Sturges, among others, pledged itself to 'the Amelioration of the Condition of the Unhappy Children of Africa, and especially of Female Negro Slaves'. Their activities galvanized the formation of a network of ladies' associations against slavery across the country, who, in turn, contacted missionary wives and their spouses, and sent money to schools in the West Indies.[23] Embracing the idea that British women represented the highest level of civilization, and assured of their own superiority as a result, female abolitionists felt entitled to dominate other women of the empire, to serve as 'teachers of nations' and manners to the less well-positioned. Those who failed to exhibit these qualities – which included British working-class women as well as colonized and enslaved women – were denigrated as savage, monstrous or depraved, and redeemable only by acquiescing in the division of labour and standards of domesticity set for them by their betters.[24]

The model of middle-class femininity and family relations endorsed by evangelicals became the touchstone of political economy and of English liberals' attempts to reform the imperial and domestic polities. Britain's successes in single-handedly defeating Napoleon did much to restore belief in the manliness and merit of the nation's leaders and British men: effeminacy became a charge levelled most often at colonized peoples, whose childishness, weakness, and languor necessitated stern but benevolent British tutelage. The Christian gentleman, whose justness, probity, and family values could be relied upon to bring order into dangerous times and climes, marked the hegemony of a masculine ideal meant to complement that of feminine domesticity and virtue. This was fortuitous, since by 1820, the British Empire had absorbed almost a quarter of the world's population. A version of settler colonialism, geared towards developing Australia and New Zealand, began to absorb Britain's 'surplus' inhabitants (felons, radicals, and paupers, as well as the ambitious or stymied), further diffusing British people across the globe, just as the principles of 'free trade' or 'Pax Britannica' became the slogans and justification for wielding British power across the world. Imperial reforms attempted to disseminate liberal principles of liberty and *laissez-faire* through the coercive apparatus of empire. William Bentinck, as governor-general of India, implemented reforms in law, education, and administration geared towards educating Indian peoples – regarded for the most part as indolent and sensual inhabitants of the 'torrid zone' – in the mores of British 'civilization', by which was meant English ways of life and gender roles. His work in abolishing *sati*, or widow-burning, in British India (1829) was commemorated by a statue meant to 'elevate the moral and intellectual character' of Indians, depicting a bare-breasted Indian woman being torn from her children for the funeral pyre.[25] Saving indigenous and British women from indigenous men would become a *cause célèbre* of British imperialism as the nineteenth century unfolded, just as the abolition of *sati*, infanticide, human sacrifice, and slavery in British colonies, and the formation of parliamentary committees to protect indigenous peoples within the empire, vindicated the nation's identification with liberty, law, and justice.

The liberal principles and reforms of empire also drew attention to the plight of poor working women 'at home'. The clergyman, Thomas Malthus, had brought the knowledge and theories forged by empire back to Britain by turning the precepts of stadial theory on the domestic population: he predicted that savages and the European poor, conjoined in their inability to control their sexual urges, were doomed to reproduce beyond the food supply. Only the European, and especially the English middle classes, were able to exercise the 'moral restraint' necessary to liberate reason from the forces of instinct and avert apocalypse.[26] British working women in particular were targeted as more 'profligate and perverted than the Hindoos'.[27] Poor Law and factory reform thus attempted to save the degraded British working classes from themselves by instilling the sexual restraint and industry necessary for civilization's advance. The Reform Act of 1832, which consolidated the middle class's image of itself as the agent as well as the beneficiary of progress, also inaugurated a period when the 'bourgeois' virtues of domesticity and separate spheres for men and women began to be codified in forms of state and social power that targeted the immoral poor, the *enragé* radical working class, the idle aristocracy, and the heathen *indigène* as its objects.[28] Significantly, Victorian languages of class, imperialism, and reform would continue to use the status and treatment of women, and their conformity to the standards of domesticity, as the marker of civilization, respectability, and national belonging itself.

British women in the Atlantic world

The definitions and practices of gender roles and relations within Britain were certainly carried with them to colonial environments, but in the act of crossing – oceans, territories, and cultures – these meanings and practices acquired new uses. Colonial encounters generated a 'gender frontier', where contending ideas about gender and nature met and confronted one another, forcing the invention of new identities and social practices.[29] At the same time, the different sites of empire, which varied from metropolitan society to sugar plantations, white settler colonies, factories, fortresses, and outposts across the globe, meant that relations of gender and power were differently articulated, always in flux, and difficult if not impossible to maintain in the familiar forms of 'home'. The *instability* of gender and national identities are thus brought into relief in colonial settings, as desire and recognition, as well as disavowal, shaped the categories of difference that empire was believed to discover, vindicate, and sustain.

Gender roles consequently provided a key to British assessments of the stage of civilization of indigenous societies and to the type of treatment meted out to recalcitrant local people. This had long shaped English relations with Celtic peoples within the British Isles. In Scotland, the commercial and property reforms instituted by the British government following the Jacobite uprising of 1745 targeted Highland clan culture which was said to 'barbarically' subordinate women (despite the greater freedoms allowed them in Scottish law and custom). The culture and gender order of the Highlands continued to shock English missionaries into the nineteenth century.[30] Centuries of English domination of Ireland was continually legitimated by the allegedly backward character of native Irish gender relations: the women were 'brazen' and lascivious, partial to strong drink, and wielded too much power over their husbands; Irish men were lazy, tyrannical, and lacking proper ties to property (indicated by their serial use of common lands for pasturage). Early-modern English writers asserted that the Irish were non-Europeans, descended from the Scythians, and sharing customs with the Tartars. The so-called 'Celtic fringe' thereby provided models of 'primitive' peoples who both required and benefited from English civility and rule.[31]

In eighteenth-century America, intercultural and sexual exchange between English colonists and Native Americans, and wars with France, coaxed British settlers, fur traders, missionaries, and soldiers, from Canada to Carolina, to scrutinize Native American societies in order to gauge their progress, if any, from 'savagery' to civility, defined as their willingness to cooperate with the British.[32] Gender and sexual relations were deemed of particular importance, as English emissaries sought to find some evidence of a household order from which they could extrapolate or coax stable political relations. But male authority seemed conspicuous in Indian communities by its lack.[33] The women's sexual 'libertinism', the effort-lessness with which they gave birth (that infallible indicator of savagery the world over, in British eyes), and the ease with which heterosexual partnerships were made and dissolved underscored the problem of masculine deficiency and debased femininity. 'To cuckold her Husband is so little a [crime] that no notice is taken of it . . . Their Maids do not keep that Name . . . they lie with whom they please before marriage,' noted John Oldmixon disapprovingly.[34] Significantly, of the women taken captive by

Native Americans in this period, some would prefer the native way of live to that of the Europeans.

But what most animated British observers was Indians' apparently anarchical domestic life, which was (mis)translated as an index of social disorder. Historians of British America are in substantial agreement on this point: 'patriarchy', in the form of the supreme authority of the white, predominantly property-holding, male heads of household, was the building-block and organizing principle of British-American societies, and the household was the main unit of social order and indigenous reclamation. The power of the male heads of households in law and practice from New England to Carolina owed much to colonization and to the novel forms of servitude and slavery it generated.[35] It was also a response to the relative weakness of the regulatory apparatus of Church and State in societies where whites could be a minority. Claiming the right to 'dispatch wives, children and slaves', the patriarch's will was expressed and enforced by the whip. As the notorious sexual profligate and successful planter, William Byrd, wrote in 1726.

> Like one of the patriarchs, I have my flocks and my herds, my bond-men, and bond-women, and every soart of trade amongst my own servants, so that I live in a kind of independance [sic] on every one, but Providence.[36]

A great deal of the work of male authority took its most potent form in the regulation of sexual behaviour of household and family members, which was enforced or extended by colonial law. Female sexual access was a jealously guarded and valuable commodity. Laws against interracial unions, legal limitations on the freedoms of free blacks, and prosecution of white women for bearing mixed-race children (while being indifferent to those fathered by white men with enslaved or native women), meant masters intervened in the most intimate of connections. When combined with measures to establish legal standing for definitions of 'race', as occurred in Virginia and Maryland, legal constructions of patriarchal privilege and female honour provided 'assurance that white female domesticity and sexuality would remain the preserve of white men'.[37] The gender power of patriarchy reinforced that of colonialism, as the appropriation of land, labour, and sexual entitlements went hand in hand.

Women's experience of colonization was shaped by their positions within these various hierarchies. In the early years of settlement, white British women immigrated to the New World as family members or as indentured or forced labourers. Impoverished Irish women were recruited by promises of money or new clothes, or impressed into emigration to relieve the 'vagrant' problem; in either case, once in the New World, they suffered the highest number of miscarriages and stillbirths in the hemisphere, in an unsavoury anticipation of the fate of African women.[38] On the mainland, frontier conditions undermined traditional distinctions between men's and women's work, ranging them both in a variety of intensive agricultural and domestic employments, and allowing some women to pursue freedom as farmers, merchants, nurses, innkeepers and moneylenders. Among the labouring poor, however, female indentured servants were liable to sexual abuse or harassment by masters or their sons; and, as high rates of natural reproduction in the mainland colonies balanced sex ratios, and enslaved labour increased, the demand for female indentured servants' productive and sexual labour slackened. Women who were not servants were largely excluded from the skilled trades, while law and custom limited the social significance of women's work, subordinating them to fathers, husbands, and masters, as 'good wives' and 'helpmeets'.[39] Women's initial increased opportunities in the New World in law, medicine, and labour similarly declined over the eighteenth century.[40] The gender frontier closed down rather than opened up opportunities for many women, especially the poorest, for whom the promise of good marriages and social betterment was cruelly belied.

As the harsh conditions of frontier settlement gave way to greater prosperity and diversification, British women were enjoined to bring their special moral qualities to bear on the arts of colonization and direct the social practices that maintained the boundaries of nationality and entitlement. The requirements of 'politeness' in the colonies ensured the adaptive reproduction of English culture and stock far from home. In the colonial towns such as Philadelphia, Boston, Williamsburg, and Charleston, where the growth of urban culture promoted the principles and practices of politeness and sensibility on the metropolitan model, women's roles as arbiters and polishers of manners placed them at the centre of social life. However, strategies of social engineering (of which 'patriarchy' was certainly one) collided with individual motivation and condition to produce unexpected results. For example, where the men greatly outnumbered women, as in the Caribbean, New South Wales, or India, British women from fairly petty backgrounds could aspire to good marriages; widows, as women of property, were also highly desirable. 'Widowarchy' prevailed in other Atlantic colonies too, from Virginia to St Helena, where the regulation of marriage as a means of transmission of property was of critical import.[41] The strategy could also work in reverse. Teresia Constantia Phillips, notorious courtesan, immigrated to Jamaica in the 1750s to use the time-honoured strategy of 'marry and bury' to gain the fortunes of a string of wealthy men and perform the role of English lady with great aplomb, becoming Mistress of the Revels. Even the penal colony of New South Wales afforded social mobility: Esther Abrahams, a Jewish convict transported for stealing lace, became the mistress and then the wife of a future governor of the colony, serving as a beacon of hope to other convict women.[42]

Most women in the southern American and Caribbean colonies did not have the same opportunities for self-invention, for most were caught within the complex webs of power and debasement of the Atlantic plantation, which cast its shadow over many aspects of local life. Here, the division between free and slave was bolstered by perceptions and legislation of national origin: white people, with the exceptions of Jews, were assumed to have the protection of 'British rights and liberties' of people back home; black people were assumed to exist beyond the bounds of this protection. In fact, as numbers of people of African descent made clear, slave and free, both before and after the American Revolution (when numbers immigrated back 'home' to Britain), 'Britishness' could not be neatly demarcated or contained, legally or imaginatively. Both enslaved and free blacks declared themselves to be British, as did the ex-slaves Mary Prince (the first black British female emancipationist) and Olaudah Equiano (who poignantly declared himself to be 'almost an Englishman' in his *Narrative* of 1793).[43] Yet the fates of black people could be hampered not only by colonial laws which attempted to circumscribe their rights, but also by contemporaries' assumption that national 'origin', however distant, largely determined one's character and social place.

The vast majority of slaves in British America were of African descent and worked on the sugar, tobacco, and rice plantations of the Caribbean and Chesapeake.[44] Men outnumbered women two to one in slave importations until the 1760s, although the rates of reproduction in the mainland colonies created a rough parity between the sexes by the middle decades of the century. Nevertheless, in a very real sense, slavery was first and foremost a system of gender and racial power: black women were made responsible, materially and symbolically, for the reproduction of plantation slavery.[45] In order to ensure a future supply of slaves, all children at birth took their legal status from their mother, thereby reversing the custom of male lineage typical of British law. This meant that white women, white men, and black men, free or slave, could, at least theoretically, produce free children; but enslaved mothers could only produce more slaves.

The black woman's body and the internal character it was mobilized to convey had long been objects of intense scrutiny. Stereotyped images of African women as 'masculine', unfeminine, and monstrous had circulated in European culture since the sixteenth century; old and new images got a fresh lease on life with the popularity of voyagers' accounts in the eighteenth century. Depictions of West Africans and the so-called 'Hottentots' of South Africa appeared in English narratives as perfect examples of the way in which 'each Nation has retained certain Lineaments or Features' as 'infallible signs of their Dispositions'. Their supposedly lascivious and over-sexualized natures also made their modes of reproduction suspect. This strategy of using gender and sexuality as ways to set the British off from non-European peoples had a long history and future.[46] In the 1700s, these tropes of difference were reorganized and formalized through the taxonomies of natural history and the rigours of plantation life. All observers agreed that in terms of civility, morality, capacity for progress, and the treatment of women, Africans lagged far behind Europeans, existing in an anterior historical time of savagery that only slavery itself could modernize.[47]

Not surprisingly, enslaved women's bodies were acute sites of struggle between the contending hierarchies of authority that sought to claim a stake in the property of slavery. Masters and overseers alike forced themselves on slave women at will; sexual duties were considered part and parcel of an enslaved woman's work; the master's claims trumped those of any other men. Enslaved women's exploitation caused them trauma and suffering, and aroused the hostility and occasionally the violence of enslaved men. Although impossible to calculate precisely, 'there was a deep and sullen hatred for what happened to the women'.[48] Yet, despite the impossibility of truly 'consensual' intercourse between master and slave, deep attachments sometimes formed. The notorious overseer, Thomas Thistlewood, whose diary (1750–86) records forced sexual relations with thousands of black and coloured women on Vineyard Pen and Egypt plantation in Jamaica, took his favourite lover, Phibbah, as his 'slave wife'. However, she had sometimes to stay at home to attend her master (and Thistlewood's employer), rather than spend her nights with Thistlewood, to the distress of them both.[49]

While masters depended on their enslaved mistresses for gossip about slave relations and potential conspiracies, their 'wives' frequently used their positions to gain advantages for themselves and their children, or to seek retaliation for ill-treatment through domestic sabotage. Mulatto women, in particular, used their colour and attractiveness to ensure a favourable place within the hierarchies of plantation life; in the West Indies, they almost never worked in the fields, but were favoured servants in the household. Enslaved women of all hues could exploit their sexual or emotional intimacies to acquire property or establish themselves in trade – or even to obtain their freedom. By the time of Thistlewood's death, Phibbah had secured the freedom of their son, John, and her own future manumission, as well as a small estate and two slaves of her own. Significantly, despite their clear emotional involvement, Phibbah and Thistlewood never married. As Bryan Edwards remarked, '(so degrading is the melancholy state of slavery) [that] no man who has the least respect for himself will think of marrying a female slave'. Nor, he concluded, 'is it within the reach of Human Authority to restrain the Appetites of Nature': hence sexual liaisons between white men and black women (although not, apparently, between black men and white women), and their product, mulatto children, would continue to be inevitable.[50]

Within the theatres of power and debasement in plantation societies, white women played crucial but complicated roles. Despite their varied social and economic positions in plantation and urban economies, law and custom worked to put white women on a pedestal that emphasized the cultural distinctions of 'race' as it endowed planter society with respectability. Against the black woman's alleged voracious sexuality and primitiveness, white women were idealized as fragile, maternal, and inviolable. As economic agents and mistresses of slave-based households, however, white women often appropriated the 'paternalism' of the masters with a vengeance. Certainly many who left records displayed repugnance towards the institution of slavery and compassion for the slaves. Elizabeth Fenwick of Bridgetown, Barbados, who ran a school for privileged white children, was distressed by the plight of slaves, yet when her female slaves flouted her authority, lied and stole, and otherwise caused her 'endless trouble and vexation', she sold them and purchased male slaves.[51] Others, like Mary Ricketts or Lady Maria Nugent, found the flora and fauna of the West Indies threatening, and disliked the bodies and presence of the ubiquitous black slaves.[52] Most mistresses brooked no insubordination, meting out physical punishment for the slightest perceived offences; the cruel white mistress became a notorious sign of the degrading effects of slavery on masters and enslaved alike. Mary Prince, a Bermudian slave who became the first black British woman to publish a record of her experiences, left a devastatingly vivid account of the abuse she suffered at her mistress's hand in her *History* (1831):

> She taught me to do all sorts of household work; to wash and bake, pick cotton and wool, and wash floors, and cook. And she taught me (how can I ever forget it!) more things than these; she caused me to know the exact difference between the smart of the rope, the cart-whip, and the cowskin, when applied to my naked body by her own cruel hand. And there was scarcely any punishment more dreadful than the blows I received on my face and head from her hard heavy fist.[53]

Prince's narrative, which also documented the murder and torture of slaves and their children by British masters in Bermuda and Antigua, inflamed public opinion in Britain and pushed the abolitionist cause forward.

The cruelty of many white women to their slaves may have been retaliation for the low esteem in which they themselves were held by their men. Although socially and symbolically superior by law and custom, white Creole women were considered pallid imitations of 'real' English ladies: gauche, indolent, extravagant, and prone to display the 'vulgar manners' of their black servants. The young ladies wanted 'that indispensable requisite of complete beauty, the glow of youthful vermilion', Bryan Edwards opined, 'which heightens the graces of the English fair'.[54] The high rate of concubinage was thus blamed on white women's cultural and physical insufficiencies. On the other hand, white, black, and mulatto women organized slave brothels that serviced urban populations of slaves, merchants, planters, sailors, and soldiers, or even bought and sold slaves themselves, exploiting the formidable power of slaveowners over their property.[55]

Beginning in the 1810s, numbers of British women began arriving in the Caribbean as missionaries' wives and sisters. They meant to serve, by example, as moral beacons, reforming the family and gender relations of 'backward' enslaved Africans along a Christian model. Their presence as 'helpmeets' and domestic anchors eased the burdens of missionary men, while also securing them, it was thought, from the temptations of concubinage and excess sexuality associated with African and creole culture. British women also bolstered the goals of conversion and reform in the pre-emancipation periods. Indeed, after slavery and apprenticeship were ended, British women continued to serve as teachers, nurses, counsellors, and leaders, dedicated to elevating their black brothers and sisters within the family of man.[56] In the event, their convictions were sorely tested and in the post-emancipation period many became convinced of the unredeemably 'heathen' and depraved nature, not only of black and coloured people, but also of the whites who had lived their lives on the islands.[57] The complexities and symbolic politics of the systems of power, entangling gender, sex, class, and race in plantation societies meant that the categories of 'white' and 'black,' 'men' and 'women', 'slave' and 'free', were continually at risk, undercut by the performances of difference that all groups enacted in the tasks of everyday life and the commodification of 'freedom' and 'civilization' themselves.

British women in India, Australia and Oceania

British women's role in the 'eastern' empire of the eighteenth and early nineteenth century has been less well documented by historians, but recent work is beginning to investigate the regulation of gender relations and its link to the consolidation of a racialized dynamics of British rule.[58] For example, in British settlements in Madras and Calcutta, the absence of white women had led officers and servants of the East India Company to make 'connections' with local women. These 'connections' were less romantic than contemporaries or some historians have suggested. Unlike America, which had been conceptualized as a 'virgin land', free to be taken and shaped at will, India was recognized as an ancient, if barbaric, nation and imagined as Oriental exoticism incarnate, conjured through images of the 'female mystery' of the *zenana* and the veil, the 'Oriental despotism' of polygamy, child marriage, *sati*, or widow immolation, and the 'effeminacy and resignation of spirit' of Hindu men.[59] In this setting, romance and marriage between a high-ranked Company official and an Indian noblewoman, such as that of orientalist, James Kirkpatrick, Resident at the Hyderabad Court, and Khair-un-Nissa, added to the mystique. But having and maintaining 'bibis', as they were called, was widespread among Company officials and servants. George Bogle, Secretary to the Company at Calcutta in the 1770s, maintained an alternative family of Indian mistress and children, which he kept secret from his relations 'at home', as did surveyor Richard Blechynden. In the case of the latter, his 'wife' (a paid servant) and their children were 'betrayed' to his English relatives through the gossip and correspondence networks created by Company employees.[60] British and native conjugal relations would be discouraged and even prohibited by officials like Lords Cornwallis and Wellesley, in order to maintain the boundaries between British and native, and to keep people of colour from becoming a significant factor in local politics, as they had in the West Indies and the Cape. Still, the practice of maintaining native mistresses and slave concubines continued into the nineteenth century, even if the strategies of managing them changed. [61]

From the 1770s onwards, East India merchantmen were carrying small but significant numbers of married, betrothed, or marriageable British women – English, Scottish, and Irish, but particularly the former – to the male servants of the Company on the subcontinent, perhaps in a move to stabilize the Company's transition from a trading to a political, fiscal, and territorial power. British women changed the tenor of Anglo-Indian life, presiding over the rituals and social performances of cultural affiliation, with the result that, for the moment, they had greater freedom to engage in public and social life than they would in the next century. For Eliza Fay, who accompanied her husband to a legal post in Calcutta, dangerous surfs, marauding pirates, and shipboard fevers were but the prelude to a fifteen-week imprisonment of her party by Haidar Ali at Calicut. But once in Calcutta, she was greeted with an 'astonishing spectacle'. 'Asiatic splendour, combined with European taste exhibited around you on every side', she exclaimed, 'under the forms of flowing drapery, stately palanquins, elegant carriages, innumerable servants, and all the pomp and circumstance of luxurious ease, and unbounded wealth.'[62] Here, British women maintained the hectic schedules of balls, concerts, plays, races, visits, and elaborate masquerades that were central to the performance of British social and cultural affiliation.[63] Almanacs for the ladies, printed at the mission office, marked Hindu feasts and Muslim religious holidays as well as important days of British national commemoration, from the monarch's birthday to the anniversary of Clive's victory at the Battle of Plassey (1757). Lady Frances Chambers, wife of the Chief Justice of Bengal and Eliza Fay's patroness, kept her appointments and memorandums in such a diary. She noted the dates of the births – and deaths – of her children, the plays she attended, the quantity of rupees she won in the local lottery, the visits she made, the treatment meted out to recalcitrant slaves, and the romantic and political alliances and patronage networks that animated and orchestrated local British society.[64] Other women, such as Charlotte Barry, moved in polite circles as the companions of East Indian Company servants without sanctity of marriage (although she travelled under the name of 'Mrs William Hickey'), thus continuing the tradition of unconventional sexual arrangements that distinguished British imperial culture. Nevertheless, the *Calcutta Gazette* liked to boast about 'our numerous beauties, who charm the eye and enthrall the ear', and declared them central to 'the rapid progress we are daily making in all those polite and refined entertainments, which have so strong a tendency to humanize the mind, and render life pleasing and agreeable'.[65]

British women's place within Anglo-Indian society began to change in the first half of the nineteenth century, when British influence was extended to encompass the princely states located between the Bengal, Madras, and Bombay Presidencies, and liberal and evangelical reformers targeted Hindu society for education and elevation along the British model. Women's bodies and status, British and Indian, were crucial objectives. As a society 'refines upon its enjoyments, and advances into that state of civilization', Utilitarian and East India Company official James Mill declared, 'the condition of the weaker sex is gradually improved, till they associate on equal terms with the men, and occupy the place of voluntary and useful coadjutors'.[66] Such an improvement in Indian women's position necessitated, in British eyes, an end to the social segregation of the *zenana*, or women's quarters of the household, as well as the abolition of *sati* and the raising of the age of consent for marriage for girls to age twelve – all of which became rallying points around which reformers tried to ameliorate the 'barbarity' of Indian culture.[67] Reformers also objected to Anglo-Indian women's frivolous socializing and indolence, which were seen as dangerously reflecting the *zenana*, where women 'wiled away the time in silly obscene conversation'. British women were enjoined instead to occupy their days in useful employments, to dress demurely, and to keep up appropriate distinctions between themselves and local native society. As early as 1813, Anglo-Indian women had begun to exclude 'half-casts', or mixed-race people of European and Indian descent who had formerly moved in polite circles, from their company, in a pointed commentary on the unconventional sexual arrangements and their issue accepted in the army.[68] Hence, even before the Indian Mutiny of 1857 solidified the negative view of Indians as 'savage' and 'treacherous', British people on the subcontinent had begun to argue for the need to separate the 'races' as the means of preserving English culture from Indian 'degeneracy and effeminacy,' and to socialize by example the 'Indian character' in the ways of civilization. Handbooks for Anglo-Indian women prescribed methods for making the household a more 'British space', where cleanliness and godliness could predominate and the intimate contact between the family and their many Indian servants could be better limited and controlled.[69] As in the Caribbean, men and women used the issues of women's status and standards of domesticity to define themselves and their civilizing mission, and to give visible embodiment to the personal and political boundaries of rule. British women held a social and symbolic position that defined appropriate relations of power and subordination and clarified who was entitled to claim the 'rights and privileges' of British people – and who was not.

European women were absent in the South Pacific and Australia prior to 1787 and thereafter they made their dichotomous appearance as missionaries' wives or convicts. For example, the voyages of Captain James Cook (1768–80) and reports of the godless, lascivious, but friendly peoples of the South Seas had sparked the formation of a new spate of missionary societies geared towards saving the debased savages from heathenism and French Catholicism alike. Several women, wives of the artisans and trades- men who made up the missionaries, set sail for Tahiti in 1797 on the first mission organized by the London Missionary Society. It was hoped that they would be able to access female space in Polynesian society and serve as 'improving' models of Christian womanhood and evangelical family values for their charges.[70] In the event, their example may have been more convincing to the natives than to their own men. In the second year of the mission on Tahiti (1798), Thomas Lewis's decision to take a local woman as his wife caused great distress among the rest of the fellowship, who promptly excommunicated him.[71] The problem of British men 'going native' with local women also plagued the missions to the North Island of New Zealand organized by the evangelical cleric, Samuel Marsden, chaplain to the colony of New South Wales. The independence, courage, and intelligence of the fierce Maori nations had so impressed Marsden that he concluded that the Maoris may have been the 'Jews of Old', one of the Lost Tribes of Israel. Yet when one of his missionaries, school-teacher Thomas Kendall, became so enthralled with native culture that he ended up living with a Maori girl in 1823, he was expelled from the mission. It was not until after 1837, with the formation of the New Zealand Land Company to further British settlement and make the islands 'the Britain of the southern hemisphere', that significant numbers of British women were willing to brave this new frontier and anchor the social and sexual life of British men. Even then, of course, cross-cultural alliances continued to be made.[72] The cultural and topographical mappings of the Pacific suggested that British conflation of gender and national difference could be disrupted, rather than confirmed, by colonial encounter and the practices of everyday life.

This was self-consciously the case in the penal colony of New South Wales in 1788, where an insular British colony of convicts, guardians, and soldiers were deposited on the edge of a vast continent only partially charted by Cook and inhabited, in British eyes, by a 'savage' and strangely incurious people. Governor Phillip wanted the colony to be a model of enlightened reform, efficiency, and reclamation, where slavery was prohibited, humane and mutually beneficial relations with native peoples established, and convict men redeemed by hard work and, eventually, freedom as labourers, artisans, even landholders. In fact, familiar patterns of coercion, subordination, and multi-directional cultural traffic quickly established themselves in relations between men, men and women, and British and aboriginals. The initial shortage of white women led to 'gross indecencies' that led Phillip to want to make sodomy a capital crime. Women felons were soon sent out by the boatload, a situation described by contemporaries as a 'floating brothel'. Phillip had hoped that arriving women could be ranked according to 'degree of virtue', with some prepared for marriage and others, 'the most abandoned', encouraged to live as prostitutes.[73] In the event, men and women, British and Aboriginal, made unconventional arrangements that crossed the spectrum from rape to marriage to concubinage. Many British men came to prefer their Aboriginal mistresses, who they found to be 'soft and feminine', and British women would escape their 'husbands' for better prospects, sometimes with other women.[74] Convict women inside the Female Factory (the women's prison) in Paramatta could also better their lot through trade, exchanging flour for bread, sex for lodging in town, and marriage for release from the factory.[75] Nevertheless, as we have seen in the case of women within Britain elsewhere in this volume, convict women were widely deemed to be worse than their male counterparts.[76] Arthur Bowes Smyth, surgeon on board the *Lady Penryn*, the ship carrying the first load of female convicts to Australia, declared 'there was never a more abandon'd set of wretches', and they were routinely referred to by British officials as whores – not, significantly, because they were selling sex, but because they had broken the rules and did not behave like ladies or sober workers.[77]

The customary and casual violence undergirding officially sanctioned relationships was revealed by the policy of Governor King (1800–6) and his successors which allowed newly arrived convict women to be 'selected and applied for' by 'industrious' settlers, 'with whom they either marry or cohabit' despite the will or desire of the women themselves.[78] Aboriginal women, too, were abducted as sexual partners by British men, leading to intensifying violence between blacks and whites on the frontier. Missionaries, who began arriving in New South Wales in the 1810s, decried Aboriginal women as 'bond-slaves of Satan', mistranslating the complex gender and lineage systems in which female-exchange played an important diplomatic role. The consequent depiction of Aboriginal women as oppressed by cruel menfolk, and of the absence of recognizable households through which Aboriginals could be redeemed, gave rise to the practice of collecting children in the effort to attract their kin to the missions.[79] When the first influx of free immigrants began to reach Australia in the 1820s, women became part of the sojourners to the 'whole, vacant earth', as Thomas Carlyle called it, of South Australia, Victoria, and Gippsland. Frontier warfare with Aborigines in this instance gave rise to legends of white women taken captive and converted to native ways, in a resonant echoing of earlier New World myths. Held by 'savages' who were believed to treat their women as drudges, captive white women's real and imagined plights were widely publicized in newspapers, magazines, and novels in Britain and Australia, cementing the identification in the British mind of Aborigines as demonic and subhuman.[80] Clearly, British constructions of civilization and proper womanhood could make themselves felt even in the antipodes, but their utility in effecting change and stabilizing the boundaries between 'them' and 'us' would continue to be contested and uneven, in the nineteenth century, and beyond.

Notes

1 'The journal of Charlotte Browne, Matron of the General Hospital with the English Forces in America, 1754–56', in Isabel Calder (ed.), *Colonial Captivities: Marches and Journeys*, New York, 1935; reprinted 1967, pp. 169–200.

2 See Linda Colley, *Britons: Forging the* Nation, New Haven, CT, 1992; Patricia Lin, 'Citizenship, military families and the creation of a new definition of "Deserving Poor" in Britain, 1793–1815', *Social Politics* Spring, 2000, pp. 5–46; Margaret Hunt, 'Women and the Royal Navy', in Kathleen Wilson (ed.), *A New Imperial History: Culture, Identity and Modernity in Britain and the Empire*, Cambridge, 2004; Holley Mayer, *Belonging to the Army: Camp Followers and Community during the American Revolution*, Columbia, 1994; Kathleen Wilson, *The Sense of the People: Politics, Culture and Imperialism in England 1715–1785*, Cambridge, 1995; also Kathleen Wilson, *The Island Race: Englishness, Empire and Gender in the Eighteenth Century*, London, 2003; Myna Tristam, *Women of the Regiment: Marriage and the Victorian Army*, Cambridge, 1984.

3 Wilson, S*ense of the People*, Chapter 1; James Walvin, *Fruits of Empire: Exotic Produce and British Taste, 1660–1800*, London, 1997; David Shields, *Civil Tongues and Polite Letters in British America*, Chapel Hill, NC, 1997.

4 Tessie Liu, 'Teaching the differences among women from a historical perspective', *Women's Studies International Forum*, 1991, vol. 14, pp. 270–1.

5 Colley, *Britons*, p. 154.

6 Wilson, *Sense of the People*, pp. 49–50; Gateshead Public Library, Ellison MS, A54/11, George Liddell to Henry Ellison, 15 Mar. 1739.

7 Wilson, *Island Race*, pp. 110–20.

8 This paragraph is based on Wilson, *Island Race*, Chapter 3.

9   Samuel Johnson, *A Dictionary of the English Language*, London, 2nd edn, 1775; Michèle Cohen, *Fashioning Masculinity*, London, 1998, p. 17.

10 *The Female Volunteer*, London, 1746; Eliza Haywood, *The Female Spectator*, London, 1746, vol. 2, pp. 117, 121.

11 John Brown, *An Estimate of the Manners and Principles of the Times*, 2 vols, London, 1757, vol. 1, pp. 51–2, 66–7.

12 Wilson, *Island Race*, pp. 112–15; *The Female Soldier: of the Surprising Life and Adventures of Hannah Snell*, London, 1750, repr. *Augustan Reprint Society*, ed. Dianne Dugaw, no. 257, Los Angeles, 1989, pp. 1–2.

13 Wilson, *Sense of the People*, Chapter 5; Stephen Conway, *The British Isles and the War for American Independence*, Oxford, 2001, pp. 89–90.

14 Colley, *Britons*, pp. 253–4 ; Katherine Binhammer, 'The sex panic of the 1790s', *Journal of the History of Sexuality* (1996), vol. 6, pp. 409–34.

15 Mary Wollstonecraft, *A Vindication of the Rights of Women*, ed. Miriam Brody Kramnick, New York, 1985, pp. 186–92, 256–8.

16 Harriet Guest, *Small Change: Women, Learning, Patriotism*, Chicago, 2001; Charlotte Sussman, *Consuming Subjects*, Stanford, CA, 2000; Wilson, *Island Race*.

17 G. J. Barker Benfield, *The Culture of Sensibility*, Chicago, 1993; Jane Rendall, 'Virtue and commerce: women in the making of Adam Smith's political economy', in Ellen Kennedy and Susan Mendus (eds), *Women in Western Political Philosophy*, New York, 1987; Susan Kingsley Kent, *Gender and Power in Britain 1660–1990*, London, 1998, pp. 67–71.

18 William Robertson, *The History of America*, 4 vols., London, 1777, vol. 2, p. 98; Adam Ferguson, *An Essay on Civil Society*, London, 1766, pp. 146–7, 201.

19 William Alexander, *The History of Women, from the Earliest Antiquity to the Present Time*, 2 vols, London, 1779, 1782; Hannah More, *Essays on Various Subjects*, London, 4th edn, 1785.

20 Susan Thorne, *Congregational Missions and the Making of an Imperial Culture in Nineteenth Century England*, Stanford, CA, 1999, pp. 23–88.

21 Leonore Davidoff and Catherine Hall, *Family Fortunes: Men and Women of the English Middle Class*, London, 1987; Thomas Laqueur, *Making Sex: Body and Gender from the Greeks to Freud*, Cambridge, MA, 1990.

22 *Manchester Mercury*, 6 Nov. 1787, as quoted in Clare Midgley, *Women Against Slavery: The British Campaigns*, London, 1992), pp. 21–2. This paragraph on abolition is based on Midgley's excellent monograph.

23 Midgley, *Women Against Slavery*, pp. 43–4, 45–71; Catherine Hall, *Civilizing Subjects: Metropole and Colony in the English Imagination, 1830–1867*, London, 2002, pp. 314–15.

24 Deborah Valenze, *The First Industrial Woman*, Oxford, 1995; Anna Clark, *The Struggle for the Breeches: Gender and the Making of the British Working Class*, Berkeley, CA, 1995.

25 Kent, *Gender and Power*, pp. 205–6.

26 Thomas Malthus, *An Essay on the Principle of Population; or a View of its past and Present Effects on Human Happiness; With an Inquiry into our Prospects, Respecting the Future Removal or Mitigation of the Evils which it Occasions*, version publ. in 1803, with the variora of 1806, 1807, 1817, and 1826, 2 vols., ed. Patricia James, Cambridge, 1989, vol. 1, pp. 1–3, 21, 47.

27 Susan Thorne, ' "The Conversion of Englishmen and the Conversion of the World Inseparable": missionary imperialism and the language of class', in Frederick Cooper and Ann Laura Stoler (eds), *Tensions of Empire: Colonial Cultures in a Bourgeois World*, Berkeley, CA, 1997, p. 249.

28 Ibid., pp. 238–62; Jenise DePinto, 'Re-imagining the nation in early Victorian Britain: class, race and gender in the "Condition of England" question, 1830–1850', PhD dissertation, SUNY–Stony Brook, NY, 2005.

29 Kathleen Brown, *Good Wives, Nasty Wenches and Anxious Patriarchs: Gender, Race and Power in Colonial Virginia*, Chapel Hill, NC, 1996, pp. 33, 45.

30 R. A. Houston, 'Women in the economy and society of Scotland, 1500–1800', in R. A. Houston and I. D. Whyte, *Scottish Society*, Cambridge, 1989, pp. 119–47; Leah Leneman, *Alienated Affections: The Scottish Experience of Divorce and Separation*, Edinburgh, 1998; Thorne, 'Missionary imperialism', pp. 238–9.

31 David Dickson, 'No Scythians here: women and marriage in seventeenth-century Ireland', in Margaret MacCurtain and Mary O'Dowd (eds), *Women in Early Modern Ireland*, Edinburgh, 1991, p. 224; Nicholas Canny, 'The ideology of English colonization', *William and Mary Quarterly*, 3rd Ser., 1973, vol. 30, pp. 575–98.

32 Nancy Shoemaker (ed.), *Negotiators of Change: Historical Perspectives on Native American Women*, Chicago, 1995; Richard Godbeer, 'Eroticizing the middle ground: Anglo-Indian sexual relations along the eighteenth-century frontier', in Martha Hodes (ed.), *Sex, Love, Race: Crossing Boundaries in North American History*, New York, 1999, pp. 91–106.

33 Richard White, 'What Chigabe knew', *William and Mary Quarterly*, 3rd Ser., 1995, vol. 52, pp. 152–3.

34 Colin G. Calloway, *New Worlds for All: Indians, Europeans and the Remaking of Early America*, Baltimore, MD, 1997; David Milobar, 'Aboriginal peoples and the British press, 1720–1763', in Stephen Taylor, Clyve Jones and Richard Connors (eds), *Hanoverian Britain and Empire: Essays in Memory of Philip Lawson* Woodbridge, CT, 1998, 76; John Oldmixon, *The British Empire in America*, 2 vols, London, 1708, vol. 1, p. 279.

35 John Demos, *A Little Commonwealth: Family Life in Plymouth Colony*, Oxford, 2000; Carole Shammas, 'Anglo-American household government in comparative perspective', *William and Mary Quarterly*, 3rd Ser., 1995, vol. 52, pp. 104–44.

36 William Byrd, as quoted in Brown, *Good Wives*, p. 265; Philip D. Morgan, *Slave Counterpoint: Black Culture in the Eighteenth-Century Chesapeake and Low Country*, Chapel Hill, NC, 1998, pp. 274–5.

37 Brown, *Good Wives*, pp. 195–7, 203.

38 J. Casway, 'Irish women overseas', in MacCurtain and O'Dowd (eds), *Women in Early Modern Ireland*, pp. 126–7.

39 Karen Kupperman, *Providence Island, 1630–1641: The Other Puritan Colony*, Cambridge, 1993, pp. 199, 155–8; Sharon Salinger, '"Send no more women": female servants in eighteenth-century Philadelphia', *Pennsylvania Magazine of History and Biography*, 1983, vol. 107, pp. 29–48; Lisa Wilson, *'Ye Heart of a Man': The Domestic Life of Men in Colonial New England*, New Haven, CT, 1999; Laurel Thatcher Ulrich, *Good Wives: Image and Reality in the Lives of Women in Northern New England, 1650–1750*, New York, 1991.

40 Cornelia Hughes Dayton, *Women before the Bar: Gender, Law and Society in Connecticut, 1639–1789*, Chapel Hill, NC, 1995; Brown, *Good Wives*; Elaine Forman Crane, *Ebb Tide in New England: Women, Seaports and Social Change, 1630–1800*, Boston, 1998.

41 Brown, *Good Wives*, pp. 253, 257.

42 Wilson, *Island Race*, Chapter 4; Suzanne D. Rutland, *At the Edge of the Diaspora: Two Centuries of Jewish Settlement in Australia*, Sydney, 1997, p. 11.

43 *The History of Mary Prince, A West Indian Slave, Related by Herself* (1831), ed.

Moira Ferguson, Ann Arbor, MI, 1993, p. 56; Olaudah Equiano, *The Interesting Narrative of the Life of Olaudah Equiano*, ed. Robert Allison, New York, 1995, pp. 132, 340.

44 Morgan, *Slave Counterpoint*, pp. 479–81.

45 Hilary McD. Beckles, *Centering Women: Gender Discourses in Caribbean Slavery*, Kingston, 1999, pp. 2–22.

46 Awnsham and John Churchill, *A Collection of Voyages and Travels*, 4 vols., London, 1704, pp. 835–6, 838; Jennifer Morgan, '"Some could suckle over their shoulder": male travelers, female bodies and the gendering of racial ideology, 1500–1770', *William and Mary Quarterly*, 3rd Ser., 1997, vol. 54, pp. 167–92.

47 *Gentleman's Magazine*, 1735, vol. 5, p. 91; Edward Long, *The History of Jamaica*, 3 vols (1774), vol. 1, p. 271.

48 James Walvin, *Black Ivory*, p. 172.

49 Douglas Hall, *In Miserable Slavery: Thomas Thistlewood in Jamaica, 1750–86*, London, 1989.

50 John Carter Brown Library, Edwards MS, f. 17v.

51 Beckles, *Centering Women*, pp. 168–9.

52 British Library [hereafter BL], Add. MS 30,001, Ricketts Family Correspondence, f. 5, 23 June 1757; *Lady Nugent's Journal*, ed. Frank Cundall, London, 1907, pp. 72, 103, 131–2.

53 *History of Mary Prince*, ed. Ferguson, p. 56.

54 Bryan Edwards, *A History Civil and Commercial of the British Colonies in the West Indies*, 2 vols, Dublin, 1793, vol. 1, pp. 127–8.

55 Beckles, *Centering Women*, p. 25; Lillian Ashcraft-Eason, '"She voluntarily hath come": a Gambian woman trader in colonial Georgia in the eighteenth century,' in Paul Lovejoy (ed.), *Identity in the Shadow of Slavery*, London, 2000.

56 Hall, *Civilising Subjects*, pp. 91–6, 178–9.

57 Ibid, pp. 140–208.

58 See, for example, Ann Laura Stoler, *Carnal Knowledge and Imperial Power: Race and the Intimate in Colonial Rule*, Berkeley, CA, 2002; Indrani Chatterjee, *Gender, Slavery and Law in Colonial India*, Delhi, 1999.

59 Robert Orme, *Government and People of Indostan*, London, 1753, bk IV, pp. 38–44; Thomas R. Metcalf, *Ideologies of the Raj*, Cambridge, 1995, pp. 8–9, 92–3.

60 C. A. Bayly, *Empire and Information*, Cambridge, 1996, pp. 92–4; Kate Teltscher, 'Writing home and crossing boundaries', in Wilson (ed.), *A New Imperial History*; Peter Robb, *Clash of Cultures? An Englishman in Calcutta in the 1790s*, London, 1998, pp. 40–3.

61 See Chatterjee, *Gender, Slavery and Law*, *passim*; Sudipta Sen, 'Colonial aversions and domestic desires: blood, race, sex and the decline of intimacy in early British India', *South Asia*, 2001, vol. 24, pp. 36–7; P. J. Marshall, 'The whites of British India, 1780–1830: a failed colonial society?' *International History Review*, 1990, vol. 12, pp. 26–44.

62 Eliza Fay, *Original Letters from India*, ed. E. M. Forster, New York, 1925, pp. 161, 170.

63 See, for example, *Hicky's Bengal Gazette*, 16–23 Dec. 1780, 6–13 Jan. 1781.

64 British Library, OIOC MSS Eur/A172, January–December, 1784.

65 *Calcutta Gazette*, 21 Oct. 1784.

66 James Mill, *The History of British India*, 1818, as quoted in Margaret Strobel, *Gender, Sex and Empire*, pamphlet for the American Historical Association's series Essays on Global and Comparative History, 1992, p. 36.

67 E. M. Collingham, *Imperial Bodies: The Physical Experience of the Raj, c.1800–1947*, London, 2001, pp. 76–7; Lata Mani, *Contentious Traditions: The Debate on Sati in Colonial India*, Berkeley, CA, 1992, pp. 11–205; Strobel, *Gender, Sex and Empire*, pp. 12–13.

68 Collingham, *Imperial Bodies*, pp. 62–3, 76–7.

69 Ibid., pp. 100–3.

70 Wilson, *Island Race*, pp. 81–4. For the intended ideological impact of the English family, see *Evangelical Magazine*, 1800, vol. 8, p. 9.

71 James Wilson, *A Missionary Voyage to the Southern Pacific Ocean, Performed in the years 1796, 1797, 1798, with the Ship Duff, Commanded by Captain J. Wilson, Compiled from Journals of the Officers and the Missionaries*, London, 1799 p. 157; Richard Lovett, *The History of the London Missionary Society 1795–1895*, 2 vols, London, 1899, pp. 156–7.

72 K. R. Howe, *Where the Waves Fall: A New South Sea Islands History from first Settlement to Colonial Rule*, Honolulu, 1996, pp. 223–5.

73 Alan Atkinson, *The Europeans in Australia: A History*, Oxford, 1997, pp. 129–30.

74 Tim Flannery (ed.), *Watkin Tench, 1788*, Melbourne, 1996, p. 55; Joy Damousi, *Depraved and Disorderly: Female Convicts, Sexuality and Gender in Colonial Australia*, Cambridge, 1997.

75 Paula J. Byrne, 'A colonial female economy: Sydney, Australia', *Social History*, 1999, vol. 24, pp. 287–93.

76 See Anne-Marie Kilday, 'Women and crime in Britain, 1700–1850'.

77 Deborah Oxley, 'Representing convict women', in *Representing Convicts: New Perspectives on Convict Forced Labour Migration*, London, 1997, pp. 91–3.

78 Michael Flynn, *The Second Fleet: Britain's Grim Convict Armada of 1790*, Sydney, 2001, pp. 99–100.

79 Annette Hamilton, 'Bond-slaves of Satan: aboriginal women and the missionary dilemma', in Margaret Jolly and Martha McIntyre (eds), *Family and Gender in the Pacific: Domestic Contradictions and the Colonial Impact*, Cambridge, 1989, pp. 236–58.

80 Julie E. Carr, '"Cabin'd, cribb'd and confin'd": the white woman of Gipps Land and Bungalene', in Barbara Trade and Jeanette Hoorn (eds), *Body Trade: Captivity, Cannibalism and Colonialism in the Pacific*, New York, 2001, pp. 167–79.

Index

Aborigines 279–80
Acland, Lady Harriet 263
agriculture, commercialization of 2, 125–30
Aikin, Anna 16–17, 21, 23, 104, 110
almshouses 163
Americas 260, 265, 269–75
Anglicanism 102, 109; *see also* Church of England
anti-Corn Law movement 248–9
anti-slavery movement 111, 113–14, 206, 246–8, 266–7
Astell, Mary 18, 92, 103
Austen, Jane 23
Australia 279–80

Bailey, Joanne 63
Baker, Judith 203
Ball, Hannah 110–11
Barbauld, Anna *see* Anna Aikin
Berg, Maxine 126, 133, 143, 204
Bible Christians 107, 115
Bible Society 112–13
bluestockings 19
Bodichon, Barbara Leigh Smith 219, 248
bondage system 128–9
Bosanquet, Mary 106
Bourne, J. M. 229–30
breastfeeding 68
Brook, Hester 230
Browne, Charlotte 260

Buchan, Elspat 108
Burdett-Coutts, Angela 225
Burke, Edmund 15, 21–2

Calvinists 108
capitalism 4–5, 125
Cappe, Catherine 35, 36
Carlyle, Jane 64
Caroline, Queen 223
Catholicism 101–2, 105–6, 109, 115
'Celtic fringe' 269
censuses 124, 135, 141
Chapone, Hester 24
charity 103, 109–12, 163–4, 166–7, 225
Chartism 206, 245–6, 248
childbirth 69–70, 164
childhood 35, 68; *see also* education
Church of England 101; *see also* Anglicanism
Church of Scotland 101, 237–8; *see also* Presbyterianism
civilization 22–3
Clark, Anna 65
class 3, 36–7, 62, 85–6, 196–7, 209–10
Clearances, Highland 185
conduct books 23–6
Connelly, Cornelia 109, 115
consumer revolution 208–9
Corfield, Penelope 140
Court *see* royalty
courts *see* crime
Crawford, Patricia 89

Cressy, David 162
crime 174–88
Cullwick, Hannah 135–6

dairy industry 130
Davidoff, Leonore 130, 137
debating societies 49, 78
department stores 208
desertion 62, 66–7, 156
dissent *see* nonconformity
divorce 66
domestic service 135–6
domestic violence 64–6
domesticity *see* separate spheres
Douglas, Peggy, Duchess of *see*
    Douglas cause
Douglas cause 231–2
Drake, Judith 18–19
dress 88, 207–8

Earle, Peter 137
Edgeworth, Maria 25, 45
education 18, 24–5, 33–56, 143; home
    41–3; religious 48–9; *see also*
    universities
Edwards, Bryan 273, 275
effeminacy 264–5
elections 218, 219, 233, 234, 239
electoral reform 220–1, 244; *see also*
    suffrage
Elliott, Charlotte 114–15
elopement 60
Empire, British 196, 260–80
enclosure 129–30, 186, 236–7
Enlightenment 9–32, 35, 45, 81
erotica 86, 90
Evangelical Revival 102–3, 117, 198–9,
    205

Female Spectator 13
Fenwick, Ann 105–6
family 68–70, 162–3, 219–20, 230–4
fathers 42–3, 68
Fay, Elizabeth 276
Feeley, Malcolm 174–5
Finch, Lady Cecilia Isabella 223
fishing 127
Fox, Charles James 218
French Revolution 17, 23, 24, 107,
    187, 264–5
Friendly Societies 165
Fry, Elizabeth 111–12, 116
funerals 204–5

gendered division of labour 127, 130,
    133, 142–4
Georgiana, Duchess of Devonshire
    218, 220, 263
Gilbert, Ann 42–3
gleaning 129–30
Gregory, John 24
Guest, Lady Charlotte 63
Gurney, Betsy 112

Habermas, Jürgen 9–10
Hall, Catherine 130, 137
Hallahan, Margaret 115
Hamilton, Elizabeth, Duchess of 231–2
harvesting 128, 129
harvests, effects of poor 155
Heyrick, Elizabeth 113
highwaywomen 180
history writing 22–3
Hollen-Lees, Lynn 167
hospitals 68–9, 108, 166
hostesses, political 227–9
Hume, David 13, 14, 15, 20, 23
humours 80
Hunt, Margaret 65, 143
Huntingdon, Selina, Countess of 108,
    199
Hutcheson, Francis 13, 21

illegitimacy 62, 69, 85, 156
illness 153, 155–6
India 267–8, 275–8
'Indians' *see* native Americans
industrialization 2, 125–6, 133–5,
    158–9
infanticide 184–5

Jebb, Ann 21
jews 101

Kerr, Cecil Chetwynd 108

labour disputes 239; *see also* Trade
    Unions
Lady Huntingdon's Connexion *see*
    Huntingdon, Selina, Countess of
Lamb, Frederick 232
Laqueur, Thomas 79–84, 93
legal status of women 58, 64–5,
    139–40, 176, 195, 203–4; *see also*
    crime *and* divorce
Leicester, Lady 227–8
Leinster, Emily, Duchess of 63, 70

Lister, Anne 67, 219
Little, Deborah 174–5
Locke, John 12, 14, 18, 34
Londonderry, Frances Anne, Lady 233
Luddites 239
luxury 197–9

Macaulay, Catherine 20–2, 24, 46
Macdonald, Lady Margaret 230–1
Mackenzie, Henry 16
magazines 206–7
Mandeville, Bernard 197
Marlborough, Duchess of 224, 233
marriage 59–65, 85, 156, 201–4
Marriage Act, 1753 (Lord Hardwicke's) 59–61, 85
medical literature 14–15, 18–19, 78–84, 89
medicine 141
menstruation 89
Methodism 102–3, 106–7
Middleton, Margaret 111
midwives 141
migration 3, 59, 61–2, 105, 129, 132
Militia Act 238–9
Mill, John Stuart 218–19
Millar, John 22
millenarians 108
mining 130–1
missionaries 112–14, 278
Montagu, Lady Mary Wortley 19, 92, 199, 229
Moravians 104
More, Hannah 25–6, 35, 37–8, 44, 45, 110–12, 205, 264
mothers 35, 42, 65–6, 68–70, 143, 156

'nation', meaning of 262
native Americans 269–70
New Zealand 278
newspapers 196, 242–4
nonconformity 104–5; see also individual sects
Northumberland, Duchess of 199
nuns 109

Owenites 244

Paine, Thomas 21
Palmerston, Lady 226
patronage 228–34
pawnbrokers 164–5
Peterloo massacre 241–2

Pilkington, Laetitia 90–1
pin money 203
poisoning 182
politeness 13–14, 271
Polwarth, Lady 228
Poor Laws 152–3, 159–62, 166, 169, 244–5
population growth 3, 59
Poullain de la Barre 18
preachers, women 100–1, 104, 106–7, 111, 115
pregnancy 88, 143; see also childbirth
Presbyterianism 105; see also Church of Scotland
Primitive Methodists 107, 115
Prince, Mary 272, 274
professions 140–2
prostitution 91, 136–7, 279
proto-industrialization 131–2
Pullin, Nicola 138

Quakers 104, 107, 112, 205

race 270–80
radical societies 240–3
Ramsden, Isabella 226
Rational Dissenters 104
reading 14, 38–9; see also conduct books
reproduction 80–3
republicanism 20–1
Reynolds, Kim 224, 227
Richardson, Samuel 15–16
rioting 185–7, 235–9
Roberts, Michael 128
Robertson, William 23
Rousseau, Jean-Jacques 16, 21, 25, 35, 46, 68
royalty 205, 222–4

Savile, Gertrude 91–2
schools 38, 43–5; charity schools 38–9, 164; see also education
Scott, Mary 19–20
Sellon, Priscilla Lydia 109
sensibility 14–15, 206, 265–6
sentiment 59, 62–3, 68–9
separate spheres 5, 70, 103, 176
servants see domestic service
sex 78–99, 156, 269–70
Shackleton, Elizabeth 64
Shaftesbury, Lord 12–13
Sharpe, Pamela 126, 128, 132, 168

Sharples, Eliza 243
slavery 272–3
Smith, Adam 15, 22, 23, 45, 198
Snell, Hannah 265
Snell, Keith 128
Society for the Propagation of
    Christian Knowledge 112
Southcott, Joanna 108
spinsters 67, 143, 157, 162, 204
spirituality 107–8, 114–15
Stewart, Lady Susan 223–4
Stone, Lawrence 59, 68
suffrage 218–19
Sutherland, Countess-Duchess of
    221–2
sweated industries 134–5

Tahiti 278
Talbot, James 37
Taylor, Helen 219
tea 200–1
teaching 141–2; *see also* education
textile industry 133–4
theft 178–80
Thistlewood, Thomas 273
Thompson, E. P. 154, 185, 235
Thynne, Lady Louisa 199–200
Tractarianism *see* Anglicanism
trade 137–40
trade unions 134

Trimmer, Sarah 36, 39

Unitarians 104
universities 50–1
unstamped press 243–4
urban renaissance 10, 14
urbanization 2, 157–8

Valenze, Deborah 130, 132, 166–7
Verdon, Nichola 128
Vernon, Admiral 263
Vickery, Amanda 125, 204
violence 175, 176–7, 180–5, 185–7
Vries, Jan de 195

wages 127, 133, 154
Waldegrave, Lady Betty 225–6
Walker, Garthine 179
war 154–5
weather 155
Wedgwood, Josiah 200, 202
Wesley, John 106–7, 205
Wesley, Susanna 103
widows 66–7, 138, 143, 157, 162, 204,
    230–2, 271
Williams, Helen Maria 17
Wollstonecroft, Mary 21–2, 23, 24–6,
    44–6, 92, 104, 142, 265
work 39–40, 124–51, 154–5, 271
workhouses 159–62

WOMEN'S HISTORY FROM ROUTLEDGE

A History of European Women's Work: 1700 to the Present

Deborah Simonton

In *A History of European Women's Work*, Deborah Simonton takes an overview of trends in women's work across Europe.

Focusing on the role of gender and class as it defines women's labour, this book examines:

- a wide range of occupations such as teaching and farming
- contrasting rates of change in different European countries
- the definition of work within and outside patriarchal families
- local versus Europe-wide developments
- demographic and economic changes.

1998: 352pp
Hb 0-415-05531-8
Pb 0-415-05532-6

Women's History: Britain, 1850–1945

An Introduction

June Purvis

Women's History: Britain 1850–1945 introduces the main themes and debates of feminist history during this period of change, and brings together the findings of new research.

It examines the suffrage movement, race and empire, industrialisation, the impact of war and women's literature. Specialists in their own fields have each written a chapter on a key aspect of women's lives including health, the family, education, sexuality, work and politics. Each contribution provides an overview of the main issues and debates within each area and offers suggestions for further reading.

It not only provides an invaluable introduction to every aspect of women's participation in the political, social and economic history of Britain, but also brings the reader up to date with current historical thinking on the study of women's history itself.

1997: 352pp
Pb 0-415-23889-7

For credit card orders: call +44 (0)1264 343071
or email book.orders@routledge.co.uk

For more information, or for a free History catalogue please call Jenny Hunt on 020 7017 6118 or email jennifer.hunt@tandf.co.uk

Routledge
Taylor & Francis Group

www.routledge.com   available from all good bookshops

eBooks – at www.eBookstore.tandf.co.uk

A library at your fingertips!

eBooks are electronic versions of printed books. You can
store them on your PC/laptop or browse them online.

They have advantages for anyone needing rapid access
to a wide variety of published, copyright information.

eBooks can help your research by enabling you to
bookmark chapters, annotate text and use instant searches
to find specific words or phrases. Several eBook files would
fit on even a small laptop or PDA.

NEW: Save money by eSubscribing: cheap, online access
to any eBook for as long as you need it.

Annual subscription packages

We now offer special low-cost bulk subscriptions to
packages of eBooks in certain subject areas. These are
available to libraries or to individuals.

For more information please contact
webmaster.ebooks@tandf.co.uk

We're continually developing the eBook concept, so
keep up to date by visiting the website.

www.eBookstore.tandf.co.uk